POWERING
PROSPERITY

POWERING PROSPERITY

A Citizen's Guide to Shaping the 21st Century

INDRANIL GHOSH

BOMBARDIER
BOOKS

A BOMBARDIER BOOKS BOOK
An Imprint of Post Hill Press

Powering Prosperity:
A Citizen's Guide to Shaping the 21st Century
© 2020 by Indranil Ghosh
All Rights Reserved

ISBN: 978-1-64293-308-6
ISBN (eBook): 978-1-64293-309-3

Cover design by Cody Corcoran
Interior design and composition by Greg Johnson, Textbook Perfect

BOMBARDIER BOOKS   Post Hill PRESS

Post Hill Press
New York • Nashville
posthillpress.com

Published in the United States of America

To Priyanka, Kabir, and Raphael—
my enduring sources of inspiration.

CONTENTS

PREFACE

As a child of the 1980s, I am a committed capitalist who believes in the *extraordinary spirit of the empowered individual* to affect positive change. Central to my world view is the importance of private enterprise operating in open and competitive markets and a meritocratic culture that rewards hard work, creativity, and risk taking—all supported by *government that is smart, lean, and catalytic.*

But having straddled many worlds through my British Indian heritage and my experiences working around the world, I am also a capitalist who passionately believes that *strong society is a positive-sum game.* Over the past decade, my experience as a development investor has left me with no doubt that a culture of investing in other people's success is the way to build thriving communities. During my tenure as head of strategy and macroeconomics at Mubadala, the investment and development company of Abu Dhabi, I helped shape a portfolio of investments in new industries and infrastructure that engaged thousands of local citizens. Through this and other experiences, I've learned that people are our biggest asset. The more we empower innovators and entrepreneurs, the more we create new markets which make goods and services more accessible to a broader array of consumers in a more sustainable manner. In doing so, we increase demand and productivity growth—global economic goals that have been so elusive of late.

In order to *strike the harmonious balance* between empowered individuals and a strong society, I believe that government plays a key role in managing trade-offs by engaging the private sector and civil society in a constructive manner. For example, in walking the fine line between keeping taxes low while providing universal access to public goods and driving economic development, government can enlist the help of investors by setting incentives to steer private capital into public projects such as affordable housing, infrastructure development, and accelerating small enterprises. It can also devolve power to states and local communities, empowering them to shape their own development strategies for attracting businesses, capital, and top talent.

I believe that these principles, taken together, spark the dynamo of a vibrant socio-economy. But unfortunately, most of the world has found it difficult to achieve this balance over the past thirty to forty years. Runaway inequality has led to an upswelling of disillusioned, marginalized citizens and a breakdown in the public trust. In liberal democracies, this has opened the door to populist movements and to chaotic decisions such as Brexit. In more state-controlled regimes, simmering discontent is boiling over into public protest, forcing the regimes in power to tighten their control over pubic life even further.

In this book, I put forward a different path—a new way of thinking— which rejects divisive politics and seeks to unite citizens behind a common vision for restoring the balance between free enterprise and healthy society. My roadmap, or **Citizen's Guide**, casts aside dogmatic political leanings to either the left or the right and focuses on pragmatic solutions organized around the following three themes:

- ▶ **Advancing Inclusive Governance** to win back the public trust.
- ▶ **Investing With Purpose** to address the long-term Sustainable Development Challenge.
- ▶ **Empowering Local Communities** to become innovative, connected, entrepreneurial hubs in a globalizing world.

In the course of my lifetime, whenever humanity has pulled together to achieve common goals, incredible watershed moments have followed: the fall of the Berlin Wall in 1989, the end of apartheid in 1994, the first legalization of same-sex marriage by the Netherlands in 2000, and the Paris Agreement on climate change in 2016. These dramatic achievements can all be traced back to the courageous leadership of a few citizens who were ultimately able to rally humanity to raise the high-water mark of freedom.

As citizens, each of us holds a portfolio of roles in society—as voters, parents, school principals, public officials, judges, union representatives, employees, consumers, investors, board members, bloggers, journalists, and the list goes on. Each role endows us with the power to express our values, influence others, and shape the future. The personal choices we make about how we select political representatives, what products we buy, the work we choose to take on, the companies we support with our investment, and how we educate the next generation all leave a lasting imprint.

The more we act with consistent authenticity across all our roles in society, the greater our personal impact. When, as bold citizens, we make principled choices, our voices inspire followers. And when, as a society, we unify around a common vision, large-scale change becomes possible.

It's time to set aside differences and to focus on our shared interests in order to make the big changes that are required. In this book, I have laid out a common vision for Advancing Inclusive Governance, Investing With Purpose, and Empowering Local Communities—all of which, I believe, will be essential to power prosperity in the 21st century.

CHAPTER 1

INTRODUCTION

Brexit: The First Tremor

On June 23, 2016, as London was lashed by a torrential downpour, Londoners dutifully trekked out to their local polling stations to cast their vote in the UK's referendum on European Union membership.

In the run-up to the election, Britain had experienced the most aggressive and divisive campaigning it had seen in decades. Opinion polls in the final days before the vote suggested a narrow lead for "Remain" of around 2–4 percent.[1] This certainly seemed to be the sensible choice for British voters to make. Membership in the EU, after all, affords British citizens extensive access to live and work in continental Europe and trade freely with their European neighbors. Moreover, leaving the Union would isolate Britain from its neighbors and harm its standing in the world. Surely, the British people, following their long-standing traditions of moderation and pragmatism, could be relied upon to make the rational choice. Or could they?

As the rain subsided the next morning, such hopes for the "rational" choice lay in ruins. The morning's newspapers proclaimed the surreal news. Some headlines screamed with jubilation—"We're Out!," "Take a Bow, Britain!," "See EU Later"—while others, overwhelmed by the stunning 4 percent "Leave" victory, solemnly tried to process the shock. By 8:15 a.m., Prime Minister David Cameron announced that he would resign.[2]

The news that morning sent equity markets reeling. The FTSE 100 stock index fell by almost 9 percent in the first hours of trading,[3] while the pound plunged to its lowest level since 1985, dropping 10 percent in six hours.[4] Stocks of UK companies continued to hemorrhage over the coming days.[5]

The epicenter of the hysteria was London, which stood to lose the most from Brexit. Much of London's economy had been built on professional services, especially financial services, which are delicately interwoven with the EU's Single Market. Many large corporations have located their global or EU headquarters in the British capital, drawing on a large white-collar workforce from the continent. Brexit jeopardized the city's global preeminence in these fields—the one sector in which Britain's economy truly excelled. It also threatened to displace thousands of Europeans living in London, where they had diligently constructed their lives and careers.

The election result was particularly difficult for the business community to accept, because it seemed so economically irrational. Prior to the vote, the well-regarded consultancy Oxford Economics estimated that in the best-case Brexit scenario, the UK's GDP would barely grow between 2016 and 2030; in a worst-case scenario, it would be almost four percentage points lower.

Most astonishing of all was how utterly unprepared Britain seemed to be for Brexit. What was the process for leaving the EU? What would happen to all the advantages the British people had recently come to take for granted, such as frictionless trade and freedom of movement? The "Leave" campaigners had focused single-mindedly on why the EU was allegedly bad for Britain, but they had done precious little to sketch out a vision for an alternative future. The government had treated Brexit as a perfunctory referendum that would quell irritating voices of dissent once and for all—but it had never laid out clear, specific plans for how Britain would continue to thrive outside the EU if the citizenry actually voted to leave. In a related failure, many in the media chose to amplify incendiary rhetoric rather than asking the tough questions, interrogating the facts, and informing the public.

At the time of writing, three years after the Brexit vote, uncertainty runs as high as ever, as permanent agreements regarding the movement of goods, capital, and people remain under negotiation. Many of the economic fears shrouding Brexit are being realized. Prior to the referendum, Britain boasted the fastest-growing economy among G7 nations, peaking at 3 percent annual GDP growth in 2014. By 2018, Britain languished at the bottom of the rankings, posting annual GDP growth of only 1.4 percent.[6] British business has been starved of investment to an extent that will certainly be toxic for its long-term economic health. Notable casualties have been industries such as automotive—where investment is down 80 percent since 2016[7]—aerospace, and pharmaceuticals, with leading multi-national corporations such as Astra-Zeneca[8] and Airbus freezing their investment in Britain.

So why did so many Brits—almost 17.5 million, or nearly 52 percent of those voting—opt for Brexit? Why did they inflict the "economic self-harm" that David Cameron had warned about during his "Remain" campaign?[9]

In the days following the referendum, analysis of the voting patterns began to shed light on this critical question. It emerged that "Leave" voters fell into several segments: deindustrialized regions that consecutive governments had allowed to decay, middle-income districts where wages had stagnated, socially-conservative pockets of the country such as the "Home Counties," and communities such as seaside towns with large elderly populations that had been used to resettle refugees.

Far removed from the thriving, cosmopolitan micro-economies of London and the affluent corridors reaching out to Oxford, Cambridge, Surrey, and a few other urban centers—which had voted resoundingly to remain—these communities felt betrayed by successive governments that had been out of touch with their realities. They had lost trust in policies such as membership in the EU, which they felt were tailored to promote the success of London and its satellite regions.

Troublingly, plummeting trust in government was accompanied by suspicion of its experts. Contrary to Treasury projections, which forecast that a Brexit vote would precipitate a dramatic decline of the British economy, polls showed that the majority of "Leave" voters believed that Brexit would be economically neutral or even positive for their future. So, paradoxically, most "Leave" voters were attempting to follow their economic interests—or at least what they perceived those interests to be.

Redcar, a town in the northeast of England, could well claim to be a community that had been neglected with the kind of callous indifference that had so deeply inflamed British voters. Steelmaking had been the lifeblood of Redcar's economy for 170 years. But this tradition ended in October 2015 with the collapse of the large steelmaking firm SSI Steel UK—the final act of a long, drawn-out story of decline. Prior to the liquidation of SSI, steelworkers earned on average a £33,000 annual salary; after the collapse, they were lucky to earn £24,000 a year in other jobs. Resentment undoubtedly played a role in Redcar's thumping 66 percent support for "Leave."[10]

But the resentment in Redcar, and in other economically disadvantaged communities in Britain, runs deeper than the mere frustration with the slow, painful economic deterioration they've endured. The stark contrast between their own declining fortunes and the optimism of London and the South East has caused visceral sentiments of unfairness and neglect to well up.

These disadvantaged communities could only look on as investment poured in from the public purse and from overseas investors, upgrading London's real estate and infrastructure and making it highly attractive as a global destination for elites to live and do business. Conversely, investment to retain the prowess of the industrial and manufacturing clusters dotted around the rest of Britain has been systematically neglected, in many cases dating as far back as the Thatcher era.

Open-border policies with the EU proved to be tremendously favorable for London, since they allowed the best talent from the continent to be drawn in to power the city's professional and financial-services hub. By contrast, the struggling regions of Britain often viewed open borders as a gateway to a host of serious problems. Local economies were opened to competition from foreign firms but were rarely empowered with the investments required to rejuvenate and re-invent themselves. These dynamics reinforced the structural impact of automation, outsourcing, and other labor-cost savings that took place across many of the developed economies. Hundreds of thousands of migrants entering Britain from Central and Eastern Europe were perceived to be crowding out domestic workers and, ultimately, altering the very fiber of local culture.

Brexit has shown us that the wounds in Britain cut much deeper than economic issues. Far too many Brits now feel they are getting a "Raw Deal." There is a broad perception of a loss in public trust, frustration over too little investment in the future, and resentment that too many local communities have been left behind in the rush to globalize. The people feel divided, insecure, and powerless.

These sentiments are in no way exclusive to Britain. They are echoed around the world. Even before the Brexit referendum, early signs had been visible in disparate quarters, such as the rising vote-share for the far-right National Front in France, particularly in deindustrialized areas, and the rise of Hindu nationalism in India. But the Brexit vote was the first major tremor that set in motion a seismic shock that is shaking the foundations of our current world order. Understanding how we arrived here—and what solutions we can apply to chart a more positive course—is the subject of this book.

Collapse of the Washington Consensus

If Brexit represents the beginning of a sharp break from the current international system, it's important to consider how the system arose, and how it ultimately failed to serve the needs of so many around the world.

The sentiments driving the Raw Deal can be traced back to an ideology that rose to prominence in Western policymaking circles during the 1980s. For the last thirty years, global economic policy has been heavily influenced by the free-market ideals championed by US President Ronald Reagan and British Prime Minister Margaret Thatcher. The core policy positions of both leaders centered on lower tax rates, privatization, deregulation of markets, and liberalization of trade and capital flows. Many of these policies were adopted into key financing programs organized by the Washington-based International Monetary Fund (IMF) and various regional development banks. Eventually, these principles were codified into ten broad policy recommendations that became known around the world as the "Washington Consensus."

Initially applied to struggling Latin American economies and other emerging-market economies in order to steer them toward recovery from the various crises they encountered during the 1980s and 1990s, the Washington Consensus gained prominence due to forceful backing by international institutions such as the IMF, the World Bank, and the World Trade Organization (WTO), as well as the prevalence of US-trained economists—often from the University of Chicago, where "free-market" Washington Consensus thinking was refined—in the ministries of many developing countries.

A common strategy employed by these multilateral institutions to spread the doctrine to developing economies was to link the availability of loans (or debt forgiveness) to the adoption of the ten-point Washington Consensus policy package—an approach that produced a mixed track-record. For example, during the Asian Financial Crisis of 1997–98, the combination of restrictive monetary and fiscal policy imposed by these institutions hurt consumption and business activity in several countries, such as South Korea and Indonesia. Eventually, these countries found the cost of IMF financing to be too expensive and decided to insure their economies through greater saving.

In the original formulation of the Washington Consensus, the authors were careful to temper its articles of faith. The emphasis on cutting trade subsidies, which would open the doors to foreign competition, was to be balanced with the redirection of some public spending "to the broad-based provision of key pro-growth, pro-poor services." Moreover, limitations on market deregulation were advocated in cases "justified by safety, environ-mental and consumer protection grounds, and prudential oversight of financial institutions."

Unfortunately, in the years that followed, the Washington Consensus became increasingly associated with a neo-liberal mutation, which pro-ceeded to burrow into the political fabric of many developed and emerging economies. The mutated strain featured a fanatical zeal for shrinking the footprint of government, expanding the role of free markets to all extremi-ties of the socio-economy, and promoting unfettered globalization.

In the circles that embraced the mutated neo-liberal form of the Wash-ington Consensus, government itself was widely believed to be incompetent. Even the best-intentioned regulations, or so the thinking went, diminished the power of free markets to allocate capital and resources efficiently and drive prosperity on a national and global scale.

In many ways, I am a child of this ideology. Growing up in Thatcher's Britain, I witnessed the economic revival that it brought after decades of malaise in a socialist economy. The demise of Communism soon followed. What greater validation could there be of liberal democracy and free-mar-ket capitalism?

During the late 1990s, I spent the internet boom as a graduate student at MIT. Widely recognized as one of the great research hubs for science and technology, MIT is also a cradle for the commercialization of trans-formative new technologies worth billions of dollars in market value. Early in my professional career, I worked for McKinsey & Company, advis-ing large corporations on investment and business strategy. What better training ground to learn the conventions of corporate "best practice"? Sub-sequently, my capitalist education was rounded out as a senior fundraiser for Bridgewater Associates—the world's largest global macro-hedge-fund and a perfect vantage point for observing the machinations of the financial markets. Technological ingenuity, entrepreneurial energy, corporate disci-pline, all fueled by global markets for goods and capital—surely a complete formula for free markets to create prosperity.

The Global Financial Crisis of 2008–9, and its aftermath, shook many people's faith in this formula. The crisis was a turning point for the cred-ibility of the Washington Consensus, which had already been somewhat discredited in emerging markets—and it proved to be a wake-up call for my own beliefs as well.

Many in the financial world, including my colleagues at Bridge-water Associates, had seen the meltdown of financial markets coming.

Irresponsible lending and securitization had over-leveraged banks to a point that was simply unsustainable. The crisis exposed the economic devastation that could result from the financial deregulation and liberalization of global capital flows espoused by neo-liberal policymakers and their intellectual cheerleaders. Worse still for the neo-liberal ideology, it took unprecedented government intervention in many Western economies to bail out banks and to provide the necessary stimulus to keep the real economy from crashing into the abyss.

The Washington Consensus had received a formidable body blow, but it managed to stutter on, albeit with a diminished insistence on its most extreme policy positions, such as the total elimination of capital controls. But once the main economies were pulled back from the brink of collapse, and their financial sectors were functionally repaired, the IMF and other global institutions reverted to their well-rehearsed policy prescriptions.

But criticisms continued to grow. Stagnating wages for the middle classes, growing inequality, and industrial decline became so palpable in most advanced economies that they could no longer be denied or ignored. Climate change also entered the popular vernacular.

In the wake of these challenges, citizens began to question the central tenets of the Washington Consensus more openly. Could free markets stimulate growth in faltering, deindustrializing regions of a country? Could market forces be relied upon to narrow the income gap and avert environmental crises? Were the trade-offs between globalization and national interest—even sovereignty—worth it? It was a striking failure of the policy intelligentsia that no one seemed able to step forward with a compelling alternative to address these legitimate concerns.

In the ideological vacuum that followed, the discontent of forgotten communities and the "squeezed" middle class fomented in many Western economies, waiting for an opportunity to mount a revolt. If the Brexit vote was the first tremor, then the election of Donald Trump as the 45th President of the United States was the seismic quake that brought about the final collapse of the Washington Consensus.

In many ways, the issues that resonated among Trump voters reflected similar issues that had inspired British "Leave" voters on the other side of the Atlantic. Once in office, the Trump administration's nationalist rhetoric, fiscal profligacy, belligerence toward free trade, and disdain for global institutions were entirely antithetical to the global-policy ethos of the previous three decades.

In this ironic twist, the two nations that most emphatically advocated for the Washington Consensus have both witnessed their citizens abandon it at the polls.

The Search for a New Paradigm

As the violent tremors caused by the collapse of the Washington Consensus continue to ripple outward, and the perception of a Raw Deal festers and grows, citizens in an ever-expanding list of countries have begun to rebel against the systems they believe have abandoned them.

In the midst of this swelling global rebellion, people have begun to search for new political and economic paradigms to secure a more broadly shared sense of prosperity in the 21st century. Among the many alternatives now battling for ascendency, three models have emerged as the most prominent contenders: **populism**, **state-capitalism**, and **localism**.

Each of these three models highlights a valuable perspective that has been neglected by the defects and blind spots of the Washington Consensus:

- ▶ **Populism** elevates the perspective of Marginalized Citizens, typically from economically and socially disadvantaged segments of society, who have been overlooked and ignored due to the tendency of the Washington Consensus political doctrine to concentrate wealth and power in the hands of elites.
- ▶ **State Capitalism** responds to a critical flaw in Washington Consensus thinking—the lack of emphasis placed on long-term savings to support investment, particularly as applied to sustainable economic development. This is the perspective of a long-term Development Investor.
- ▶ **Localism** takes the perspective of a Community Builder. The focus is on empowering local communities to create an environment that is highly attractive to residents, businesses, and external investment. This is in stark contrast to the Washington Consensus model, which encourages countries to hurtle toward a frictionless, hyper-globalized world without shoring up the unique capabilities of their own regions.

During the first phase of my career, I was fortunate to work at several of the world's vaunted temples of capitalism and become trained in the nuances of Washington Consensus thinking.

But, during other phases of my life and career, these three additional perspectives—the **Marginalized Citizen**, the **Development Investor**, and the **Community Builder**—have profoundly influenced my worldview and helped me decode the stream of increasingly chaotic social, political, and economic developments unfolding around us.

Throughout this book, I will use each of these three perspectives as a lens to analyze the challenges that must be solved in the post-Washington Consensus world.

Marginalized Citizen

A wave of populism is sweeping across the globe, infecting countries as diverse as the US, Italy, Mexico, Brazil, and the Philippines. It's no surprise that many of these countries once experimented with the Washington Consensus—a model with a knack for creating a majority out of the marginalized.

Populist governments, by their very design, tend to affect a posture of concern for marginalized citizens and often promise to be their champions. They vow to fight off the establishment, the elites, and other forces such as globalization and immigration that are to "blame" for the plight of their "victims." Left-wing populist governments, such as the one in Mexico, prize social justice while attacking capitalism and threatening to expropriate private property. In contrast, their right-wing counterparts in countries such as Brazil, Italy, and the Philippines prioritize such policy goals as nationalism, an aggressive domestic-security stance, and curbing welfare expenditures.

But populist governments often struggle with longevity, when they don't invoke outright authoritarianism, because they are inherently divisive themselves. They replace one set of marginalized citizens with another and deploy questionable economic policies that pander to their electoral base rather than generating a broad and genuine prosperity.

Notwithstanding their shortcomings, the merit of populist governments is to acknowledge the frustrations of the marginalized and give them voice and legitimacy. As the son of an Indian immigrant family that settled in the northwest of England in the late 1970s, I experienced the bitterness of marginalized communities firsthand. Living in various towns in the corridor between Liverpool and Manchester, we fell squarely in an economically challenged part of the country due to Britain's stark north-south economic divide. Many of my school friends were the children of unemployed parents. Poverty was commonplace, and for some kids, the only meal of the day was the school lunch. For many, it was difficult even to envision a way out. Manchester had once been the world's biggest producer of textiles and the world's first industrialized city, while Liverpool had been one of the world's great seaports. These cities experienced a devastating industrial decline during the late 20th century. And until recently, this region had not seen the arrival of industries to replace the ones that had disappeared.

My family arrived in Britain at the tail end of the immigrant wave from the Indian subcontinent, the Caribbean, and other Commonwealth countries during the postwar years. In many communities, these immigrants were perceived as a threat to the national identity—the very culture and heritage of Britain. Tensions sometimes ran high, occasionally flaring up into ugly violence, as in the Brixton race riots of 1981.

One of the early lessons I learned in my life is that acceptance, integration, and the change of social attitudes towards immigrants takes time. Growing up, I remember my parents having to seek out restaurants in an ethnic part of town to enjoy an Indian meal. Today, forty years later, many Brits consider curry chicken to be the national dish. Perhaps thirty years from now, Polish pierogi will be commonplace on the menu of British pubs. Accelerating the integration of migrant groups while ensuring that neither the migrant nor the native groups feel marginalized or repressed is one of the toughest socioeconomic challenges facing the modern world today.

Drawing on these early experiences, I cultivated a keen eye for the marginalized. Long after the worst years of the Global Financial Crisis had passed, I remember striking up conversations with cab drivers, accountants, corporate managers, and other workers across America only to hear the same stories echoed again and again. Good jobs had become hard to find. Middle-income people were struggling to provide financial security for their families. Healthcare and other required expenditures were rising. The vast swathes of people who felt marginalized were on the rise, and there was a growing sense that the public trust had been betrayed.

Such stories are not a vague sentiment, but a quantifiable phenomenon. According to the Pew Research Center, trust among Americans in their government is now hovering near historic lows. Recent data shows that only 18 percent of voters trust the federal government in Washington "always" or "most of the time" to do what is right, which is significantly lower than under presidents Clinton or George W. Bush, when Americans' rate of trust in the federal government fluctuated but was regularly above 30 percent and even in the forties.[11]

Other examples of unsustainable marginalization have also caught my eye around the world: idle youth roaming the streets in the sprawling shanty towns of Cairo in the years leading up to the Arab Spring movement of 2011; the jarring gap between the affluence on Ipanema beach and the poverty in the favelas of Rio de Janeiro—especially galling considering the corruption scandals that have been exposed throughout Brazilian government and business since 2014.

If they had taken the perspective of **Marginalized Citizens**, politicians would have recognized that the **Loss of the Public Trust** had become a serious challenge long before it was ultimately exploited by populist movements led by the likes of Donald Trump, Andrés Manuel López Obrador, and Jair Bolsonaro.

Development Investor

Many observers—especially those in emerging economies—point to the successes of the state-capitalist model that has evolved in China. It is a hybrid approach that encourages market development in many sectors and gradually opens up the economy to foreign investment. It tends to pool capital locally, encouraging savings of local individuals and firms to meet long-term development needs. On the other hand, the strong hand of the state maintains a powerful grip on the media, academia, and many other aspects of society. This brand of governance also features a state-led, long-term strategy for investing to incubate new industries in a protected environment.

I became intimately familiar with the state-capitalist model, in which government acts as catalytic "development investor," as I began the second phase of my career. After leaving the hedge-fund world, I was appointed as the head of strategy and macroeconomics of Mubadala, one of Abu Dhabi's sovereign-investment companies. Mubadala's mission is to support Abu Dhabi Vision 2030, a strategic roadmap to diversify the economy away from the production of oil and gas. It's extraordinary how far Abu Dhabi in particular, and the United Arab Emirates overall, have come on this journey. In the few short decades since the early 1990s, the UAE has invested part of its surplus hydrocarbon-wealth to build the thriving cities of Abu Dhabi and Dubai. Perhaps most famous as a destination for luxury tourism, shopping, and iconic real estate, the Emirates is also a world leader in industries such as logistics, aerospace, and aluminum smelting, many of which were incubated by sovereign-investment vehicles such as Mubadala. Moreover, it is now charting a path to capture significant influence in the technology sector through its $15 billion[12] investment in the Softbank Vision Fund.

Although the success of state capitalism in propelling the development of the UAE and lifting China from poverty to superpower status is undeniable, it may be too early to judge the long-term sustainability of the model. In China, for example, overall economic growth has decelerated in the last few years, debt has risen, and the prosperity enjoyed by China's eastern coastal regions has yet to spread fully to its central provinces. Moreover, instead of offsetting the slowing pace of economic progress with advances in civil liberties and political participation, President Xi Jinping has set about reversing some of the liberalizing work of set in motion by Deng Xiaoping. In 2018, the Chinese government announced the elimination of the two-term limit on the presidency, in what some China scholars suggest could pave the way toward making Xi "president for life." In the coming years, the Chinese people's tolerance for centralized power and curbs on individual freedoms may be severely tested.

State capitalism is unlikely to find a home in countries where civil liberties and self-expression have a long tradition, or where people value local autonomy over centralized control. However, these countries could make use of the key strength of state capitalism, which is to recognize the shortcomings of markets in making large-scale, early-stage, or long-term investments that are necessary to catalyze economic development, and financially provisioning for public liabilities or future costs to society.

Some of these future costs are relatively easy to quantify, such as the social-security obligations for an aging population and an under-educated, unhealthy workforce. The same goes for high costs of energy, transportation, and communication if infrastructure is poor. Other future costs, such as damage resulting from climate change or lost output from the lack of innovation, may be more difficult to estimate but are equally threatening. In aggregate, these future costs are usually far beyond the annual fiscal capacity of most countries, which live hand-to-mouth and are barely able to fund their annual public-expenditure obligations.

Many state-capitalist countries—such as China, the Gulf States, and former Soviet Republics—take a more proactive approach than their market-economy counterparts. State-owned enterprises or investment vehicles are tasked with developing infrastructure, creating social-service enterprises, incubating new innovations and industries, and breathing life into communities. Once the development stages are de-risked, so the thinking goes, it is much easier to attract private capital to take a stake in these projects.

Long-term state-investment vehicles are not the sole preserve of state-capitalist systems. They have been adopted by liberal democracies such as Canada, Australia, New Zealand, and the Nordic countries. Although their primary purpose has been to invest in financial assets to grow financial wealth for future generations, there is now a trend to increase their allocations for domestic economic-development projects.

Most countries, however, fail to provision and invest adequately in their economies. For example, in the United Kingdom, the substantial revenue generated from North Sea oil wealth since the 1980s was largely squandered, whereas Norway managed to build up sovereign funds worth approximately $1 trillion from its North Sea reserves. As we will explore later in the book, perhaps with smarter provisioning and investment, the UK government could have saved more of its natural-resource surplus and deployed it to address the economic blight affecting many regions of the country.

Taking the perspective of a long-term **Development Investor**, the **Failure to Provision and Invest** in long-term economic development and in addressing public liabilities is a significant challenge facing most countries.

Community Builder

Localism advocates devolving greater powers to communities and empowering them to take control of their destinies. Successful community builders understand that this model relies on creating an attractive environment that draws in talent, businesses, and outside investment. Rising cities and clusters, such as Pittsburgh in the US and Copenhagen in Denmark, epitomize this trend. Each one has built or rejuvenated a community to create a magnetic hub for business and cultural life.

In the last few years, I have turned the attention of my own advisory firm towards helping local and regional authorities around the world to develop strategies for attracting more businesses and investors into their communities.

From the perspective of the community-builder, I have learned the importance of catering to the needs of many different stakeholders. For local residents, what matters most is the availability of jobs and the quality of life on offer to individuals and their families. People seek a location with multiple employment options, high quality and reasonably priced housing, a clean environment with recreational spaces and cultural venues, good schools, and affordable healthcare.

Employers, on the other hand, value a business-friendly environment, good transport and communication infrastructure, as well as universities and vocational colleges that can supply a steady stream of trained workers and offer partnerships in research and development.

To build such attractive destinations requires strong local governance that is empowered to raise funds from local taxes and make critical investment decisions. Local authorities must also develop strong capabilities in urban planning and forging close partnerships with the private sector and civil-society organizations.

Of course, localism is not without its challenges. Thriving communities can become victims of their own success. As they've become over-concentrated, early success stories such as San Francisco, Boston, and Singapore are now grappling with problems of congestion, pollution, and lack of affordability. Escalating land and property prices are generating higher rents for owners, but those rents are driving out workers and smaller businesses to suburbs, satellite towns, or other locations entirely. This economic "sorting" can become a trigger for the sentiments of marginalization—and, ultimately, for the kind of populism that was discussed earlier in this chapter.

On the other hand, localities can get sucked into a "race to the bottom" as they compete with each other to lure in business activity with inducements such as tax breaks. In a recent example, New York State and City governments were reported to have offered an estimated $3 billion package of tax breaks to Amazon[13] to locate its second headquarters in Long Island City, Queens. If Amazon had not withdrawn from the deal, it may have ended up as a case of the "winner's curse" for the local government.

Localism should not be confused with isolationism. Unlike isolationists, community builders thrive on connectivity. They promote transportation, communication, and social networks that enable linkages to customers and suppliers, and they make great efforts to nourish their locality with ideas, people, and capital from around the world. In a globalizing world, where industries are at risk of shifting to new locations with lower costs or superior skills, community builders believe that a region's best defense against competition is investment that builds up the area's capabilities.

But while advocates of localism accept open economies, they resist forces that remove their ability to make optimal decisions for their local needs. Loss of national sovereignty on matters such as lending rates, currency, taxation, working conditions, or product standards can be very problematic for the prospects of local communities.

Many communities have been seriously harmed by excessive moves towards global integration at the national level. Perhaps the most salient example of the phenomenon is the eurozone. In the wake of the financial crisis, the debts of some eurozone countries—notably Portugal, Ireland, Greece, and Spain, which are often referred to by the derogatory acronym "PIGS"—spiraled out of control as governments rushed to prop up failing banks that had overextended themselves during the boom years. The resulting austerity policies imposed upon these countries illustrate how attempts at economic integration can also lead to a loss of local autonomy.

The country that has suffered the most pain is Greece, which now finds itself in a terrible debt-trap. Because it is part of the eurozone, Greece cannot loosen its monetary policy by cutting interest rates to stimulate growth. Moreover, the "troika" of supranational organizations, consisting of the European Commission (EC), the International Monetary Fund (IMF), and the European Central Bank (ECB), urged Greece to cut public spending and increase taxes in return for a bailout.

Prime Minister Alexis Tsipras called a referendum in June 2015 to decide whether to accept the austerity measures. The "No" vote won with a resounding 61 percent popular support. Yet seven days later, with long lines at ATMs, businesses hemorrhaging money, and the threat of even greater austerity to compensate for the crisis caused by the referendum, Prime Minister Tsipras signed the very deal he had publicly railed against.

Ominously, the democratic prerogative of the Greek people was ignored so that the country could remain a part of the eurozone project. Greeks rightly feel they have lost control over their own policymaking authority and national sovereignty. Worse still, the austerity policy turned Greece into an economic disaster. It reduced Greek economic demand and caused unemployment to shoot up to 25 percent in 2015—higher than the US during the Great Depression.[14] Only now is Greece crawling out of its economic tragedy,[15] but unemployment is still at around 18 percent.[16]

Taking the perspective of a **Community Builder**, I have come to understand the problem of **Communities Forgotten in the Rush to Globalize**.

A New Vision for Prosperity in the 21st Century

This book will outline a new vision for prosperity in the 21st century, by offering ideas to solve the problems that make up the Raw Deal. I have organized the roadmap of potential solutions under three themes:

- ▶ Advancing Inclusive Governance to win back the public trust.
- ▶ Investing With Purpose to address the long-term Sustainable Development Challenge.
- ▶ Empowering Local Communities to become innovative, connected, entrepreneurial (ICE) hubs in a globalizing world.

Under each theme, there are various political, regulatory, technological, and investment prescriptions. While these are all important considerations, positive change will require each of us, as citizens, to make good choices.

As citizens, each of us holds a portfolio of roles in society—as voters, parents, school principals, public officials, judges, union representatives, employees, consumers, investors, board members, bloggers, journalists, and the list goes on.

Each role endows us with the power to express our values, influence others, and shape the future. The personal choices we make about how we educate our children, what products we buy, the jobs we choose to take, and the companies we support with our investment all leave a lasting imprint. For better or worse, our choices profoundly affect important outcomes such as the civic engagement of our youth, the social responsibility of businesses, and the sustainable stewardship of the environment.

The more we act with consistent authenticity across all our roles in society, the greater our personal impact. In this book, I will share many inspiring stories of citizens who are infusing a common purpose into all their endeavors. We will meet students who are turning away from "traditional" high-paying careers to launch social enterprises that solve problems they deeply care about. We will see how the leaders of many faith-based organizations are making the conscientious move to remove hydrocarbon stocks from their investment portfolios. We will also encounter city mayors who are enacting sustainable policies in their local community—even when national government remains too paralyzed to act.

When bold citizens make principled choices and generate prosperity from purpose, they inspire followers. And with the collective support of a population, large-scale change becomes possible.

Throughout this book, I will endeavor to distill how people can think about key choices in order to make a positive difference—a Citizen's Guide, if you will.

Advancing Inclusive Governance

Part 1 of this book focuses on **Advancing Inclusive Governance** to win back the public trust. In chapter 2, I begin by recounting the various factors that led to what I refer to as the Great Trust Crisis—the low point in social capital that we are experiencing today.

As I argue in chapter 3, a critical first step in restoring their diminished legitimacy is for governments to repair frayed social contracts. Too often in the past, policies have been skewed to favor one segment of the population over another, or to achieve a short-term benefit at the expense of a much larger longer-term cost. These Faustian bargains have come home to roost in the form of masses of marginalized citizens. New accords must be made that bring together all segments of the citizenry under a common vision of the future—and a cohesive social contract.

Chapter 4 calls for inclusive governance—a system of laws, institutions, and culture that promotes political participation, civil liberties, and socioeconomic mobility for the entire population, and which is resilient to "capture" by a ruler or special interests. It is the critical framework for upholding cohesive social contracts and reversing divisive ones.

Investing With Purpose

Part 11 of the book explores a collaborative model of long-term investing to meet the world's sustainable-development priorities, which I refer to as **Investing With Purpose**.

In chapter 5, I begin by outlining the key elements of the Sustainable Development Challenge—a broad set of long-term investments across both developed and developing economies that aims to graduate millions of people from poverty to opportunity, adapt infrastructure and industry to be more environmentally sustainable, and nurture human creativity and innovation.

The next three chapters deep-dive into each of these topics in detail. Chapter 6 explores the key principles for combating poverty and providing social services and infrastructure that increase socioeconomic mobility. Chapter 7 looks at the urgent initiatives required to avert environmental catastrophe: decarbonizing infrastructure and industry, managing the use of water, which is fast becoming a scarce resource, and reducing waste through a circular economy. In each case, I will focus on how emerging solutions can be scaled up rapidly to achieve the impact required. In chapter 8, I discuss the impact of intelligent machines on the automation of many forms of work that are currently the preserve of humans. We will need to move towards a lifelong model of human development so that workers displaced by automation can be quickly re-skilled and redeployed into emergent areas of well-paid, cutting-edge work.

To conclude part II, we examine the total magnitude of the investments required by the Sustainable Development Challenge and how it can be funded. In chapter 9, I will show that the scale of challenge is too vast for most countries to fund either by increasing taxes or by using other public monies. Instead, it will be essential for governments to partner with the private sector to co-invest in long-term development projects that generate socioeconomic impact as well as a healthy financial return. Increasingly, private investors are also looking to deploy their capital into sustainable investments such as direct-impact projects, stocks of companies that meet high corporate-responsibility standards, and green bonds. This growing movement—if properly harnessed through reliable frameworks and standards to ensure that well-meaning capital achieves its intended impact—could prove to be the tipping point to a sustainable future.

Empowering Local Communities

Part III of the book looks at **Empowering Local Communities** in a globally connected world.

It has become apparent that the globalization wave spanning the past thirty years has pulled millions of workers in the emerging world into the middle-class; it has increased the profits of multi-national corporations, and it has helped to reduce the cost of goods and services everywhere. However, it has also contributed to stagnating wages of middle-class workers in many developed countries. As a reaction to the gap in the fortunes of the "winners" and "losers" of the current globalization paradigm, the debate over global economic integration versus local sovereignty has reached fever pitch.

Chapter 10 calls for the devolution of decision-making on issues of economic development and public finances to local communities, since they are best placed to carve out an economic niche that plays to their unique set of assets and competitive advantages. Local governance is also more likely to forge close partnerships between the public and private sector to co-develop ICE hubs, which will be magnets for talent, capital, and ideas. As I mentioned earlier, this model has already proven effective in many towns and cities around the world and deserves to be extended more broadly.

Chapter 11 argues that in the coming decades, as China, India, and some other large, emerging-market countries catch up economically with North

America, the EU, and developed Asia, there will be a greater convergence of interests among a much-enlarged group of countries on key issues such as digital trade, labor standards, intellectual property, sustainable investing, and reduction in carbon emissions to mitigate climate change. The opportunity to upgrade global rules so that they support and connect local economic dynamos should not be missed.

The three parts of this book, taken together, provide a practical roadmap for achieving social and economic prosperity in the 21st century.

In my view, there could hardly be a more important topic for dialogue, given the state of the world today. As the father of two young children, it is painful for me at times to reflect on the state of our planet and its grim trajectory. It is easy to become discouraged and imagine my children growing up in a culture of deep mistrust between people, government, and business; a world of inequality where privilege triumphs over meritocracy; an era of growing censorship and repression; perhaps even a dystopian future of environmental catastrophe and a disastrous repetition of the 20th century's global wars.

It is imperative that we avoid such a tragic outcome. Accordingly, the concluding chapter is set out as a "Citizen's Guide," pulling together the suggestions made throughout the book that empower citizens to shape a prosperous future through the myriad of roles they hold in society.

PART I

INCLUSIVE GOVERNANCE

CHAPTER 2

THE GREAT TRUST CRISIS

Generational Blues or Existential Crisis?

On a chilly spring evening in 2018, I found myself walking to the Flower Shop, a curiously named restaurant in New York City's East Village, to meet with three young college students who were all driving impressive social initiatives. The students had been selected as Dalai Lama Fellows, a program in the University of Virginia's Contemplative Sciences Center, dedicated to nurturing young leaders in solving global challenges through the discipline of mindfulness.

In all honesty, I felt a little intimidated by them. Most of my college and graduate-school years had been spent between the books and the pubs—with my primary focus being getting ahead academically and professionally. In those days, I spent very little time outside the blinders of my own personal ambition, wondering how to make a meaningful social contribution. Now, here I was with a group of bright and well-informed students who had each made a ninety-degree turn from the rat race, and who were already devoting a great deal of their energy and time to making the world a better place.

Over appetizers we made our introductions, and then my new friends began to share stories about their experiences. R.J. Khalaf, a Palestinian-American sophomore at NYU, had founded LEAD Palestine, an NGO focused on providing summer programs on English and leadership to adolescent children in Palestinian refugee camps. Azza Cohen, a Jewish-American film student from Princeton, told me about her life-changing experiences working in a legal-aid clinic in Varanasi, which helped victims of human trafficking take action against their captors. She had made a documentary—Specks of Dust: A Better World—giving voice to children born into the sex trade, in order to raise awareness of the stigma and discrimination they face. And Hannah Dehradunwala, a Pakistani-American from Columbia University, who was running a social enterprise called Transfernation that used a digital app to ferry leftover food from the bounteous catering at Manhattan professional service firms to shelters in the surrounding boroughs; the tax relief the donating organizations received paid for the distribution costs—and then some!

Ultimately, my intimidation gave way to sheer admiration—and I felt compelled to ask the question every fan would want to ask their idol: What motivated you to take on these impossible challenges? The conversation, which had been very upbeat and lively to this point, suddenly took on a more somber tone. The students took turns trying to crystallize the driving force behind their labors, until one simple comment struck a resonant note: "We don't fit!"

Being confident and popular students, they weren't referring to a lack of social acceptance by their peers. What didn't "fit" was the disconnect between their profound sense of social purpose and how they saw the social fabric unraveling in the world around them. As firm believers in tolerance, they sympathized with the millions living under repression or persecution in places like Syria, China, and Venezuela. As guardians of truth, they balked at the bias and sheer misinformation they saw in the media. As champions of opportunity, they were appalled by the unconscionable inequality they encountered every day in and around New York City. And as environmentally concerned citizens, they were alarmed at the lack of action being taken to avert a climate and environmental crisis.

A central thread running through their discontent was a deep disappointment in political leadership and a jaded distrust of institutions. They found little inspiration in the fractious rhetoric from the recent crop of populist leaders such as Trump, Orbán, and Duterte. But the "establishment" had also proven itself to be thoroughly corrupt. In Brazil, President Dilma Rousseff had been impeached in 2015 on criminal budget-misconduct charges. Just two years later, in 2017, the president of South Korea, Park Geun-hye, was also impeached on charges stemming from allegations of abuse of power and influence peddling.

The students' trust in large corporations was also in short supply. Volkswagen's wholly false claims about the emission levels in their cars had been a particularly shocking revelation. The Volkswagen fraud put into doubt every piece of "scientific" data used to persuade consumers to buy a product. It's not unreasonable to wonder: Can any of us really trust the safety of our shampoo, our medication, or even our food supply? Moreover, in the wake of recent social-media scandals involving the leakage of personal data to third parties for use in micro-targeting political campaigns, the students already knew that tech companies could not be trusted with their private information.

My companions clearly felt let down. They felt that their voices were not being heard. They felt marginalized. Without a clear channel to express their views, or a reliable mechanism to work within the system, they now felt compelled to take matters into their own hands to make a difference.

As I left the restaurant, I began to reflect on the bind my new friends found themselves in. Were they simply suffering from a case of generational blues—the angst that each cohort of young people must navigate as a rite of passage—or did their creeping sense of not "fitting in" have a more ominous cause?

Social Capital and the Three Freedoms

The Malady of Social Capital

When I think about the bright young university students I first encountered in the East Village, I can't help but wonder if they were suffering from a more serious malady than the age-old dance of each new generation finding its place in the world. They instinctively understood that there's much more to prosperity than financial and material well-being, valuing the importance of human dignity and fulfillment, a clean environment, and a strong social fabric to secure the long-term well-being of fellow citizens. Yet they were genuinely troubled by the vision of a world besieged by the serious challenges looming ahead.

These young people weren't underprivileged. In fact, quite the opposite. They were excellent students at elite universities looking ahead to a future filled with promises and opportunities. They were ideally positioned for rapid advancement and success in the wealthiest and most technologically advanced society the world has ever known. So, what was missing from their lives?

One data point that might help to explain this seeming paradox is a recent study from Edelman, the global-powerhouse PR firm. Each year, Edelman conducts a survey on the levels of public trust in various types of institutions. According to the Edelman data, 2016 saw a record plunge in public trust. The study observed declines in twenty-one out of the twenty-eight countries surveyed. Trust fell in every type of institution measured—government, the media, business, and NGOs—and these trust scores have picked up slightly at the time of writing, three years on. But the majority of populations are still distrustful of their country's institutions.[1]

So how does the concept of trust relate to the future lives and careers of my young friends? Let's turn for a moment and take a look at the way most of us think about our own professional and financial futures. We are all familiar with idea of capital. In finance and economics, we use this word to describe certain types of assets. It may refer to financial assets such as money, stocks, and bonds held in a brokerage account, or real assets such as land and real estate. In a business, capital may refer to tangible assets such as buildings, computers, plant equipment, and heavy machinery. But capital could also refer to intangible assets such as a brands or intellectual property. These "hard" types of capital show up on the balance sheets and income statements that accountants prepare for companies, individuals, and governments. To a greater or lesser extent, the pursuit of these forms of capital motivates much of our daily thinking.

But what if, in order to understand the plight that my student friends faced, we need to expand our definition of what capital is? What if the traditional notions of capital don't adequately describe the choices our students were making?

If my student friends wanted to acquire financial capital as cash paid out in salary and bonuses, they might aspire to go to work at a tech giant like Google, a prestigious law firm, or at an investment bank like Goldman Sachs. But that was not their calling. To understand what motivated their decisions—what they truly valued—we need to broaden the idea of capital to express the needs and desires the students felt.

A model that can help us to do this has been developed by the Forum for the Future, which views prosperity as the balance of Five Capitals: manufactured capital, financial capital, social capital, human capital, and natural capital.[2]

Economists will instinctively react to a framework like this by asserting that all Five Capitals could, in some way, be translated into the terms of financial capital. This is certainly true of manufactured capital, which includes intellectual property. They might point out that natural capital can be "priced" for key commodities such as oil, metals, water, and maybe even carbon. Human capital can be expressed as a wage, they might say. And maybe social capital could be linked to costs incurred—for example, in social services—to unlock additional economic output. There is some validity to such statements, and I would certainly encourage improvements in the discipline of financial accounting as applied to these "softer" forms of capital.

But the truth is that narrow financial metrics can barely keep up with pricing basic commodities such as water, common pollutants, and carbon— let alone placing a value on the rich biodiversity of the planet. A wage does little to measure the true value of individual human potential. And what value do we put on social capital when the outcome from its depletion is civil unrest and conflict? But it is precisely these values—as represented by natural, human, and social capital—that profoundly motivated my student friends. And with good reason. Across the broad sweep of human history, what all successful civilizations have had in common is their ability to maintain high levels of all Five Capitals.

In acknowledgement that our standard financial and economic metrics are wholly inadequate for capturing the important values embedded in the Five Capitals, many commentators and international agencies have written about additional measures that should help steer our action.

The UN has been at the forefront of efforts to expand our measure- ment of prosperity. The UN Environment Programme, for example, leads the Inclusive Wealth Index, which aggregates scores for produced capital, natural capital, and human capital for 140 countries. And the UN's "17 Sus- tainable Development Goals" (SDGs) have identified 165 targets that they believe are essential to securing a sustainable future.

Although these efforts are laudable contributions—and the SDGs represent a landmark achievement in global alignment to drive positive action—I believe most people would benefit from a more compact set of considerations, accompanied by a small set of indicators, to help guide their choices and actions. To that end, this book endeavors to offer a simple Citizen's Guide that I believe is much needed to help us shape a prosperous 21st century.

But where to start? Taking a cue from my young friends, the most palpa- ble deficit they felt was "trust in the system," stemming from the erosion of social capital all around them. Indeed, among the Five Capitals, I believe that social capital—the true metric of which is trust—has a special role because it provides the unifying force that holds a society together. The greatest civilizations all managed to build up the Five Capitals, but those that endured stand apart because they were able to regenerate their social capital. Moreover, the ultimate demise of these great civilizations can usually be traced back to the moment when their accumulated social capital eventually began to crumble. Let's take a brief look at one prominent example from history.

Enduring Empire

The British Empire's inclusive political governance, social meritocracy, and highly developed public administration—which were all highly advanced for their time—helped to create a high level of social capital for British citizens and allowed their country to hover at the apex of global power for nearly 200 years.

The extraordinary ascent and enduring power of the British Empire has captivated historians for generations—and for good reason. At its peak, Britain's dominance in industrial power and naval might allowed it to rule an extraordinary 25 percent of the world's landmass. Understanding just how this came to pass requires a brief look into the history of Britain's rise to supremacy.

After the English Civil War ended in 1651, a new locus of power emerged outside the monarchy and nobility. Parliament consummated a more inclusive form of national governance by passing the Bill of Rights, which greatly expanded its own powers as a collective of elected representatives and limited those of the king. Over the following century, other segments of society—agricultural combines, newspaper barons, factory owners, traders, and the military—began to thrive in this environment of expanding freedom. Innovation and entrepreneurship blossomed, ultimately sparking the Industrial Revolution in its wake.

In order to hold together such a vast and flourishing empire, Britain required considerable administrative sophistication and expertise. The demand for such administration became not just a cost for Britain, but also an opportunity—one that relied on the collective social capital of British citizens. By extending its civil service institutions in each of its colonies, and by populating them with local staff and ruling indirectly through local elites, Britain was able to run the empire with around 40,000[3] British civil servants in the UK by the turn of the 20th century.

Similarly, at home in Britain, the British Empire responded to the massive social disruption that had been caused by the Industrial Revolution with brilliant innovations in the public services that the state provided to its citizens. During the Victorian Era (1837–1901), Britain's population almost doubled from 25.5 million to 41 million. Simultaneously, the proportion of Britons living in cities rose dramatically from approximately one third in the early 1800s to nearly 80 percent by 1911.

During this wave of urbanization, cities in Britain became overcrowded and squalid due to a shortage of affordable housing, clean water, sanitation services, and public-health facilities. Working conditions were harsh, and child labor was ubiquitous. In the framework of the Five Capitals, we might say that the turmoil created by the rise of manufactured capital threatened to ravage the nation's social capital.

However, throughout the 19th century, Britain addressed this looming crisis by continuously improving the social infrastructure of British society. The proportion of children in Britain who received some schooling increased from 20 percent to 50 percent, a police force was created to enforce law and order, tolerable standards of labor were introduced, and many charities sprung up to offer health services. By 1911, Britain had introduced limited national-health benefits and unemployment insurance as the green shoots of the social-welfare model grew in scope. In 1900, the Labour Party was established to further advance the cause of the working class of Britain, and it greatly expanded the welfare state upon reaching government a few short years later in 1924.

But as the rest of the world caught up in its standards of social welfare, the empire's moral inconsistencies led to its ultimate demise. The British Empire was meritocratic only for a relatively small proportion of its subjects. While the growing class of merchants and tradesman could find opportunity in Britain's imperial trade and industry, there was still relatively little mobility between Britain's social classes. Furthermore, the vast majority of subjects in the colonies were systematically discriminated against and regarded by the empire as second-class citizens.

Over the next several decades, the empire disintegrated, as it became clear Britain no longer had the moral authority to rule over its colonial subjects. At root was the fact that the empire was extractive. Take India— evidence suggests its per capita income declined by 8 percent over the period 1757–1947, compared with a 300 percent increase in the UK. Now, it's possible this could have been due to poor levels of productivity in India and excellent levels in the UK. While this undoubtedly played a large part, research by Utsa Patnaik suggests that Britain used about a third of the revenues it gained from taxing Indians in order to pay for goods produced in India for British consumption.[4]

After a major revolt against British rule in 1857, the British government took direct control over governing India from the East India Company. Although Britain did consult with the Indian population more than before—for example, by including Indians in the Legislative Assembly—the mutiny became a turning point for the rise of Indian self-determination. Similar movements rose up in Britain's other colonies, especially after colonial subjects fought for the empire in World War I, yet still were not rewarded with the dignity of self-determination.

In many ways, the British Empire provides an excellent example of how successful civilizations are innovators in creating new forms of social capital—one that is still relevant and resonant today. It demonstrates how social capital must be dynamic and continuously evolve to higher standards in order to sustain a healthy society. But it also offers a warning from the past about how societies can lose their way and diminish in stature when their stores of social capital are not replenished and updated.

The Three Freedoms

The history of the British Empire provides an interesting case-study to think about the workings of social capital. But how can we put a little more definition on what social capital is and how it can be measured?

To understand social capital, let's start by thinking about the fundamental relationship between the rulers of a society and the citizens they govern. Citizens consent to being governed by their rulers, and in exchange, they put their trust in the ruling establishment to provide the broadest possible scope of freedom. If this trust is perceived to have been breached, and the adequate freedoms are not provided, citizens will agitate to change their rulers—either through an orderly, pre-defined process or by more disruptive and even violent means.

I believe that it is helpful to think of social capital as the strength of the relationship between rulers and the citizens they govern. In turn, the strength of this relationship is reflected in the trust that binds rulers and citizens, as well as different parts of a society, together. This is why I view trust as an insightful metric of social capital. And since it is a metric that we have been measuring for many years—albeit with crude tools such as surveys—it does provide an important barometer of social cohesion.

Unfortunately, most countries are distrustful of their institutions, indicating that social capital has been depleted around the world because rulers are not delivering the level of freedom that their citizens expect. In other words, we are in the depths of the Great Trust Crisis.

In order to lift ourselves out of this crisis, we must now probe deeper into what social capital consists of, so that we can gather clues for restoring its depleted levels. A good place to start in addressing this challenge is to consider the critical commodity that citizens are exchanging in return for their consent to be governed: freedom.

But since freedom itself is a dynamic concept, it is important to take a moment to define the term. Our notion of freedom has evolved—and expanded—over the centuries, and we rightly expect much more today than in past centuries. Some of our earliest ideas about freedom come from religious teachings. In Christianity, Jesus says that the truth will set us free—that is, repenting our sins and following his teachings will lead to spiritual freedom. The theme of righteous actions leading to salvation— freedom from suffering—seems to be a common theme among religions. Many religions go into detail on other aspects of liberty. Islam speaks of the liberties of "life, religion, reason, property, and lineage." Confucius paints freedom as a state of stable, unified, and enduring social harmony—a state that only arises if rulers concern themselves with justice and compassion for their subjects, if rank is conferred based on merit, and if people treat others as they would wish to be treated.

In Western philosophical thought, freedom had narrow beginnings. Hobbes's Leviathan, written during the English Civil War (1642–51), called for an absolute monarchy to keep control of the forces of human anarchy. Hobbes argued that the constraints on individual liberty were worth "keeping the peace," that is, freedom from violence. In the 18th century, Adam Smith espoused the benefits of free trade and railed against the rigging of markets by businesses and governments. He also argued for public goods such as universal education.

By the 19th century, J.S. Mill encouraged utilitarianism—maximizing happiness and well-being for all members of society—and government action only where necessary, such as ensuring public security or intervening in times of recession to prevent extreme social hardship. From the 1850s, the freedom to participate in the political process became a focal point as the right to vote was extended to progressively broader segments of society.

The 20th century also saw significant improvements in human rights and the alleviation of poverty. Friedrich Hayek and Joseph Schumpeter made the powerful case for markets to be as free as possible. And gradually freedom came to encompass the welfare state, which provided citizens with education, healthcare and other public services necessary to achieve their full potential.

In recent decades, we've been inundated with a host of new indices for measuring freedom. Freedom House, the US-based NGO, measures twenty-five variables, including freedom of the press, religious liberty, rule of law, right to form and join political parties, and electoral transparency, among others. The World Bank's Social Progress Index is more socioeconomic in scope and measures a society's ability to combat poverty and meet citizens' basic welfare needs. The Economist Intelligence Unit's Democracy Index, by contrast, focuses more on democratic institutions, political culture, and civil liberties.

Within this plethora of indices, I find no single satisfactory standard that holistically captures our modern-day expectations for freedom. However, when we zoom out from the chatter and skim along the high-water marks of human liberty, I believe that modern societies aspire to freedom in three basic categories: **political participation**, **civil liberties** and **socioeconomic mobility**. Let me summarize what I mean by these terms:

- ▸ **Political participation:** Political participation offers every citizen the right to engage equally in choosing their rulers. There is space for differing opinions and ideas and a political culture that fosters constructive dialogue and respectful conduct. An independent media, committed to accurate reporting, enables citizens to make well-informed decisions in free and fair elections. Adequate powers are devolved to local communities to afford them control over local resources and policies to shape their own economic-development pathway.

- ▸ **Civil liberties:** Civil liberties, upheld by the impartial rule of law, protect a citizen's basic human rights and render all people equal before the law. Citizens also enjoy freedom of expression and beliefs based on access to truthful information, associational and organizational rights, and the right to own property. An effective security apparatus is maintained to enforce the rule of law, but it does so without infringing on the rights of innocent citizens.

- ▸ **Socioeconomic mobility:** Socioeconomic mobility is the provision of equal opportunities for individuals to advance materially and socially, regardless of their beginnings in life. All segments of society are equally active in the workforce, and advancement is based on merit. Competitive markets are preserved by the active curtailment of monopolies and rent seeking, while innovation is strongly incentivized and supported. Moderate levels of economic inequality are accepted to motivate hard work, but high-quality public goods and services—such as education, healthcare, childcare, infrastructure, and protections for vulnerable social groups in society—are readily available to all. Meanwhile, robust financial provisions are put in place to cover the society's long-term investment priorities.

Modern societies must provide all of these freedoms to maintain high levels of social capital and thereby achieve sustainable prosperity. When the citizenry, or marginalized segments within it, no longer believe that they are receiving these freedoms from their governments, a crisis in trust results.

In the remainder of this chapter, I will look at how these three freedoms have been eroded globally over the last few decades, leading to the Great Trust Crisis.

Freedom in Retreat

By all the metrics and indices mentioned so far, freedoms have been in retreat over the last few decades, and this has only intensified since the Global Financial Crisis.

The Rise of "Strongman" Rulers

Let's first look at the retreat of the first of the three freedoms: political participation.

As my young friends look ahead toward an uncertain future, and we sort through the complexities of the present, are there clues from the past that might help us untangle what has caused our current crisis of trust?

In 1991, Samuel Huntington released his seminal book The Third Wave: Democratization in the Late Twentieth Century. His work drew attention to the unprecedented increase in political freedom that had occurred during the preceding 150 years. Huntington laid out a model that showed freedom surging in three successive waves of democratization: the first took place between 1828 and 1926 with the granting of suffrage to the majority of citizens in Western countries (women much later than men); a second wave occurred after Allied victory in World War II, up until 1962; and the final wave started with the Carnation Revolution in Portugal in 1974 and sped up with the collapse of communism after 1989.[5] Since the period starting just before 1850, the number of democracies in the world exploded from just three to almost ninety by 2000, as reported by the Center for Systemic Peace (see Figure 1-1). This seemingly inexorable trend led many to speculate that we were riding a one-way train to full democratization across the world.

FIGURE 1-1: GLOBAL TRENDS IN GOVERNANCE (1800–2016)

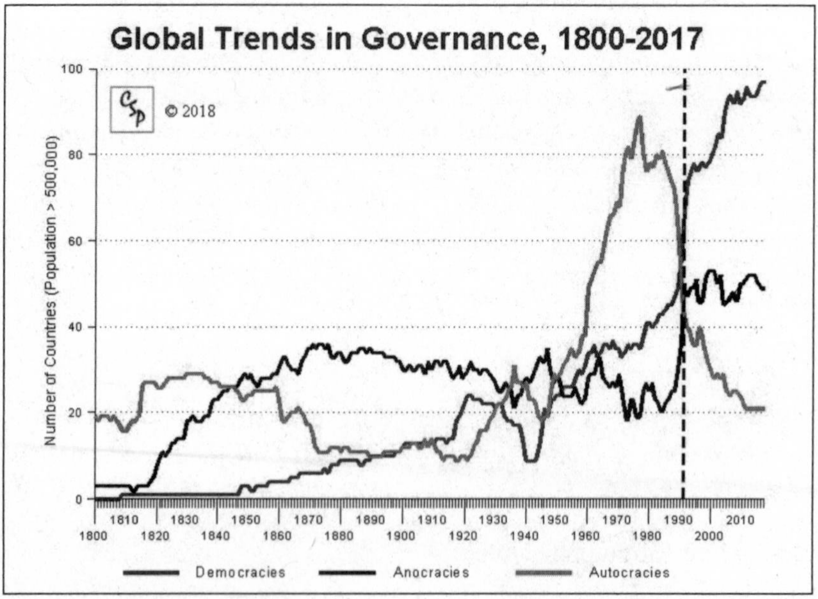

Source: Center for Systemic Peace[6]

For example, the prominent hedge-fund Renaissance Capital observed that once a country reaches the $10,000 income level, as measured in per capita purchasing-power terms, it would become an "immortal" democracy—meaning that the nation would remain a democracy in perpetuity.[7] And Francis Fukuyama famously predicted the "end of history"—a final victory of liberal democracy over all other political models—based on the success democracy experienced during the 20th century in pushing aside rival totalitarian political systems, such as communism, socialism, and fascism.

These predictions—which took the successes of the last 150 years and projected them forward indefinitely into the future—now seem premature. Since the mid-2000s, the number of democracies in the world has declined while the number of autocracies has increased.[8] Meanwhile, the charitable organization Freedom House has reported a global decline in political and civil rights every year since 2006. Specifically, according to the 2018 report,[9] political participation is declining because of the rise of populism perpetrated by strongman leaders. These strongmen operate in radically different environments: some in weak democracies, others in autocratic states, while others have penetrated the heart of liberal democracies. Critically, wherever strongmen operate, they follow a remarkably similar script—one that stifles the democratic process and weakens its core institutions.

Vladimir Putin, the Russian President, is perhaps the most notable example of this strain of modern strongman leader. Let's take a closer look at his playbook—one that many others have emulated. The first strategy is the rise to power on a platform that promises to "right perceived wrongs" for marginalized groups of citizens.

Before Putin came to power in the year 2000, Russia had experienced a decade of humiliation. In the wake of the breakup of the Soviet Union, Russia had lost its empire, its GDP had declined by 30 percent between 1991 and 1998, and much of its economy had been siphoned off to oligarchs during Boris Yeltsin's botched privatizations of state-owned enterprises. Within a decade, Russia had plunged from being a superpower to the brink of a failed state.

Strongmen thrive in such environments. They champion the marginalized and position themselves as a savior from outside the establishment. In Russia's case, the marginalized group was the broad population of the country, who had suffered while the oligarchs enriched themselves. Putin positioned himself as a traditionalist with economically liberal views, while distancing himself from Yeltsin's legacy. He publicly stated that he regarded the disintegration of the Soviet Union as a "geopolitical catastrophe" and was scathing of the oligarchic elites who had brought on Russia's decline.

Populist strongmen often notch up early successes by addressing the drivers of popular discontent that propelled them into power in the first place. For example, Putin set to work with bold policy actions such as renationalizing many of the companies that Yeltsin had privatized during his spell as prime minister. Yukos Oil was a notable example. By renationalizing many of Yukos' assets, Putin demonstrated his own political strength by wresting back control from one of the country's most powerful oligarchs. Putin also reversed some of the lawlessness of the Yeltsin years and put into place several sound macroeconomic policies such as keeping public spending low and creating financial buffers in case of harder times.[10]

Greatly aided by rising oil and gas prices, Russia's average annual real GDP growth was 6.9 percent during the period between 2000 and 2008, and the average purchasing power of Russian citizens more than doubled to US $21,600. Putin used the economic windfall to solidify his base of supporters by splashing out on pensioners and increasing military spending. But perhaps most importantly, he won broad support among the populace by restoring some measure of national pride.

In order to build up their own stature, strongmen rulers deploy a second strategy to galvanize support from their populaces. They begin to craft a national narrative and paint those who deviate from it as "public enemies." In Putin's case, the narrative was centered on Russia once again regaining its position as a great global power. Over time, the conveyor belt of "public enemies" he put forward to the Russian people have included: Chechen terrorists; "extremist" opposition voices at home; the expansionist ambitions of NATO and the European Union; and the United States. In the national narrative, each has been portrayed as stirring up trouble in the former lands of the Soviet Union.

Putin appears to have systematically neutered opposition voices via intimidation and criminalization. For example, the prominent critic Boris Nemtsov, once a senior member of Yeltsin's government, was arrested multiple times for attending protests against Putin's rule. He was assassinated in Moscow in 2015. Another significant critic of Putin, the lawyer and anti-corruption activist Alexei Navalny, has been arrested numerous times, including twice for embezzlement. He was barred from standing against Putin in the 2018 election on the basis of a criminal conviction, which insulated Putin from his most significant opponent in the election.

Control of the media is essential to promulgate Putin's narrative, elevate the strongman's personal image, and demonize the public enemies. After Chechen terrorists sieged Moscow's Dubrovka Theater in 2002, leading to the death of 150 hostages, Putin was furious at television coverage by one of Russia's major TV networks for what he said was "publicity on blood." He moved swiftly to replace its management, and by 2003 Putin had closed Russia's last independent TV station.

Thereafter, Putin ramped up his nationalist rhetoric. By the late 2000s, television stations were saturated with coverage of Putin, emphasizing him as the guarantor of Russia's social and political order and chief problem-solver. The regime destroyed faith in alternative narratives, smearing anti-Putin protestors, political activists, and NGOs. He would later fall out with Russia's liberals, who had been among his strongest supporters early in his rule and had praised his economic liberalism. However, when this group turned on Putin, protesting alleged electoral fraud in the 2011 parliamentary elections, he expanded the legal scope of the security services to include cracking down on "extremism"—a vague term designed to ensnarl opponents.

Strongmen also thrive by painting themselves as protectors against foreign adversaries, who are portrayed as saboteurs of the national narrative or oppressors of "countrymen" in neighboring states. Putin has used this strategy on several occasions. In 2008, Putin intervened to support the pro-Russian breakaway regions of South Ossetia and Abkhazia in Georgia. In 2014, Russia attacked the Ukraine on the grounds of aiding ethnic Russians in Crimea and the Eastern Ukrainian oblasts of Donetsk and Luhansk. Putin's propaganda machine went into overdrive after the Ukrainian invasion. Russian TV news barely covered anything else, projecting an image of Russia as a strong and capable nation that could protect its interests without asking permission from the West.

As their power grows, strongmen rulers use their third strategy—securing power by changing the institutions of governance. In 2004, Putin began this process by abolishing elections for regional governors and conferring the power to select them directly to himself. He also cracked down more overtly on the opposition. Those deemed a serious threat were simply not allowed to register in elections, with the Kremlin's powerful Presidential Administration body from 2007 demanding previously independent parties submit electoral party lists to the Kremlin before elections.[11]

While Russia's courts have been politicized since Soviet times, Putin's regime has regained primacy over the courts, following a period when business interests held more influence under Yeltsin.[12] The examples of opposition leaders convicted on spurious charges is testament to this fact. However, as Ella Paneyakh and Dina Rosenberg have argued, the picture is mixed, since Russians have also successfully challenged the government in courts, even sometimes in highly political cases such as human rights cases, where courts have ruled that the government wrongly persecuted a citizen.[13]

As the economy faltered following the Global Financial Crisis, Putin's authoritarianism has intensified. Oil prices have collapsed, and Western sanctions continue to bite in response to his invasion of Ukraine in 2014. The purchasing power of the average Russian is now lower than it was in 2013, and the poverty rate is again rising. On my recent trips to Russia, working with multi-national firms, I have found Moscow and St. Petersburg to be as visibly wealthy as any European city—while the rural areas surrounding them remain desperately poor. The patience of the Russian people may be wearing thin. Since 2016, fewer than half of Russians trust the government, with 9 percent and 10 percent declines in trust in 2016 and

2018, respectively. Russia has been at the bottom of Edelman's Trust Index of twenty-eight countries for three years running.[14]

Still, to many, Russia under Putin looks strong, even if it is in structural decline. Putin's strongman model has admirers in the populist governments of Central and Eastern Europe, which rule in seven out of fifteen countries in the region. Chief among them is Viktor Orbán of Hungary, who has similarly hollowed out democratic institutions under the nose of the EU. Populist strongmen are also in power in Turkey, the Philippines, Mexico, and Brazil. But most troubling is that the world's two largest powers have strongmen at their helm: President Xi has appointed himself ruler for life in China, while President Trump is attacking democratic institutions in the US—though he is facing stronger resistance from America's liberal democratic norms.

The War on Truth

Civil liberties—the second freedom that contributes to social capital— have experienced some gains over the past forty years. Although there is still a long way to go, women, various ethnic and minority groups, and the LGBTQ community have made great advances in their fight for equality. However, since the mid-2000s, the US NGO Freedom House has reported steady erosion in most measures of core civil liberties: freedom of expression and belief, associational and organizational rights, personal autonomy, and the rule of law.

While the overall decline is alarming, perhaps the most pernicious trend is the attack on the ability of citizens to access the truth. One of the most striking elements of Edelman's 2019 survey of public trust is the finding that the media is the least trusted institution around the world—with citizens in sixteen out of twenty-six countries surveyed ranking it as untrustworthy. Among the general population, sixty-three percent of Edelman's survey respondents in their 2018 study agreed that the average person does not know how to tell good journalism from rumor or falsehoods; 59 percent said it is becoming harder to tell if a piece of news was produced by a respected media organization.[15]

In roughly the last fifteen years, an accelerating trend of attacks on the free press has been in evidence, according to Freedom House's 2018 study. In countries where citizens live under anti-liberal rule, there has been a rising trend of government influence—and even outright takeover—of traditional media. For example, most TV stations in Russia and Turkey are controlled by Putin and Erdoğan's allies, respectively. But traditional media is also under pressure in the EU across countries such as Hungary, Czech Republic, and Austria. In the latter case, the state broadcaster has come under attacks from the country's right-wing government over spreading "lies."[16]

Perhaps most disturbing of all is the rising trend of journalists being murdered or attacked while reporting on political corruption. In the supposedly democratic EU, there were three such cases resulting in journalists' deaths in the two-year period between 2017 and 2018 alone. Moreover, autocratic regimes like Russia and China have now moved to control online news by arresting their critics and requiring the social-media companies inside their own borders to register the names of their users.

These recent trends have not simply curtailed the freedom of expression of citizens around the world; they have damaged the overall state of political accountability and pluralism.

Citizen Manipulation through Digital Media

One of the newest—and potentially most ominous—threats against the public trust is the rise of social manipulation through digital media, which is becoming a deeper and more pervasive presence in the lives of citizens across the globe.

Social media apps such as Facebook, WeChat, WhatsApp, Qzone, Twitter, and others have made it far easier to collect citizens' personal information—making them increasingly vulnerable to targeted manipulation and discrimination in ways that had not been previously foreseen.

Perhaps the most serious threat to our civil liberties from digital media comes from the micro-targeting of citizens during election campaigns. The best-known example of this disturbing phenomenon is the Cambridge Analytica scandal. The story began in June 2014, when a researcher named Aleksandr Kogan from Cambridge University in the UK developed a personality-quiz app that 270,000 Facebook users installed on their accounts. In addition to survey results, Kogan was also able to access data from the users' Facebook friends. Kogan then made a private database containing information from a staggering fifty million citizens, which he passed on to Cambridge Analytica, who subsequently made thirty million "psychographic" profiles of voters.

Cambridge Analytica then bought political ads and used the profiles to micro-target them to voters on behalf of the Brexit Leave campaign, the 2016 campaign for the presidential nomination of Ted Cruz, and the 2016 Trump campaign. Swing voters were targeted on platforms such as YouTube and the political news website Politico, using "sponsored content," such as a purported list of "10 Inconvenient Truths About the Clinton Foundation," to look like real journalism. The algorithms they used could be continuously updated and refreshed to deliver thousands of different messages to voters depending on the contents of their profile.

Although Cambridge Analytica has yet to be found guilty of breaking the law when it used the data during political campaigns,[17] the story highlights how voters are being manipulated through political advertising in the digital age with more calculating and intrusive tactics than prior generations of campaign managers could have ever dreamed possible.

Such manipulation damages the collective capacity for open debate, as citizens are fed only stories that conform with their preexisting biases (and often fears), stifling the shared experience of free expression and public discourse. In nearly every country throughout the world, political advertisers are not required to disclose the source of their funding for digital advertising.

Stories like Cambridge Analytica's algorithm scandal have further harmed voters' already deeply shaken faith in politics. The company, which is no longer active after negative publicity from the British and American scandals forced it to close, is also thought to have influenced campaigns in India, Mexico, Malta, and Kenya.

It seems quite likely that the world will see many similar examples of voter manipulation using digital means, as technology's power becomes irresistible to candidates and campaigners.

Social media's capacity for manipulation is by no means limited to electioneering. As examples of the underlying trend, two disturbing cases in the field of medicine have recently come to light. In the US, there are growing concerns that healthcare companies are using online data to socially profile patients based on attributes such as race to unfairly manipulate pricing for their healthcare plans.[18] Moreover, anti-vaccination groups have also been successful at whipping up fears that measles vaccinations cause autism, leading to an uptick in the incidence of measles itself.

Perhaps more sobering is the evidence that has emerged showing that state actors entered the fray with cyber-manipulation campaigns of their own. Egged on by the success it experienced domestically, Russia's Internet Research Agency (IRA) has trained its misinformation bazooka on other countries. Formed in mid-2013, the IRA was highly active in the US 2016 election,[19] using fake social media accounts to promote the Kremlin's position and sow discord abroad.

In the "post-truth" era of digital media, falsehoods can proliferate remarkably rapidly, and even the most absurd and outlandish tales can gain traction and warp public opinion. This was precisely the case when nearly 50 percent of Trump voters were led to believe that Hilary Clinton could be linked to a pedophilia ring—a bizarre tale that came to be known as "Pizzagate."[20]

The "story" had initially circulated among relatively obscure chat-board websites and included lurid tales that Clinton was sexually abusing children while taking part in Satanic rituals in the basement of a Washington, DC, pizza joint. After spreading virally on social media, it was picked up by right-wing platforms like Breitbart and InfoWars. Eventually, it morphed into a mainstream news event when a right-wing vigilante, Edgar Maddison Welch, took it upon himself to conduct a one-man "raid" on the pizza parlor armed with an AR-15 semiautomatic rifle, a .38 caliber revolver, and a folding knife. Needless to say, Edgar did not find what he was looking for.

This example illustrates just how easy it can be to mislead broad swathes of the population using fake news stories. The Clinton "Pizzagate" myth is believed to have arisen somewhat organically but was aided and abetted by a combination of online activists and Russian bots, who added layer upon layer to the story until it emerged as a full-blown conspiracy theory. It was exactly the sort of discord the IRA's foreign-activities group sought.

Experts in digital-media manipulation fear that fake videos—using a frighteningly believable technology known as "deepfakes"—are the next dangerous frontier in this trend. In an experiment, the University of Washington has already created believable doctored footage of a young Obama giving a speech he made years later.

Debasing of Expertise: A Fundamental Attack on Knowledge

The manipulation of information in digital media has been highly damaging to social trust, but it is by no means the only factor threatening our ability to access the truth. At an even more fundamental level, the basis of truth generation itself—scientific and academic inquiry—is also under assault. This frightening trend has recently been on display in both the corporate world and in academia.

At the corporate level, "greenwashing" a product or service to create an exaggerated impression of its environmental responsibility has become common. While it is unfair to belittle the progress made by some corporations, which we will explore later in this book, many corporate overtures to social responsibility or environmental sustainability are simply thinly veiled PR stunts or hollow gestures intended to influence investors and consumers.

One recent and prominent example, which came to light in 2015, is the massive scandal involving the German carmaker Volkswagen. Volkswagen fabricated test results for its diesel car fleet, making it seem that its cars had achieved low emissions while simultaneously maintaining stellar fuel economy.

As a penalty for their malfeasance, Volkswagen was forced to pay $25 billion by US authorities, and a single, mid-level VW manager was sentenced to seven years in prison. In the EU, however, which is VW's home market, the company still has not been prosecuted. Based on the absence of European fines and the lack of high-level criminal prosecutions, the relative impunity of VW in this case hardly seems likely to serve as a significant deterrent for other corporations to rein in a culture of deceit.

In academia, the number of scandals involving fabricated data has increased markedly in recent years. The case of the once-promising social psychologist Diederik Stapel, of the School of Social and Behavioral Science at Tilburg University in the Netherlands, serves as an example of just how simple it can be for academic professors to dupe the world.

Stapel's research on "priming" achieved global-celebrity status, with articles about his work appearing in the New York Times and the Los Angeles Times. "Priming" is the psychological theory that very small stimuli can affect human behavior in significant ways. It has been applied to demonstrate that background factors—like interviewing a test subject on a dirty street—can make people respond more negatively to questions they are asked.

The problem was that Stapel's data turned out to be entirely fabricated—the former rock-star professor had simply invented his own data in the kitchen after his wife and kids had gone to bed.

Reports suggest there are now 8,000 fake science journals online, which are known as predatory publishers. These journals convince scientists to submit their research, typically for exorbitant fees, but have no peer-review mechanism to validate the quality of the work.[21]

China is currently a hotbed for fake research. In 2017, the respected cancer-research journal Tumor Biology had to retract 107 papers it had published due to doubts about the integrity of the research. All 107 papers had been submitted by researchers in China.

Due to such broad, systemic manipulation of academic and commercial research, it's becoming ever more difficult for scientific knowledge to be taken seriously by the general public. The creeping sense of doubt sown by consecutive frauds underlines yet another mechanism by which citizens' power to access the truth is under threat in the most fundamental ways. In this toxic environment, politicians of questionable integrity can thrive. They take advantage of the overall debasing of knowledge and truth to broadcast their own self-serving falsehoods.

Inequality Reaching Extremes

Let's now turn our attention to the gradual decline over the past three to four decades of the third freedom: socioeconomic mobility.

There can be little doubt that the gap between rich and poor has widened markedly over this period in both developed countries and emerging markets such as India and China. Theories abound about why inequality has spiked in recent decades relative to the moderate levels that were the norm throughout much of the 20th century.

Thomas Piketty's seminal work, Capital in the Twenty-First Century, provides a very instructive historical perspective on the topic, looking mostly at France, Britain, and the US. In his book, Piketty argues that the world is returning to the high levels of inequality that were the historical norm before World War I. Piketty points out that prior to this period, private wealth—concentrated in a narrow band of rich families—tended to dwarf national wealth. By wealth, Piketty means assets that generate income—as opposed to money earned from wages and salaries.[22]

According to Piketty, inequality shoots up when the rate of return on capital remains greater than the rate of income growth, since capital tends to be held by a narrow group of the population.[23] It was only the effect of two World Wars, which destroyed a large amount of capital and were followed by higher taxes, inflation, economic growth, and welfare spending, which brought down the ratio of wealth to income. This was the so-called Golden Age of capitalism. However, by the 1980s these effects appear to have worn off, and we are now at levels of inequality approaching those of the Gilded Age before WWI. While his thesis has great merit, there is much more to the story.

Unpacking the complex interplay of factors that have led to the latest chapter of inequality, two themes emerge as the primary drivers. First, the structure of the global economy has shifted to become inherently more concentrated. Wealth and income in an increasingly global, knowledge-intensive economy have become concentrated in a narrow group of companies, a class of highly skilled creative workers, and a clutch of super-cities. Second, a wide array of policy choices has systematically favored the owners of capital over workers. Gradually, this trend has eroded the types of public services that enhance and promote socioeconomic mobility among citizens.

Let's take a look at both of these themes in more detail, with special attention paid to the United States, where inequality has reached the most extreme levels in the Western world.

A Concentrating Global Economy

Over the past several decades, structural concentrations have arisen in the world economy as the result of three key trends.

First, globalization has reduced trade frictions and allowed economic activity to aggregate where it enjoys significant comparative advantage.

Second, the growing knowledge-economy—powered by highly scalable, intangible assets such as intellectual property—has turned markets into "winner takes all" competitions and concentrated industry profits into relatively few companies. In addition, since the 1970s there has been a shift in corporate governance to elevate the interests of shareholders over those of all other corporate stakeholders. The practice of shareholder "primacy," in turn, has increased the share of corporate profits channeled to a relatively narrow class of shareholders and senior executives, while the share accruing to workers has declined.

Third, knowledge-intensive businesses have tended to cluster in big urban centers, creating a feedback loop that further concentrates the top "creative" talent and the owners of capital in our biggest cities.

Global Economic Integration

Since the creation of the World Trade Organization (WTO) in 1995, and the proliferation of regional trade deals that followed during the late 1990s and 2000s, the global economy has experienced a dramatic increase in the international trade of goods and services. As trade levels have increased, so too have mounting concerns that globalization has caused middle-class jobs to leak from developed to developing countries, driving up inequality in both parts of the world.

In 2012, a single chart published by the Serbian-American former World Bank economist Branko Milanović and his colleague Christoph Lakner took policy circles by storm. The chart seemed to illustrate that the worst fears about globalization and inequality were justified and supported by clear evidence. Commonly known as the "elephant chart," Milanović's analysis provides a lucid snapshot of the sharp rise in income inequality in the two decades leading up to the Global Financial Crisis.[24]

Plotting income growth for each percentile of the global income distribution, Milanović's elephant chart clearly shows the winners and losers of globalization since the late 1980s. The two groups that have benefitted most are the top 10 percent of the income distribution, who are mostly concentrated in developed countries, and the middle-class in emerging markets, particularly those in emerging Asia and parts of sub-Saharan Africa, who occupy the thirtieth to seventieth percentiles. By contrast, the biggest losers have been middle- and low-income workers in developed countries, who occupy the seventy-fifth to ninetieth percentiles of global income: their real wages have stagnated for the past twenty years.

These uneven trends in income growth have created chasms between the rich and poor in both emerging and developed countries. While hundreds of millions of citizens in developing countries have been lifted out of poverty, many millions have been left behind. In India, by 2014, the average person in the three richest states (Kerala, Tamil Nadu, and Maharashtra) earned three times as much as the average person in the poorest three states (Bihar, Uttar Pradesh, and Madhya Pradesh),[25] with just as bad interstate inequality reported more recently.[26] So, too, in China, where the Eastern-seaboard provinces are vastly wealthier than the interior provinces.

In the United States, the share of income earned by the richest 1 percent of the population doubled as a percentage share of national income—rising from 10 percent in 1980 to 20 percent in 2016. By 2016, the richest 1 percent also owned 38.6 percent of the country's wealth—a record high.

During the same period, the bottom 50 percent of the US population saw their share of income plunge from about 21 percent to 13 percent. To make matters worse, a substantial chunk of the population in the top 1 percent of US earners has become concentrated in cities of the Eastern and Western seaboards, such as San Francisco and New York City, whereas the bottom 50 percent disproportionately have come to occupy the deindustrialized heartland regions of the United States, such as the Midwest.

Now that we have an overview of the evolution of global wage-inequality, let's take a deeper look at the factors that have caused inequality to grow.

The Winner-Takes-All Economy

Consider this: one of the world's largest companies, Apple, has relatively few physical assets.[27] That, as Jonathan Haskel and Stian Westlake outline in Capitalism without Capital, is a stark example of how knowledge-intensive companies with intangible assets—such as a design, a brand, or a business process—are becoming increasingly dominant in developed and emerging economies alike.

Haskel and Westlake explain how the key features of intangible assets—the Four Ss: Scalability, Sunkenness, Spillovers, and Synergies—set them apart from their physical counterparts.

What makes intangible assets scalable is that they can be used by one person without depriving another of their benefits. As an example, think of computer code, which can be reused an infinite number of times, or the ability of a brand to extend its goodwill into another product line. Scalable intangible assets can be consumed repeatedly at virtually no additional cost to the company that owns them.

Intangible assets have another unusual property, which limits their value to competitors. Unlike land and factory equipment, which are physical assets that can be resold, a brand or a business process may have no value to any business outside of the firm that owns it. This property is referred to as sunkenness, because the development costs are, in effect, already sunk.

Intangible assets are also leaky and can easily spillover to other players in the industry. Although some intellectual property can be protected, it can be relatively easy to copy a design, circumvent a technological patent, or poach an employee with relevant know-how.

The final property that separates intangible assets from traditional assets is their tendency to create synergies. With intangible assets, disparate ideas, technologies, and designs can be combined in new permutations to create useful products and services. Google's search algorithm benefited from both spillovers and synergies from countless antecedents, such as the US military's research into networks between the 1960s and 1980s, as well as the work of competitors like Lycos, AltaVista, Internet Explorer, and Netscape. Eventually, in the 1990s, Google software engineers iterated those early efforts into one of the most powerful intangible assets ever created—the Google search engine.

Taken together, the Four Ss of intangible assets help to explain how a knowledge-intensive economy is inherently prone to concentration. As a hypothetical example, let's imagine a company that develops a new service that can be delivered digitally through a phone app. If the company's service meets customer needs better than any of its rivals, it's conceivable that the company can scale to near 100 percent market share—since the service can be delivered anywhere in the world at almost zero marginal cost.

Once that company has a lock on the relationship with the vast majority of customers, the company's valuation will likely soar, since the market expects that additional services will be sold to the customer base, and extraordinary profits will result. A growing valuation will enable access to additional funding, which can be invested in developing new IP or buying up innovative players in adjacent industries.

As the company's scope expands, it becomes better positioned to capture the spillovers and synergies within its own ecosystem and avoid the sunk costs of failed innovation. For example, if an innovation project fails at a large firm involved in a wide variety of business sectors, it is more likely that the firm will be able to recycle the IP into a future product elsewhere in its own portfolio. By contrast, a smaller independent firm would be more likely to experience the failure as a sunk cost. It is an interesting dynamic that scale—one of the Four Ss—enables a firm in an intangibles-intensive industry to overcome the challenges posed by spillovers and sunkenness—two of the other Four Ss.

In this winner-takes-all economy, size begets size. Bigger companies are best positioned to leverage their capabilities to grow into adjacent areas, gradually disrupting and conquering entirely new sectors. Companies such as Alphabet (the parent company of Google) and Amazon, as well as many other scale-players in fields where intangible capital matters most, illustrate this trend. They have each migrated from core markets into diverse areas such as payments, grocery retail, self-driving cars, biotechnology, utilities, healthcare, and more. In a winner-takes-all economy, market share and industry profits become concentrated in fewer firms—and, ultimately, in the hands of a narrow group of shareholders.

Although the concentration of market share and profits into fewer firms is most extreme in knowledge-intensive sectors such as technology, the manufacturing and services sectors are also showing similar trends as they progressively become more reliant on intangibles. We can observe this process accelerating as intelligent robots move onto the factory floor and AI enables faster service transactions and improved customer experience.

In addition to these technological drivers, legal and regulatory changes have also exacerbated the problem of economic concentration. Since the late 1970s, the United States and other Western capitalist economies have modified how profits are distributed among various stakeholders: shareholders, executive management, workers, customers, and suppliers. The shift to shareholder primacy—a view forcefully articulated by Milton

Friedman in the 1970s—has channeled a greater proportion of profits to shareholders and corporate executives. According to Friedman's view:

> So the question is, do corporate executives, provided they stay within the law, have responsibilities in their business activities other than to make as much money for their stockholders as possible? And my answer to that is, no they do not.[28]

This view of the corporation has led to various practices that arguably prioritize short-term cash distributions to shareholders—and the executives they hire. It has also led to the use of excess cash on the corporate balance-sheet to buy back shares, thereby increasing the stock price and increasing shareholder value. However, this means fewer resources are invested in longer-term growth drivers of the company, such as research-and-development that fuels the pipeline of new products, training that drives worker productivity, and benefits that encourage employee retention. Executive compensation packages have also contributed to the share-buyback mania in recent decades because, often, executives' long-term incentive plans are tied to performance metrics such as earnings per share, which go up when share buybacks leave fewer shares outstanding.[29]

The net result of such changes is significant: American CEOs now earn 312 times the wage of an average employee—compared with just twenty times the wage of an average employee in 1965. And European CEOs only earn 150 times their average employee's wages. Furthermore, in the United States the labor share of income has fallen from 70 percent during the 1970s to 62 percent today.

Urbanization and the Rise of the Creative Class

Increasingly, there is a geographic component closely linked with income-distribution issues. Knowledge-intensive companies, and the higher-paying jobs they create, have become ever more concentrated in leading global cities. In the US, cities such as New York, San Francisco, Los Angeles, Seattle, Denver, Chicago, Boston, Washington, DC, Philadelphia, Houston, and Dallas are at the forefront of this trend, which can be visualized by viewing the map of US income on CityLab.com.[30] These jobs have been taken by what American academic Richard Florida refers to as the "creative class." At its core, this class consists of scientists, engineers, professors, artists, designers, architects, and other thought-leaders. The creative class also encompasses knowledge-intensive workers in the high-tech, financial services, legal, and healthcare industries.

In the US, creative workers have grown from a quarter of the working population in 1980 to a third by 2010. Their wages are 66 percent higher than the US average. The phenomenon has replicated in many other countries around the world. The US is only thirty-fourth on the list of countries with the highest proportion of creative workers. Countries such as Singapore, Sweden, and Australia lead the rankings.

Knowledge-intensive companies are relatively mobile. After all, it's a lot easier to move IP from one city to another than to move a factory. Since they are less bound to physical assets or supplies of raw materials, these companies will tend to migrate to wherever they can find their key input—highly skilled creative workers.

After decades in which developed-world cities lost population and jobs to verdant suburban towns, the trend has reversed dramatically. The creative class is unequivocally congregating in urban centers that, according to Richard Florida, offer the "Three Ts"—Talent, Technology, and Tolerance.

Creative workers understand that the knowledge economy thrives on the cross-fertilization of disparate ideas, fostered by a dense network of connections between people. Even in an increasingly virtual world, this intense dialogue and exchange still requires face-to-face interaction with a wide variety of people. As a result, creative workers are drawn to cities where they can find high densities of top talent like themselves. It is from the resulting organized and serendipitous collisions—in incubators and co-working spaces, in coffee shops and in pubs and bars—where the big ideas are born.

But cities must offer more than just a high density of people to attract creative workers to them. They must be at the cutting edge of technology in specific fields. Research universities, government labs, and corporate research centers are essential ingredients. As reservoirs of the latest technological breakthroughs—and the young scientists and inventors that make them—universities are an indispensable source of ideas and talent. They help form the nexus for an ecosystem of start-ups, venture capital, and corporations all striving to translate technologies into useful products and services to benefit society.

Creative workers are also drawn to cities that are attractive and tolerant places to live. They must be accepting of outsiders, open to different cultures and lifestyles, and encouraging of self-expression. This, in turn, leads to an active scene for fashion, design, arts, and entertainment, a vibrant nightlife, and green spaces with outdoor recreation. These three factors, when present in sufficient quantities, create the high quality of life that creative workers crave.

Over the last twenty or thirty years, cities that have managed to harness the "Three Ts" have experienced extraordinary success. Dublin, the capital city of Ireland, is a prime example. Dublin has long been recognized as a seat of learning, boasting famous universities such as Trinity College and University College Dublin. Boosted by government investment, these universities and numerous tech colleges produce a strong supply of Irish graduates, 60 percent of whom receive degrees in computer engineering, digital design, or business studies. Since the 1990s, Dublin has attracted leading technology companies such as Oracle, Microsoft, IBM, and Apple with its value proposition of a technologically savvy talent base, competitive tax rates, and its position as an English-speaking staging point for the EU market.

Over this period, Dublin has also transformed itself into a diverse cultural hub with an alluring lifestyle for creative workers. Blessed with a rich literary and musical heritage and one of the youngest populations in Europe, Ireland took $255 million in EU structural funds[31] and transformed the Temple Bar district into Dublin's cultural quarter.

Dublin was an early mover in a worldwide trend of cities refashioning themselves into dense hubs for creative, knowledge-intensive industries. New York City, San Francisco, London, and Singapore also marked the first wave, but they have now been joined by many other cities around the globe—Boston, Austin, Denver, Pittsburgh, Lisbon, Tallinn, Santiago (Chile), and Eindhoven. But the top tier of global cities remains in a league of its own: 70 percent of ultra-high net-worth individuals—those with investable assets of $30 million or more—now live in just ten cities around the world.[32]

While leading cities have risen in prosperity, they have also paid a price for their success. These metropolitan areas now attract huge pools of capital, which pushes up property prices to levels that quickly become unaffordable for many longtime residents. Meanwhile, the wealthiest segments of the population, or older generations, who own the land and real estate in urban centers are well-positioned to realize the rents created by these inflated asset-prices—further entrenching existing inequality. The result is that much of the middle and working classes, as well as younger workers, are pushed out, reducing their access to the jobs and resources available in the city centers.

Through these dynamics, the geographic concentration of wealth in urban centers is creating numerous barriers to cultural diversity and socio-economic mobility, while contributing to the erosion of social cohesion in modern societies.

Policies Favoring Capital Owners

As the concentration of wealth has grown dramatically over the last thirty to forty years, it's perhaps not surprising that elites have translated their financial power into political influence. As a result, most Western countries have witnessed a shift to policies that favor capital owners over workers in this period.

A central feature of this era has been loose monetary policy, which has inflated the value of real and financial assets alike, clearly favoring richer people who are overwhelmingly the owners of such assets. During the twenty years prior to the Global Financial Crisis, the low-interest-rate environment and easing of credit regulations marked a prolonged, leverage-fueled bull run in the Western economies for most asset classes—but especially for equities, real estate, and commodities. In the decade since the crash, governments printed money to restore liquidity and economic growth. Yet, once again, cheap money found its way into pushing up asset prices.

At the same time that asset prices have soared, the taxes paid on them have fallen. This has been an era when capital-gains taxes, property taxes, and inheritance or estate taxes have all declined precipitously. For example, the US capital-gains tax has been cut in half—providing a windfall to the wealthiest Americans, who earn much of their income from capital invest-ments. Although the US has one of the highest rates of estate tax in the OECD at 40 percent,[33] the exemption has crept up to over $11.2 million per individual,[34] which is considerably higher than similar exemptions in other developed countries.

Corporate shareholders have also benefited from a declining corporate tax burden. Despite the fact that the headline US corporate tax rate had remained at 35 percent until recently, a slew of exemptions allowed the average company to pay an effective tax rate of around 24 percent. Under President Trump's new tax bill in 2017, however, the headline rate itself was slashed to 21 percent. Since companies have long had excess cash on hand, it seems highly likely that most of the tax cuts will find their way to share-holders and executives through increased dividends and bonuses.

Although tax receipts as a proportion of GDP have risen in OECD nations from about 25 percent of GDP in 1965 to 34 percent in 2017, much of the increase is the result of mushrooming pension and social-security liabilities due to aging populations. This has left a shrinking public purse to pay for the types of services that enable socioeconomic mobility—education, healthcare, infrastructure, and affordable housing. The net result is that affluent segments of society, such as the urban creative class, have enjoyed huge income gains and falling taxes, while the socioeconomic ladder has been pulled away from lower-income segments of society.

To top it all off, prosperous cities around the world are experiencing a housing crisis. With the knowledge economy and its creative workers concentrating in cities, rents and property prices have skyrocketed. Younger workers and even middle-income families who cannot afford to pay city rents, let alone buy a house, are being pushed progressively further out to suburbs and commuter towns.

In 1940, the median house price in the US was $30,600, adjusted for inflation based on year 2000 prices. By 2017, the median house price was almost $200,000—though the median home prices in cities such as San Francisco or New York were far higher.[35]

Finally, what of the social safety nets for the most vulnerable members of society? President Lyndon B. Johnson's "War on Poverty" introduced Medicare and Medicaid to provide subsidized healthcare to the poor and elderly. Although they have provided much relief, they have failed to keep up with soaring healthcare costs—and now President Trump intends to drastically slash federal funding for Medicare, Medicaid, and Social Security.[36] Moreover, Social Security is now underfunded, as the worker-to-retiree ratio falls—and most people's pension savings will not see them through retirement as lifespans increase.

The reality of the American experience today is that forty million citizens are living hand to mouth. A recent study, for example, showed that 44 percent of Americans have insufficient savings to cover even a $400 emergency expense.[37] This environment hardly provides the kind of security required to take on the risk of starting a new business—or even to enter an education or training program that could lead to enhanced professional opportunities and socioeconomic mobility.

The Raw Nerve

The Raw Deal experienced by so many individuals around the world, in developed and developing nations alike, has exposed a raw nerve among disaffected citizens. In recent decades, political participation has atrophied, civil liberties have fallen into retreat, and socioeconomic mobility has been slowly grinding to a standstill. Because of these and other challenges, the global stock of social capital has been depleted—and the world has fallen headlong into the throes of the Great Trust Crisis.

During the Global Financial Crisis a decade ago, coordinated global action from institutions such as the International Monetary Fund (IMF), the US Federal Reserve, and the European Central Bank (ECB) helped narrowly avert another Great Depression. The US government instituted an unprecedented $700 billion Troubled Asset Relief Program (TARP) to purchase toxic assets and equity from financial institutions to shore up the banking sector. Ominously, as we enter the third decade of the 21st century, there is no analogue for similar remedial action to address the challenges we now face from the global crisis of trust.

When the trust in a society is broken, there are no quick fixes on offer. Rather, the immediate trajectory is one of blame, acrimony, and turbulence in politics. At a time when national and global institutions are most urgently needed as forums for dialogue, they are being torn down by populist leaders. It augurs a dangerous period in which the risk of misunderstandings and miscalculations run dangerously high. As noted earlier in this chapter, aggression towards domestic and international "enemies," real or imagined, is a routine strategy in the populist strongman playbook. In an age of misinformation, where social media and information authoritarians can wage a war on truth from laptops and smartphones, it is not difficult to imagine that any one of many local skirmishes could spiral into an unplanned and unintended national or global conflict.

If reserves of trust are to be rebuilt, it will be through thoughtful dialogue, rational policy planning, and the strengthening of democratic institutions.

What chance is there of such improvements in national and global institutions of governance? My faith lies with the three social entrepreneurs I met in the East Village and the upswelling of social purpose they represent. It is a force whose magnitude is gradually making leaders around the world sit up and take notice.

Larry Fink, CEO of BlackRock, an asset management firm with $6 trillion invested in the world's largest corporations, captured it well in his annual letter to investee companies in 2019:

> *Over the past year, we have seen some of the world's most skilled employees stage walkouts and participate in contentious town halls, expressing their*

perspective on the importance of corporate purpose. This phenomenon will only grow as millennials and even younger generations occupy increasingly senior positions in business. In a recent survey by Deloitte, millennial workers were asked what the primary purpose of businesses should be—63 percent more of them said 'improving society' than said 'generating profit.' In the years to come, the sentiments of these generations will drive not only their decisions as employees but also as investors, with the world undergoing the largest transfer of wealth in history: $24 trillion from baby boomers to millennials. As wealth shifts and investing preferences change, environmental, social, and governance issues will be increasingly material to corporate valuations.[38]

In his letter, Fink points to the immense impact that can result when social purpose is infused into corporate and investment practices. The same weight of social purpose can rebuild social capital by rewriting our social contracts to be more cohesive and reshaping our institutions to be more inclusive. These will be the subjects that occupy us for the remainder of part 1 of this book.

CHAPTER 3

COHESIVE SOCIAL CONTRACTS

Joe the Plumber

At a campaign stop in the blue-collar town of Toledo, Ohio, during the 2008 presidential campaign, a man made his way through the crowd to ask candidate Barack Obama a question. "I'm getting ready to buy a company that makes $250,000 to $280,000 year," he said. "Your new tax plan's going to tax me more, isn't it?"[1]

The question came from an Ohio plumber named Joe Wurzelbacher. Obama responded that, under his new plan, Mr. Wurzelbacher would get a small tax cut for healthcare costs—but that he would, in fact, pay a little more tax. Wurzelbacher's small-business tax rate would rise from 36 percent to 39 percent for income above $250,000.[2] Raising taxes on the 5 percent of small businesses making more than $250,000, Obama said, would allow him to cut taxes on the 95 percent of small businesses earning less than quarter of a million dollars a year.

Obama justified his proposed policy in terms of the benefits it would create by redistributing income. "It's not that I want to punish your success," candidate Obama explained. "I just want to make sure that everybody who is behind you, that they've got a chance at success, too.... Just put yourself back ten years ago when you were making less, maybe $60,000 or $70,000.

Under my tax plan, you would keep more of your paycheck, save more, and you would've gotten to where you are faster. My attitude is that if the economy's good for folks from the bottom up, it's gonna be good for everybody. If you've got a plumbing business, you're gonna be better off if you've got a whole bunch of customers who can afford to hire you, and right now everybody's so pinched that business is bad for everybody. And I think when you spread the wealth around, it's good for everybody."[3]

That explanation didn't satisfy "Joe the Plumber," as Mr. Wurzelbacher quickly became known—and he wasn't shy about expressing his views: "Because you're successful you have to pay more than everyone else?" he protested during a television interview. "It's a basic right," Wurzelbacher continued, referring to paying the same tax as everyone else. "Obama wants to take that basic right and penalize me for it...and that's a very socialist view, and it's just incredibly wrong."[4]

Joe the Plumber's message had a strong resonance with a certain segment of the American electorate, and he became an unexpected cult hero during the campaign. So much so, in fact, that Republican presidential candidate John McCain seized on his story and made Joe the Plumber's argument one of the central themes of his campaign.

McCain went on to argue, "[W]e need to cut people's taxes, we need to encourage business, create jobs—not spread the wealth around."[5] In essence, McCain's pitch was that by putting more money in people's pockets, that money could be more effectively spent in the economy, since the individuals themselves are best placed to decide how to spend it.

McCain's argument was a sympathetic one, and he appeared to score powerful rhetorical points with his charge: namely, that Obama was "penalizing success" by increasing the federal tax burden that small business owners assumed.

Looking back, it's clear why the exchange between Joe the Plumber and Obama became a lightning rod in the 2008 presidential campaign, transcending tax issues and sparking a debate about the heart of the social contract in America.

America's Social Contract

As I described in chapter 2, citizens consent to being governed in return for the protection and enhancement of their freedoms. The "terms" of this agreement constitute a social contract. Some aspects of a social contract can exist explicitly in formal documents, such as national constitutions, economic-vision statements, or a national body of law. However, aspects of a social contract can also be part of a popular narrative represented by specific events in a nation's history, national stories, slogans, symbols, and so on. As we have seen, successful societies are pioneers of social innovation. As a result, their social contracts are dynamic—while retaining a set of enduring values, they can also evolve to adapt to the changing realities of a particular period in history.

In 2008, and even more so today, there is growing sentiment that the US must write a new chapter in its social contract to keep up with changing attitudes and restore social capital. We see this reflected in historically low levels of trust in the federal government. Pew Research reports that just 19 percent of Americans trust the government in Washington to do what is right "just about always" or "most of the time." Indeed, less than three in ten Americans have expressed trust in the federal government in every survey since 2007.[6] This contrasts sharply with 1958, when 73 percent said they trusted the government just about always or most of the time. Interestingly, though, such views are not mirrored towards local government. Two-thirds of Americans have a favorable view of their local government, and nearly three-quarters say the quality of candidates in recent local elections have been good, while only 41 percent say the same about presidential candidates.[7]

One area where there has been a marked change in public opinion over the last thirty years is whether the prevailing level of inequality helps or hinders the motivation to work hard and achieve success. Signs have emerged that wealth inequality is now being viewed as a progressively more urgent problem in the US and around the world. Writing in Foreign Affairs, Ronald Inglehart says that the annual World Values Surveys in the late 1980s and early 1990s found that there was general agreement with the belief that income inequality generates aspirations and drives productivity. In 1989, the survey found that people in fifty-two out of sixty-five countries supported the assertion: "Income differences should be larger to provide incentives for individual effort." But since then, the trend has steadily reversed. In fact, today there is a widely held belief that the current levels of inequality are intolerable. The 2016 World Values Survey results showed that respondents in fifty-one out sixty-five countries, including the United States, overwhelmingly supported the statement: "Incomes should be more equal."[8]

It's not surprising that such a dramatic shift in the public perspective should precipitate a reexamination of social priorities. And given the growing public concerns about inequality and the desperate need to stimulate the economy during the depths of the Global Financial Crisis in 2008, it's easy to see that Obama's proposals had great merit for the urgent requirements of the time, as well as more universally.

It's well known to economists that if you want to stimulate demand, one effective way to do so is to invest in the economic development of the poorest citizens in a society. This can be done through tax cuts, other types of transfer payments, or investments in infrastructure and services that increase their access to new economic opportunities.

Poorer citizens in an economy tend to spend far more of their disposable income than those who are wealthier, because more of the essential needs of the poor remain unmet. Richer households, on the other hand, tend to save or invest a higher proportion of any additional income they receive.[9] Because of these effects, putting more money in the hands of those who have the least generates greater consumption, increases total demand for goods and services, and ultimately creates more business for entrepreneurs such as Joe the Plumber.

In order to succeed, entrepreneurs also rely on a broad set of social investments. They need robust social services to provide a steady supply of educated workers, transit systems to enable workers to get to and from their jobs, and good transportation and communications networks to move goods to their point of sale and enable business interactions.

Businesses also require new discoveries from basic research, which is quite often publicly funded. It's tempting to think that shiny new products, such as iPhones, are developed exclusively by corporations like Apple. But as the work of the Italian-American economist Mariana Mazzucato demonstrates, many of the technological breakthroughs that made the iPhone possible were because of research carried out by public institutions.

The World Wide Web was made possible by the work of British scientist Sir Tim Berners-Lee working at CERN, the particle-physics research center in Switzerland funded by European governments. The internet was first started by an unprecedented network of computers funded by the US Department of Defense in the 1960s. The inventor of the touch screen was an engineer named E.A. Johnson, working for an agency of the British government. And Siri—the virtual voice assistant on iPhones—was made possible by research funded by the US Defense Advanced Research Projects Agency (DARPA). The agency, responsible for developing emerging technologies for use by the military, commissioned Stanford Research Institute in 2000 to create a virtual office-assistant to help military personnel to do their jobs.[10] These are only a few of the examples of how government research made the iPhone possible.

All this being said, I also believe that the arguments of Joe the Plumber and John McCain had several merits. First, McCain was right to pick up on Obama's clumsy comment about "spreading the wealth around." While Obama did say he wanted taxes to be used as a way to ensure others had a "chance at success," as Joe the Plumber had achieved, he still slipped into the unhelpful way many see taxes—as a form of redistribution. Instead, I find it much more helpful to think of taxes as public contributions to socioeconomic investments that benefit the whole of society. When viewed through this lens, it would make sense to most people that taxpayer money be used to fund public investments, if such investments generate more economic activity than if the money remained with individuals or with private-sector firms.

But we should go beyond mere rebranding and move to greater transparency on how taxes are used. The public deserves to know exactly what beneficial goals their "contributions" will serve and what financial return may be derived from these "investments." For example, a new water tax is being considered in California, where the water situation has reached crisis proportions. Alarmingly, one million people in the state do not have access to safe drinking water. The proposed tax would raise $150 million in revenues per year for water action. But how should the money be spent? One promising suggestion that's being considered is that some of the money be put into a fund to invest in infrastructure projects and businesses that lead to the conservation of water. Such a fund could be professionally managed and governed in a way that achieves the required public accountability.

The benefits of this approach would be numerous. It would create a clearer line of sight between the public investments made using taxpayer money and the socioeconomic impact achieved. If the investments were fruitful, the public money would generate a financial return that could be reinvested or used to reduce the tax burden in the future. Finally, if structured as investments, it is also easier for public projects to attract private capital as co-investment.

Second, Joe the Plumber was right that taxation should not be too high. Although changing public opinion may indicate a greater willingness to collect more public contributions for social investments that address the distortions caused by inequality, this is not a license to be profligate with public funds.

As mentioned in chapter 2, the average tax take in OECD countries was only 25 percent in 1965, 9 percent lower than it is today.[11] And while the

US may appear to be a low-tax country—with tax revenues at 27 percent of its GDP today[12]—this is misleading because it under-invests in public goods, such as infrastructure, and transfers substantial social costs directly onto citizens. For example, spending on social services like healthcare is highly inflated and inefficient—the US spends twice as much on healthcare than other high-income countries but has the lowest life expectancy and highest infant mortality among all of them.[13] And only 45 percent of the total spending on US healthcare comes from public funds.

One point that neither Obama nor Joe the Plumber made was that the US could impose less tax on labor and more on wealth. In OECD countries, 50 percent of tax revenue on average is labor-related (individual income taxes and payroll or social-security contributions), but in the United States it represents a 64 percent share.[14] These are taxes that hit middle-income citizens like Joe the Plumber most directly.

Since most Americans suffered a substantial write-down in the value of their assets during the Global Financial Crisis, it's not surprising that wealth taxes did not feature as a key issue in the 2008 election. Additionally, while the OECD average for wealth taxes is 6 percent, the US is higher at 10 percent because property taxes are used to fund education and other local services.[15]

However, given how unequal the US has become today, with the three wealthiest people owning the the same amount of assets as the bottom half of the population, it may be worth re-visiting tax increases on land, property, capital gains, and estate taxes—at least for the ultra-wealthy. For now, President Trump has gone in the opposite direction, by raising the thresholds on estates tax to $11.2 million for singles and $22.4 million for couples. Taxes on long-term capital gains, the source of a significant chunk of the wealthiest Americans' earnings, have also dropped precipitously in the last thirty years.[16] At least some of these tax cuts might be better invested in infrastructure and public services or put in the hands of average citizens like Joe the Plumber.

Another area where Americans' attitudes are changing rapidly is on how they view the environment. In 2008, just 41 percent of Americans thought protecting the environment should be a top priority for the president and Congress. Now almost 60 percent think it should be. As we will discuss in chapter 7, we have not adequately priced the negative impact caused by carbon and other pollutants, and we treat water as a free resource when it is, in fact, a scarce commodity. From a taxation standpoint, consumption taxes comprise 32 percent of total public revenues for the OECD on average, but only 17 percent in the US—very little of that being in the form of environmental taxes. In a similar vein, we ought to have more tax incentives to encourage good behavior. In the US, for example, we should expand the scope of programs such as the 45Q tax credit for carbon capture and investment tax-credits for solar panels.

As well as changing attitudes on inequality and the environment, there have also been seismic shifts in public attitudes on key issues such as gender quality and LGBTQ rights. Because of all these changes, America's social contract needs a radical update. Neither Obama's vision nor Trump's seem to have set the course towards a cohesive social contract that brings the country together and accounts for these attitudinal shifts. If and when such a compelling social contract is offered, it will likely precipitate a significant revision of many policies such as taxation.

In this chapter, I will examine examples of both good and bad social contracts and put forward a framework to help citizens better assess and evaluate them.

The Faustian Bargain

As we try to navigate the Great Trust Crisis, in search of cohesive social contracts that can unite a nation, we are at heightened risk from a dangerous breed of political promise that I refer to as the Faustian bargain. These bargains lead to harmful social contracts that ultimately erode the fabric of society.

In German folklore, Faust makes a pact with the devil, selling his soul in exchange for knowledge and worldly pleasure. In the myth, the deal with the devil destroys Faust's life, leading to the damnation of his lover, Gretchen, and the death of their child. The lesson of Faustian bargains is that they are ultimately self-defeating because what is surrendered is far more valuable than anything that could be gained in the deal.

Faustian bargains are responsible for the falling levels of freedom and trust that we observed in chapter 2. These bargains come in several varieties but never result in a cohesive social contract. One common type of Faustian promise—often used by populist politicians—is to offer a short-term advantage to one group of citizens at the exclusion or disadvantage of another. This is an expedient way to win votes, by exploiting societal fault lines such as identity, religion, or wealth. Alternatively, citizens may be promised more of one type of freedom, such as rapid economic growth and socioeconomic mobility, at the expense of greater state control, which will curb other freedoms such as civil liberties and political participation. However, there is rarely a good reason why all segments of the population cannot be empowered to thrive. Nor is there any good reason why a society cannot enjoy all three freedoms in good measure. Faustian bargains are false choices that are encumbered with hidden costs that only become apparent with the passage of time and leave the entire society feeling cheated.

Unfortunately, as trust declines, Faustian bargains are to be found on offer with ever-greater frequency. These "deals with the devil" have become more popular not just with political leaders but also with corporations and even civil institutions. This isn't surprising, given the urgent need for solutions to pressing challenges. But in the long-run, as in the myth of Faust, the damage and the costs incurred by these quick fixes is often far greater than anyone ever imagined.

In this section, I will discuss two further Faustian bargains in detail. The first is China's state-capitalist model, which has powered its extraordinary economic rise in the past three to four decades. The second example explores the darker side of the digital business revolution.

China's State Capitalism

China's rise as an economic superpower has been nothing short of astounding. The strength that China has gained through its economic achievements has now begun to spill over its borders, creating broader cultural and geopolitical influence in Asia and elsewhere in the world. China's success was achieved using state capitalism—a model that has attracted many would-be followers, especially among developing nations that wish to emulate China's "economic miracle."

A critical factor in the success of Chinese state-capitalism, as mentioned in chapter 1, is the aggressive long-term investment that the nation has made to build up strategic industrial sectors and, more recently, to enhance its public services and place its infrastructure on a sustainable footing. Such long-term investments in sustainable development are required in all nations, as we will explore in more detail in part II of this book.

However, despite its seeming advantages, state capitalism is a Faustian bargain: it promises growth in material well-being in exchange for significant limitations in political participation and curtailment of civil liberties. However, when economic growth slows, as it inevitably will, the state typically tightens its grip on control, rather than expanding the freedoms of its citizens, and the long-term costs of the model begin to emerge.

For the citizens of other countries poised to embrace state capitalism, it's important to understand the challenges they are likely to face. So, let's explore in greater detail how the model has evolved in China.

Deng's Visionary Leadership

To understand China and its state-capitalist model, let's begin the tale in the 1970s, when the country was still in the repressive stranglehold of Chairman Mao's extreme socialist regime, long before China had attained global-superpower status.

Back then China was an impoverished nation. Mao had ravaged the country as a result of his failed "Great Leap Forward" campaign between 1959 and 1962. The goal of the program was to increase China's industrial output—but it did the opposite, leading to one of the worst famines in world history, which claimed forty-five million lives, according to recent estimates.[16] Recognizing his failure, Mao initially allowed moderate voices to gain more ascendency in the party leadership, which led to Deng Xiaoping and Liu Shaoqi assuming control of Chinese economic policy in 1959.

But, several years later, still stinging from his loss of prestige among the party leadership, Mao launched the Cultural Revolution, which lasted from 1966 until his death a decade later. The goal of the Revolution was to purge allegedly "bourgeois" elements from Chinese society and from the Chinese Communist Party (CCP), which he accused of wanting to return to capitalism. Deng and Liu were sidelined, and the Revolution deprived the country's bureaucracy of many other competent officials.

By 1976, the repression and economic decline stemming from the Cultural Revolution brought on widespread civil unrest in China, eventually culminating in a protest of two million people who gathered in Tiananmen Square in opposition to the so-called "Gang of Four"—the four officials the populace held most responsible for the excess of the latter stages of the Cultural Revolution, which included Chairman Mao's wife. Following Mao's death later in the same year, Deng Xiaoping quickly rose to prominence again, ascending to the role of "paramount leader," which he held from 1978 to 1989. If one man can be said to be responsible for overseeing the country's transformation, it would be Deng. But, as we shall see, the rise of China was not a simple linear narrative where Deng's vision was faithfully executed over several decades. The evolution of state capitalism took many twists and turns, as the Chinese leadership worked through the many ideological tensions and socioeconomic crises that they encountered along the way, continually searching for a more coherent model of governance.

Viewed in retrospect, these gyrations have revealed a clear pattern: a wave of economic liberalization that raises living standards and legitimizes the CCP regime, followed by conservative retrenchment to shore up the CCP's grip on power whenever growth stutters.

This cycle has repeated, approximately every twenty years. The first reversion to centralized rule was the Cultural Revolution, which occurred between 1966 and 1976. The next backlash against liberalization was catalyzed by the student protests in Tiananmen Square and the fall of the Soviet Union and lasted between 1989 and the mid-1990s. Most recently, another reversion to consolidating state control began in 2012, when Xi Jinping ascended to the position of paramount leader and consolidated power into strongman rule, which continues until this day.

The object lesson from China is that state-controlled regimes generally do not permit political and social freedom to arise in the wake of economic liberalization. Rather, economic progress is used to perpetuate state control. Moreover, when economic progress declines, the state clamps down its controlling grip to suppress the cries for democracy made by its citizens. Let's look in more detail at how this Faustian bargain has played out in China over the last forty years.

From the moment Deng became paramount leader, he was fixated on making China an economic powerhouse. Impressed by what he saw during his visits to Singapore, Thailand, and Malaysia in 1978, Deng launched the "Four Modernizations," which focused on agriculture, industry, science and technology, and the military.

In 1982, Deng also took the first steps toward a more democratic system by mandating that no leader should rule for more than two consecutive five-year terms. He stressed the principle of collective leadership and instituted a model in which the Politburo Standing Committee, a small group of China's most powerful leaders, would rule through consensus.

Throughout his tenure, Deng strived to reduce the role of ideology in decision-making, imploring his citizens to "seek truth from facts." He advocated for the broad use of advanced management techniques that had become common in capitalist countries. Deng also allowed for the establishment of private enterprise and for industries to sell products beyond what was demanded by government quotas. These steps toward economic liberalization helped banish the industrial shortages that had haunted the Chinese people throughout much of the Mao era.

By 1989, however, discontent and unrest had begun to rise again. Anger at inflation, frustration with corruption by party officials, and calls for more political freedom eventually boiled over into the now-infamous student protests in Tiananmen Square. The demonstrations, which lasted over six weeks, exposed a deep division in the party between conservatives, who demanded greater centralized control, and reformists, who appealed for greater democracy and transparency in government. Eventually, the government declared martial law and crushed the rebellion—but the clashes within the party's leadership continued. As a conservative movement gained ascendency, Deng resigned later in the year.

The fall of the Berlin Wall in November of 1989 and the subsequent breakup of the Soviet Union two years later became a kind of cautionary tale for the fate of single-party socialism when openness and democracy were given wings too quickly. This geopolitical backdrop added fuel to the Chinese conservative counter-movement, which was led by the new premier, Jiang Zemin.

However, it remained clear that economic reforms were necessary to continue improvements in the material well-being of the populace. Even without official titles, Deng Xiaoping remained the most powerful leader in the country. Deng's "Southern Tour" in 1992, which drew attention to the "economic miracle" that was beginning to take shape in the Pearl River Delta and in other southern cities that had benefited from economic liberalization, helped to reinvigorate Deng's reformist agenda within the Communist Party.

Eventually, the dueling ideologies in the Communist Party reached consensus that China's economy needed to continue on its path to liberalization, but that single-party political control must be maintained in order avoid a repeat of the disastrous collapse of the communist regime in the Soviet Union. In an attempt to achieve both objectives, the Communist Party defined three key policy imperatives, as outlined by Edward Tse in his book The China Strategy, that would provide the underpinnings of the state-capitalist model.

The first was to pursue economic growth as the guiding goal. This was encapsulated by Deng's remark: "What is good for growth is good for China." After the early 2000s, this came to incorporate a focus on sustainable growth, such as paying more attention to environmental effects and increased spending on healthcare and education, to tackle the excesses that characterized China's initial economic burst in the 1990s. The second was social stability, which included the government's ability to direct and respond to public opinion, as well as more equal growth. This necessitated strict control over the media. The third was to ensure the continuance of

Communist Party rule by strengthening its organization and standards for admitting members.[17]

State Capitalism's Economic Miracle

By the 1980s, Deng Xiaoping had established the model of collective leadership and presidential term-limits. He had also introduced a more orderly and meritocratic path for government promotions, which demanded much greater accountability from local officials. Initially, bonuses were tied to economic growth targets; in more recent years, performance scorecards have grown to include additional metrics linked to new priorities, such as reduced pollution and improved social services.

To administer an increasingly complex economy, the capability of Chinese public officials had to be upgraded across the board. Accordingly, China implemented one of the most ambitious talent-enhancement programs in history. Tens of millions of party members passed through an assessment-and-development process. Older, ineffective members were rooted out, while younger, more capable members were promoted. The Communist Party has also waged a long war against corruption. The anti-corruption measures began with small changes, such as allowing citizens to make administrative payments through banks rather than directly to public officials, which helped to stamp out petty corruption through increased transparency.

China's "Reform and Opening Up" economic policies, begun by Deng Xiaoping in 1978, have transformed the country into an economic superpower. The economy has grown rapidly under Jiang Zemin (1992–2002), Hu Jintao (2002–12), and Xi Jinping (2012–present) as a result of four strategies.

First, China allowed foreign companies to enter the country and produce goods in China, reversing its stance of self-reliance. In particular, the Chinese government relaxed regulations in Special Economic Zones (SEZs), which it created in coastal cities. These special zones allowed China to learn modern management techniques from Western companies and to absorb investment from abroad. Over time, well-known multinationals, such as VW, IBM, KFC, and Kirin, entered China. The ensuing cut-throat competition drove productivity and innovation, ultimately leading to the emergence of giant Chinese companies such as Kweichow Moutai, which is now the world's largest alcoholic-beverages company, and BYD automotive, which has also become a global leader in its sector.

Second, the Chinese public sector was liberalized. In addition to de-collectivizing agriculture, China began privatizing State-Owned Enterprises

(SOEs) in non-strategic sectors in the 1990s (for example, industrial sectors such as garment and appliance manufacturing). State- and collectively-owned organizations fell from a peak of more than 7.6 million in 1994 to less than 0.6 million in 2008. During the same time period, local private companies in China increased from 140,000 to almost 6.6 million.[18] Despite implementing market reforms, China has retained state control in strategic sectors such as media, financial services, petrochemicals, oil and gas, aerospace, automotive, power, and shipbuilding.

Third, China has aggressively pursued investment-led growth in export sectors, especially in its Special Enterprise Zones. The original Special Enterprise Zones were Shenzhen, Zhuhai, and Shantou in Guangdong, and Xiamen in Fujian. They were initially small towns but ballooned in size as they found success in light-manufacturing and consumer-goods industries. Capital to fund development inside the enterprise zones was earmarked by the Chinese government and sourced from consumer deposits and from the banking system.

In 1984, encouraged by the success of the Special Enterprise Zones, the Chinese government opened fourteen larger cities along the coast to foreign trade and foreign investment. Special Enterprise Zones still contribute heavily to Chinese exports; however, the enterprise zones have slowly moved up the value chain. Today, Shenzhen is the center of China's high-tech industry and is now home to world-leading companies such as Huawei, Tencent, BYD, ZTE, Gionee, TP-Link, and OnePlus.

In 2013, under Premier Xi Jinping, China embarked on a grand foreign adventure to passport its investment-led development model beyond its borders through what became known as the Belt and Road Initiative. Under the Belt and Road umbrella, China plans to invest over $1 trillion in loans for energy, transportation, and digital-infrastructure projects across Europe, Asia, and Africa. This initiative could position China to become the dominant political and economic player across the Eastern hemisphere, spanning an area that covers over half the Earth's population.

China is also positioning the Belt and Road Initiative (BRI) to help build overseas markets for its construction and industrial sectors in a bid to relieve overcapacity and to allow China to sustain its investment-led growth. China's goals for BRI are in some ways analogous to the Marshall Plan, the United States strategy to provide loans for European redevelopment after the wholesale destruction of World War II, which provided the US an overseas market for goods and helped relieve American industrial overcapacity. BRI, however, is much larger in terms of its geographic scale and the capital deployed.[19] It is also a huge source of national pride for the Chinese and an excellent diversionary tactic from potential problems at home.

Fourth, in a move that has come to define its economic model, the Chinese state empowered its local governments to pursue their own economic growth through investment-led urban and industrial development. With local officials rewarded for achieving targets related to growth in GDP and tax revenues, incentives to pursue aggressive development were very strong. Local authorities raced to sell land—which accounts for as much or even more public revenue than taxes in many provinces today[20]—for the development of factories, office buildings, malls, power plants, and transport infrastructure. Eager developers gobbled up cheap debt from local bond-markets.[21] To avoid an economic slowdown following the Global Financial Crisis, the Communist Party pushed local development into overdrive by expanding the availability of low-interest loans even further.

One critical tool that the CCP has used to maintain its power is a commitment to shaping and responding to public opinion. Previously, China held the media on a short leash and used it to promote its own views, while simultaneously restricting the spread of dissent.

But, over time, the Communist Party became savvier in its communications strategy, developing its capacity to poll public opinion and use print, TV, and digital media to respond to the concerns of its citizens. In recent years, the party has allowed the publication of opinion polls on smog in public-run media and has vowed to launch a "war on pollution" in response to widespread discontent among its citizens on the issue. The party has also noted that corruption is frequently listed as one of the public's main concerns, and Xi's corruption crackdown is in part a reflection of this realization.

Occasionally, China has allowed for some moderated debate around issues of economic policy as an effective trial-balloon. It also regularly uses consultations with focus groups to gauge public opinion on new initiatives.

Apart from political messaging, the press and media enjoy huge freedom to broadcast sports, lifestyle, and entertainment programming, according to the tastes of the Chinese public. In fact, the Communist Party wants to support a great revival of Chinese arts and culture and then export the image of a "harmonious society" across the world.

China has also taken its penchant for influencing public opinion to the rest of the world. The little-known United Front Work Department of the Communist Party spends $10–12 billion a year on soft-power initiatives. Its activities vary from traditional lobbying, to PR campaigns, to more clandestine forms of influence-building. Through Confucius Institutes abroad and scholarships to foreign students to study domestically in China, the party gains great influence. China has committed to 10,000 scholarships for citizens of Belt and Road countries each year. In 2016, it increased places for African government officials, journalists, and students from 200 to 1,000 per year.

Invariably, scholarship recipients return from China with a positive impression of the country and a ready-made network of Chinese contacts. Ethiopia's ruling EPRDF party has assiduously copied the Chinese model by controlling business and investment and reproducing the Central Party School and party cadre-system of China. In South Africa, more than half of the ruling African National Congress has attended political training programs in China, and the party now refers to China as its "guiding lodestar."

The Faustian Bargain Emerges

After break-neck growth of over 10 percent between 1990 and 2008, China's growth has slowed since the financial crisis, averaging 7.4 percent (2011–18), with a brief sugar rush in the immediate aftermath of the crisis as the government flushed the country with a huge stimulus to keep growth rates at around 10 percent. It's clear that China's growth is slowing due to decreasing global demand and because it is reaching the limits of investment-led domestic development.

As soon as the central proposition of state capitalism was challenged— increasing material well-being in return for single-party rule with curbed political participation and civil liberties—the Faustian bargain became evident.

Instead of offsetting a slowdown in the improvement of living standards with greater political participation and expanded civil liberties, the government's response has been to step up its control of every aspect of the economy and society, worried that the regime's legitimacy won't survive slower growth. As a result, the hidden costs of the Faustian bargain have become palpably visible in the retreat of all three freedoms.

Political Participation

Since he rose to power in 2012, Xi Jinping has concentrated power not just in the Communist Party, but also in himself personally. By abolishing presidential term-limits in 2018, he has made himself the most powerful Chinese leader since Chairman Mao and abandoned Deng Xiaoping's principle of collective leadership. His regime has inserted "Xi Jinping Thought" into China's constitution. A powerful personality-cult has developed around him, pump-primed by China's propaganda machine. Although the recent Chinese anti-corruption drive represents, in part, a genuine desire to combat political malfeasance, the campaign has also been used as cover to quash political rivals. As China falls into the strongman trap, the long-term cost will be poor decision-making that will prioritize preserving the leader's control at the expense of inclusive growth. In such a "yes-man" culture, the supply of talent that China has successfully cultivated for public service over the past few decades will also likely slow to a trickle.

Civil Liberties

The regime's tightening grip on the social sphere will come at the cost of further curbs to its citizens' civil liberties. The new "Citizen Score," based on surveillance of a Chinese citizen's online and offline activities, will be used to determine a person's ability to get a job, obtain a loan, and admit their children to good schools. Even their travel choices and internet speed will be affected. Harassment of activists, NGOs, and lawyers has already stepped up since Xi came to power. It is a disturbing prospect to think that such a wealth of personal information could be weaponized for political control, as often happens with information from other sources under strongman rule.

Socioeconomic mobility

Chinese state-capitalism has failed to install good social-safety nets. As the population ages briskly in an overhang from the single-child policy, the government will be faced with tens of millions of disaffected elderly citizens unless pensions are raised from their meager level of approximately $60 to $75 per month for urban residents.[22] China is also at risk of "getting old before it gets rich," and younger workers will increasingly have to shoulder greater responsibility for the elderly, but without the rapid rise in wage levels workers were accustomed to in the past. Healthcare coverage has improved marginally. Ten years ago, only 13 percent of Chinese citizens had medical insurance; now, almost everyone has public insurance—but the coverage is still vastly inadequate. The current system consists mostly of overcrowded hospitals and relatively little primary and secondary care. Fifty percent of Chinese healthcare spending is still absorbed by patients as an out-of-pocket expense.

But, worst of all, the ranks of marginalized citizens in China are rapidly growing. The economic-development spurt in the coastal cities drew in swarms of rural-to-urban migrants, who now represent a huge underclass that is hundreds of millions strong. Due to China's hukou residency-status system, they are not recognized as city dwellers, rendering them second-class citizens in their own country. The hukou residents are barred from holding certain jobs, their children are sidelined by the education system, and their pensions are less than one-sixth of those with urban-residency status.[23]

Taking the regime's recent assault on the three freedoms into account, it may not be surprising that the UN-sponsored World Happiness Report has ranked China in the bottom half of countries for reported happiness, below even Russia—a true warning indicator that China's social capital is at risk.

Warning Signals in the Economy

The hidden costs of the Faustian bargain are also becoming evident economically in the form of unproductive industrial and urban-development projects and rising levels of bad debt.

Chinese state control is now showing signs of penetrating business. The government has mandated that all companies—private and public sector alike—have Communist Party members on their boards. There's growing anxiety among entrepreneurs of guojin mintui—a phrase that can be translated as, "The state advances, the private sector retreats."

Despite initially pledging to give market forces a more significant role in the Chinese economy, Xi has instead empowered inefficient State-Owned Enterprises (SOEs). Attracted to government guarantees provided to SOEs, the share of new bank-loans to state companies has more than doubled between 2012 and 2019—from 32 percent to 80 percent[24]—even though the return on assets from SOEs is less than half of their private sector peers.[25] Meanwhile, private-sector companies received just 11 percent of new loans in 2015, compared with 52 percent in 2012,[26] the year before Xi came to power.

Debt has also fueled the overdevelopment binge at the local-government level. Rife with corruption, many projects were poorly conceived and badly constructed. The result of these debt-fueled projects is vast numbers of half-empty office buildings and the spectral presence of nearly empty shopping malls. Moreover, now that local governments have sold off their most valuable plots of land, they risk running out of mechanisms to generate new economic growth and expand their tax base.

Runaway lending—often to unproductive SOEs and local-government projects—has caused the total level of Chinese debt to soar from 150 percent of GDP in 2008 to 250 percent in 2018.[27] Going forward, this trend could be exacerbated if Chinese loans to Belt and Road projects are not paid back—a very real possibility since many of the Belt and Road countries are high-risk emerging markets with corrupt regimes. With Beijing courts set to rule on Belt and Road related disputes, geopolitical tensions may arise if the verdicts are deemed to be unfair. Chinese courts, after all, do not yet have a track record in independent international arbitration.

Overall, the rapid rise of Chinese debt is worrying to many observers. In the past, similar debt pileups have precipitated damaging shocks such as the Global Financial Crisis and the implosion of a real estate bubble in Japan in the 1990s, which resulted in three decades of Japanese stagnation, continuing even to this day.

China remains on course to be the United States' primary strategic rival and the world's second superpower, contending with the US for leadership in many global industries, such as clean energy, technology, and artificial intelligence. Moreover, the Chinese state will progressively wield greater cultural, social, and diplomatic influence on the world stage in the process.

China's great success over the past thirty years is inextricably linked to moves that advanced the Three Freedoms: namely, collective leadership and greater fact-based dialogue in the CCP, increasing openness to the world economy, the unleashing of market forces that created a vibrant private sector, and the empowerment of a stronger cadre of local officials to drive local development.

But the price the CCP exacts for economic progress is the concentration of power and control. This Faustian bargain at the core of China's state-capitalist model will always be an Achilles' heel that impedes the country's progress—and may even cause it to crumble.

The Digital Revolution

The digital revolution is a force that's radically reshaping the way we live. Technology giants currently offer us valuable services that are "free," or that are distributed at deeply reduced prices relative to that prehistoric era before the internet.

But there's an important question worth raising about the brave new world that's been ushered in by our new digital economy: How is it that we can receive all these free, or nearly free, products and services while the giant tech-companies that supply them become the largest and most profitable companies on Earth?

Part of the answer to the question is suggested by the Four Ss we discussed in chapter 2: namely, that digitization creates remarkable productivity improvements. But is it also possible that another part of the answer is that we—collectively, as consumers—have given up something more valuable than the free and convenient services we receive? Have we signed up for a Faustian bargain with Big Tech?

If there is a Faustian bargain on offer, the daily benefits it provides to my family and me are quite clear. Like many other contemporary families, we use social-media apps such as Facebook, Twitter, and Instagram to share ideas, photos, and stories with friends and family. As parents, my wife and I are grateful for YouTube, Khan Academy, and the many other learning apps that allow our kids to satisfy their curiosity and help them with their studies. London, the city where we live, is congested and has limited parking, so we take advantage of e-commerce to order our groceries from Sainsbury's, our lunch through Deliveroo, our clothes on Net-a-Porter, and everything else on Amazon—all of which saves us precious hours of time each week. And when my wife and I use some of that time to go to dinner—in an Uber, naturally—we can pay the babysitter with PayPal. Professionally, Google allows me to pinpoint relevant information from the unfathomably large pool of content on the internet. I can use low-cost voice- and video-communications services from Skype and Zoom to collaborate seamlessly from my office in London with colleagues and clients in New York, San Francisco, Chicago, Lagos, Kuwait, and Mumbai. On the backend of my business, most of my company's administration gets handled by a suite of Software-as-a-Service applications accessed through the cloud.

But all the convenience that technology delivers to me in London seems quaint when compared to the vast digital platforms that cater to nearly every aspect of life in China. For example, in China it's increasingly difficult to pay for anything with cash. The fashion is to buy your latte with facial recognition linked to your digital wallet. Platforms such as WeChat have combined social media, commerce, and payments—configuring them together to provide an increasingly diverse set of services. For example, you can now access a doctor via WeChat, consult with him or her via video or voice call, and pay for your digital office visit using your integrated digital wallet.

But what are the hidden costs of all the convenience that this bewildering array of technology gives us? What consumers don't always appreciate is that there are typically two sides to a digital business. On the consumer-facing side, I've given a brief tour of the cornucopia of products and services that so many of us now benefit from. But on the other side of the bargain, the product is our personal data. Facebook, WeChat, Amazon and the other tech giants monetize the data they collect from our website clicks, social-media chats, payment histories, and e-commerce transactions. The data may be used to profile users and micro-target them for further product promotion using predictive models—or it may get sold to a range of other third-party advertisers, political groups, or other organizations.

In liberal democracies, the law is often fuzzy on how personal data can be used by political parties. To date, there's enough latitude to allow political parties to micro-target voters with news stories or other political messages. We've already seen how this type of activity can help subvert democracy, as in the case of Cambridge Analytica's role in the Brexit vote. In countries with strong state control, such as China, technology companies are required to share their data with governments; in turn, that data forms the backbone for state surveillance and social censorship, using mechanisms like China's "Citizen Score."

The wonders of today's digital economy harbor a darker side in which personal data is traded without regard for user preferences, making those users vulnerable to unwanted product solicitation, political influence, surveillance and censorship, cyber-security attacks, and potentially other forms of discrimination.

Until more robust frameworks and institutions are developed to establish the rights of the data owner (meaning us), to allow the data user (meaning tech companies), these digital businesses will remain at the center of an extractive Faustian bargain, which not only powers the war on truth but also erodes individual civil liberties in the process.

As our digital-economy example illustrates, corporate bargains, just like their political counterparts, are an essential component of the social contract. The deals we enter into with corporations are just as likely to be interwoven with costly and deceptive Faustian bargains. Citizens need to be vigilant and ask questions about their hidden costs. And when corporate offers come with hidden tradeoffs, citizens must be empowered to demand a resolution to safeguard their freedoms.

Cohesive Social Contracts

We've seen the damage that society can suffer when Faustian bargains burrow into the fabric of a nation's social contract. But if Faustian bargains are the hallmark of bad social contracts, what are the characteristics of a good one? With many political manifestos on offer in the age of the Great Trust Crisis, how can citizens differentiate between a social contract that brings a society together and one that pulls it apart?

In my experience, cohesive social contracts adhere to four key principles, which may be a useful guide for assessing a social contract and thinking about how it could be adapted for the future. Let's take a look at these four principles and explore the templates of best-in-class social contracts that embody them.

Principle I: Commitment to Balance in the Five Capitals

The first principle of a cohesive social contract is a commitment to the balanced growth of all Five Capitals: financial, manufactured, natural, human, and social.

There will always be a strong temptation to exploit and degrade natural, human, and social capital for short-term financial benefit, but the very awareness that the temptation exists and that the long-term costs are so high, can help us to resist the myopic drive for short-term gains.

One attempt at establishing a framework that focuses on prudent, balanced, longer-term thinking is provided by the United Nations' seventeen "Sustainable Development Goals." While the UN's framework is somewhat broad and unwieldy, its approach makes a good-faith attempt to identify many of the key issues that should be addressed in a modern social contract. Moreover, all of the UN's social-development goals are congruent with the need to grow the Five Capitals in a balanced manner.

Among other diverse topics, the UN's Sustainable Development Goals touch on: the elimination of extreme poverty by 2030, the elimination of hunger, improvements to education, gender equity, clean water, renewable energy, and greater action to battle climate change. The complete list of all seventeen goals can be found on the United Nations website.[28]

Principle II: Commitment to the Three Freedoms

The second principle of cohesive social contracts is that they recognize the special importance of social capital and the Three Freedoms in building resilient societies. Fortunately, there are excellent templates to follow for maximizing political participation, civil liberties, and socioeconomic mobility. Let's look at each one in turn.

Political Participation

Many national constitutions now declare the rights of citizens to vote for elected representatives to government. For example: via amendments, the American Constitution guarantees the right to vote for the country's representatives to all citizens. The Fourteenth Amendment states "[The] right of citizens of the United States to vote shall not be denied or abridged by the United States or by any state on account of race, color, or previous condition of servitude,"[29] thereby enfranchising minorities such as African Americans. And the Nineteenth Amendment extended the vote to women by declaring, "The right of citizens of the United States to vote shall not be denied or abridged by the United States or by any State on account of sex."[30]

As government institutions mature and public administration capabilities grow, countries should devolve power to their subnational governments and local communities. Out of the necessity to forge a union among its constituent states at the time of American independence from Britain, the US was particularly explicit on its framework of devolution from the outset. Three out of the seven articles of the United States Constitution outline the principles of federalism, describing the responsibilities of state governments and their role in relation to the US federal government. Germany is another example of a country that has devolved power downwards. Its Basic Law, which forms its constitution, states that all legislative and administrative functions are first and foremost the jurisdiction of Germany's sixteen states (the Länder), unless otherwise specified.

Civil Liberties

After the devastation of World War II, and the wholesale abuses of human rights committed by the Nazi regime, the world formalized the first charter of inalienable human rights in the form of the UN Universal Declaration of Human Rights in 1948. These rights are now embedded in the constitutions of over ninety countries and constitute an explicit commitment to civil and human rights on behalf of those nations.

Among charters and declarations, the most evocative statement of the theme is contained in the US Declaration of Independence:

> We hold these truths to be self-evident, that all men are created equal, that they are endowed by their Creator with certain unalienable Rights, that among these are Life, Liberty, and the pursuit of Happiness.[31]

Socioeconomic Mobility

Social contracts must focus assiduously on improving socioeconomic mobility. Citizens should support governments that provision for such key enablers for socioeconomic mobility as education, worker training, infrastructure, and healthcare, and who provide social safety nets such as adequate healthcare coverage, basic pensions, and unemployment assistance.

A telltale sign of upholding socioeconomic mobility is a commitment to preserving and growing the middle-class. America has been a pioneer in this regard. In his book The Crisis of the Middle-Class Constitution, Ganesh Sitaraman correctly argues that America was different from other nations in the way that it came into being because it was founded on the premise that there was, and should be, a middle-class and economic opportunity.

Since the time of Aristotle, constitutionalists had tried to incorporate different classes but had accepted as inevitable that there would be economic conflict between the classes. But in the American Constitution there are no provisions that refer to a specific economic class, in contrast to other countries where "thousands of years of constitutional design explicitly incorporated economic class into the structure of government."[32] The founding fathers had internalized the writings of the British philosopher James Harrington, who argued that only if economic power were spread widely would republicanism be possible.[33]

Sadly, as Sitaraman argues, middle-class America is under threat due to widening inequality. This needs to be addressed as part of a new social contract.

Principle III: Balancing the Four Major Pillars of the Socio-Economy

When people are asked, "How should your economy be organized?" they often seem trapped in a dangerous dichotomy: one camp tends to advocate for unfettered market capitalism, with a limited role for the state or public-sector intervention; conversely, the other side tends to argue for some form of a largely state-driven approach, such as state capitalism.

Cohesive social contracts, however, take a less binary and more nuanced view of the issue. They acknowledge the unique roles that the **public** and **private sector** are each best equipped to play in a society and seek to foster a constructive partnership between the two. But they also recognize the important role of **civil society** and **the commons** and place them alongside the public and private sectors—creating the *four* key pillars of the socio-economy.

The Public and Private Sectors

Despite the dogma that obscures much of the public-versus-private-sector debate, there tends to be broader agreement on many of the core ideas than much of our political discourse would suggest.

Most people, for example, would agree that the goal of the state—and its various public-sector entities—is to preserve the long-term prosperity of its citizens. As a result, the state takes on the role of providing effective mechanisms for governance, defense, law and order, and diplomatic relations with other nations. It is also responsible for controlling the money supply and providing macroeconomic stability, as well as regulating the private sector, civil society, and the commons in order to ensure fair competition, protect people's rights, and safeguard the natural environment. Due to its long-term outlook, the state is uniquely responsible for thinking across multi-generational time horizons. As a consequence, the public sector is well placed to make investments involving risks that are long-range and large-scale, and that involve projects or innovation at a very early stage of development. In modern societies, this leads to the public sector's key role in provisioning basic services such as education, healthcare, and social security, as well as making investments in infrastructure and basic research.

Similarly, there is usually broad agreement that the goal of the private sector—which I take to include listed or unlisted private corporations as well as private wealth—is to invest in or produce useful goods and services in a manner that generates financial returns. In contrast to the long-term focus of the state, the creative destruction of a vibrant private sector means that relatively few firms will last beyond one or two decades. As a result, in most cases, private-sector firms and their investors tend to be focused on short-term investments with a moderate risk-profile. As part of their operations, firms make investments in equipment and innovation and employ workers who are paid wages that support household consumption and savings. However, in order to operate successfully, the private sector relies on a stream of skilled, healthy workers, critical infrastructure to ship goods and connect with business partners, and cutting-edge research from universities to support the development of innovative products and services. Since companies cannot individually pay for highways, school systems, and university research, they rely on the state to raise tax revenues from companies and individuals to pay for such public infrastructure and services.

Of course, the devil is in the details, and the arguments tend to flare up in three main areas. The first point of debate is often about where the boundaries are drawn between assets that are owned by the public sectors and those that belong in private hands. On this matter, Dag Detter and Stefan Fölster have made a significant contribution by demonstrating how the state can play a critical role in the stewardship and value-creation of publicly owned assets. In their groundbreaking book The Public Wealth of Nations, Detter and Fölster examine such public assets as natural resources, government-owned land and real estate, public infrastructure, and state-owned enterprises. On a global level, the pair estimates that such public assets are worth $75 trillion.[34]

Rather than selling off public assets for one-time windfall gains or leaving them to decay, as was the case in the privatization dogma of the UK in the 1980s and 1990s, Detter and Fölster advocate professional management of public assets to commercial standards. The latter approach has been successfully implemented by countries such as Denmark, Sweden, and Singapore. For example, Copenhagen's municipal government transferred vast amounts of public land by the city's harbor and between the airport and its downtown into a newly created, publicly owned but privately managed corporation. It then rezoned the land for commercial and residential use and used the projected revenues to obtain financing to fund a major infrastructure upgrade, including a transit system. Three decades ago, the city had a budget deficit of $750 million and unemployment at 17.5 percent. The development corporation is one of the major reasons for its revival.[35]

As the authors point out, increasing the yield on public assets by just 1 percent would release $750 billion annually to the public purse on a global basis. As the value of the assets increases, offering co-investment opportunities to the private sector can bring in public receipts at progressively higher valuations—capital which could then be invested for future generations through vehicles such as a sovereign-wealth fund.

A second area of controversy often arises when determining where the private sector should be allowed to operate. The profit-seeking motive of private sector operators in social-service settings can lead to some distorted outcomes. For example, the decision to privatize some prisons—leading to an increase of the privately-run prison population from 69,000 in 1999 to about 128,000 in 2016[36]—has had some perverse impacts. A recent study by economists Christian Dippel and Michael Poyker found that states that had private prisons caused judges to give out longer sentences because they (incorrectly) assumed the cost to the state would be lower in private prisons.[37] Another study by economist Anita Mukherjee, looking at private prisons in Mississippi, found that they gave out more conduct violations than state prisons, thereby extending average time served by prisoners by ninety days and increasing their companies' revenues.[38] Similar challenges can arise when mass-transportation systems are turned over to private operators who promptly shrink—or even cancel—services on rural lines with low passenger volumes. While it may boost corporate profits, it can leave many remote communities even more isolated.

A third point of contention centers on how to provide protections for workers, consumers, and the environment without adding excessive costs to business. Corporations are increasingly expected to behave in a socially responsible manner to all their stakeholders, as well as towards the environment—and rightly so. But the added responsibilities have come with a variety of costs in the form of healthcare benefits, social-security taxes, and local taxes to pay for utilities and infrastructure—to name just a few. And these costs are at risk of rising further in order to address the sustainable development challenges that lie ahead, such as providing workers with lifelong learning, building renewable industry and infrastructure, and providing security for our aging populations. In some cases, targeted taxes could be raised to pay for the investments required. For example, a carbon tax on hydrocarbon-intensive sectors of the economy could generate funds to plow into public investments in renewable infrastructure and new green technologies.

However, as we shall see in part II of this book, the scale of the investments required to secure a sustainable future cannot be paid for by higher taxes alone. Instead, the private sector must be incentivized to be part of the solution. Corporate tax breaks for investing in apprenticeships and employee training, retrofitting buildings for higher energy efficiency, or investing to capture their carbon emissions are simple examples of steering the private sector to make sustainable investments with long-lasting benefits. But perhaps the biggest lever of all could be to mobilize the $200 trillion of global private wealth by serving up opportunities to pursue social investments with an attractive financial return. On this front, one example that seems directionally correct is the creation of "Opportunity Zones" under the Trump administration—low-income rural and urban areas designated by the chief executives of every US state and territory. These areas qualify for reinvestment of unrealized capital-gains into Opportunity Funds, which are then pledged to building up economic activity in these disadvantaged areas. Although there has been much criticism of inadequate oversight to ensure that investments in opportunity zones are actually benefitting disadvantaged communities, the scheme—properly administered—does have the potential to channel private investment into projects that deliver social impact as well as a good financial return.

A cohesive social contract will articulate an active relationship between the private and public sectors that best addresses the social priorities of the day. This may involve raising the bar on the financial returns that the public sector is expected to generate from its portfolio of assets. It could involve redefining or regulating how the private sector participates in social services. It may even reinvent the role of the private sector (and private wealth) in making social investments. It's time to end the senseless debate about the relative "size and power" of the private and public sectors and explore more creative and productive partnership between them.

Civil Society and the Commons

Civil society and the commons are two key pillars of the socio-economy because they provide critical checks on the public and private sector, while providing valuable resources to both.

Civil-society organizations provide a vehicle for citizens to organize around an issue or cause, helping to amplify their voice, develop innovative solutions, and bring about accountability and policy change. These organizations can include labor unions advocating for worker rights, ecological groups organized to preserve the environment, NGOs and charities campaigning for human and civil rights, think tanks addressing policy issues, or centers of worship providing spiritual guidance. Civil society also comprises a host of citizen-organized associations such as amateur sports leagues and neighborhood-watch schemes, which form the backbone of local communities.

Cohesive social contracts legally protect and encourage an active civil society. In many countries, civil-society organizations can operate with non-profit or charitable status to receive special tax exemptions. People donating funds to these organizations can write off their contributions against their personal tax liabilities. Nigeria and Israel, which are countries that demand mandatory community service from young adults, supply civil-society organizations with cohorts of volunteers every year. In the UK, civil society has been dubbed as the "Third Sector," and successive governments under both Conservative and Labor parties have channeled public funds through qualifying charitable organizations to implement social and welfare work, such as ambulance services, housing, legal advice, social care, and metal health.[39]

If there is any doubt about the power of civil-society organizations, we only need to look at Brazil, South Africa, and Malaysia, where they have been pivotal in ousting corrupt national leaders. In South Africa, for example, the South African NGO Organization for Undoing Tax Abuse has played an important role in bringing charges against high-ranking South African politicians, helping precipitate the resignation of disgraced President Zuma. Or we can look to the Cystic Fibrosis Foundation in the US, which has been instrumental in discovering breakthrough treatments,[40] or the Smile Foundation, which provides free education to 400,000 underprivileged children and their families across twenty-five states in India.

The commons refer to resources that are open to everyone and are owned by neither the public nor the private sectors, such as water and common land used for recreation or grazing. The term gained prominence in the 1960s after Garrett Hardin published the article "The Tragedy of the Commons," in which he lamented the spoiling of these mutually owned resources because no individual or institution was responsible for their maintenance.[41] Back then, discussions about the commons usually referred to the "depletive" kind such as fish or forest stocks—where users subtract value each time they use the asset, and where the focus remains on preservation.

But the term has gained renewed meaning since the advent of the "digital" commons, which are viewed as additive resources—where users tend to add value to the common asset by using it. The World Wide Web and its digital offshoots comprise the most powerful commons ever established. Wikipedia, for example, provides access to verifiable facts and information to billions of people worldwide for free. Another great example is the open-source software movement, whose goal is to foster cooperation and innovation within the global programming community by placing code online for others to share and build upon.

Relatively few countries explicitly champion the commons, but some are better than others. South Korea's government is particularly impressive in its promotion of the digital commons. The Open Data Barometer, which monitors the level of openness of government data, ranks South Korea as by far the most advanced nation globally on this metric. The government's strategy has spurred the creation of new companies in technology, advertising, and business services as a result of commonly available data created by the government. Mapping data released by the Ministry of Land, Infrastructure and Transport, for example, has been used by the company Archidraw to provide 3-D visualization for interior design and property modeling.[42]

Principle IV: Appreciation of the Long-Term National Interest

The fourth and final key characteristic of a cohesive social contract is that it places the long-term national interest over the self-imposed constraints of a nation's historical legacy—and above any short-term tradeoffs that may be facing the country.

While a cohesive social contract should connect to a nation's heritage, culture, and economic roots, it also must reflect a nation's future roadmap. For example, backward-looking nationalist fervor is unhelpful when a country's demographic structure is changing rapidly. A cohesive social contract must embrace non-native citizens when immigration has created a diverse ethnic mix. It must focus on achieving full employment for young people if there is a youth bulge, as in Nigeria or Saudi Arabia. It must harness the capabilities of the elderly and provide a robust care platform in aging societies, such as Japan.

Good social contracts also provide an economic vision backed up by coherent long-term policies, so that it is clear to citizens what economic opportunities will be on offer and how individuals and families will be supported in the process of capturing them. For example, Abu Dhabi's Economic Vision 2030 is a public document that was commissioned in 2006 and declares the Emirates' goal to achieve a diversified economy that is far less dependent on oil and gas by 2030. But Abu Dhabi Vision 2030 is also, in effect, a very explicit social contract, because the document lays out a detailed roadmap of commitments that will change the experience of its citizens. For example, Vision 2030 outlines regulatory changes and investments that will promote a much greater role for the private sector and capital markets. The Vision also features a significant commitment to developing the talent of the Emirates to occupy high-paying, knowledge-intensive jobs, particularly in business and technology, as well as enhancing the healthcare ecosystem to promote a healthier population. According to the Vision, citizens of Abu Dhabi can also expect great improvements in hard infrastructure, combined with a much wider selection of arts, entertainment, and recreational offerings to increase the overall quality of life.

Many other countries have been proactive about providing clarity to their own long-term social contracts through powerful vision-statements. For example, Kenya's Vision 2030 "aims to transform Kenya into a newly industrializing, middle-income country providing a high quality of life to all its citizens by 2030 in a clean and secure environment." Kenya's Vision is broken down into three pillars: economic, social, and political. The economic and social pillars lay out a very sensible set of initiatives to boost economic activity by developing key sectors such as agriculture and financial services and to increase socioeconomic mobility through the provision of affordable housing and much-improved basic education and health. However, my attention was drawn to the political pillar, which promises a major investment to build up the capabilities of local authorities as a

FIGURE 3-1: STOCKHOLM VISION 2040

1. A Stockholm that stands united

In 2040, Stockholm will be a cohesive city, where all children have the same opportunities to achieve proficiency targets, apartments are available at reasonable rents, the elderly are guaranteed a secure life, and equal opportunity, gender equality, and accessibility are never questioned.

2. Eco-smart Stockholm

In 2040, Stockholm will be a climate-smart city that prioritizes cycling, walking, and public transportation. An efficient, climate-smart transportation system is combined with greater consumption of renewable energy. Children are guaranteed a non-toxic environment, and more organic food is served at city facilities.

3. Financially sustainable Stockholm

In 2040, Stockholm will be a financially sustainable city, where financial accountability is combined with labor market initiatives based on easy access to available jobs, education, and housing.

4. Democratically sustainable city

In 2040, Stockholm will be a democratically sustainable city that promotes human rights, combats discrimination, and guarantees all inhabitants equal rights and opportunities.

prelude to decentralizing decision-making around economic development. This kind of explicit support to the empowerment of local communities is essential to prosperity in the 21st-century economy, as I will discuss in part III of this book.

Among explicit long-term social contracts, my personal favorite is Stockholm Vision 2040, which is shown above in Figure 3-1. Stockholm's goal is to realize a "cohesive city" that is rich in all Five Capitals. The vision statement calls for "financial sustainability," sustainable transportation and energy infrastructure, an "eco-smart" environment, and "labor market initiatives" to emphasize the city's commitment to financial, manufactured, natural, and human capital. The importance of social capital is a central theme in the manifesto: Stockholm aspires to be a "democratically sustainable city that promotes human rights, combats discrimination and guarantees all inhabitants equal rights and opportunities." In calling out the specific provisions the city plans to make for children, working-age people, the elderly, and both genders, Stockholm's inclusive approach across demographic segments can be in no doubt. Stockholm's social contract is also very vocal on affordable housing, smart transportation, education, and healthcare—recognizing them as key enablers that provide citizens with equal access to opportunity. Although not explicitly mentioned, Stockholm must foster a strong partnership between business, government, civil society, and the commons to achieve its vision. When viewed in its totality, Stockholm Vision 2040 is a great credit to the city's people and government.

Where Next for the American Dream?

Now that we've taken a detailed look at social contracts—both good and bad—how would we characterize the social contract we have in America today? And how does that social contract need to evolve to adapt to the realities of the 21st century?

To understand the present, let's begin by looking at the past. The US is blessed to have had one of the most powerful social contracts ever conceived: the American Dream. As a PhD student at MIT in the 1990s, I remember hearing the phrase "the American Dream" all the time—in the news, in sitcoms, and in casual conversation. It was a narrative anchored deep in the hearts and minds of the American people that celebrated the spirit of liberty, equality before the law, and opportunity.

The spirit of the American Dream had been enshrined generations earlier in the US Declaration of Independence, the Federalist Papers, the US Constitution, and in the Bill of Rights in the late 18th century. The spirit was so unique that foreign visitors were immediately struck by its optimistic and empowering message. French sociologist Alexis de Tocqueville, who traveled to the US in 1831, referred to this spirit as the "charm of anticipated success" in his classic work of 1835, Democracy in America.

The American Dream makes the promise that people can work hard to achieve a better life, regardless of their national origin, humble beginnings, or other barriers to success. It is not merely an aspiration, but a promise that has been validated by generations of immigrants from all over the world. While the American Dream inspires a sense of national unity, even patriotism, it doesn't require conformity to any ethnicity, religion, or native language. Industrious people of every stripe have achieved the American Dream. At its core, the promise is simple—broad freedoms to undertake private enterprise for self-betterment within a robust framework of political participation and impartial rule of law ensured by government.

The term "American Dream" itself was first coined in 1931 by the American writer and historian James Truslow Adams in the depths of the Great Depression. In his book The Epic of America, Adams sought to remind Americans that with a "can-do" attitude, individuals have the power to bring about change. And yet, as the Depression dragged on, it became woefully apparent that individuals and communities alone could not mount an adequate response to a crisis of the magnitude of the Great Depression.

By 1933, when it became clear that a far greater national effort than individual initiative was required, Franklin D. Roosevelt's New Deal ultimately raised the bar for the responsibilities that governments undertake on behalf of their citizens. The New Deal planted the early seeds of the civil rights movement, replaced "Hooverville" shantytowns with federal-housing camps, and put millions to work on infrastructure projects, based on the idea that handouts to the destitute would over time destroy personal dignity. These projects often created great public "commons"—like Colorado's Red Rocks Amphitheater, public pools and parks from Los Angeles to South Carolina, sea walls in Newport, Rhode Island, and flood abatement and electrification projects in the backwaters of the Tennessee Valley.

The New Deal also elevated the role of civil society by strengthening labor unions and raising the standards of corporate responsibility. Retirement and elderly medical care were previously funded through individual means, but it now became a responsibility jointly shouldered by individuals and employers through payroll taxes. Despite many changes and attacks over the years, the New Deal's broad redefinition of the public sector, private sector, civil society, and the commons has survived even to the present day.

After the challenges of the Great Depression and World War II had passed, the United States entered a period of previously unknown prosperity. During the post-war years, the American Dream became embedded within the framework of material abundance. Working hard in a meritocratic society became associated with such mid-20th-century staples as owning a home and a car, providing a college education for one's children, and a broad array of consumer delights.

However, from the 1980s onward, a more consumerist and individualist ideology began to take root in America. The small-government and light-touch approach of Washington Consensus politics pivoted the US to a focus on free-market capitalism—establishing such norms as the supremacy of shareholder profits in corporate governance, a more muted role for labor unions, and the reversal of progressive taxation. Allied with the concentrating forces of 21st-century economics outlined in chapter 2, the outcome has been widening inequality, the capture of public and political institutions by wealthy elites, and, ultimately, the loss of public trust.

In the United States today, in stark contrast with the 1990s, one hardly hears any mention of the American Dream at all. The promise the concept once represented seems to have disappeared from the American vernacular. On the rare occasion when the American Dream is mentioned, it is referenced wistfully by older generations as a faded or outdated ideal. For younger people in the US, the American Dream is an alien concept that simply does not relate to the reality of their life experience. In the throes of the Great Trust Crisis, America is crying out for a new social contract to fit the challenges of the 21st century.

And yet, at this crucial juncture in US history, the most prominent option on offer is "America First," a social contract put forward by President Trump that seems to embody his policies and worldview. America First is fundamentally inward-looking and nationalist in its perspective. It abandons such values as inclusiveness, transparency, and accountability, while attacking venerable American institutions in the bargain. America First appears to extinguish the last vestiges of the spirit of the American Dream and is directly at odds with the principles of cohesive social contracts outlined in this chapter.

To begin with, Trump's America First model does little to balance the growth of the Five Capitals. Despite winning the presidency by rallying support from middle-class Americans left behind in the deindustrialized heartland of the US, Trump has focused on providing a short-term tax stimulus to the economy rather than a clear, actionable plan to stimulate job growth in these communities. Trump's agenda is also light on how to restore America's position as a leader in developing the human capital that was so important to its rise in the early 20th century and after World War II. His apprenticeship program for 3.8 million workers, pushed through by executive order in 2018, comes across as a mere smokescreen to distract attention away from his executive proposals to slash funding for federal job training programs by 40 percent.[43] There are also no new ideas or incentives to promote lifelong learning that help retrain workers displaced by automation into open jobs in the digital economy, which are now suffering from significant skills shortages. America First has put natural capital in jeopardy by promoting the extraction of hydrocarbons from US shale deposits and renewing the focus on coal. To legitimize this sort of short-term economic and political gain, Trump has gone so far as to assert that climate change may not be manmade and has pulled the US out of the Paris Agreement on climate change. The resulting costs to the whole world—including to the US—from climate change will be staggering, as we will see in chapter 7.

Second, America First is further eroding social capital by curtailing the three freedoms of political participation, civil liberties, and socioeconomic mobility.

Trump's presidential election victory itself was another reminder of some deep flaws in the US model of political participation. Trump won the Electoral College vote but not the popular vote—receiving almost 2.87 million votes (2.1 percent) less than Hilary Clinton. Trump has sowed doubt into the electoral process by insisting before the election that the vote would be "rigged."[44] Following the election, he alleged that Clinton won the popular vote due to fraud, setting up a task force to investigate, but then disbanding it in January 2018 after it produced no evidence.[45]

And then there has been the constant stream of allegations that Trump conspired with the Russians to undermine Clinton's campaign. Trump has himself said, "I think I'd take it," if he was given dirt on an opponent from a foreign government.[46] It must be said that Special Counsel Robert Mueller, in the conclusion of his investigations on the alleged collusion with Russia, said that he found no evidence to suggest conspiracy. However, he did pointedly say that he had not cleared Trump of obstruction of justice for his conduct in the investigation.[47] More recently, of course, Trump has again been the subject of electoral malfeasance. His suspected abuse of presidential power in pressuring Ukraine to launch an investigation into discredited allegations against Joe Biden and his son Hunter Biden, led to his impeachment by the House of Representatives.

On civil liberties, Trump is a leading player in the war on truth. He regularly attacks the media, branding them as "enemies of the American people," while his own tweets are frequently laced with falsehoods. He has tried to stymie investigations into his own alleged election misconduct at every opportunity.

America First also has a nationalistic fervor that takes a harsh view towards immigrants. In stark contrast to the American Dream, America First no longer welcomes newcomers to the country, and, per the Trump administration's stated policy, intends to physically close the border with Mexico with the infamous Trump Wall.

Moreover, it is extremely troubling when the implementation of immigration policy flagrantly disregards international standards for human rights. The most salient example was the Trump administration's deplorable decision to separate parents and children at the border when they were seeking asylum or attempting to enter into the US as illegal immigrants. The decision was quickly reversed due to widespread public outrage, but it remains a clear indication of the ethos of America First.

America First will also further suppress socioeconomic mobility in the US. The tax cuts implemented at the beginning of 2019 are skewed heavily toward reducing the tax burden on the wealthiest Americans. These fiscal policy choices are reducing the government's ability to invest in socioeconomic mobility enablers—such as education, healthcare, and infrastructure. Trump has already cut funding for Medicare and Medicaid and has still yet to find funding for his infrastructure plan—or even for his wall.

Third, America First seeks to erode the public sector, civil society, and the commons while furthering corporate interests. Trump has showered the corporate sector with significant tax cuts—a large portion of which will end up flowing through to shareholders as dividends, rather than being deployed into wages or investments into worker training and innovation, for the reasons we discussed in chapter 2. The reduced tax-base will also deprive the public sector of money with which to pursue the same objectives by funding basic research and workforce-development plans.

But the Trump administration has gone far beyond starving the public sector of capital; his administration has actively attempted to hobble key government agencies through the appointment of leaders who have key philosophical differences with the missions of their respective agencies. Scott Pruitt, Trump's first appointment to head the Environmental Protection Agency (EPA), was formerly the attorney general for the oil-producing state of Oklahoma and spent much of his time there fighting the EPA—the very same agency he was tasked to lead. Pruitt's appointment was widely seen to be an assault on climate change and a means to remove barriers for the oil and gas industry. In a similar vein, Ben Carson, who is known to have a deep aversion to social safety-net programs and fair-housing initiatives, was appointed to lead the Department of Housing and Urban Development; the appointment of Carson was also perceived by many as a move designed to cripple that agency's impact. Similarly, Betsy DeVos, the education secretary, has been a long-time supporter of private-school vouchers, a policy that many critics claim undercuts the public-school systems at the core of the Education Department's mission—again in favor of the private sector.

The Trump administration's attitude toward civil society marks a shift from previous conservative US presidential administrations. Republicans have historically been champions of charitable organizations. George H.W.

Bush spoke of "a thousand points of light" when referring to them. His son, George W. Bush, set up a new White House office to engage directly with non-profit organizations. Trump himself, meanwhile, seems generally apathetic toward the non-profit sector as a whole.

The Trump administration has also taken an axe to a most vital element of the digital commons—net neutrality. In 2017, the administration reversed previous rulings in favor of net neutrality to introduce a new model, whereby telecom giants like AT&T, Comcast, and Verizon will be able to block or slow down access to other websites, while prioritizing their own content or paid "fast lanes." The move will restrict citizens' freedom of speech by restricting their access to information unhindered, and it will restrict competition on the internet, thereby furthering America's oligopolistic digital economy.

Fourth, America First is inflicting grievous harm to America's long-term national interest by attacking US and global institutions and, in the process, retreating from its role of respected global superpower and "leader of the free world." Rather than shaping a new world order grounded in shared interests that calls for a fairer framework on issues such as security, trade, and climate change, America First has persistently taken a unilateralist stance by chiding America's NATO allies, sparking trade wars with China and other major trading partners, and withdrawing from global climate accords.

Domestically, Trump's disdain for public institutions is on daily display. In addition to his attacks on the media and key government agencies that we have already outlined, he routinely lambasts law-enforcement agencies, denouncing the criminal justice system as "a joke" and berating the FBI and Justice Department for not investigating his political opponents. James Comey, the former director of the FBI, alleges that Trump dismissed him after he refused to offer his personal loyalty to the president. Trump has also spoken publicly of his desire to interfere more in the Justice Department and has expressed his deep frustration at not having been allowed to do so.

As an overall proposition, if Americans took off their partisan blinders for a moment, most would agree that they deserve a better social contract for the 21st century than America First provides. But in order for that new social contract to emerge, I believe that Americans must get back to basics— to their roots as the land that's always been a global leader in freedom and inclusiveness.

When America's social contract has veered off course, it's usually been caused by the loss of its inclusive vision. This was true before the American

Civil War with the issue of slavery. It was evident in the pitiful response to the Great Depression by President Hoover's administration. The denial of rights to African Americans and their struggle during the civil rights movement was yet another critical failure. And now we see America veering off course as it struggles to pay heed to public concerns around growing inequality, the environment, and faith in government to do the right thing.

America has always been able to get back on track because it is empowered by strong democratic institutions and the norms of political dialogue those institutions have created. These norms have provided a strong bulwark against would-be strongman leaders intent on wreaking havoc— and they've created the time and space for great leaders to enter the scene to lead a political and spiritual renewal: Abraham Lincoln's role in ending slavery, FDR and the New Deal, and Martin Luther King Jr. and others during the civil rights movement remain inspiring examples for many Americans. Now the stage is set once again for other great leaders to renew and reenergize America's social contract for the 21st century.

While the American people await a more compelling and cohesive social contract that unifies the country and leads to an inclusive prosperity, I remain very concerned about the damage being caused by America First's assault on public institutions. Americans are fortunate to live in a country with strong institutions that—thus far—have endured. But, as we will see in the next chapter, this is far from the case in every country around the globe. Inclusive institutions that are resistant to capture by special interests make the difference between countries that enjoy sustained prosperity and those that crumble quickly when strongman rulers ascend to power.

CHAPTER 4

INCLUSIVE GOVERNANCE

The Price of Weak Institutions

In the spring of 2018, I was following the state visit of President Erdoğan of Turkey to the United Kingdom. He was to visit the queen at Buckingham Palace and to hold a joint press conference with British Prime Minister Theresa May. Erdoğan has ruled Turkey since 2003, first as the prime minister until 2014 and then as president. His visit had a dual purpose. One was to solidify the relationship between the UK and Turkey, which have been pulled together by their relationship with the EU—Turkey on its periphery looking in, and the UK about to join the periphery at the time. The other was to reassure investors that Turkey's economy was strong despite the battering the Turkish lira was facing in the financial markets.

I have been visiting Turkey on and off for the last fifteen years and have witnessed its miraculous transformation from economic crisis in the late 1990s into a vibrant, globally connected, modern economy. For a time, it was an investment darling for asset-management funds, private-equity firms, and corporations looking for opportunities in the Middle East region.

Therefore, I was surprised to watch a bizarre interview with Erdoğan from his trip in which he espoused a highly unusual—and erroneous—theory on monetary policy. The president believes, contrary to any rational economist, that higher interest rates cause, rather than curb, inflation. Coming from the head of state of a country credited with stable economic management in the last fifteen years, his statement was mind-boggling. It sent the lira into a tailspin.

Due to its persistent current-account deficit, Turkey is highly dependent on foreign investment. But after Erdoğan's interview and further missteps, investment has crumbled. The currency has stabilized somewhat since then, but the economy has gone through a crippling recession. At the time of writing, inflation is still above 15 percent, and the government has resorted to setting up food banks.

How could Turkey, once a genuine candidate to join the EU, have fallen to such depths? On the surface, the answer seems simple: Turkey is yet another country now ruled by a strongman ruler. Erdoğan narrowly won a 2017 referendum to transform Turkey's political system from parliamentary to super-presidential, handing him supreme power. In the eyes of the capital markets, however, this meant that the central bank's independence—and its position as an institution—had been compromised. Erdoğan's views on the relationship between inflation and interest rates could no longer be considered as his own "pet theory," but were now the basis of Turkish monetary policy.

The key question is how Erdoğan has so easily turned the country into an autocracy. Upon clearer examination, I realized that what has most let Turkey down are its institutions. Despite Trump's best efforts, the US's institutions have so far stood up to his attempts to curtail democratic norms. They will probably continue to succeed.

But in Turkey's case, the institutions have failed to protect the three freedoms because they were never inclusive in the first place—they have always marginalized a significant segment of society. And, once again, they have allowed special interests—namely Erdoğan and his political supporters—to capture the apparatus of the state. While before the favored segment of society was a secular elite that was closely tied with state institutions, now it is a new class of businessmen which Erdoğan and his Justice and Development Party (AKP) have nurtured.

Modern Turkey was founded by military commander Mustafa Kemal Atatürk, who threw out occupying Allied Forces after World War I. Crucially for him, this state had to be "secular" and progressive. Turkish women gained the right to vote a decade before women in Western European countries like France, Italy, and Belgium. Atatürk—an honorific title that means "Father of the Turks"—was highly revered for establishing a modern country out of the ashes of the collapsed Ottoman Empire.

But despite his modernizing reforms, Atatürk's brand of secularism did not translate into tolerance. As Turkey adopted European codes of law and increasingly leaned towards Western cultural norms, the state often discriminated against the country's majority Muslim population. Headscarves were prohibited in public institutions such as universities—effectively barring conservative women from gaining degrees. Ethnic Kurds, who account for roughly 20 percent of the Turkish population, were also singled out for persecution—at times, not even being allowed to speak their language in public. The Turkish state was run by a secular elite and felt remote to most of Turkey's conservative citizens.

The institutions of Atatürk's republic were as polarizing as its policies. Turkey remained a one-party state until Atatürk's death in 1938, except for a brief experiment in 1930 to allow an opposition party headed by one of Atatürk's confidants. Even though it towed the secular line, the party was closed in the same year after Atatürk deemed it to be too much of a threat.

Turkey didn't transition to multi-party democracy until 1945. There were elections, but they were largely ceremonial, given that, legally, only one party was allowed—the national assembly was supposed to reflect the views of the Turkish people and had the power to select the government and prime minister. The government also tightly controlled social and cultural organizations so that they aligned with the state's ideals of secularism and republicanism. It banned any newspapers that leaned to liberal or socialist values. Only government-controlled ones were allowed.[1]

During the multi-party era (until the AKP), democratic governments of different political stripes came and went, but the secular foundations of the state were never seriously challenged. At various stages, the organs of the state made sure a truly Islamist party could not take hold. For example, the National Order Party was banned by the Constitutional Court in 1971 after being founded in 1970. The National Salvation Party was likewise banished after the 1980 military coup. And in 1998 and 2001, the Constitutional Court banned two other Islamist parties.

Erdoğan himself was even put in prison briefly and stripped of his position as mayor of Istanbul in the 1990s because he recited a poem that promoted a religious view of government. Despite being the leader of the AKP, which won the 2002 elections, he was initially barred from becoming prime minister because of the conviction.

Once Erdoğan did ascend to the role of prime minister in 2003, he positioned himself as an inclusive leader. He reopened peace talks with the Kurds following a long-running conflict in the southeast of the country. And he allowed Kurdish to be used in all media and political campaigns, as well as restoring Kurdish names to cities and towns that had forcibly been given Turkish ones. He even launched the Democratic Initiative Process, consisting of a series of meetings with representatives of civil society, in an attempt to deepen human rights and democracy.

The central theme of Erdoğan's international posture was to secure Turkey's membership in the EU. He swiftly set about enacting a series of liberal reforms necessary to join the Union. But he also used the EU's membership criteria as a means to pursue his own political goals. For example, Erdoğan sidelined the Turkish Armed Forces on the pretext that the EU required a non-politicized role for the military in its member nations. This was a major step to strengthening his grip on power, since the Turkish military had always been the bulwark of secularism—even staging coups in 1960, 1971, 1980, and 1997 to preserve Turkey's secular regime.

During his first decade in power, Erdoğan went further to hobble potential opposition from the military, by increasing the ratio of civilians to military officers in the National Security Council and giving it a civilian head. He also removed the military's representatives from the state boards for education, radio, and television. When the military issued a memorandum threatening to intervene in the proposed appointment of an Islamist to the traditionally secular position of president in 2007, Erdoğan called an election and dramatically increased his support, due to his refusal to bow to military pressure. He thereby significantly diminished the military's power.

In retrospect, Erdoğan's rule fits neatly into the strongman playbook. His early reign had similarities with Putin's. Erdoğan came to power as an outsider who championed the marginalized. He thrived by presiding over a recovery of the Turkish economy—Turkey had suffered a major economic crisis in 2001. While in his early years he was careful not to go too far in attacking Turkey's secular character, all the while he built a power base separate from the secular elites. He used government infrastructure contracts to reward his business allies, who he then encouraged to purchase media outlets as part of their portfolio and trumpet his message.

Like Putin, Erdoğan's rule took a more authoritarian turn once he faced multiple threats. While Putin's turning point appears to have been in 2011, for Erdoğan it was 2013. In 2013 Turkish police launched a sprawling corruption investigation, arresting the sons of three government ministers. To make matters worse, leaked audio of Erdoğan seemingly telling his son to hide money appeared on social media. The same year saw the Gezi Park protests—a large and nationwide uprising against the government's increasing authoritarianism, sparked by the government's plan to build over one of Istanbul's few remaining public parks.

In response, Erdoğan began to craft heavily nationalist narratives that excluded secular voters and Kurds. Once the man knocking on the EU's accession door, he became increasingly anti-European, while his allies in the media whipped up conspiracy theories about the West attempting to clip the wings of an Islamic power.

Turkey's authoritarianism grew even greater after a failed coup attempt in 2016, orchestrated by a conservative faction once loyal to the AKP. Erdoğan capitalized on the coup to brutally crack down on any form of descent. According to Freedom House:

> *His response to the July 2016 coup attempt has become a sprawling witch hunt, resulting in the arrest of some 60,000 people, the closure of over 160 media outlets, and the imprisonment of over 150 journalists. The leaders of the third-largest party in the parliament are in prison, and nearly 100 mayors across the country have been replaced through emergency measures or political pressure from the president.*[2]

As strongman typically do once they fear their power slipping away, Erdoğan systematically hollowed out institutions. The judiciary was stuffed with AKP loyalists so that it can no longer be considered independent. It is routinely used as a tool to silence political opponents. In a striking resemblance to Russia, more than 90 percent of the media is now under government influence. Turkey has reached this sorry state after years of Erdoğan putting pressure on independent outlets via arbitrary fines that crippled their finances or politically motivated court cases. For example, Turkey's largest media group, Doğan, had no choice but to sell to allies of the president in 2018 following years of pressure, including a $2.9 billion fine (later reduced to $600 million) in 2009 after it reported corruption allegations against a religious charity close to Erdoğan.[3]

Elections since 2014 have also been grossly compromised. On the day of the 2017 referendum, which asked Turks if they supported turning Turkey into a presidential system, Turkey's supreme electoral board lifted a ban on counting ballots that did not have an official stamp—affecting up to 1.5 million votes. In the 2018 presidential and parliamentary elections, the public broadcaster TRT gave the ruling AKP and Erdoğan 181 hours of coverage, compared with just sixteen hours for his main opponent Muharrem Ince and his party. And when the main opposition, the Republican People's Party (the party Atatürk founded), narrowly won the mayoralty of Istanbul in 2019, Erdoğan put huge pressure on Turkey's electoral board to annul the result. Tellingly, it did not call for a new poll for Istanbul's districts, where the AKP did comparatively better. In the rerun of the election, with the opposition's vote-share rising dramatically as the public reacted with outrage, Erdoğan had to accept defeat.

Modern Turkey is a sad example of how easily progress can be lost if institutions are weak and non-inclusive. Since the times of Atatürk, one group has always marginalized another rather than ruling for the whole country and building institutions that promote the three freedoms. The result has been a deeply polarized society and severe erosion of social capital. Once a beacon for Middle Eastern success, Turks are turning their back on their own country. Since the 2016 crackdown, there's been a sizeable brain-drain to the US and other European countries, dealing a heavy blow to the nation's economic prospects. The outlook is bleak.

Inclusive Governance

To avoid polarizing politics and the marginalization of broad segments of citizens, I believe it is essential to adopt what I will call Inclusive Governance:

> *Inclusive Governance is a system of laws, institutions, and culture that promote political participation, civil liberties, and socioeconomic mobility for the entire population. It is resilient to "capture" by a ruler or special interests. It is the critical framework for upholding cohesive social contracts and reversing divisive ones.*

Inclusive Governance is more than democracy, which is a system of political participation through popular voting. Instead the focus is on inclusion and good governance. It is a very challenging summit to reach—indeed no country in the world today truly reaches it, but countries like Singapore, Germany, Canada, New Zealand, Australia, and the Nordic countries come close. And even when they approach the summit, countries can quickly regress if their gains are not protected by strong and inclusive institutions.

Figure 4-1 shows a selection of the institutions that I hold to be the most critical in upholding the three freedoms and cohesive social contracts in the 21st century. Some institutions, like property rights, will be familiar to the foundation of any successful society. Others, like anti-trust commissions,

FIGURE 4-1: INCLUSIVE INSTITUTIONS

Political Participation	· Inclusive constitutions
	· Checks/balances between executive, parliament, and judiciary
	· Free and fair elections administered by an independent electoral commission that regulates campaign financing, has the broad support of political parties, and enforces strict adherence to pre-determined rules of the game
	· Inclusive electoral systems such as proportional representation (PR) instead of first-past-the-post (FPTP)
	· Limits to campaign financing, gerrymandering, and the "revolving door between government and the private sector"
	· Devolution of powers to subnational levels: election of local governors, taxation, and spending
	· Competent and well-paid civil service
Civil Liberties	· Judicial independence and effectiveness
	· Strong land and property rights with pragmatic processes to enable sustainable development
	· Regulators that enforce fiduciary responsibility on users of personal data and veracity of news on all media
Socioeconomic Mobility	· Well-funded mobility enablers: health, education, affordable housing, and economic infrastructure
	· High-quality, broadly accessible lifelong learning
	· Long-term national and regional investment and development vehicles with independent governance
	· Powerful and well-staffed anti-trust commission
	· Greater stakeholder engagement in corporate governance

desperately need adapting in the winner-takes-all global economy we find ourselves in. And new institutions may be required to address emergent challenges such as the misuse of personal data.

The list is by no means exhaustive but represents what I hold to be most significant. But, in addition to institutions, political culture is vital for Inclusive Governance. Indeed, culture shapes institutions just as institutions shape culture. There must be space for vigorous debate, new ideas, and a constructive dialogue among the major stakeholders, with the common goal of finding the best solution for society's long-term interests. Sadly, the tenor of political dialogue has declined significantly in the US over the last thirty years, with notable culprits such as Newt Gingrich and President Trump setting the bar ever lower.

In what follows, I will show how Germany and Singapore—two highly successful countries in terms of economic performance and political stability—each have elements of Inclusive Governance. I will also talk about the need for new institutional mechanisms to deal with the emerging challenges in the 21st century, such as freedom of expression, the winner-takes-all economy, and shareholder primacy versus stakeholder capitalism.

Germany: A Beacon of Political and Civic Freedom

Following the defeat of the Nazi regime in World War II, Germany was a humiliated nation. Battered into submission, it was cleaved into two rival states—East and West Germany—by the ideologically incompatible victors: the USSR and the US-led allies of the West. Germany's rise as an economic power and an inclusive society from its devastated state after the war is a source of great optimism for the entire human project. And I believe that Germany's adoption of strong inclusive-governance elements was a fundamental driver of success.

Political and Civic Institutions

Germany owes a lot to the jurists who crafted West Germany's equivalent of a constitution, known as the Basic Law, after WWII. Adopted in 1949, the Basic Law embraced full political and civil rights for its citizens under a proportional-representation (PR) system. Written by German lawyers and politicians and approved by all four victorious Allied powers, the Basic Law was framed to try to ensure a dictator could never again take over the state. Upon absorption of the collapsing East German state in 1990, it became the official constitution of the reunified Germany.

Germany's Basic Law specifically guarantees democracy, republicanism, forms of inclusiveness, and federalism. It is the foundation of Germany's cohesive social contract. Here are a few excerpts of its most powerful tenets:

All state authority is derived from the people. It shall be exercised by the people through elections and other votes and through specific legislative, executive and judicial bodies.

No person shall be favored or disfavored because of sex, parentage, race, language, homeland and origin, faith, or religious or political opinions. No person shall be disfavored because of disability.

All Germans shall have the right to resist any person seeking to abolish this constitutional order, if no other remedy is available.[4]

Immediately after WWII, defendants of the remaining leadership of Nazi Germany argued at the Nuremberg war-crimes tribunals that they were just following orders from above, so they could not be held responsible for their actions. The "right to resist" unconstitutional orders protected by the Basic Law is therefore a direct response to the Holocaust revelations aired at the trials.

The Basic Law has survived remarkably well and has helped instill an inclusive political culture into Germany's body politic. Germany, like the US, has a robust system of checks and balances between the chancellor's office (the executive), the bicameral legislature, and the powerful constitutional court. As mentioned in chapter 3, Germany's Basic Law elevates the role of its states, thereby acting as another check on centralized power.

Inclusive Governance ideally demands a free and fair electoral system, which ensures as many viewpoints as possible are considered. However, even in regimes with tight state control, inclusiveness can be sewn into the political fabric. We saw this in China with the government's increased use of polling and focus groups to gauge public opinion.

We've already seen how the FPTP systems of the US and the UK effectively disenfranchise millions. Germany's mixed-member proportional representation (MMP) system is much more inclusive of the whole population, while maintaining a link between candidates and a local area. MMP, which is also used in New Zealand, allows voters to select both a candidate in their local district and a party they'd like to win a majority in the nation as a whole. Each candidate that wins a district is awarded a seat, and additional seats are distributed to make sure parties are represented proportionate to their overall vote.

While PR systems are more inclusive than the FPTP systems of the US and the UK, they must guard against the political fragmentation that occurs when too many parties enter the legislature. Germany imposes a 5 percent threshold, below which smaller parties cannot win a seat. Brazil demonstrates what happens when such minority-party thresholds are not installed. The result is unstable coalitions and pork-barrel politics—corruption, in other words—as governments need to grease too many wheels to cajole smaller parties into supporting them. Additional areas that require careful safeguards are campaign financing, gerrymandering, and the "revolving door between government and the private sector."

There must be limits on campaign financing. US courts have, since the 1970s, allowed corporations to spend huge sums in campaign financing—defending it as a corporation's right to free speech.[5] A 2010 Supreme Court ruling allows US corporations to fund campaign financing without any cap on their contribution whatsoever, as long as donations were not made directly to a candidate's campaign—opening the door to donations to nominally independent bodies called Super Political Action Committees.[6] Even more worrying because of the unaccountability it makes possible, a super PAC can also accept money from donors that don't reveal their identities, through shell corporations and political nonprofits.[7] The Supreme Court's decision has enhanced corporations' lobbying powers and distorted politics by making it beholden to narrow interests, often against the wider public interest. For example, according to Business Insider, Koch Industries has donated to the American Legislative Exchange Council, a nonprofit organization of conservative state-legislatures and private enterprises that work together to draft state legislation, which has promoted limiting lawsuits from people with terminal illness as a result of asbestos. Koch Industries owns Georgia Pacific, which has been subject to such lawsuits.[8]

Germany does fall short in this regard, since by law there are no limits on private and corporate campaign giving. In the late 1990s, Chancellor Helmut Kohl was even brought down by the Schwarzgeldaffäre ("black money scandal"), in which undisclosed donations were made to his Christian Democratic Union party. By contrast, the UK has much more restrictive campaign-financing laws. For the 2019 election, parties were allowed to spend only £30,000 in each of the UK's 650 constituencies on campaigning in the year before the election.

Finally, Germany scores very highly for its independent judiciary and protection of civil liberties, with its judiciary being regarded as one of the most independent and effective in the world.

In summary, the institutions of German democracy—from the chancellor's office, to the bicameral legislature, to the constitutional court—have been proven to be inclusive and resilient. They have stood firm in the face of severe challenges posed over the past seventy years: decades on the front line of the Cold War, left-wing terrorism in the 1970s, German reunification in 1990, right up to the massive influx of refugees from Syria, Iraq, and elsewhere in recent years.

Germany's Economic Success

Inclusive institutions of political participation and civil liberties in West Germany, undergirded by the security umbrella of NATO, laid the foundations for Germany's post-war Wirtschaftswunder (economic miracle). Also key to Germany's economic success has been its devolved system of governance. The Länder (states), each with its own parliament, wield significant power. While areas such as foreign policy and defense are the exclusive responsibility of the federation, all other areas are shared or are the exclusive competence of the Länder. The Länder have wide discretion over areas like education, local economic development, justice, and policing.

Unlike centralized countries such as the UK, in Germany subnational governments (the Länder, and below them, districts and municipalities) collect a significant proportion of taxes and have greater latitude on how revenues are spent than in most countries. Specifically, subnational governments collect 50 percent of all tax revenue in Germany, well above the OECD average of around 30 percent, and local government is responsible for almost 50 percent of all public spending—double that of the UK.[9] Subnational taxes include local business tax, inheritance tax, vehicle tax, real estate purchase tax, lottery tax, beer tax, and so on. Personal income tax, corporate income tax, and VAT are shared taxes.[10]

Most states have also historically benefited from their Landesbanken and below them the Sparkassen—state-owned and municipal banks, which invest heavily into German industry, particularly export-oriented businesses—channeling funds made available by Germany's high savings rate. Since 2001 the Landesbanken's role has been curtailed somewhat due to EU state-aid rules, which deemed unlimited guarantees from states as illegal state-aid. This had the adverse effect of encouraging the Landesbanken to disastrously invest in riskier assets abroad to compensate, such as the American securities, which helped cause the financial crisis in 2007–8.[11]

To its credit, Germany also managed with relative ease to reintegrate East Germany into a united country after the fall of the Berlin Wall in 1989.

It's true that this involved large fiscal transfers to the East, and West German incomes still remain one-third higher than those of East Germans. Nevertheless, it is a testament to Germany's institutions that such a complex process was managed without any significant conflict or unrest. And there is no doubt that the three freedoms have increased for East Germans since the Wall fell.

Today, Germany's economy is envied the world over. In contrast to most developed economies, it has managed to hold on to well-paid manufacturing jobs. It is the world's third largest exporter—just behind the US, even though its population is a quarter of the size. It is also one of the most equal societies in the world terms of income distribution, with a Gini Coefficient (a measure of inequality where 0 represents complete equality and 1 complete inequality) of 0.29, compared with the OECD average of almost 0.32 and a score of 0.39 in the US.[12]

If one were to point to a flaw in Germany's socioeconomic system, it would be its record on socioeconomic mobility. Despite the collapse of the American Dream, the US still performs better in this regard than Germany. A poor German child would need 180 years to reach the average German income, compared with 150 in the US.[13] One key obstacle is Germany's system of educational tracks, which funnels German children into different types of schools based on academic performance. In Germany, at the age of ten or twelve, kids are streamed into different "tracks."[14] Track one is for the brightest students; track two is the next step down and is intended for average or better white-collar jobs. Track three trains kids to work in the trades and blue-collar jobs. While the system has been credited with helping sustain well-paid manufacturing jobs for people in the lower tracks, it does tend to limit their ability to move into other higher-paying, non-manufacturing sectors.

Another factor driving poor socioeconomic mobility is Germany's excessive licensure of the labor market. Specific qualifications are often absolutely essential to move into a particular profession. Licenses are even required to become a hairdresser. However, it is difficult for many adults to gain these qualifications later in life because of inadequate funding or childcare options to give them the time to study and train.

Upwardly Mobile Singapore

Looking around the world, there are relatively few advanced economies that perform well on socioeconomic mobility, except for a select group of

Nordic countries and Singapore. Indeed, I believe Singapore offers clues for how we can improve socioeconomic mobility in the long term.

In general, Singapore's institutions provide a good foundation for growing the Five Capitals and preserving the three freedoms. Let's take a look at how it performs on all these dimensions, with a deeper dive on its performance in socioeconomic mobility.

In the early 1960s, Singapore was part of the independent Federation of Malaysia, formed in 1963. But Malaysia soon became fearful that the ethnic Chinese of Singapore, under a dynamic young leader named Lee Kuan Yew, would embolden ethnic Chinese in other parts of the country to challenge the dominance of the predominantly Muslim Malays. So, in what surely must rank as one of most shortsighted moves of the post-colonial era, Malaysia's parliament expelled Singapore from its national umbrella in 1965.

Most expected Singapore to flounder. It had little going for it upon independence. While it held the remnants of an important Royal Navy base, it had no military forces with which to defend itself, little indigenous industry, no natural resources, and almost no fresh water. Most of its two million citizens were poor and illiterate.

Yet today, Singapore is one of the world's most prosperous nations. It does not perform especially well on political participation and civil liberties, but it outperforms on socioeconomic mobility. In contrast to many Western societies, inter-generational mobility is still positive in both absolute and relative terms. What's also noteworthy is the relative inclusiveness of its economic growth. Singapore became a little more equal—not less—during recent periods of economic growth.[15] Therefore, the mechanisms Singapore has used to foster income mobility are worth reviewing, and they offer lessons for other countries. But even Singapore needs to be aware of threats to its future socioeconomic mobility. The city-state has no inheritance tax, and as property prices have risen in recent decades, wealth inequality has risen—1 percent of adults in Singapore hold a third of the country's wealth. Also, its system of allocating pupils into tracks, as in Germany, could hurt the mobility it has worked so hard to build up.

Political Participation and Civil Liberties

The bedrock for Singapore's success has been its first-rate economic institutions, as well as the visionary leadership of its founder Lee Kuan Yew, who was Prime Minister from 1959 to 1990. With Asia's version of the Cold War raging around him, Lee concluded that Singapore could leap from "Third World to First" in a series of steps. Singapore has followed this vision remarkably well. The first, which lasted roughly from independence to the early 1980s, was survival. Lee decided this required a strict, though not quite dictatorial, form of paternalism. He also formed an alliance with the US—the one power that could secure a freckle of a nation from potential predators like Mao's China, Communist Vietnam, Sukarno's Indonesia, or vestigial Malaysia.

The second step was opening up to international capital. From roughly 1980–96, Singapore courted multinational banks and corporations, many of which set up their Asia headquarters locally. The third step—which began in the survival era but received a boost from 1997 onwards—has seen Singapore continue to invest heavily in education as part of its bid to capture the most high-tech sectors of the global economy.

But Singapore has also thrived due to its inclusiveness, which has helped underpin a cohesive social contract. The city-state has always had a multicultural citizenry, with a Chinese majority but also sizeable Malay and Indian minorities. On the day Singapore became independent, Lee proclaimed that Singapore is "not a Malay nation, not a Chinese nation, not an Indian nation. Everybody will have a place in Singapore." This spirit was enshrined in the constitution and in the "National Pledge"—an oath to Singapore devised in 1965 and recited at state events—which reads we "pledge ourselves as one united people, regardless of race, language or religion."

Lee saw the direct link between inclusiveness, tolerance, and prosperity that the British had failed to live up to before their empire crumbled. "Throughout history, all empires that succeeded have embraced and included in their midst people of other races, languages, religions, and cultures," he once remarked.

This philosophy laid the groundwork for a superior political culture. Lee stressed the rigorous application of meritocracy in public office, with "the best and brightest doing the most outstanding jobs." In a portend to a key governmental innovation that would power China's success, Lee aligned officials' incentives directly with economic growth. Singapore's civil service also attracts the best and brightest by continually linking salaries to comparable jobs in the private sector via a mathematical formula.

The same rigor is applied to the ruling People's Action Party (PAP). The party actively recruits individuals with academic brilliance and distinguished careers across a wide spectrum, such as think tanks, religious groups, businesses, and community organizations. All representatives must pass an IQ test and an incredibly thorough—and arguably invasive—background check, illustrating the stringent standards required.

But most importantly, they must have completed grassroots community work. Lee even disapproved of some outstanding officials because of
their lack of ability to work in the grassroots. He was also wary of "ideological inbreeding," as he called it, and encouraged a diversity of ideas, as long
as politicians agreed on some core values and handled problems logically.
This fact-based approach chimes with Deng's approach in China.

One of the first institutional steps independent Singapore took was to
give its corruption-fighting body more teeth. Founded in 1952, the Corrupt
Practices Investigation Bureau (CPIB) initially had little power to fight corruption, which had been rampant under colonialism. However, under Lee,
the CPIB was radically revamped in 1960. New legislation made the penalty
for corrupt behaviors much more severe and the legal permissions to clamp
down on it more powerful. CPIB offices were given the authority to arrest a
person suspected of corruption and the ability to access a suspect's financial
accounts. Today Singapore is regarded as one of the least corrupt nations
on Earth—ranking the third-least corrupt in Transparency International's
Corruption Perception Index.[16]

The government's drive to clean Singapore of corruption infused its
approach to justice more broadly. Singapore has carved out a reputation
for itself as a country with a strong rule of law—ranking thirteenth out of
126 countries for this measure, according to the World Justice Project.[17] It
ranks particularly highly (number five) in civil justice—the ability of ordinary citizens to resolve their grievances peacefully and effectively through
the civil-justice system.[18]

However, Singapore by no means has a perfect record in political participation and civil liberties, performing more weakly on these metrics
compared to many of its Western peers. While the PAP has been critical to
Singapore's economic success, it has also shaped political institutions in its
favor. As with FPTP systems in the US and UK, Singapore's electoral system
makes it extremely difficult for minority parties to achieve representation
in proportion with their popular support. For example, each constituency
is allocated between one and six members in parliament, but all seats are
allocated to whichever party receives the most votes in that constituency.
As the most powerful and well-funded party, the PAP wins most constituencies and therefore the vast majority of seats. It remains extremely difficult
for new parties to break through.

In terms of civil liberties, Singapore is also certainly no angel. In April
2019 Singapore introduced legislation which will give any government minister the power to order social media companies and news sites to remove

or "correct" material they deem to be "false or misleading" and "against the public interest."[19] Those who publish false statements with malicious intent face criminal sanctions, including jail terms of up to ten years.[20] The law is worrying for the freedom of expression because it does not give any clear definition of what a false statement is and also fails to define what it means by "public interest." Therefore, it gives the government almost a carte blanche to define the truth, although citizens can appeal to the courts.[21] We'll return to this issue later in the chapter when we look at necessary institutions of the future for Inclusive Governance.

Furthermore, much of Singapore's media follows the ruling party's narrative and there are relatively few independent media outlets. Singapore also does not get everything right in its race relations. Public-ownership regulations restrict homeowners from minority communities selling or renting to the majority Singaporean Chinese community. While originally this was intended to maintain a 'racial quota' in a particular area, it has also unfairly stymied the ability of minorities to accumulate wealth because it means that market demand, and therefore prices, are lower for property they rent or sell because of the smaller pool of potential buyers.

Excellence in Socioeconomic Mobility

Notwithstanding its shortcomings in political participation and civil liberties, where Singapore does shine is in socioeconomic mobility. Fourteen percent of young Singaporeans in their thirties whose parents were in the lowest income quintile when they were young were able to move into the top quintile of earners. That's impressive compared with other countries. The comparable figure is 11.7 percent in Denmark, 9 percent in the UK, and only 7.5 percent in the US.[22] Furthermore, a Singapore Ministry of Finance study of adults born between 1978 and 1982 shows that they earn more than their parents, even after correcting for changes in cost of living,[23] and are also more likely to move up into a higher income-decile. But the study also cautions that this socioeconomic mobility may be at risk of slowing down.

Singapore's impressive performance is derived from its excellent educational system, its openness to foreign capital, talent, and ideas, as well as its long-term investment model. And running through all these factors is a strong and continuously evolving economic-development vision.

Of course, Singapore's economy has developed much more recently than most of its Western counterparts. Therefore, it's reasonable to argue that the higher mobility of the age cohort mentioned above resulted from the many opportunities available in Singapore' high-growth economy of the 1980s and 1990s. Yet what's remarkable about Singapore is the speed at which it has converged with developed countries, far outperforming even China. In fact, Singapore now has a higher median household income than the UK,[24] suggesting that there is more to its socioeconomic mobility than merely timing.

Education

A key principle that has guided Singapore's transformation from independence to today has been the ongoing refinement of its national curriculum to align with Singapore's evolving economic-development vision, and a belief in the central role of human capital in economic growth. Its education model has also been guided by equal opportunity for all citizens regardless of race, maintaining unity in diversity, and an emphasis on mathematics, science, and technical subjects. It has evolved in three distinct phases, in line with the evolution of Singapore's economic-development vision.

The first phase, from 1965 to 1978, focused on preparing citizens to work in labor-intensive export manufacturing industries. After a massive state-funded school-building program, primary and secondary school enrollment grew by 66 percent between 1959 and 1968, and the supply of teachers increased by 80 percent. By 1970, universal lower-secondary-school education was achieved.[25] From 1960 to 1980, Singapore hugely increased technical education to feed the manufacturing industry and attracted foreign multinationals to Singapore, in the process obtaining valuable technology and skill-transfers. Also, by 1966 bilingualism had been made mandatory in secondary schools, with English teaching seen as essential to Singapore's quest for making the entire world its marketplace.[26]

By the 1980s, it was clear Singapore's comparative advantage in low-cost labor was wearing out as other developing countries industrialized. Therefore, the second phase, from 1978 to 1997, focused on transitioning Singapore from a 'third-league' labor-intensive industrializing country to a 'second-league' capital-intensive economy. This transition would require more engineers, research professionals, and managerial employees—a tall order since only 9 percent of Singapore's students attended universities or polytechnics in the early 1980s. However, by 1990 Singapore had managed to increase its pool of research scientists and engineers by 270 percent, thanks to government incentives like increasing the starting salaries for these careers in public-private partnerships.

The next stage in Singapore's education system and its economic model came in the late 1990s. It presciently identified the need to reform education in line with the shift of value creation in the global economy away from production and towards innovation and creativity. Its "Thinking Schools, Learning Nation" program focused on instilling values of lifelong learning—a critical element for a nation to prosper in the 21st century, as we'll see later in the book (chapter 8). It also changed the national curriculum to concentrate more on higher levels of technological literacy, a spirit of innovation, and enterprise and risk-taking, and it mandated that 30 percent of curriculum time be devoted to learning with computers.

Furthermore, in recognition of the vital role of teacher quality in educational outcomes, it made teachers' remuneration comparable with or better than lawyers, engineers, and even medical doctors in the government service, established bonuses for long service, and introduced one hundred hours per year of subsidized professional training.

And more recently, Singapore's education system has continued to keep up with the new challenges of its economic-development aspirations. For example, in the past decade the country's focus on the biomedical sciences and digital media sectors was supported by reforms to the science and mathematics curriculum to concentrate more on life sciences and the application of scientific, mathematical, and technological knowledge to the real world.[27]

Of course, no system is perfect. Like Germany, Singapore also streams pupils into different tracks: Express, Normal Academic, and Normal Technical. The Normal Academic and Normal Technical tracks set pupils up for non-academic tertiary education. But even though they learn valuable skills, students in these tracks usually do not attend university, which limits their lifelong earning potential. Singapore's highly adaptable education model has worked well so far, but it needs to be careful that its tracking system doesn't undermine mobility overall, as it has in Germany.

Attracting Global Capital, Talent and Ideas

From its inception, Singapore's growth formula has also included opening up to foreign sources of capital, talent, and ideas in order to gain a leadership position in emerging industries of the future. This has helped generate job opportunities, and therefore mobility, for its citizens.

Once again, Singapore's excellent institutions have contributed in large part to its success. Singapore's Economic Development Board (EDB)—a quasi-governmental agency established to generate economic growth by providing a friendly business environment for multinationals to invest and expand—has been especially important. After being expelled from Malaysia,

Singapore lost access to raw materials and export markets. Faced with an unemployment crisis and potential for civil unrest, it took action to attract multinationals to invest in export-oriented, labor-intensive industries. The EDB set up its first overseas centers in New York and Hong Kong to create awareness of Singapore's capabilities.

As with Singapore's education system, the EDB has intelligently adapted to changing economic winds over time. By the late 1960s it began to move away from cheap manufacturing and began to refashion Singapore into the "precision engineering" destination, which required more investments into capital and skills. In the same period, Singapore also took advantage of foreign capital to upgrade its port and make the most of its strategic geographic position. The containerization of cargo had barely begun by the late 1960s when Singapore made a bold bet by investing in its first container port at Tanjong Pagar in 1969, backed by a $45 million loan from the World Bank.[28] Singapore's port is now the busiest container handler in the world. It also benefited from the state-of-the-art Paya Lebar airport, which was built in the 1950s. Once it outgrew this, it constructed the award-winning Changi Airport, opened in 1981, to solidify its position as a regional air-transportation hub.

In the 1980s, the EDB enticed multinationals to set up management hubs in Singapore, while locating their manufacturing in neighboring Malaysia and Indonesia. As globalization gathered pace in the 1990s, the EDB again adapted to position Singapore as one of the world's leading professional services and R&D hubs. In yet another iteration, the EDB is now helping to make Singapore one of the world's foremost centers for biotech and clean manufacturing.

A great example of the EDB's success in attracting capital to spawn new R&D-focused business activity is Biopolis—an R&D center for biomedical sciences in Singapore. In contrast to other biomedical hubs like Cambridge, Massachusetts, which already had world leading life-sciences research universities such as MIT and Harvard to build on, Singapore started off with very little experience in this field. Begun in 2000 as the Biomedical Sciences (BMS) Initiative, with a budget of $2 billion,[29] few would have expected Biopolis to become the success that it is today.

Biopolis was the result of the Singaporean government's vision for biomedical sciences as the next major driving force for economic growth in the city-state. It proceeded in three phases. In the first (2000–5), it built biomedical sciences institutes close to Singapore's most prestigious university—the National University of Singapore—and its medical schools.

It attracted top-notch veteran scientists to lead the institutes. Phase two (2006–10) saw further funding ($1 billion[30]) poured into translational and clinical research capabilities. Phase three (2010–15) was focused on attracting businesses, and it has been highly successful, with the settlement in Biopolis of companies like Roche, Novartis, GSK, Chugai, P&G, and Nestlé.

We can link Biopolis directly to economic opportunities for Singaporean citizens. It has created 25,000 new jobs in the last ten years, mostly highly paid. Already by 2014, biomedical-sciences manufacturing in Singapore generated $10 billion—or 3.2 percent of overall GDP. Through the initiative, Singapore has attracted more than fifty manufacturing plants and fifty new research-facilities, while settling more than thirty regional headquarters of multinationals in the sector. This is just one highly successful example of Singapore's knack of creating high-paying jobs for its citizens over the decades.

Singapore owes a lot to the EDB's skill in attracting overseas capital, talent, and ideas. Its employees are public service oriented but entrepreneurially spirited and are organized according to different sector-focused physical "clusters." Each cluster has talented account managers that work with clients looking to invest and expand in Singapore and network between them and the local government. The government induces investors through various incentives such as tax incentives, cheap land, availability of infrastructure, and vital resources such as clean water.

Aside from the EDB's work, Singapore is generally attractive to international investors because the overall business environment is so favorable. According to the World Bank, Singapore ranks second among 190 economies for its overall ease of doing business (New Zealand is first). It is the third easiest country in the world for setting up a business. It is first for the enforcement of contracts, and it scores in the top ten of countries for the ease of the tax system, gaining construction permits, and protections for minority investors.[31]

Long-Term Investment Model

Also integral to Singapore's success in socioeconomic mobility has been its long-term investment model, which makes the most of its assets and reserves of surplus money.

Singapore recognized early on that it needed to establish a strong presence in new industries due to a lack of natural resources to fall back on for revenue. In 1974 it formed Temasek as a holding company for its state-owned enterprises. Over the next thirty to forty years, Temasek would perform its role as an asset manager of government companies, nurturing them into competitive multinationals. Ultimately, the fund performed its role so well that most of its holdings were privatized, leaving it free to become a financial-investment vehicle. It now has $235 billion in assets under management and a global portfolio.

The government has also used its healthy financial position to stoke new R&D-intensive industries. For the 2016–20 period, it has allocated $13.7 billion[32] to its Research, Innovation and Enterprise (RIE) Plan, which is steered by the Prime Minister Lee Hsien Loong himself. This has helped fund projects like Biopolis.

Furthermore, Singapore has recognized the need to provision for the very long term. In 1981, Singapore formed Government Investment Corporation (GIC), a sovereign-wealth fund, in which to tuck away economic surpluses and grow the capital pool for use in future generations. The GIC has well over $100 billion in assets in forty countries—an impressive feat for a country with just 5.6 million people and no commodity wealth. The GIC's portfolio is an important buffer against any potential downturns and liabilities. When needed, it can also provide an important supplement to government revenues to invest in Singapore's mobility enablers.[33]

Despite being famed for its low-tax and light-regulation regime, Singapore has always viewed social equity as a key plank of its growth strategy. The government subsidizes education, housing, healthcare, and public transportation for all citizens. Under colonial rule in 1955, Singapore established the Central Provident Fund as a compulsory savings scheme to help workers provide for their retirement. Employers and employees were initially required to contribute 5 percent of salary. This was progressively increased to the high rate of 25 percent, but lowered to 10 percent after a recession in 1986 and is now at 20 percent up to age 55. In 1986, the Fund was also expanded to cover housing. Singaporeans can access savings from the fund to purchase a house, typically from public-housing stock. Furthermore, in 1990, the fund introduced the MediShield health-insurance scheme to provide universal healthcare to all Singaporeans. Over time, supplements to the Fund have also been introduced to provide pension and medical provision top-ups for low-income older workers.

As wealth inequality persists, provisions like these are likely to increase in importance to Singapore's performance in socioeconomic mobility. In light of this, the government has increased the supply of social housing and sought to increase private supply as well. It has also indicated that it will intervene further if property prices rise faster than income. The government has proved before that it can help stoke mobility through its long-term vision and investment, and continued proactiveness will be needed if Singapore is to continue to perform strongly on this measure.

Institutions of the Future

While no system is perfect, the examples of Germany and Singapore, collectively, show us how embracing inclusive political, economic, and civic institutions helps to create a stable environment in which countries can drive sustained socioeconomic progress.

However, as we saw in previous chapters, modern strains of problems relating to the growing market-power of top firms, rent-seeking by owners of capital, and the misuse of personal data may need to be addressed by innovative, new institutional approaches. Interestingly, the world's three big power blocs—the US, China, and the EU—are approaching these critical issues in markedly different ways.

To date, the US is opting for a broadly laissez-faire model. Since the 1970s, American policy towards antitrust, corporate governance, and taxation of wealth has been strongly influenced by the free-markets philosophy advocated by the Chicago School of Economics. Followers of this line of thinking believe that the regulator should only step in to break up firms in the most egregious cases,[34] that the sole objective of corporations is to maximize profits for shareholders, and that lower taxes on the wealthy will "trickle down" to the rest of the economy. As a result, US antitrust authorities haven't brought any major cases against a tech giant for twenty years.[35] The primacy of shareholders in corporate governance has not been challenged until very recently. And capital gains and other taxes on the wealthy have gradually been chipped away for the last thirty to forty years. The US also has a much more relaxed view of privacy compared with Europe. No legislation is in play at the national level to prevent the use of consumers' data without their consent.

The EU is generally more interventionist than the US, with the objective of protecting consumer interests. When it comes to antitrust, it has slapped fines worth €8.2 billion on Google, a smaller one on Facebook (€110 million), and is investigating Amazon for anti-competitive behavior. Many European countries—such as Germany, France, and the Nordics—also take a broader stakeholder view of corporate governance, with these states mandating worker representation on company boards.[36] And the EU has also enacted General Data Protection Regulation (GDPR), which requires companies to obtain consumers' explicit consent for the use of their personal data for a specific purpose.

Predictably, China also takes a more interventionist approach than the US, but with the primary goal of increasing state control. Under Xi Jinping, China is far from an antitrust champion. Instead, it is empowering SOEs, especially those that have global ambitions, to gain market power. It is also increasing party intervention in large private corporations, although it is unclear whether this will result in greater or lesser competition in key sectors. A byproduct of China's meteoric rise over the past thirty years has been skyrocketing inequality. However, there appear to be few attempts to tax the vast amounts of land, real estate, and financial capital that have accrued to throngs of newly minted millionaires and billionaires. When it comes to the use of personal data, China's social-credit system appears designed to tighten control over society by hoovering up as much personal information as possible. There are virtually no protections against government and corporations using consumers' personal information for political and commercial purposes.

The debate on how to address these three issues is in its infancy, and much could change in the directions ultimately taken in the US, EU, and China. While it may appear that the EU is leading the way by evolving regulation and institutions to tackle the dominant trends, some in the US and China would argue that the Europeans have less to lose, since they have given rise to very few platform-based technology giants. And perhaps additional regulation would squash the very dynamism that allows these innovative businesses to thrive. However, many in the US are becoming vocal about their model also needing to change. For example, California has introduced similar legislation to GDPR, which will come into effect in 2020. Many Americans support a push for similar rules at the federal level. And on corporate governance, presidential candidate Senator Elizabeth Warren is also advocating changes that would increase the considerations given to workers and the local community.

In the remainder of this chapter, I'll look at various options being considered to adapt or innovate institutions to achieve greater competition, lower inequality, and increased consumer-choice—without harming the dynamism of the broader economy.

Antitrust Institutions in the Winner-Takes-All Economy

According to Chicago-school economic thinking, we shouldn't be concerned about monopolies because monopoly power is temporary in an innovative economy. The contest among companies to become the monopoly player maximizes innovation and consumer welfare, they claim. Any attempt by a firm to increase prices is met by new firms entering the market, willing to sell at a lower price.[37]

These outcomes have clearly not come to pass in the US. As the Nobel Laureate economist Joseph Stiglitz argues, prices relative to costs (i.e. markups) have risen in many industries in the US.[38] Just look at telecoms prices, which are much higher in the US compared with other countries, while the quality of service falls short. Traditionally, in antitrust regulation the measure of market power used to justify investigations has been whether or not companies can raise prices without losing customers. However, by narrowing the scope of what constitutes anti-competitive behavior, Chicago-school economists have made it much harder to justify antitrust measures. US antitrust regulators see it as their duty to intervene only when it can be shown that consumers are currently negatively impacted by monopolistic behavior. In Europe, regulators are much more likely to view too much market power as a negative in and of itself.

The EU, taking the cue from German regulators, has also started to evolve this thinking in light of digital platforms that may offer services free of charge. If they command very high market share, consumers have little choice but to part with their personal information in order to receive those services. Now the ability to collect personal data is seen as akin to raising prices: the more a platform like Facebook is able to collect personal data without losing subscribers, the more it warrants an investigation.

Based on this new interpretation of market power, EU and British regulators are planning to force the Big Tech companies to share the customer data with other companies if it is deemed to give them too much of a strategic advantage. A consumer would be able to move their data about their Google searches, Amazon purchasing history, or Uber rides to rival services.[39]

Such an approach will achieve two main aims. First, it will give the consumer more choice for the services they effectively "pay" for through their passing on of valuable data to companies. Second, it will allow smaller players to gain more of a foothold in digital marketplaces.

If there is too much market power, consumers are not only hurt by rising prices and losing control of their data, but also by a reduction of their choice of new products due to stifled innovation. Taken together, Alphabet, Amazon, Apple, Facebook, and Microsoft have acquired a company every week on average for the past five years. Across the US economy more broadly, the rate of formation of small- and medium-sized entrepreneurial businesses fell steadily from 1980 to 2015.[40] By acquiring potential rivals, large companies are staving off the threat of being disrupted themselves—all the while increasing their market power.

When firms are allowed to become too large, they are also able to turn their power on the public purse. By dangling the carrot of bringing jobs to a community, large firms can lobby for special exemptions from local taxes, to the detriment of public revenue. We saw an example of this phenomenon in the way New York offered Amazon very generous tax inducements to locate its second headquarters in New York City. The deal eventually fell through due to a public backlash.

But we only need to turn back the clock by a decade to be reminded of the calamitous consequences of allowing firms to become "too big to fail." Deregulation that allowed financial-services firms to swell in the 1990s and 2000s eventually brought the global financial system—and many national economies—to their knees in the Global Financial Crisis. Banks that were "too big to fail" in the US had to be bailed out to the tune of $700 billion. Perhaps European regulators are on the right side of history as they proactively try to limit the market power of mega-firms arising from "winner-takes-all" economics.

Beyond Shareholder Primacy

For the first two decades after World War II it was common for most American companies to follow a "good neighbor" policy in which CEOs regarded themselves as "corporate statesmen." Frank Abrams, chairman of the Standard Oil Company of New Jersey, summed up the mood in 1951 when he said, "The job of management is to maintain an equitable and working balance among the claims of the various directly interested groups...stockholders, employees, customers, and the public at large."[41]

But as we saw in chapter 2, things started to change in the 1970s as Milton Friedman of the Chicago school of economics promulgated the "shareholder primacy" view of corporate governance, which states that maximizing profits for shareholders should be the sole purpose of a corporation.[42, 43]

His message was as powerful as it was simple. There was never a change in law that precipitated its dominance, but rather a change in culture. Over time, however, this perspective on corporate governance has led to several negative outcomes: excessive focus on short-term profits to plough into shareholder dividends and share buybacks over longer-term investment in

R&D and talent development; soaring executive compensation relative to the average worker pay; and a falling labor-share of corporate income.

Shareholder primacy in its purest form is practiced in Anglo-Saxon economies—such as US, UK, Canada, and Australia—as well in the city-states of Singapore (another reason why Singapore is not perfect) and Hong Kong. But this is by no means the norm everywhere. While profit generation for shareholders is a foremost concern in European countries such as France and the Nordics, workers also gain a prominent voice through a stronger role for trade unions. Also, it is mandatory in France, Finland, and Denmark for companies over a certain size (fifty employees in France, thirty-five in Denmark, and thirty in Finland[44]) to have works councils representing employees. And at the opposite end of the spectrum lies Germany, which upholds the "stakeholder primacy" view of corporate governance, giving much greater prominence to workers, customers, and local communities in which businesses reside. For example, by law, just under half of a company's supervisory-body board members must be representatives of workers.

But, recalling the sentiments of my young companions in New York City in chapter 2—a sentiment echoed in Larry Fink's letter to BlackRock's investee companies—the pendulum of public opinion seems to be swinging back to the belief that a corporation's social responsibility is to benefit all its stakeholders and the overall environment. This does not mean that the drive for profitability and shareholder return ought to be blunted in the pursuit of improved outcomes for society. In fact, a global study by UBS showed that most investors now expect businesses to deliver a broader positive impact, without compromising returns to shareholders. Regardless of the corporate-governance debate on shareholder-versus-stakeholder primacy, the force of investors calling for broader environmental, social, and governance (ESG) will have an increasingly strong impact on corporate behavior. Corporate executives will need to respond by being much more creative about achieving multiple financial and social-impact goals simultaneously.

Perhaps we can take a glimpse into how this brave new world might work by learning from the recent experiences of Anglo-Dutch consumer-goods giant, Unilever. The company takes pride in a staunchly stakeholder-centric view of corporate governance. It won plaudits for its Sustainable Living Plan, launched in 2010, which aimed to double its revenues while halving its environmental footprint and improving the health and well-being of more than one billion people by 2020. By 2017, it announced that it had reached 80 percent of its commitments in the plan.[45] All the while, Unilever outperformed the FTSE 100 and matched the growth of its global peers.[46]

However, notwithstanding the successes in its social and environmental mission and its strong long-term financial performance, Unilever was not—and should not—be immune to the pressure of the capital markets. Without it, managers can too easily take their eyes off short-term opportunities to increase profits and create economic value.

In 2017, American competitor Kraft-Heinz launched a takeover bid for Unilever, which was supported by Kraft's legendary investor Warren Buffett. In prior years, Kraft had built a reputation for aggressive growth by acquiring rivals and slashing costs. Within days, Unilever was able to fend off Kraft-Heinz with the support of its shareholders and network of stakeholders. As a powerful symbol of opposition, the company was able to mobilize 100,000 signatures from concerned citizens rallying against the takeover by Kraft-Heinz.

Unilever's stakeholders were no doubt passionate about preserving the company's social and environmental mission, which they felt could be jeopardized by the takeover. But ultimately, the shareholders also needed assurance that senior management was not unnecessarily leaving money on the table. Once the company committed to raise its profitability margin target from 16 percent to 20 percent by 2020—which Unilever planned to achieve through increased sales and €6 billion in cost saving[47]—the bid failed, and the company's share price soared.

As the Unilever example shows, in capital markets where investors with diverse objectives co-exist—some focusing on short-term shareholder returns and others caring more about long-term, double bottom-line impact—firms will increasingly feel the pressure to deliver both financial and social impact. Indeed, it appears that business can step up to the challenge. Meta studies show that companies with high ESG standards outperform their peers financially, with 62 percent of studies showing a positive relationship between ESG and corporate financial performance and only 8 percent a negative correlation.[48] And in my own experience advising start-ups and larger corporations, the leaders of more and more companies are building their business strategy around a compelling social purpose that is central to the way they attract customers, employees, and business partners.

Notwithstanding these positive trends, as public attitude tips away from Friedman's narrow view of shareholder primacy, it is inevitable that some politicians, such as US Senator Elizabeth Warren, will call for legislative changes that will "hard-wire" the voice of other stakeholders and local communities into stakeholder governance. Such proposals deserve careful consideration.

For example, to curb some of the negative effects of shareholder primacy, Senator Warren calls for US corporations to be required to have workers elect 40 percent of the membership of board of directors. Strong worker representation on boards may help to increase workers' share of corporate income—a share that has fallen persistently since the 1970s. To encourage a shift away from blinkered short-termism, Senator Warren wants to limit executives' ability to sell shares of stock that they receive as pay to five years after they were received and three years after a share buyback. And she also proposes that corporate political activity be supported by 75 percent of shareholders and 75 percent of board members. This may go long way to ensure that corporate lobbying is truly aligned with the interests of all stakeholders, rather than an elite executive class.

It appears to me that proposals such as these may mitigate the key problem—that corporate governance is exacerbating social inequality, rather than contributing to the growth of social capital. Perhaps some additional measures focused on environmental sustainability, such as mandatory reporting of a company's environmental impact, could also have a place in the legislative upgrades.

However, we should be cautious of legislation that goes too far in blunting the pressure of capital markets and introducing too much bureaucracy. For example, Senator Warren's additional proposal that companies with revenues over $1 billion should obtain a federal charter of corporate citizenship may fall into this category. This would require directors to consider the interests of all major stakeholders such as workers and the communities they operate within, as well as shareholders. In my view much of this rebalancing would probably be achieved by Warren's earlier proposals. However, Senator Warren's charter would weaken the fiduciary duty of companies to maximize shareholder returns, since it would shift significant management attention in too many directions. Although shareholders would still be able to sue if they believed companies weren't considering their interests, this seems to introduce unnecessary ambiguity in the operation of capital markets.

Taking on Rents

Blunted antitrust policies and an overly shareholder-centric view of corporate governance have allowed corporate profits to accrue disproportionately to shareholders and executives over the past few decades. Over the same period, owners of real assets such as land and real estate—who are often the same people that have gained from corporate returns—have also been earning outsize rents.

The increasing concentration of knowledge-intensive businesses and creative workers in urban areas has raised land and real estate rents in cities around the world. Quite often, rents have soared even when land and property owners have done little to improve their assets. These asset owners have often benefitted from the increasing desirability of their location as businesses have clustered nearby or public investments have improved the quality of amenities and infrastructure.

Worse yet, rising property rents are becoming a severe drag on economic growth and socioeconomic mobility, since they are leading to shortage of affordable housing and office space, while making it more difficult to build critical infrastructure. In almost all metropolitan areas above two million people in North America, UK, and Australia, the median house price is three times higher than median income.[49] And globally, McKinsey estimates the affordable housing gap to be at 330 million urban households—a figure that is expected to grow to 440 million households, or 1.6 billion people, by 2025.[50]

Since land and property owners have benefitted from much higher rent, often without doing anything to improve their assets, increased land and property taxes would seem like a natural way to address a key source of wealth inequality.

Although prevalent in only thirty countries, land taxes have been favored by economists of different ideological hues, from Friedman to Adam Smith. This is because land taxes make land more affordable and encourage landowners to make their land available for development. Since the supply of land is finite, imposing a land tax reduces the price of land by the same amount as the discounted value of future tax payments. Furthermore, since landowners would need to pay a tax even on idle land, they are incentivized to develop the land to avoid incurring a cost with no gain. Despite its merits, land taxes have not caught on in most countries because they are often strongly opposed by landowners—a group that usually wields considerable lobbying power. However, we have reached a stage where land—especially in urban areas—is an asset class that has helped to fuel record levels of inequality, and its lack of availability is holding back the development of affordable housing, job-creating businesses, and critical transport-infrastructure. It seems like it is time to reconsider land taxes as key measure for enhancing economic opportunity—especially for people lower down the income spectrum.

Property taxes are another avenue for moderating inequality, although the case for increased property taxes is a little more complex. First, taxes based on the value of property are already levied in the vast majority of countries and are quite considerable in some developed countries such as the US, UK, and Australia, where they account for roughly 10 percent of total tax revenues; in Israel they make up over 30 percent of revenues.[51] Second, property taxes can act as a disincentive to property development and improvement, since rising property values incur higher tax liabilities. Third, and worse still, other property-related taxes such as stamp duty—a tax levied when a property is purchased—can be yet another barrier for people to gain a foothold on the property ladder. However, with the appropriate exemptions or reductions in taxes and stamp duties for primary homes below a threshold value, the negative impact of property taxes may be minimized while still taxing those who have benefitted from property as a financial asset.

Combating Fake News and the Misuse of Personal Data

The world's come a long way since the New York-based The Sun, the first modern newspaper, ran a series of articles in 1835, since dubbed "The Great Moon Hoax." They claimed a civilization was discovered to be living on the moon. After the incident was exposed as bogus by rival newspapers, the media learned the hard way that in the long-run, more money is to be made by telling the truth. They had a reputation to protect, and if readers suspected stories were made up, they would no longer buy that newspaper. Over the years, a variety of defamation and privacy laws were introduced to institutionalize the media's obligation to report the truth and respect people's privacy.

This all changed with the internet. The proliferation of social-media platforms and "digital native" news sites have mounted an onslaught on truthful reporting. "News" has also become a relative term, as many news sites are actually more opinion-based. While newspapers have a brand and profits to protect, commentators on the internet are not exposed to the same incentives to remain truthful. And even if they were, the sheer amount of online content makes it hard for readers to ascertain what the truth is.

Regulation of content on the internet clearly needs to get tougher, and much of the onus lies with the social-media platforms. They must do more to immediately block harmful content, such as that livestreamed by terrorists. They also clearly have a clear role to play in reducing fake news.

Germany has approved a law that imposes fines of up to €50 million on social-media firms that fail to remove criminal content like defamatory and hate-inciting posts quickly enough. Also, in Germany, Facebook has teamed up with a fact-checking organization called Correctiv to check the veracity of stories. Users can report fake or misleading stories, and Correctiv then flags whether they are untrue or not. So far, the project is only in the experimental phase, but the idea that social-media platforms should be required to pay for third-party fact-checks is an important step towards regulating fake news.

France's 2018 law to ban "fake news" during election campaigns is another example of this trend. Candidates and political parties will be able to appeal to a judge to stop "false information" in the three months before an election. But judging what is false and what is opinion will prove difficult. In Singapore, the government has the power to define what is a fact—a dangerous position to be in because, if abused, it could restrict citizens' access to the truth. Balancing truthful news with freedom of expression will be a difficult challenge for many governments. However, fact-checkers will at least provide the basis for rating social media according to their track record on veracity.

We must develop ethical standards for digital news as newspapers have done over time. For example, it is generally accepted that journalists must corroborate facts with at least two sources, but this convention took a while to develop. Comparable codes of conduct should develop over time in the digital sphere. It will probably require bold moves from governments.

An emerging policy position in the UK looks promising. Under proposals published by the government in April 2019, any company that enables people "to share or discover user-generated content or interact with each other online"[52] would be subject to a statutory "duty of care" to keep its users safe. A regulator will publish guidelines, oversee complaints, and issue fines and other penalties, such as holding executives personally responsible.

Untruthful information is a form of negative market externality—a cost to society akin to environmental pollution. We expect factories to abide by environmental regulations to reduce pollution, and the same standards should apply to social-media platforms in cleaning up the erosion of social capital caused by fake stories.

Towards a More Inclusive Future

The world has in many ways made enormous strides over the last half century. In 1981, a shocking 44 percent of the population was living in extreme poverty—defined as living on less than $1.90 a day, in 2011 prices.

Today it is 8.5 percent.[53] Yet, as we've seen, faith in the world's dominant economic and political systems, such as the Washington Consensus, has broken down. Too many communities—whether they be blue-collar workers in the West, smaller towns and rural areas, the hundreds of millions of rural migrants in China, or unemployed youth across southern Europe, Africa, and the Middle East—have been left behind.

Social capital has declined because political, civil, and economic freedom have been curtailed for too many people. This has bred marginalization and resentment, leading to populism and the Great Trust Crisis. It has created opportunities for political opportunists, such as strongman leaders, who will perpetuate the Faustian bargains that led us to the current predicament.

Instead, citizens will need to demand more cohesive social contracts. That requires a healthy balance between the state, civil society, the private sector, and the commons. Yet only with resilient institutions can an inclusive social contract embed itself into the body politic. Some of these institutional mechanisms are familiar; some will need to be invented to deal with challenges such as the winner-takes-all economy, too much shareholder power, and fake news. Without them, we are at risk of special interests entrenching marginalization even further, as we see in Turkey and other countries.

However, Inclusive Governance is merely the framework for prosperity. For it to truly thrive, countries will have to Invest With Purpose and Empower Local Communities that have been forgotten in the rush to globalize. I will address these issues in the remainder of the book.

PART II

INVESTING WITH PURPOSE

CHAPTER 5

THE SUSTAINABLE DEVELOPMENT CHALLENGE

Dual Imperatives

In part 1 of this book, we discussed how winning back public trust in the time of the Great Trust Crisis will require an inclusive model of governance that consists of cohesive social contracts supported by inclusive institutions that prevent state capture by special interests, such as strongmen rulers, corporations, ideological factions, or an oligopolistic elite.

Inclusive governance builds social capital, which, as we've already seen, has always been the key to enduring prosperity in successful civilizations. We observed the role that elements of Inclusive Governance played in the rise of the British Empire, and how the erosion of those principles led to the empire's eventual decline. We also explored how Inclusive Governance powered modern success stories, such as the American Dream in the United States, the Wirtschaftswunder of post-war Germany, and the Tiger Economy of Singapore. Even in the flawed model of state capitalism being pursued by China, we witnessed how many of the positive aspects of its economic growth in the past thirty years can ultimately be traced back to steps taken towards Inclusive Governance by Deng Xiaoping.

Although Inclusive Governance is a necessary foundation for long-term prosperity, it does not guarantee it. An object lesson is the tragic case of Flint, Michigan—the birthplace of General Motors. Flint, which was once known as "Vehicle City," boasted the highest median income for American workers under the age of thirty-five and employed 75,000 workers through General Motors alone at its peak in the 1970s. But as Flint gradually bled car-making jobs to lower-cost, offshore locations such as Japan and Mexico, middle-class flight shrank Flint's population from a peak of around 200,000 in the 1970s to 96,500 in 2017. Flint is now one of the most impoverished cities in America, according to US Census Bureau data.[1]

While such circumstances would pose serious challenges to any city in the country, Flint, due to the many advantages provided by its industrial success, arguably had the resources to arrest its own decline. After all, the town has been home to a campus of the University of Michigan since 1956. The university has an enrollment of over 8,000 students—a wellspring of skilled and willing workers. Throughout the automotive industry's gradual decline, the town remained full of people with automotive experience and know-how who might have been supported to create other businesses in the auto parts-and-services value chain. As employers and residents began to leave the town, a great deal of industrial land and housing became available at very competitive prices.

Given these advantages, Flint might have seized the opportunity to invest in redeveloping its "brownfield" industrial sites to encourage entrepreneurship in automotive services. The town might also have attempted to attract companies in new industries such as renewable energy, technology, or food services, to name just a few. Additionally, it could have encouraged more retail and entertainment businesses to improve the quality of life in its downtown area. The combination of new jobs, as well as affordable housing and a vibrant cultural life, may have persuaded more families to stay in the town and helped to lure new residents.

Sadly, Flint has only woken up to some of these possibilities today. Partnerships between local entrepreneurs, foundations, and local government have begun to show green shoots of the early stages of an entrepreneurial revival. But for the past thirty to forty years, the city had responded to the falling tax-base caused by its population exodus merely by slashing spending. Until very recently, neither state nor local government appears to have had much success in breathing life back into this former economic jewel.

Ultimately, the spending cuts in Flint became simply preposterous. In April 2014, a decision was made by a state-appointed acting-mayor to switch the municipal water source from Lake Huron to the local Flint River. Despite warnings that the river was toxic because of industrial sludge that had been poured into it for decades—locals say the river twice caught fire—the local government pushed ahead with its plan. The town even refused to spend the very small amounts necessary for anti-corrosion agents, which would have prevented lead from leaching out of the pipes and into the town's drinking water. Had it done so, the city would have prevented thousands of its citizens from being poisoned by lead and bacteria, which have caused lifelong debilitations.

As we've already seen, the United States falls short of the highest standards of Inclusive Governance in several key ways, but I would argue that Flint's demise was due to additional factors. Unlike city-regions such as Singapore, neither Flint nor the State of Michigan had the foresight to build and maintain institutions during the heyday of the automotive industry that could have acted as an economic bulwark against the inevitable downturns to come. For example, the presence of public vehicles for long-term developmental investment—such as the Central Provident Fund in Singapore—could have helped to ease the transition in Flint as the automotive industry ebbed away.

But I would argue that the primary public-policy oversight was that the city of Flint and the state of Michigan lacked a long-term economic development strategy and an investment plan to support it. Based on my experience in several national and regional development efforts in a diverse range of countries, I have come to understand how important it is for any country, region, or locality to follow dual imperatives to secure long-term prosperity.

As we mentioned in chapter 1, the first strategic imperative is Investing With Purpose in order to meet the Sustainable Development Challenge (SDC). This will be a focus of the discussion in part II of this book. Meanwhile, the second strategic imperative is Empowering Local Communities to build innovative, connected, and entrepreneurial hubs (ICE hubs), which I will explore in greater depth in part III.

Investing With Purpose

In places like Flint, Michigan, the overwhelming neglect and the pain caused by the Faustian bargains struck over many decades have stored up substantial long-term costs to society. At a global level, the problems have become so large that we are now at risk of breaching sustainable environmental and societal limits unless a significant program of investments—which I refer to as the Sustainable Development Challenge—is made. It is not possible to delay these investments any longer. Without them, we will soon face existential threats in the form of social unrest, conflict, and the potentially devastating impact of climate change.

The SDC requires investments in three broad areas: 1) Basic provisioning; 2) Cleaning up infrastructure and industry; and 3) Human-capacity building, as shown in Figure 5-1 opposite.

In this chapter, I will provide an overview of the key investment areas making up the SDC. I will also explain the urgency surrounding it. Unfortunately, humanity doesn't have the luxury of time when implementing these sustainable solutions. It has taken one hundred and fifty years to bring electrification and telecommunications to all corners of the world—and it is still a work in progress. This pace is simply too slow for the changes we must now embrace. Our solutions need to be nimble enough to be deployed in a few decades, rather than centuries.

Chapter 6 will focus on basic provisioning—a series of measures to combat poverty and to deliver modern infrastructure and the enablers of socioeconomic mobility. I will explore programs that can free millions of people from the vicious cycle of poverty, hunger, and homelessness, as well as the safety nets that can prevent them from slipping back into them. I will illustrate how basic infrastructure, such as electricity, roads, mobile communications, and internet access can improve lives and unlock enormous economic activity. I will also explore how investments in socioeconomic mobility enablers, such as affordable housing, education, healthcare, and financial inclusion, can help people gain access to new opportunities. Finally, I will look at some of the requirements associated with demographics: job creation for youth, engagement and caring for the elderly, and empowerment and equality for women.

In chapter 7, I will dive deeper into initiatives that have the potential to clean up the environmental footprint of infrastructure and industry. This is a vast topic, so I will focus on three areas where I believe we have the means to reap the greatest impact: decarbonization of the economy, adapting to water scarcity, and the circular economy—an economic system that decouples economic activity and consumption from the use of finite resources. In addition to keeping the devastating effects of climate change in check, investments in these areas have the potential to create millions of green jobs, as well as setting the factors of production at competitive levels for other industries.

FIGURE 5-1: INVESTMENT AREAS OF THE SUSTAINABLE DEVELOPMENT CHALLENGE

Investment Areas	Sustainable Development Initiatives
Basic provisioning	· Combating poverty · Housing and infrastructure: affordable housing, electrification, clean water and sanitation, transport links, mobile telecommunications, internet access · Universal education and healthcare · Demographics –Youth Bulges –Aging populations
Cleaning up infrastructure & industry	· De-carbonizing the economy to mitigate climate change –Renewable energy such as solar, wind, hydro, and nuclear –Energy storage and smart grid –Electrified or hydrogen-powered smart mobility –Low-carbon industrial processes –Carbon capture and storage · Adapting to water scarcity · Waste reduction and circular economy
Human-capacity building	· Lifelong learning to safeguard against displacement by intelligent machines

Chapter 8 will discuss how to build up human capacity. In a world where we face extreme demographic challenges—youth bulges in the Middle East, Africa, and South Asia, contrasting with rapidly aging societies in Western Europe, East Asia, and China—it will be essential to engage the capacity of human talent of all ages and both genders to provide economic security for individual households, while sharing the cost of social security as broadly as possible.

Superimposed on these demographic challenges, is the rise of intelligent machines that are on course to make redundant hundreds of millions of jobs—whether they be in shoe factories in rural Bangladesh or financial-services firms in London. All countries must have a clear plan to build up human capabilities on an ongoing basis so that displaced workers can be rapidly redeployed in high-wage work.

In chapter 9, I will review how much the SDC will cost globally and how we might pay for it. It will quickly become apparent that the investment requirements are far too big to be funded by tax increases or pools of public money. I will look more closely at how we can mobilize public and private capital—at both the national and local level—to pay for the SDC. These principles are at the heart of what I call Investing With Purpose—the key paradigm in this section of the book.

Empowering Local Communities

Briefly looking ahead, we will address the second long-term strategic imperative (empowerment of local communities) in part III of this book. At this stage, it is enough to note that local communities become economic success stories by drawing upon their key assets (such as raw materials and research universities), their sustainable-production advantages (such as low-cost solar or hydro energy), and the extent of their physical, communications, and financial connectivity to the rest of the world.

A country or region that has done a good job of meeting the first strategic imperative—the SDC—will have already gone a long way towards endowing local communities with the assets, capabilities, and connectivity that will be critical ingredients of their success.

With this groundwork in place, local government, businesses, and civil-society organizations can come together to invest in building ICE hubs, specializing in sectors that feed off the community's specific strengths. Successful hubs become strong enough to supply national and international markets, thereby creating a robust source of jobs and income. Localities that are role-modeling this approach include Dublin in software, Pittsburgh in robotics and artificial intelligence, and Tel Aviv in life sciences, technology, and water systems. In case it seems that only cities can give birth to ICE hubs, remember the map of German Mittelstands, scattered in small towns across the country.

By contrast, a failure to implement these two strategic imperatives has led to the decline of many economic powerhouses such as Flint.

All Countries are Developing Countries

I'm often asked whether the dual strategic imperatives we've discussed—Investing With Purpose and Empowering Local Communities—are different for countries at varying levels of economic development. My response runs contrary to the common, yet anachronistic way of dividing the world into "developed" and "developing" nations. I've come to believe that the investment and development model in the 21st-century economy is remarkably similar for all countries across the globe.

After all, rich and poor countries both have significant sustainable development needs that are broadly analogous. Just as many parts of sub-Saharan Africa are struggling to end extreme poverty, malnourishment, and the lack of clean water and sanitation, deprived regions of the US and Western Europe are still searching for solutions for millions of people who are homeless or trapped in poverty-stricken communities. Countries across the development spectrum face a significant challenge to decarbonize their infrastructure and industrial base. Similarly, all nations face the challenge of developing their people to take on higher-value work, as intelligent machines take on more routine tasks—both manual and cognitive. The SDC is truly a universal one.

In a highly competitive world, all countries need to empower local communities to build up ICE hubs that can generate high-value jobs and compete for national and international market share. We should be careful not to stereotype the kinds of hubs that will emerge in a given location. Just thirty years ago, who would have thought that Bangalore and Tel Aviv would leapfrog many developed-market competitors to become global technology hubs? Of course, developing and developed countries have different starting points, but the principles for building thriving local communities that have a meaningful presence on the global stage apply equally to nations across the board.

So, as we step back and look at the dual strategic imperatives for building long-term prosperity, I cannot help but think that every country is a developing country. And to avoid falling behind in the competitive milieu, every country must emphasize the mobilization of long-term pools of public and private capital to drive sustainable development and build up ICE hubs.

The Sustainable Development Challenge

At first glance, the investment initiatives that make up the SDC (see Figure 5-1), bear some resemblance to the United Nations' Sustainable Development Goals (SDGs). Indeed, it is right that there should be significant overlap, since the SDGs were formulated as a very comprehensive response to global challenges. However, with 169 targets grouped around seventeen goals, many argue that the SDGs are too unwieldy for practical purposes. In formulating the SDC, I've attempted to present a more compact set of investable areas that could form the basis of a focused policy agenda and investment plan for any country or region.

For the most part, I've focused on specific, scalable solutions that already exist—or are already within reach—to address the biggest problems. For example, large-scale investments in affordable housing, transportation, schools, hospitals, and financial inclusion will, to a high degree of confidence, improve the livelihood of millions of people and give them access to greater economic opportunity. Similarly, investments in renewable energy, electric mobility, and decarbonized industrial processes will, if deployed at sufficient scale, bring down the emissions of greenhouse gases and moderate the impact of climate change. Investments in lifelong learning and career development will catapult people into higher-paying work, even in the age of automation by intelligent machines. But, as we shall see, it will require important changes in attitudes, policies, and incentives to channel adequate investments even to these focused solutions.

A few areas within the SDC are, however, more complex. For example, reducing waste through the circular economy requires that we minimize our environmental footprint by recycling, reusing, refurbishing, and sharing products. This will require systemic changes in social attitudes, consumption patterns, investor behaviors, and the business models of entire industries. Similar systemic changes may be required in the management of fresh water. Despite their greater complexity, I believe these topics belong in the SDC because they are central to a prosperous future.

In the interest of sharpening the focus of the initiative, many important issues—such as preserving biodiversity and improving ocean health—have not been included within the scope of the SDC. While I believe these critical environmental challenges must absolutely be addressed to sustain the health of the planet, I have omitted them for three reasons. First, I believe these issues will be addressed, in part, by the efforts to clean up industry and infrastructure. Second, I also believe such environmental issues stem from overconsumption. The move towards a circular economy would do much to relieve stress on biodiversity and improve ocean health. We must make this transition, as well as doubling down on conservation efforts. Third, the scientific underpinnings of various ecological issues are not well enough understood to make it possible to recommend pragmatic interventions.

Another key difference between the UN's Sustainable Development Goals and the SDC is that my approach puts more emphasis on the issues surrounding population management and human-capacity development. As Figure 5-2 shows, world population growth was fairly steady—and at some points negative—over hundreds of years leading up the late 18th century. The Industrial Revolution changed all that, as populations increased in density in urban environments. From 1800 to 1920, annual global population growth hovered around 0.5 percent. But as waves of industrialization fanned out across the world through the 20th century, the rate of growth skyrocketed.

FIGURE 5-2: WORLD POPULATION GROWTH, 1700-2100[2]

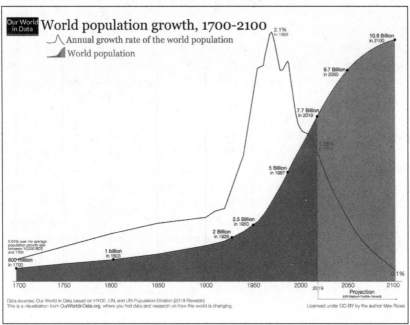

By 1940, as the industrialization wave engulfed Europe, North America, and Japan, world population growth doubled to 1 percent. The post-war period saw the wave next wash over China, India, and the rest of Asia— pushing the total global population growth rate to 1.5 percent by 1950, and ultimately to a peak of 2.1 percent during the 1960s. Since then, the global population growth rate has gradually fallen to just over 1 percent today and is projected to fall to 0.5 percent by 2050.

The net result has been that beginning with a world population of 2.5 billion in 1950, we are projected to reach a total of nearly ten billion by 2050. Is it any surprise, then, that we are testing the world's sustainable limits when we are on course to quadruple global population in a single century? That's why, in the SDC, I try to address the importance of two specific population-related issues head-on: youth bulges and aging populations.

First, let's briefly look at youth bulges. Between now and 2050, about two billion people will be added to the global population, most of them being concentrated in the poorest parts of the world: the Middle East, Africa, and South Asia (see Figure 5-3). Controlling runaway population growth will be a key priority in these regions, since it will greatly reduce the investments required for basic provisioning and clean infrastructure. In addition, population control will improve the likelihood that these countries will reap a "demographic dividend" from their bulging cohorts of young people by providing them with quality education, skills training, and jobs. As a result, investments in population control and job creation in fast-growing, youthful countries are a key feature of the SDC. Without a focus on these issues, it's quite likely that poverty and unemployment could form a toxic cocktail in many of these countries and cause famine, war, and a refugee crisis, which could easily spill over into neighboring countries.

A second alarming aspect of population dynamics highlighted in Figure 5-3 is the concentration of rapidly aging and shrinking populations in places like Europe, Russia, China, and East Asia. Transferring the burden of caring for the elderly to an ever-shrinking working-age population runs the risk of tearing societies apart. So it's no wonder that pension-plan adjustments have caused protest in many countries like Poland, Russia, and Brazil in recent years. Engaging people—especially women—in a longer working life, principally through investments in lifetime learning and the creation of work opportunities for seniors, is a key area for investment in the SDC.

FIGURE 5-3: GLOBAL DISTRIBUTION OF POPULATION GROWTH[3]

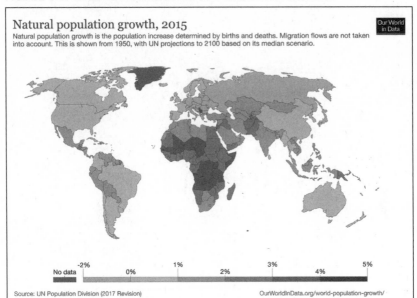

Natural population growth, 2015

Natural population growth is the population increase determined by births and deaths. Migration flows are not taken into account. This is shown from 1950, with UN projections to 2100 based on its median scenario.

Source: UN Population Division (2017 Revision)

OurWorldInData.org/world-population-growth/

But, ultimately, the solution to an aging population is to boost the fertility rate to replacement levels. Since falling birth rates are strongly correlated with increasing cost of living for middle-class households and a rising age of first-time motherhood for working women, it is imperative to make investments in affordable housing, childcare services, and fertility treatments that make it easier and more affordable for families to have more children.

In the remainder of part II, I look in detail at each aspect of the SDC. I will share many stories of solutions that have the potential to be scaled up. But, recognizing that it is a long road between a successful pilot program and mass deployment, I will always come back to the key question of how to make large-scale change happen.

Attitudes will need to change. Aspects of our lives will need to be reimagined. Policies and incentives will need to be rewritten. But, most important of all, collaboration and co-investment between government, private sector, and civil society will need to be rediscovered.

CHAPTER 6

DEVELOPMENT BASICS

Poverty Needs a Cure, Not Aid

In the village of Nanton in the Northern Region of Ghana, forty-six-year-old Abdullai Fuseina, a mother of five, makes a living by cutting down and collecting wood from the forest.[1] For Abdullai and many others like her, demand for wood collection is high since most of the Savelugu-Nanton district's 140,000 residents rely on the forest for fuel. However, the district's rapidly expanding population, which has risen by 60 percent since 2000,[2] has begun to take a heavy toll on the environment, as well as placing extreme strain on the local infrastructure. The district hospital's morgue is so overcrowded that patients are forced to share wards with dead bodies.[3] Due to a lack of toilet facilities, patients engage in open defecation.[4] As a result, the hospital is dangerous for the health of patients and staff.

Nanton's experience is not an anomaly in the Northern Region, which remains by far the poorest part of the country, and where the poverty rate—defined as earning less than $1.90 a day in 2011 PPP prices—remains above 50 percent. Rapid population-growth is a chronic challenge. According to available sources, the fertility rate in the Northern Region is 6.6 births per mother, and even though Ghana overall has managed to pull the fertility rate down from 5.5 in 1994 to just under four in 2018, it has remained stubbornly high in the north.[5]

The Northern Region is also under severe strain from climate change. Mean annual rainfall has dropped from 11.7 millimeters per year in 1900 to 6.3 millimeters in 2015.[6] And due to deforestation, the Sahara is approaching the region. The northern savannas, where subsistence agriculture is the main source of livelihoods, have also been afflicted by extreme climate events. Severe floods in 2007 left 400,000 northern Ghanaians homeless and were followed immediately by a parching drought. Needless to say, the high variability in the climate is making farming particularly challenging.[7]

Nanton and the Northern Region are not alone in their predicament. Although we have made significant strides in fighting extreme poverty over the past half-century, 650 million people were still afflicted by it globally as of 2018.[8] Of this figure, 479 million were concentrated in sub-Saharan Africa, with the remainder residing mostly in South Asia. Countries in these regions often find themselves in a poverty trap: citizens do not have enough capital and credit to kick-start businesses that would earn a sustainable living. The resulting lack of formalized private enterprise limits the opportunity to collect taxes and leads to a shortage of public money to invest in infrastructure, social services, controlling runaway population growth, and environmental remediation. Without enough domestic funds to help lift their citizens out of this vicious cycle, governments in the least developed countries find themselves turning to foreign aid.

But does foreign aid—or official development assistance (ODA), as it's known in development circles—really spark sustainable economic development? Let's explore how effective it has been in helping people in poorer nations to escape the poverty trap.

Foreign aid in response to a peacetime crisis first became to the fore in the late 1960s as millions of Americans and Europeans saw on their television screens children starving to death in Biafra—an oil-rich region that had seceded from Nigeria but was being blockaded by its one-time countrymen. The incident spurred protestors to demand action from the Nixon government, which eventually undertook the largest-ever nonmilitary airlift.[9]

Since that time, foreign aid has grown substantially.[10] Since the 1960s, the UN has called on developed countries to contribute at least 0.7 percent of their GDP to foreign aid. Few have managed that figure, but aid spending has increased markedly since then.

Over time, aid contributions have evolved from government-to-government transfers to grants or concessionary loans that are administered through various bodies such as multilateral organizations like the World Bank, international charities, and local NGOs. Aid is usually attached to a multitude of specific programs, such as campaigns to increase the number of girls in education, enabling local businesses, improving access to vaccines, or developing cheap and effective drugs to tackle malaria.

To be counted as ODA, aid must promote the economic development and welfare of developing countries as its primary objective. ODA criteria are set by the OECD's Development Assistance Committee (DAC). ODA from the thirty member countries of the DAC was reported at $153 billion in 2018, representing an overall upward trend relative to the previous decade.[11]

However, as ODA has risen, skepticism about its efficacy has heated up. In the academic world, a prominent voice among aid skeptics is Angus Deaton, a Nobel Prize winner in economics. Deaton argues that donor countries may, in fact, be making a bad situation worse, because governments come to depend on ODA, rather than doing the hard work of enabling private enterprise and building the institutions needed to increase tax collection to pay for high-quality public services.

Deaton's concern is that ODA "corrupts" the accountability of governments to their people. In some ways, it is analogous to the natural-resource curse, whereby commodity-rich countries fail to develop their economy outside of their main resource. In "resource-cursed" countries, Deaton argues that governments become less accountable to their citizens, since they earn the bulk of their revenues from resource wealth rather than taxes from private enterprise of their people.

Of course, Deaton isn't negative about all forms of ODA. For example, aid that improves access to vaccinations, malaria drugs, and other healthcare resources, are hugely beneficial. Thanks to donor programs, the number of children receiving basic vaccinations has increased from twenty million in 1980 to 200 million today.[12] Such initiatives have led to a 50 percent drop in malaria deaths since 2000, a 25 percent reduction in tuberculosis infections since 2002, and the near eradication of polio. And as Steven Radelet of the Brookings Institute documented in 2015, deaths from HIV/AIDS fell by more than a third in seven years, due in large part to aid efforts.

Notwithstanding the positive impact on health, the linkage between ODA and economic growth remains very weak. A review of 141 studies published between 1970 and 2011 by Chris Doucouliagos of Deakin University and Martin Paldam of Aarhus University found that the average effect of aid on growth was positive and statistically significant—but very small.[13]

Poverty is not a problem that is exclusive to developing countries. The UN estimated that there were 18.3 million living in poverty in the US in

2016[14] and the US Department of Housing and Urban Development noted that over half a million citizens were homeless as of 2017.[15] On a similar note, Saudi Arabia—one of the wealthiest countries in the world—is struggling to employ millions of its poor, disaffected youth. Meanwhile, Europe and developed Asia also harbor millions of people living in poverty—a situation that may worsen as many of these countries feel the economic drag from aging populations.

In a very real sense, as I observed in the previous chapter, all countries face a significant Sustainable Development Challenge (SDC). When thinking about this universal challenge, I find it helpful to start with the individual citizen before zooming out to the broader community, region, or nation. The key to launching an individual's development journey is to build up her personal assets, her skills and capabilities, and her access to infrastructure so that she can take up increasingly productive work and increase consumption—all in a sustainable manner.

In order to participate in the 21st-century economy, the key personal assets that individuals need include a home, a source of electricity like a rooftop solar-panel, a mobile phone, and a means of transportation such as an electric scooter. To reap the full value of these assets, the individual needs easy access to essential infrastructure such as a clean water supply, a sanitation and sewage system, well-paved roads, mobile-communication towers, and internet services. And finally, to participate productively in private enterprise or the public sector, the individual needs to be in good health and to be armed with reading, writing, numeracy, and computer-literacy skills, as well as a working knowledge of personal finance and small business. With these "development basics" in place, the principles of Inclusive Governance will help to hold the development model together at a national level through cohesive social contracts and inclusive institutions.

In the remainder of this chapter, I will put forward a three-part model for delivering the development basics, which, if implemented, would initiate and accelerate this virtuous cycle of sustainable development. The first part of the model is the Graduation Approach—a formula to lift people out of extreme poverty to a sustainable livelihood. The second part is to invest in the enablers of socioeconomic mobility: affordable housing, large-scale infrastructure, and key social services such as education and healthcare. The third and final part is to reap a sustainable demographic dividend by maintaining a high proportion of the population in the workforce.

The Graduation Approach

Let's start by looking at the Graduation Approach—a strategy that has been shown to have a sustainable positive impact on economic mobility in many parts of the developing world. First designed and implemented in Bangladesh by BRAC, a large Bangladeshi NGO, graduation programs provide a holistic set of services to the poorest households in some of the most deprived regions of the world. The centerpiece of the program is to transfer a productive asset, such as livestock, to a household in order to initiate a sustainable livelihood through private enterprise. Households participating in graduation programs have begun enterprises as diverse as pig farms, shoe-repair shops, and convenience stores.

In 2015, Nobel Laureates Abhijit Banerjee and Esther Duflo, along with their colleagues, reported the results of a major study to measure the impact of graduation programs in the prestigious journal Science. The study had investigated the outcomes of graduation programs involving 11,000 households across six countries: Ethiopia, Ghana, Honduras, India, Pakistan, and Peru. In each case, the programs had offered the following support to each household:[16]

- A one-time transfer of a productive asset
- Technical-skills training on managing the productive asset
- A regular transfer of food or cash for a few months, up to about a year, to support consumption
- Access to a savings account and in some instances a deposit-collection service
- Some health education, basic health services, and life-skills training
- High-frequency home visits to reinforce the skills transfer.

As Banerjee et al report, the key idea was to provide the participants with a "big push" over a two-year period, which would allow them to begin productive self-employment and sustainably increase their level of consumption. When the research team checked in on the participating households one year after the programs had been completed, they found that the impact had been transformational in nearly every country. In one program conducted in the Northern and Upper East Regions of Ghana, households had experienced a 91 percent increase in non-farm income, a 50 percent increase in livestock revenue compared with households in the control group, and three times more savings than the control group.[17]

Some observers have criticized the Graduation Approach as expensive. In the programs analyzed by Banerjee's team, the total costs for the full duration of the program ranged from PPP US $1,455 per household in India to PPP $5,962 in Pakistan.[18] But since the benefit-to-cost ratio ranged from 133 percent in Ghana on the low end, and an astonishing 433 percent in India[19] on the high end, the programs were unquestionably good value for the money.

Let's also put the costs in the context of global annual spending on ODA. If we assume that the median cost of the Graduation Approach per household is around $4,000 over the full two-year period, and that each household has on average four people—perhaps an underestimate for some developing countries, but it simplifies the estimate—the graduation cost per person works out to be about $1,000. On this basis, it would cost $650 billion to graduate all 650 million people currently in extreme poverty worldwide. This equates to $65 billion per year, spread out over ten years, which is about 40 percent of the global annual spend on ODA.

While that's a big chunk of current ODA, the sustainable impact would suggest that it's a good way to deploy these precious funds. Fundación Capital, an international development organization, has been working with governments in Colombia, Paraguay, Mexico, Honduras, and Tanzania since 2018 to implement the Graduation Approach as national policy. Instead of using in-kind asset transfers, Fundación Capital makes cash transfers and uses technology to deliver education. By doing so, it has reduced two of the biggest costs of the program: the seed capital for the productive asset as well as the coaching cost of home visits. If, as expected, graduation programs continue to succeed in their goal of lifting communities out of poverty, it will be further evidence that they would be a smarter way to spend ODA money.

Using ODA more effectively to graduate people from poverty is a good start, but is there a way to scale-up and accelerate the Graduation Approach while breaking free from the dependence on ODA altogether? Enter the market-creating private sector, which is already providing innovative solutions to graduate people from poverty. An excellent example of this paradigm is BBOXX, a London-based company that is deploying rooftop solar power and associated consumer devices across sub-Saharan Africa. They provide households with two affordable packages. The first package contains a light, a phone charger, and a radio, while the second includes all these items, plus a TV. Households pay in the range of $10 to $20 per month for the package, with no down payment due up front. After three years, the household owns the BBOXX system outright. BBOXX already sells its products in Rwanda, Kenya, Uganda, Colombia, and the Philippines and is rapidly expanding its footprint.[20]

In a similar fashion to the Graduation Approach, BBOX empowers bottom-of-the-pyramid (BOP) consumers by providing them with access to energy and vital economic assets. A source of electricity in the home frees up enormous amounts of time spent in collecting kerosene or firewood for fuel, often by women or girls in the household. A powered mobile phone opens up whole new worlds of information and transactions. Farmers can check weather reports to help with crop care and harvesting decisions, participate in auctions for their crops, and make payments through mobile-banking services.

As one customer of BBOXX, an African woman, concisely explains: "I have saved money with BBOXX, I no longer buy paraffin or dry cell batteries. I use the money for my children and buy bran for my pigs. When swine fever came many pigs became sickly, but my pigs had good food and good health."[21] As well as freeing up time and money, BBOXX products allow poorer consumers to build up a credit history, which becomes the gateway to bank loans, to investments in small businesses, and ultimately, to increased consumption.

The broader ramifications of innovative business-models such as BBOXX are very profound. First, BBOXX is helping developing countries to leapfrog a centralized electricity-generation model, especially in more remote rural areas, with a paradigm of decentralized energy generation. Second, the company is "consumerizing" infrastructure. It is offering electrification as a consumer product, sold in household-sized units by a private company with a long-term financing solution. Villagers no longer need to wait for government to fund a power scheme or to create a regulatory framework that enables private power companies to provide electricity as a utility. They can simply sign up for one of BBOXX's packages. Third, BBOXX is creating a whole new set of markets– not just for the solar panels and devices it is selling today, but for additional goods and services that households will be able to buy as their credit history builds up.

Another example of the private sector creating a new business model that is helping to graduate people out of poverty is M-Pesa. Launched in Kenya by Safaricom, and now operating across Africa, M-Pesa is transforming lives through mobile banking. M-Pesa enables poorer consumers to receive, save, and transfer money using a cheap SMS-enabled mobile phone. M-Pesa has network of 110,000 agents throughout Kenya, where customers go to put money onto their phone or withdraw funds in cash. M-Pesa agents outnumber ATMs in Kenya by a factor of forty! The service is now used by 96 percent of Kenyans,[22] and transactions made on the service represent about 40 percent of Kenya's economy.[23]

Research by Billy Jack of Georgetown University and Tavneet Suri of the Massachusetts Institute of Technology, which surveyed thousands of Kenyan households over a six-year period, suggests that M-Pesa has helped to lift an estimated 194,000 households out of poverty.[24] Crucially, in households with access to mobile money, women were more likely to move out of agriculture into higher-value business activities. This is probably because mobile money makes it easier for households to put aside savings—households with easy access to M-Pesa put away 22 percent more in sayings than those without it. As savings build up, women become more empowered to use the capital to start their own businesses and widen their occupational choice.[25]

BBOXX and M-Pesa are both examples of what the Harvard Business School professor Clayton Christensen calls "market-creating innovations."[26] Distinct from "sustaining innovations" which incrementally improve product performance or "efficiency innovations" which enable products to be made more cheaply, market-creating innovations activate new consumers by making new products and services which are more affordable and accessible. Consumption is made possible for "non-consumers." By unlocking this latent demand, or "non-consumption," both developing and developed nations have the potential to ignite significant economic growth. And unlike "sustaining innovation" which creates few jobs and "efficiency innovation" which destroys jobs, "market-creating innovations" are a factory for new jobs,[27] especially since they lead to the creation of a "whole system that often pulls in new infrastructure and regulations."[28] Furthermore, market-creating innovations tend to be relatively inexpensive to scale, since they "leapfrog" older technology or ways of doing business. For example, it would have been vastly more expensive for Safaricom to build bricks and mortar banks across Kenya than establishing its M-Pesa mobile-banking service.

Imagine how the principles of the Graduation Approach, infused with market-creating innovations by the private sector and supported by government investments in infrastructure and social services, could transform the future of Nanton. After acquiring a package from BBOXX, Abdullai Fuseina and her fellow villagers would no longer need to turn to the forest for firewood. With more free time on her hands, Abdullai perhaps could start her own embroidery business[29] and trade easily through a regional cooperative using mobile money. Following in the footsteps of successful entrepreneurs such as Abdullai, other villagers could well begin similar enterprises, often using loans made possible by their growing credit history. In a few years, Nanton might become a small regional trading hub, and create the pull for roads and logistics-infrastructure to store goods and transport them to market. As businesses take off in the region, tax receipts would increase, and further investments would become possible in infrastructure, as well as improved schooling and healthcare services. The Graduation Approach has the potential to launch countless development journeys like the one I just imagined for Nanton and to propel millions of people out of poverty towards a more prosperous future.

Investing in Socioeconomic Mobility

The second part of my model for provisioning "development basics" involves investing in the enablers of socioeconomic mobility, such as affordable housing, large-scale infrastructure, education, and healthcare. Let's take a look at how many citizens lack access to these basics, and how they can be provisioned for more effectively.

Housing and Infrastructure

There is no personal asset more fundamental than a home. Unfortunately, we seem to be in the middle of a global crisis in affordable housing, which has left hundreds of millions of people without adequate shelter, making it very difficult for them to participate in economy.

In developing countries, 881 million people, or 12.5 percent of the world's population, live in slums. Unsurprisingly, sub-Saharan Africa is the worst afflicted region, with 59 percent of urban dwellers taking refuge in shantytowns. But the scourge of homelessness afflicts developed countries as well. Many of us have witnessed the alarming rise of homelessness in American cities in recent years. And even in Western Europe, 6 percent of the population lives in "extremely precarious conditions," according to UN Habitat.[30]

By 2025, it is estimated that the global gap in affordable housing will affect 440 million urban households, or 1.6 billion people.[31] In virtually all major South American and Asian metropolises, the cost of housing is above 150 percent of net average monthly incomes.[32] And in almost all metropolitan areas with more than two million people in North America,

UK, and Australia, the median housing cost is three times higher than the gross annual median income.[33] Why is this happening, and what can we do about it?

In both the poor and rich worlds, the solution for affordable housing lies in fixing the market for land. For example, only 10 percent of the land in the African continent is registered and marketable.[34] Due to restricted supply, land prices in Africa are grossly inflated, which in turn makes housing less affordable. Even in places like Ethiopia, where the government has been building social housing at an unprecedented rate for the last decade,[35] the cheapest units are out of reach for most of the population. To complicate matters further, land rights are not well protected across the continent. Not surprisingly, the added risk of land expropriation turns off investors, choking the supply of capital to build further housing stock. The elevated risk also increases the rate of mortgage interest, making it even harder for citizens to purchase homes.

To solve the housing crisis in Africa and other poorer regions, improved land registration and enforceable land rights are required for the sector to take flight. By contrast, in rich countries where land is more marketable, the problem lies with poor zoning, NIMBY-ism (Not In My Back Yard), and misguided policies such as rent control.

The UK and California are notorious examples of such self-defeating practices at play. When it comes to zoning, the UK has classified huge tracts of land as protected "green belt." But look more closely and you'll find that much of this land consists of brownfield sites, such as disused airfields, railway sidings, and disused petrol stations.[36] In many cases, these sites would make good locations for housing developments, without damaging the natural environment.

NIMBY-ism has reached absurd levels in many developed countries. Recently in the UK, the incumbent Conservative party has been punished in local elections by single-issue parties that are vehemently opposed to the government's house-building plans.[37] Meanwhile, citizen groups in San Francisco have also been remarkably effective in preventing further house building near their homes. For example, the city council, under pressure from residents, recently unanimously rejected a new sixty-three-unit housing complex because it would cast a shadow on a Victoria Manalo Draves Park.[38]

Zoning and NIMBY-ism prevent homes from being built in job-rich areas and affect employment prospects for citizens. The results can be extremely damaging—commuters in San Francisco sometimes spend three hours each way to work in the city. In their desperation to keep rents down, citizens sometimes open the door to wrong-headed policies such as rent controls. A recent proposal by the mayor of London, Sadiq Khan, to enact rent controls in the city is supported by two-thirds of Londoners. The sentiment is understandable when you consider that the average London renter spends 40 percent of his or her monthly pre-tax income on rent.[39] Nevertheless, rent controls rarely work, because landlords react by taking properties off the rental market, thereby restricting supply even further. Alternatively, they scrimp on maintenance, renovation, and redevelopment, which eventually leads to deterioration of the housing stock. A recent study on the effect of rent control in San Francisco found that rental prices actually increased by 5 percent because landlords restricted supply in response to the measures.[40]

The only real solution to affordable housing is to build more units to tackle the severe lack of supply. At present, this isn't happening. Since 1990, San Francisco has averaged just 1,900 new housing units each year.[41] In the UK, the number of units built annually in recent years is around half of the rate of the early 1970s even though the population has grown by almost 20 percent since then.[42]

Ironically, recent proposals by Scott Wiener, a member of the California State Senate, may offer a way forward. Wiener promotes the idea of "YIMBY-ism" (Yes In My Back Yard). His bill, known as SB 50, would see the state "up-zone" land currently dedicated to single-family housing, allowing developers to build triplexes, fourplexes, and other higher-density buildings. Up-zoning powers would be assigned to "job rich" or "transit rich" areas, or those with high-quality schooling.[43] We ought to support measures like SB 50 in order to tackle the housing crisis in cities around the world.

In addition to affordable housing, large-scale infrastructure is a critical driver of human development and empowerment. Access to electricity, clean water and sanitation, mobile telephony, internet services, and transport links are essential to a citizen's quality of life and his or her ability to earn income. As with all socioeconomic inputs, we have made progress over the last thirty years, but there's still much to do.

Recent figures show that 1.1 billion people—or 14 percent of the global population—do not have electricity in their home,[44] 0.7 billion people lack access to clean water,[45] and 2.4 billion people suffer from inadequate sanitation facilities.[46] Since most of these citizens are concentrated in sub-Saharan Africa, South Asia, and Latin America,[47] it highlights the staggering degree of basic development investment still required in these regions of the world.

Mobile telephony is a critical aspect of modern infrastructure, since it is the point of entry to the digital economy—an essential source of information and services in the 21st century. Once cellular networks are installed, even the poorest citizens can use basic mobile phones to access mobile payments systems like M-Pesa and other text-based services. Unfortunately, 30 percent of people in low-income countries[48]—or around 300 million people—still did not have a mobile subscription as reported in the latest figures from 2017. And although there has been rapid growth in access across these countries, 55 percent of people go without internet services and over 70 percent of people do not have mobile broadband.

Transportation links in the form of roads, rail, ports, and airports are essential cogs that make the economy turn by enabling individual mobility as well as the movement of goods. The chronic lack of transport infrastructure presents a major barrier to development in poorer nations. For example, 70 percent of the rural population in Africa lives more than two kilometers from an all-weather road, making it very difficult to send crops to market or to bring supplies to these rural settlements. Meanwhile, on the developed world, more than 70 percent of the urban population does not have access to rapid mass-transit. The only exception to this phenomenon is Europe, where 90 percent of urban citizens enjoy easy access to public transport.[49]

While a vast amount of new economic infrastructure needs to be built in the developing world, many richer countries need to give their crumbling infrastructure a big upgrade as well. The US is a case in point. The American Society of Civil Engineers (ASCE) gave the US a D-plus in its latest "Infrastructure Report Card"[50] and identified a $2 trillion infrastructure-funding gap between 2015 and 2025. Surprisingly, mobile penetration in the US is also relatively low at about 70 percent,[51] as is access to broadband internet at home, which only 73 percent of Americans enjoy.[52]

So, what is the global investment required to meet the global demand for housing and infrastructure? McKinsey estimates that we will need to construct affordable housing for 440 million households, based on the current stock of housing and the expected rates of urbanization and income growth. To fill this gap, the land purchase value and construction cost will require $14–$16 trillion in investment,[53] which amounts to $1.4–$1.6 trillion annually over a ten-year period. In addition, according to figures from the United Nations Conference on Trade and Development (UNCTAD), we will need to spend an extra $1.3 trillion[54] on economic-infrastructure development per year, up to 2030, for developing countries to meet their Sustainable Development Goals (SDGs).[55]

Fortunately, the entire burden need not fall on public money. On average, developing-country governments are funding only about 20 percent of housing projects, 50 percent of power infrastructure, 60 percent of transport, 20 percent of telecommunication, and 80 percent of water and sanitation.[56] With the appropriate regulation and licensing, private sector investors and infrastructure operators can be attracted to participate in the build-out and operation of large-scale housing and infrastructure projects.

At the other end of the spectrum, micro-finance platforms are also becoming an effective tool for funding community-scale infrastructure. Take Water.org, an NGO championed by the award-winning Hollywood actor Matt Damon and his business partner, Gary White. Damon and White's platform has helped to mobilize $1.8 billion in capital to support small, affordable loans for water connections and toilets that help bring safe water and sanitation into millions of people's homes.[57] More than 87 percent of the borrowers are women, who are often freed up from the chore of spending many hours every day collecting fresh water as a result of the installations. Water.org reports that their loan repayment rate is 99 percent, allowing the organization to recycle its capital to future projects.

Universal Education and Healthcare

The talents of hundreds of millions of individuals will never be realized because they lack the basic reading, writing, numeracy, and computer-literacy skills required to participate in the 21st century economy. Being concentrated among the world's poor, these individuals also suffer the most from ill health—yet another barrier to capturing the economic opportunities on offer. The idea behind "universal" education and healthcare is to make basic services freely available to everyone so that nobody is excluded from economic opportunity because of a lack of access. However, in some developed countries, "universal" social services have become confused with bloated entitlement systems with offerings that are outdated or surplus to requirements. Let's look at the global gap in education and healthcare provisions and begin to calibrate the public investments required to address the problem.

Education

We are failing to educate a significant proportion of the world's citizens. In the developing world, over one billion adults are illiterate[58] and 263 million children of secondary-school age are out of school (ninety-three million in sub-Saharan Africa and one-hundred million in South Asia).[59] Even in

developed regions like North America and Europe, about 20 percent of ado-
lescents are not proficient in either reading or mathematics. And in the US,
over 6.5 million jobs are currently unfilled because employers can't find candidates with the adequate skills.[60]

The fundamental problem in education facing poorer countries is the
lack of schools in rural areas. It's safer, less costly, and less time-consuming
for kids to go to school in their own village rather than crossing over to a
neighboring town—but unfortunately, most villages do not have a school of
their own. A study conducted in 2013 by Dana Burde and Leigh L. Linden on
thirty-one villages in Afghanistan found that the construction of a school in
a village that previously didn't have one, increased enrollment for girls by 50
percent and for boys by almost 35 percent.[61] Attendance for girls is further
boosted by introducing "girl-friendly" provisions, such as separate latrines.
According to a study by Harouna Kazianga of the BRIGHT school construction program in Burkina Faso,[62] the introduction of separate female toilets
increased female attendance by over 20 percent.

But even in the areas of sub-Saharan Africa and South Asia that have
enough schools, attendance can still be quite low. This is usually because
parents believe that sending kids to school is not worth the effort if instead
they could be contributing to short-term household income by working on
the farm or in some other local business. Creating the economic cushion
that allows poorer families to send children to school seems to change the
equation. Conditional cash-transfers (CCTs), which are given to mothers
on the basis that their children regularly attend classes, were found to be
particularly effective in increasing school attendance. In addition, school
programs that provide meals, vaccines, employment counseling, and other
"utilities" have also proven to be powerful motivators for parents to send
their children to school. For example, the Oportunidades Program in
Mexico, which began in 1997, grants CCTs for schooling, nutrition, and
health-center attendance, as well as facilitating access to higher education,
formal employment, and financial services. It has been responsible for a 20
percent increase in female attendance at secondary schools and for a 10
percent increase among boys.[63] Male beneficiaries received ten additional
schooling months on average and female beneficiaries eight additional
months.[64] The program, now called Prospera, has been replicated in fifty
countries with great success.

In line with the general principles of the Graduation Approach, Prospera relieves the burden on the poorest in society to cover basic necessities
and frees up their time and energy to invest in their own future—in this

case, through education. In fact, Banerjee and Duflo report in their book Poor Economics that non-conditional cash transfers are as effective as CCTs in increasing school attendance. Education seems to be a top priority for parents once they escape the confines of the poverty trap.[65]

Beyond increasing attendance, it's vital that schools offer good-quality education that is relevant to the modern workplace. Evidence suggests that young people who attend vocational schools in developing countries fare particularly well, since they gain actionable skills for employment, not just basic literacy and numeracy skills. Recent research by Esther Duflo analyzed a ten-year program in Ghana in which 682 pupils (aged seventeen, on average) were awarded scholarships to academic or vocational schools, which they could not have otherwise attended due to a lack of funds. Duflo and her fellow researchers found that those who attended vocational school ended up earning 24 percent higher wages than academic-track awardees.[66] It seems that practical workplace skills were valued much more highly than "book-smarts."

As I will discuss in more detail in chapter 8, it's essential in the age of the "intelligent machines" that our education systems develop agile lifelong learners with problem-solving, team-work, and entrepreneurial skills that will set apart human "value-add" from automatable work for the foreseeable future. Many students and parents are rightly questioning whether the current schooling model puts enough emphasis on these skills relative to the traditional focus on absorbing technical knowledge.

In developing economies, a particularly serious problem in education is that two-thirds of the children not attending school are girls. Not only does this disproportionately close off doors to opportunity when they reach adulthood, the evidence irrefutably shows that increased education of girls leads to greater awareness of family planning, health, and gender-equality issues. This, in turn, leads to a variety of other positive outcomes, such as lower birth rates, healthier families, and higher female participation in the workforce.[67]

The connection between the level of women's education and the national fertility rate is best explained by the economic models of Gary Becker.[68] His central idea is that women with a higher level of education will have to pass up bigger economic opportunities in order to have children. In other words, the opportunity-cost of having children is higher for educated women.[69] This simple insight has tremendous ramifications in both youth bulge countries and aging societies.

In developing countries with youth bulges, educating women is a primary lever for bringing down population-growth rates to manageable levels. This, in turn, allows more resources to be invested in bringing up well-educated and healthy children with brighter economic prospects.

In developed, aging societies, in which the birthrate has fallen below the replacement rate and triggered an aging population, it's critical to increase women's participation in the workforce to balance out the growing ranks of the elderly. However, to restore a sustainable demographic balance, women will also be required to bear more children. To achieve both objectives, it seems that women must somehow surmount the trade-off presented in Becker's theory. This will require a range of societal shifts to mitigate the financial burden and increased workload faced by working mothers—shifts such as pay equality, affordable and high-quality childcare services, flexible working conditions, and a more equitable sharing of domestic responsibilities by male partners. We will explore this issue in more detail later in the chapter.

And what of the cost of basic education? A review of reports by the IMF and the UN Education for All (EFA) suggests that the incremental investment to extend basic education to the entire developing world population is approximately $670 billion per year. This would require a 7 percent increase in government expenditure on average in those countries.[70] By contrast, when it comes to developed countries, the IMF points out that improved educational outcomes could be achieved with an equal or lower budget in most cases. In other words, educational resources must be spent more efficiently and must focus on building practical skills for the modern workplace.

Healthcare

In order to understand how healthy people are around the world, it is helpful to consult a map of Disability-Adjusted Life Years (DALYs), as in Figure 6-1. One DALY can be thought of as one lost year of healthy life. The higher the average DALYs for a given population, the unhealthier it is. Armed with this definition, the map of global DALYs immediately shows the severe blight on human health in sub-Saharan Africa, the Indian subcontinent, and parts of Southeast Asia.

The tragedy is that much of this suffering could be prevented with relatively modest investments. It is widely recognized in health-policy circles that countries can dramatically improve healthcare outcomes if they focus resources more on primary care and basic surgeries.[71] For example, a study by health economist Dean Jamison has identified about 200 interventions, which if available globally would reduce premature deaths by a quarter.[72] These interventions include various preventative measures such as

FIGURE 6-1: MAP OF GLOBAL DISEASE BURDEN[73]

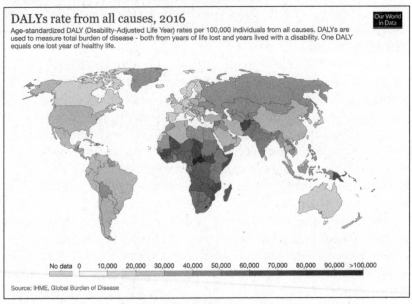

DALYs rate from all causes, 2016

Age-standardized DALY (Disability-Adjusted Life Year) rates per 100,000 individuals from all causes. DALYs are used to measure total burden of disease - both from years of life lost and years lived with a disability. One DALY equals one lost year of healthy life.

No data 0 10,000 20,000 30,000 40,000 50,000 60,000 70,000 80,000 90,000 >100,000

Source: IHME, Global Burden of Disease

immunizations, as well as surgical procedures for basic injuries, obstetrics, and cancers. Astonishingly, Jamison estimates these provisions would only cost an extra $1 per person per week and could be carried out by a GP and general surgeon, supported by a community pharmacist.

In light of these findings, it's not surprising that countries that have focused on implementing universal primary healthcare have reaped high rewards. Health outcomes in middle-income Thailand have soared with only $220 per capita spent on healthcare. This represents only 4 percent of GDP[74] compared with just over 17 percent of GDP spent on healthcare in the US. Rwanda is leading the way among low-income countries. Its success lies in expanding health insurance coverage to 90 percent of its population and focusing its scarce resources on a limited set of the most essential treatments. As an example of the scheme's success, the mortality rate for tuberculosis fell from fifty to fourteen per 100,000 people between 2000 and 2011.

These examples clearly indicate that spending modest sums on healthcare can generate very good outcomes. In fact, Figure 6-2 shows that increasing healthcare spending above about $1,000 per capita brings very limited additional gains in DALYs. Indeed, if healthcare costs become too high—as in the US and some other developed countries—it shuts off access for lower-income citizens and the nation's overall health becomes weighed down. Due largely to this effect, as well as the mushrooming opioid crisis, life expectancy in the US fell for the third consecutive year in 2019[75]—a staggering statistic for such an affluent nation.

As the health priority in both the developed and developing worlds shifts from infectious diseases to chronic conditions like diabetes and cardio-vascular diseases, the focus on primary care and preventative healthcare will become even more essential. The earlier chronic diseases can be detected and managed, the greater the likelihood of preventing acute complications that increase the risk to patients and magnify the overall cost of treatment.

Primary care is an area where AI-powered digital solutions could have a profound impact. For example, the UK venture Babylon Health started out with a diagnostic app designed in partnership with a panel of medical experts. Patients enter their symptoms, medical history, and other lifestyle information, and the app indicates possible ailments and provides triage information for relevant health services. The success of the app has allowed

FIGURE 6-2: DISEASE BURDEN VS HEALTH EXPENDITURE PER CAPITA[76]

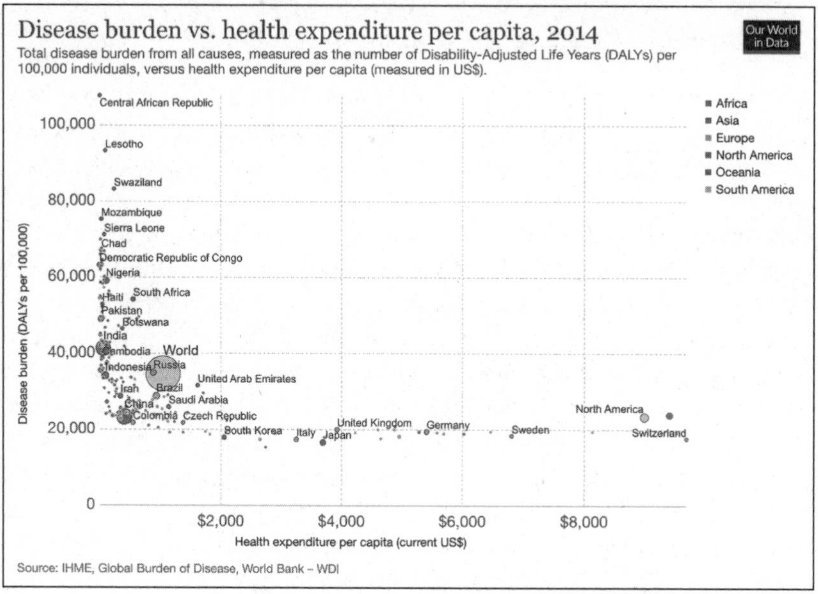

Disease burden vs. health expenditure per capita, 2014

Total disease burden from all causes, measured as the number of Disability-Adjusted Life Years (DALYs) per 100,000 individuals, versus health expenditure per capita (measured in US$).

Source: IHME, Global Burden of Disease, World Bank – WDI

Babylon Health to forge a partnership with the UK's National Health Service (NHS), whereby patients can opt for Babylon to serve as their NHS GP. Patients can use the app to investigate their symptoms, book a tele-health consultation with a doctor 24/7, or go into one of several Babylon clinics around the city. With 50,000 patients reporting a 96 percent satisfaction rate in London, the company is expanding its NHS partnership to other cities in the UK.

Telehealth has already become commonplace in many countries. Babylon already operates in Rwanda, and the popular med-tech unicorn WeDoctor is helping to relieve the stress in China's over-crowded hospitals and clinics. WeDoctor and other digital-healthcare solutions are connecting remote patients to doctors and hospitals, thereby lowering the cost of diagnosis and care delivery. WeDoctor is also helping to increase the reach of scarce medical specialists, especially into distant provincial areas.

In the case of healthcare, analysis of IMF and World Health Organization figures suggests the incremental cost to provide basic healthcare to the entire developing world population is approximately $530 billion per year—requiring a 5.5 percent increase in government expenditure on average in developing countries.[77] As with education, the report points out that most developed countries could improve health outcomes with an equal or lower budget if the resources were spent more efficiently.[78]

Demographic Dividend or Demographic Drag?

The third major element of my "development basics" model involves managing a country's demographics to keep the highest possible proportion of its citizenry engaged productively in the workforce. Unfortunately, this is an issue that most countries have failed to tackle. As a result, they now face either of the following acute challenges: youth bulges or aging societies.

Youth bulges are typically a phenomenon of countries in the early stages of the development cycle, such as India, Egypt, and Nigeria. These nations have brought down their mortality rates due to improvements in clean water supplies, sanitation, and healthcare. However, since fertility rates have not yet moderated commensurately, the cohorts of young people are ballooning. If these youth bulges can be harnessed economically through education and gainful employment, they represent a powerful economic force that could lift national output and generate new funds for critical socioeconomic investments. In short, these countries have the potential to enjoy a "demographic dividend." If, on the other hand, these countries do not generate enough new jobs, the swelling ranks of idle youth may become a significant drag on the economy, a source of civil unrest, and even a source of migrants, which creates tensions in neighboring countries.

On the other end of the demographic cycle are countries such as Italy, Germany, Japan, and South Korea, in which fertility rates have fallen far below replacement levels, and life expectancies continue to rise. As the number of retirees soars relative to the working population, the resulting "demographic drag" is dampening economic growth, stagnating productivity, and deteriorating incomes. In Italy, the world's ninth largest economy, nine tax-paying workers supported every retiree in 1950. Today, each retiree is only supported by three workers, and forecasts suggest a one-to-one ratio is not far away. To maintain the already tenuous three-to-one ratio, Yale University demographer Joseph Chamie calculates that Italy would have to raise its retirement age from sixty-two today to seventy-five by 2050.

Countries need to adopt a much more proactive approach for maintaining a sustainable demographic dividend, instead of lurching between the extremes. Let's look at how this might be achieved, by reviewing the measures being implemented in some youth-bulge and aging societies.

Youth Bulges

Let's assume a developing country with a sizeable youth bulge has already implemented the measures we've discussed: ODA funds and public money have been channeled into graduation programs to combat extreme poverty; companies with market-creating innovations such as BBOXX have gained a berth to bring private-sector solutions to the market; and investments have been made in socioeconomic-mobility enablers such as large-scale infrastructure, education, and healthcare. Even if all this were in place, the country may still be missing a critical piece of the puzzle for harnessing a demographic dividend—a vibrant private sector.

An underdeveloped private sector is debilitating for any economy, but it's particularly dangerous for countries with a large youth population. One nation contending with this predicament is the Kingdom of Saudi Arabia. While it is one of the richest countries on Earth on a GDP per-capita basis, about 10 percent of the country's thirty-three million inhabitants are thought to live below the Kingdom's official poverty line of $17 a day.[79] Saudi Arabia's economy is almost totally dependent on oil, and two-thirds of the employed citizens hold government jobs.[80] The absence of a strong private sector has resulted in an unemployment rate of 40 percent among people aged twenty to twenty-four.[81] Many other countries struggling to capture a "demographic dividend" from their bulging youth are also being hampered by a dispropor-tionately large state-sector. For example, Nigeria and Egypt have 61 percent and 41 percent employment in the public sector, respectively.[82]

Having realized that even the extraordinary wealth of the Saudi Arabian government cannot compensate for the dynamic force of private enterprise in creating jobs, the new Crown Prince, Mohammad Bin Salman Al Saud (often referred to as "MBS"), has set about charting a new course for the Saudi economy. Under the umbrella of Saudi Arabia Vision 2030, MBS aims to diversify the oil-dependent economy by stoking private enterprise and attracting foreign investment. Central to this transformational endeavor are a series of critical social, economic, and fiscal reforms.

An important early initiative championed by the Crown Prince has been a privatization drive to transfer inefficient public companies into private operatorship, while raising more than $200 billion for the public purse. However, progress so far has been slow. By mid-2019, only six deals had been completed (four in water, one in healthcare, and one in transport), with twenty-two more still to go in the lifetime of the program up to 2022.

The Kingdom is also opening up its economy to foreign investment. One hundred percent ownership of companies has already been granted in the health, education, and engineering sectors. Foreign investors can also acquire stakes in companies across a broad range of businesses such as recruitment, road transport services, audio and visual services, and real estate brokerage. The IPO of Saudi Aramco—Saudi Arabia's national oil company, which holds a series of strategic assets in oil and gas exploration, drilling, and production—has even enabled foreign investors to gain a stake in the Kingdom's most prized asset. In order to make it easier for foreign-ers to invest in the Kingdom, Saudi Arabia has already begun to reform its capital markets. As a result, the country has won endorsement from MSCI, FTSE Russell, and S&P Dow Jones Indices, which began to incorporate shares of Saudi companies into their respective emerging-market indices as of 2019.

Another core feature of Vision 2030 is to build regional economic clus-ters—even entire new cities—that will diversify Saudi Arabia's economy into new sectors outside oil and gas. For example, the Crown Prince is promoting the development of NEOM, a 26,500 square-kilometer (10,232 square-mile) zone that will focus on various sectors, including food tech-nology, advanced manufacturing, energy, and water. The mega-project will be backed by $500 billion in investment from the country's strategic-invest-ment fund. The Kingdom has also embarked on a huge tourism project to turn fifty islands near the Red Sea coast into luxury resorts. It remains to be seen whether these ambitious plans become white elephants or the next economic miracle, but the intention to generate more private-sector champions is a worthy one.

Economic reforms are being reinforced with vast social programs. The focus so far has been on building affordable housing and dramatically improving education and skill building for youngsters. The Crown Prince's reforms have already granted women the right to drive, and it seems that guardianship laws, which require women to gain the permission of a male guardian (typically a father, husband, or brother) in order to travel or conduct business, may be relaxed. These are important steps towards engaging this large pool of potential workers.

The entertainment industry is also taking off as part of Saudi Arabia's social transformation. For the first time in thirty-five years, public cinemas opened their doors in 2018, and Saudis were allowed to enjoy music concerts featuring international performers like David Guetta and Janet Jackson. Saudi Arabia is also building a 334 square-kilometer "entertainment city" outside its capital, Riyadh, with a safari, theme parks, and sports facilities. Tourist visas are also being loosened up to allow stays beyond two weeks, and beach resorts are being developed to attract visitors.

All these initiatives represent a promising start, but they are unlikely to employ the millions of unemployed youth in the country. That's because most of the measures mentioned so far stand to benefit the largest companies. But as research by the European Investment Bank (EIB)[83] and many other sources has shown, the largest source of job creation tends to come from small- and medium- sized enterprises (SMEs), run by local entrepreneurs. In this critical segment of the economy, Saudi Arabia still has a long way to go.

The most essential reforms are those that will make the country a much easier place to do business. Saudi Arabia currently ranks ninety-second out of 190 countries assessed in the World Bank's Doing Business 2019 report—marginally above Egypt (120) and Nigeria (146), and a little below India (77). If the Kingdom is serious about encouraging SMEs, it needs to relax the red tape involved in starting a private venture, registering a property, and getting access to electricity. Contractual enforcement must become more streamlined and sources of SME financing more abundant. At the moment, the banking sector in the Kingdom is completely dominated by seven big banks, which limits competition and creates little incentive to lend to riskier SMEs.

No plan to grow Saudi Arabia's private sector, especially the crucial SME segment, will succeed without women's advancement and empowerment. As I have already explained, providing access to education and an equal role in the workforce is essential to unlocking economic growth while also bringing down the birth rate—two essential ingredients to reap the demographic dividend in youth-bulge countries. Women constitute only 24 percent of the workforce in Saudi Arabia, which is just above the average of 20 percent in the MENA region. And according to a report published by Women, Business, and the Law in 2016, which measures women's ability to access institutions, get a job, build credit, and more, the MENA region contains eighteen of the thirty countries globally that most disadvantage women through laws and regulations.[84] Clearly, there's much more to do on this dimension.

Saudi Arabia has the luxury of vast government resources to build new industrial clusters, invest in sweeping social programs, and keep alive large public bureaucracies. But for countries with more limited resources, the focus needs to be on supporting entrepreneurs and nourishing small business. This is the key to job creation, engaging the youth bulge, and reaping the demographic dividend.

Aging Societies

Aging societies, such as Japan, South Korea, Germany, Italy, and China, face the opposite problem to youth-bulge countries—not enough labor. With a declining ratio of workers to retirees, governments face the challenge of a dwindling tax-base to pay for the growing burden of pensioners' benefits and the ballooning costs of social care. Furthermore, these cash-strapped governments are rarely able to build enough affordable housing for young people, who find it difficult to buy property as older generations hold onto their homes. Governments may also transfer other social costs, such as higher education, onto younger people. As the cost of living rises, it becomes more challenging for them to start families, ultimately leading to a drop in the fertility rate.

In aging societies, a suite of policies and investments are needed to boost the workforce. In the short term, the problem can be partly addressed by engaging more women and elderly people, as well as accepting more immigration. However, such changes often face significant cultural, social, and regulatory barriers. In the long-run, the fertility rate will need to be pushed up closer to the replacement level of 2.1 births per woman. This will require measures that make life more affordable for young people and make it easier for them to start a family. In many developed countries, boosting the stock of social housing and reducing the cost of higher education will go a long way towards this end. And, as explained earlier in the chapter, for fertility rates to increase significantly, the financial burden and domestic workload associated with having children must be mitigated for working women. Let's see how some countries with the most severe aging challenges have fared in reversing the tide of falling fertility.

Since Japan began aging sooner than most other developed countries, it has had more time to experiment with various policies. So far, there has been some success in boosting the active workforce. For example, Japan's biggest triumph in the past decade has been to increase female participation in the workforce from 66 percent to 76 percent, which is now on par with the US. Although much of the growth in workforce participation comes from part-time work, it is nonetheless a laudable achievement. Several policies have helped to drive this growth. Laws that restricted women's ability to work or take overtime in certain managerial, technical, or hazardous roles have been relaxed. [85] Similarly, laws restricting temporary employment have been lifted. [86] Historically, Japan has been very reluctant to expand its immigration programs. But in April 2019, in response to chronic labor shortages, a new immigration law took effect that opened the door to a larger contingent of blue-collar workers. Under this program, immigrants can stay for up to five years and are able to switch employers during that period[87].

Unfortunately, Japan has been much less successful at boosting its fertility rate, which has hovered around 1.35 since the year 2000. The government has tried a myriad of initiatives, including the introduction of one of the most generous parental-leave policies in the world—a year of paid leave for both parents, for each child. It has also significantly increased the number of daycare centers for kids. All these measures have made it much easier for women to work while raising a family, but they do not seem to have induced women to have more children.

In 2018, South Korea's fertility rate fell below 1.0 for the first time—an event that was particularly alarming for a country that has pumped $116 billion into boosting its population over the last decade.[88] South Korean parents enjoy a plethora of benefits: subsidized in-vitro fertilization services, shorter working hours for parents, monthly financial aid, subsidized medical expense for infants, free daycare in public nurseries, and the list goes on. But despite these incentives, the fertility rate has continued to decline. If current trends are not reversed, South Korea's population will decline from about fifty-one million today to forty-three million by 2065.[89]

As the experience of Japan and South Korea shows, piecemeal efforts that don't do enough to address key structural issues are unlikely to work. What seems to be holding back progress in these two East Asian countries is a shortage of affordable housing, persistent gender inequality, and an all-consuming work culture. In Japan's major cities, ongoing deregulation of zoning restrictions has led to a gradual decrease in rents over the past decade. Although rents remain very high relative to median income, the situation is better than in other mega-cities such as Hong Kong, San Francisco, London, and Seoul. Fortunately, South Korea is finally waking up to the housing crisis in its capital and recently announced plans to build a quarter of a million new public-housing units over the next five years. Most of these apartments will be allocated to young single tenants or young married couples. While there may be early shoots of progress on housing, neither country has seriously addressed its gender pay-gap, which remains the highest among OECD countries. Women are being paid one-quarter less than men in Japan[90] and 35 percent less in South Korea.[91] Similarly, in both nations, many parents complain that a competitive and intense work culture leaves too little time for family life and often makes it impossible to take full advantage of benefits such as maternity or paternity leave.

One aging country that has achieved a meaningful uptick in its fertility rate is Germany. Since the turn of the century, German fertility rate has risen from about 1.3 to almost 1.6 today. About half of this increase is attributable to Germany's relatively open attitude to immigrants, who now account for 12.5 percent of the population.[92] Women from immigrant backgrounds—for example, Syria, Iraq, and Afghanistan—give birth to 2.28[93] children on average, compared to 1.46 children for their German counterparts. The future social repercussions of this differential birth-rate remain unclear, but if immigrants and their families are integrated productively into the social and economic fabric of the country, Germany could stand to reap a demographic dividend from its immigration policy.

Besides immigration, the other half of the uptick in German fertility can be explained by the availability of relatively affordable housing in most German cities, coupled with a series of pro-family policies introduced over the past decade. For example, German law now stipulates that both parents are eligible for paid leave at two-thirds of their income for the first year after childbirth. This makes it much easier for parents to share the load of rearing very young children. Parents also have a legal right to a subsidized nursery place once the child turns one year of age, and they will receive child allowances even if they work part-time. Notwithstanding its impressive gains, the German fertility rate could receive a further boost from closing the country's gender pay-gap, which stands at 21 percent—one of the highest in the EU. Employers could also help by introducing more family-friendly work practices such as flexible working hours and working from home.

Perhaps all these countries could learn from the example of developed countries such as France, New Zealand, Sweden, Denmark, which have relatively high fertility rates (above 1.8[94]). What they seem to have in common is that their gender wage-gaps[95] are well below the OECD average, their housing is quite affordable (except New Zealand),[96] and their spending on childcare is more than 1 percent of GDP—more than double the spending in other developed countries. The OECD Family Database study shows that in addition to affordable housing and gender equality, childcare services are much more effective in driving fertility rates than other variables like cash transfers and parental leave. Indeed, long parental leave appears effective only when combined with subsidized childcare, and cash benefits to parents have proven to be relatively ineffective in boosting fertility rates.[97]

To boost fertility rates in aging countries, it seems that the key investment that we have not already accounted for is to increase the spending on childcare from below 0.5 percent to 1 percent of GDP. Childcare will also be essential in youth-bulge countries, enabling more women to work and thereby increasing the demographic dividend. The cost of increasing investment in childcare by the equivalent of 0.5 percent of GDP globally, will add over $400 billion[98] to the additional annual expenditures associated with the Sustainable Development Challenge.

Development Is an Attitude

In this chapter, I've presented a formula for advancing development basics that applies to any country, regardless of its level of development. We, as citizens holding a myriad of roles in society, can shape a positive future by supporting its three key elements: the Graduation Approach, investment in socioeconomic mobility, and managing population dynamics to reap a sustainable demographic dividend.

No doubt, we will need to invest trillions of dollars over the coming decades to address these challenges. As philanthropists, leaders of development-finance organizations, and institutional investors, we must find $650 billion of funds over the next ten years to eradicate poverty from the world. Sizeable-impact investments into platforms like BBOXX or Water. org present excellent opportunities to graduate millions to a sustainable livelihood, with the potential to earn a strong financial return as well. As government officials, we need to blend public and private capital to fund large-scale housing and infrastructure projects, as well as creating a business-friendly environment that allows private enterprise to blossom and attracts outside investment.

But when I take a step back and reflect on the collection of measures we've discussed in this chapter; it's striking how many of them will require us to re-examine our attitudes to some very fundamental issues. For example, self-defeating attitudes such as NIMBY-ism, especially in developed economies with aging societies, reduce the availability of affordable housing in the short term, but also boomerang back in the long-run to starve our businesses of workers and make it harder for our children to start families. By the time we retire, there may not be enough working-age people to pay for social security and public services for the aging.

In fact, it seems that sustainable development rests on the ability of citizens, whatever our roles in society, to navigate a minefield of such Faustian bargains. For example, as employers it can be tempting to scrimp on investments in workforce development. Not only is this bad for business, it can have a profoundly negative impact on broader sustainable development. By contrast, leading companies nurture and develop their workforce by offering apprenticeships and frequent training; they work diligently to close the gender pay gap; they encourage work-life balance and implement adequate paid leave for new parents; and they may even offer subsidized childcare. These investments make good business sense since they allow employers to attract and retain top talent, even in tight labor-markets. But these inclusive practices go far beyond good business strategy. They also help to engage youth, boost women in the workforce, and push up fertility rates—all of which are critical for maintaining a large working population and continuing to reap a demographic dividend.

Not every Faustian bargain presents itself in the form of investing more now to reap bigger benefits in the future. As taxpayers, we sometimes need to be discerning about how precious resources are spent today. For example, if healthcare spending above $1,000 per capita seems to have little incremental effect on health outcomes as measured in DALYs, does it make sense to spend five-times that amount in Germany, and ten-times as much in the United States and Switzerland? Instead, should governments focus on managing the cost structure of the public health system to make it possible to provide free, high-quality, basic healthcare to all citizens at a much lower cost?

As parents, there is no doubt that we should be committed to education with a particular focus on boosting the educational attainment of girls in those countries where there is a gap. But we must engage actively with schools and policymakers to ensure that the educational system is geared to produce agile, lifelong learners with the practical, problem-solving, and social skills that employers are demanding.

And as employers and students, perhaps it's time to reevaluate if the traditional undergraduate university degree is providing the preparation required for professions of the future, and whether the exorbitant cost is worth the debt and financial stress that it brings. Would it make more sense to take a lifetime view of investing the same financial resources through a "life account"? Perhaps students could start with a shorter university certification that is more valued by top employers. After a few years, they may want to dip into their life account to start a "market-creating" entrepreneurial venture. Throughout their careers, they could make further withdrawals to continue a lifelong practice of personal development through various courses, coaching, and other forms of learning.

To be clear, I am not suggesting that universities should become less important in the 21st century. In fact, as we will see later in the book, universities are a critical component of the development model in local communities. They act as a magnet to hold young people in a town, as well as attracting them from outside. When the educational programs are aligned with the skill requirements of the local economy, they provide a pipeline of talent for local industry. Through research partnerships with local corporations, universities also act as dynamos of innovation. The key issue that universities have to contend with is how they can deliver on the value proposition above through a model that is more affordable and more focused on developing practical skills that are in demand from employers.

As citizens, an important first step in addressing the SDC is to reexamine our attitudes to the issues I've mentioned above—as well as to topics such as the environment, which I will explore in the next chapter. This will greatly clarify our choices when it comes to how we vote, how we spend, how we invest, how we select a job, and how we run our schools, companies, and communities. Development is indeed an attitude.

CHAPTER 7

THREE EARTHS, ONE PLANET

NYC's Green New Deal

In April 2019, Mayor of New York City Bill de Blasio laid out the city's Green New Deal—a plan that would put the city on track to be net-neutral for carbon emissions by 2050. It is the most ambitious and innovative policy agenda to tackle climate change ever to be announced by a city. Like many observers, I was excited by the announcement—after all, 70 percent of global carbon emissions are generated by cities,[1] and New York, Chicago, and Los Angeles alone account for nearly 10 percent of the entire United States' carbon footprint.[2] It was inspiring that a city as big and as important as New York was taking such bold action.

The de Blasio administration projected that the plan, which covers power, transportation, building efficiency, and waste management, would lead to a 40 percent reduction in carbon emissions from 2005 levels by 2040. A quarter of those reductions will be gained from better building efficiency. At present, buildings account for one-third of the city's emissions. In a world first, New York City will require all new buildings to implement energy-efficient systems to lower emissions. Large buildings will have to reduce their greenhouse gas emissions by 40 percent by 2030 or face penalties. The city is also banning inefficient all-glass facades in new construction unless they meet strict performance guidelines.

A further 5 percent reduction in carbon emissions will come from sourcing all of the city's power from renewable sources by 2040—mostly hydropower from nearby Canada. Additionally, the Green New Deal plans to convert the city's vehicle fleet to be powered by electricity instead of gas, upgrade its creaking metro system, and ensure that buses are more reliable by boosting bus lanes.

Furthermore, de Blasio is taking on waste. The city says organic waste makes up one-third of New Yorkers' trash and is particularly harmful to the environment, since it releases methane—a potent greenhouse gas. Organic-waste collection will be mandatory, and it will be enabled by an expanded network of pick-up points. The plan will also support community composting initiatives. Although the specifics aren't clear, the plan proposes to end single-use plastic food-ware and phase out the purchase of processed meat, which has a big carbon footprint.

The OneNYC plan, as they're calling the package of policies that constitute the city's Green New Deal, is interwoven with efforts to create tens of thousands of jobs and reduce inequality. For example, retrofitting buildings and installing renewable energy infrastructure are expected to create large numbers of skilled and well-paid jobs.

In contrast to the spectacular failure of the national Green New Deal legislation in the US Senate a few months earlier—gaining zero votes from Republicans or Democrats—it is encouraging to see forward momentum at a city level. Chicago and Los Angeles have also announced ambitious action on climate change. By 2035, Chicago authorities aim to have every building running on renewable energy, and by 2040 they want to cut out fossil-fuel energy completely and convert their bus fleet to electric. Meanwhile, Los Angeles plans to obtain all its electricity from renewable sources by 2045, and 55 percent from such sources by 2025. By 2030, all new buildings will also have to be emissions-free.

Of course, these US cities are part of a growing global movement in which cities are taking the lead to place sustainable development at the center of their social contract. Remember our discussion of Stockholm's Vision 2040! As the mayor of Chicago said recently, "When we take a stand, it doesn't matter that the president wants to boost fossil fuel production because most of America will already have been moving to a low-carbon, green-energy world."

And when prominent cities put legislation behind rhetoric, it sets an example that makes corporations sit up and take note. After all, it's good business to be aligned with changing social and political currents.

Energized by these green shoots of change, let's now look at the extent of the Sustainable Development Challenge (SDC) when it comes to climate change and environmental issues. In the remainder of this chapter, we will explore where the key pain points are and how far initiatives such as New York City's Green New Deal will go in addressing them.

Overextending the Planet

The global chorus calling for more environmentally sustainable policies, as exemplified by New York's Green New Deal, is a response to the highly extractive economic model that is currently in place. Our growing industrialized, urban populations demand fossil fuels for energy; forests, metals and minerals for construction of cities and infrastructure; water for agriculture, industrial processes, and personal use; and oceans for fisheries. As countries have become affluent and many goods have become cheaper and more abundant, we have abandoned the paradigm of reuse, repair, and refurbishment in favor of disposability and waste.

According to the Global Footprint Network, a scientific consortium, the toll on the world's resources is quickly approaching ruinous levels. As early as the 1970s, we had begun to use more than one Earth's worth of ecological resources. But as the world population continued to grow and new batches of developing countries approached the living standards of their developed neighbors, our extractive practices quickly breached the Earth's sustainable ecological limit. Today we are using 1.7 Earths, and with our current extractive production paradigm, we'll be using two Earths by 2030[3] and pushing three earths by 2050.

The aggregate picture hides the disturbing truths about the huge deviation in the amount of resources being used by countries. It would require almost five Earths to sustain seven billion people at the level that the US consumes. The US isn't even the worst offender—it would take 9.3 Earths to sustain humanity if we all lived like Qatar! However, at the other end of the scale, it would take 2.2 Earths' worth of resources if we all lived like China, 0.67 Earths' worth if the global benchmark were India, and only 0.46 Earths' worth if it were Rwanda.[4]

Looking at these statistics, it is not surprising that there was such consternation from developing countries about "carbon imperialism" during the 2015 UN Climate Change Conference in Paris. India was particularly angered by US criticism that it presented a "challenge" to progress. India argued that the developed world was responsible for the majority of historical emissions.

India also countered that it burnt 35 percent less coal than the US, even though it still struggles to provide basic electricity to 25 percent of its population.[5]

The developing world understandably wants to reach the living standards of the developed. Meanwhile, the developed world is preoccupied with giving a boost to stuttering economic growth and stagnating wages. The world's collective challenge is to achieve both these objectives using three times less resource by 2050. Rich countries need to transform old infrastructure and industrial processes into cleaner and more efficient versions. Less-developed countries, meanwhile, could leapfrog directly to clean technology—getting it right the first time.

A thorough examination of the entire environmental sustainability challenge would fill many tomes by itself. In this book, I will focus on only three of the biggest challenges: decarbonizing infrastructure and industry to mitigate climate change; adapting to water scarcity; and reducing waste and transitioning to a circular economy. In most of these areas, specific solutions exist that are at—or close to—commercial viability. If they were widely deployed, supported by policies such as New York City's Green New Deal, we would go a long towards bringing humanity's production footprint back into balance with nature's capacity.

Given my attempt at focus, many other vital topics—such as plummeting biodiversity and declining ocean health—will not be covered. For example, scientific studies in as diverse places as Germany, California, and Borneo have recorded an alarming 50–80 percent decline in insect populations in recent decades. Without insects, pollination of many plants—some of which are important human crops—may be at risk. The population declines appear to be a worldwide phenomenon, but researchers are hard-pressed to pin down the true causes of the problem.[6] To an extent, issues such as these may benefit from progress on decarbonizing the economy, water conservation, and reduced pollution. But they are also topics that require greater research to ascertain the true nature of the problem before practical solutions can be formulated.

Decarbonizing Infrastructure and Industry

As far back as 1896, scientists suspected that industrialization could cause global warming. In that year Swedish chemist Svante Arrhenius argued that coal burning would enhance the world's natural greenhouse effect. In 1965, a US President's advisory council warned the greenhouse effect is a matter of "real concern."[7]

However, suggestions that man had contributed to global warming were routinely rubbished by meteorologists. It was only in the 1980s that the world started to take man-made climate change seriously. In 1990 the UN's Intergovernmental Panel on Climate Change (IPCC) produced its First Assessment Report, which concluded that temperatures had risen by 0.3°C–0.6°C over the last century, and that humans had helped cause it. It was becoming abundantly clear that our industrial economies—heavily dependent on carbon—were to blame.

The 1992 Earth Summit in Rio de Janeiro marked the first time that a group of nations forged an agreement (albeit non-binding) to reduce emissions. Developed countries pledged to keep their greenhouse gas emissions at the level they were in 1990 by the year 2000. In 1997, developed nations signed the Kyoto Protocol, agreeing to legally binding carbon emissions targets of 5 percent below 1990 levels to be reached by 2008–12. These targets were reached, but only because the US, the biggest developed country emitter, and Canada failed to ratify the agreement; if they are included, the targets were not reached.[8]

However, various follow-up summits to Kyoto made little headway, since many developed countries declined to participate. At the next major summit in Copenhagen in 2009, world leaders were unable to agree on legally binding targets. They merely "recognized" that temperature rises should be limited to no more than 2°C but made no commitments to reduce emissions that would prevent that threshold being breached.

It was not until the Paris Agreement in 2016 that the world came together for the first time to tackle climate change on a scale commensurate with the challenge—and in a legally binding way. One hundred and ninety-five nations pledged to follow these key imperatives:

▸ Keep temperatures "well below" 2°C above pre-industrial levels and "endeavor to limit" them to below 1.5°C.

▸ Reach peak emissions as soon as possible (recognizing this will take longer for developing countries).

▸ Limit the amount of greenhouse gases emitted by humans to the same levels that trees, soil, and oceans can absorb naturally, beginning at some point between 2050 and 2100.

▸ Review each country's contribution to cutting emissions every five years.

▸ Provide "climate finance" to poorer countries to adapt to climate change and switch to renewable energy, with the funding coming from richer nations.[9]

So, what happens if we are unable to achieve the goals of the Paris Agreement? The IPCC has concluded that without significant GHG restrictions and reductions, the Earth's average temperature will rise by 1.5°C–4.5°C relative to pre-industrial levels by 2100, depending on how aggressively we address the challenge.

As of today, scientists already estimate that global temperatures have risen 0.8°C. We are already feeling the effects in our daily lives in terms of hotter summers, forest fires, droughts, hurricanes, typhoons and extratropical storms, heavy rainfall, and floods. For low-lying areas—for example, the Philippine island of Luzon, Indonesia's Sulawesi, Greece's Peloponnesian Peninsula, Hong Kong's Victoria Harbour, and the US Atlantic and Gulf coastlines—sea level rise is already a noticeable reality.

According to Carbon Brief, over two-thirds of all extreme weather events since the early 2000s were made more likely or more severe by human-caused climate change.[10] The global insurer Aon believes that the top ten global economic-loss events in history were all weather-related. And they note that 2017 and 2018 were the most expensive back-to-back years for weather-related disasters on record, being responsible for $653 billion in losses.[11]

Though not ideal, the IPCC notes that if we keep the temperature rise below 1.5°C, the outcomes will be dire, but manageable. But, above 1.5°C our problems quickly escalate. A 2°C change would already double the fall in maize production and wheat production compared with a 1.5°C increase. A 2°C rise would lead to a 20 percent reduction in freshwater sources compared with today. Sea levels would rise by 50 centimeters, and 98 percent of coral would die.[12]

If our current trajectory of CO_2 emissions continues,[13] we are likely to witness a 3–4°C increase in average global temperatures, which would submerge a long list of iconic cities such as Osaka, Shanghai, Miami, and Alexandria.

With a rise of 4°C, Europe would live in permanent drought. Vast areas of China, India, and Bangladesh would be claimed by desert; Polynesian islands would be swallowed by the sea; and the Colorado River would run dry for most of the year, rendering much of the US Southwest untillable and possibly uninhabitable.

The prospect of average temperatures rising 5°C or higher has prompted some of the world's leading climate scientists to warn of the end of human civilization.

FIGURE 7-1: PATHS TO NET-ZERO AND NET-NEGATIVE CO2 EMISSIONS[14]

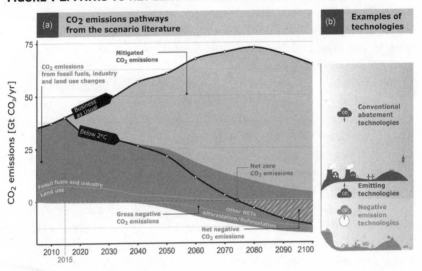

So, with these chilling prospects in mind, what needs to be done to avert a climatic Armageddon? As indicated by Figure 7-1—an infographic taken from an article in Environmental Research Letters (2018) by Sabine Fuss, William F. Lamb, Max W. Callaghan, et al.—temperatures will rise by about 3–4°C if we continue to decarbonize the global economy at a "business as usual" pace.[15] Limiting the global mean temperature rise to below 2°C requires that we decrease CO_2 emissions at a rapid clip, starting immediately. By 2040, carbon capture and storage (CCS) needs to have scaled up to play a significant role. And we must achieve net zero CO_2 emissions by the 2070s.

Taking the Low-Carbon Road

If we accept that 2°C is the maximum temperature rise we can feasibly tolerate, let's explore how we need to transform our entire industrial model to a new, decarbonized paradigm.

According to the Center for Climate and Energy Solutions, the main sources of man-made global greenhouse-gas emissions are approximately as follows: energy (39 percent), transportation (18 percent), manufacturing and construction (18 percent), and agriculture/ forestry/ land-use changes (17 percent).[16] If we can crack the code for decarbonizing these sectors, we will have advanced a long way towards avoiding a climate disaster.

Energy

Starting with energy and heat production, an obvious lever for decarbonizing the sector will be the mass deployment of renewable energy. We are making progress on this front. According to the International Energy Agency (IEA) renewables—consisting of bioenergy, hydropower, wind, solar PV, solar thermal, geothermal, and tidal—are expected to reach 30 percent of power generation by 2030, up from 24 percent in 2017.[17]

Modern bioenergy has become a major part of the energy mix, being expected to account for almost 50 percent of all renewable energy production by 2025. Modern bioenergy is close to being carbon-neutral because it only produces CO_2 that was captured by plants in the first place. It can even become carbon-negative if the CO_2 produced is captured and stored using CCS technologies. Despite its growing popularity, bioenergy has had a somewhat controversial reputation, since it has been blamed for widespread deforestation in efforts to clear space to grow the bioenergy crops. But the IEA notes that if biomass producers adhere to sustainable forestry standards and mandatory reforestation—as is the case in Finland, for example—overall greenhouse-gas emissions will be reduced.[18]

The tumbling costs for wind and solar-power generation have also propelled their rapid adoption into the energy mix in the past decade. Crystalline silicon (c-Si) PV module prices have fallen by more than 80 percent since 2010, and wind turbine costs have dropped by 30–40 percent since 2009.[19] However, the growth of solar and wind energy is currently hindered by their intermittency. Energy is only produced when the wind is blowing or the sun is shining. When intermittent renewables reach about 20–30 percent of the energy mix, their unsteady nature can create serious supply and demand mismatches. At peak demand times (usually in the evenings), this creates electricity price spikes, which can be very expensive for homes and businesses. To avoid these wild price fluctuations—or worse still, brownouts—energy storage and grid balancing become critical. However, at current price levels, this can add 30–50 percent to the cost of the renewable energy installations themselves.[20]

Numerous solutions have been explored for energy storage. Where possible, using excess energy at peak production periods to pump water to higher elevations is a convenient means of storage. When the energy is required during peak demand, the water is allowed to gush down from the elevated reservoirs in order to generate hydroelectricity. However, this solution requires large elevated reservoirs, which are generally available in mountainous areas. Unfortunately, the ideal locations for pumped hydro-storage tend to be far away from the optimal locations for generating wind and solar power, as well as being remote from the urban centers where the electricity is needed. This can lead to substantial transmission costs.

Another means of energy storage makes use of flywheels, which are rotating discs that speed up when electrical energy is supplied to them and provide electricity back to the grid when they are slowed down. Flywheel storage is good for supporting grid frequency for a few seconds but is not stable for longer durations.

Due to the limitations of the other forms of energy storage, batteries have become an attractive solution because they can provide a high frequency response as well as long-duration back up. The biggest barrier to deployment has been cost. To date, Li-ion batteries have largely been deployed in behind-the-meter electric vehicles (EVs) and residential storage systems. However, as the capital cost of Li-ion batteries continues to decline—by over 50 percent between 2018 and 2030[21]—two-thirds of investments in new battery storage capacity are expected to be at grid level by 2050.[22] In the future, other battery chemistries that rely on magnesium, sodium, or lithium-sulfur are also expected to gain traction, since they could challenge Li-ion on energy density and cost. Although some have speculated that raw materials supply may inhibit the spread of battery storage, most estimates forecast the supply of lithium and cobalt comfortably exceeding demand, at least for the coming decade.

During the ten to twenty years that it will take to bring down battery-storage prices, many countries may find that it is not cost-effective to go above the 20–30 percent limit for intermittent renewables in the energy mix. They may instead succumb to the irresistible urge to install more carbon-based power plants—as India and Turkey are doing with coal and the US with shale oil and gas. However, once these carbon-based assets are installed, at great expense, they are likely to be in place for thirty to fifty years. This makes progress in stalling CO_2 emissions much harder.

While we wait for energy storage costs to come down, thereby enabling increased deployment of intermittent-renewable-energy solutions, we need to consider other means of zero-carbon energy production. Nuclear energy, particularly small modular reactors (SMRs), could play an important role. SMRs range in size up to 300 megawatts, are much cheaper to construct than conventional nuclear power plants—the most expensive electricity source—and are also safer. Their smaller footprint and safety profile make it feasible to locate SMRs closer to cities than conventional nuclear plants.

It's not yet clear what the cost of SMRs will be. NuScale Power, which plans to build the US's first SMR plants in Idaho and Utah, predicts that its Utah plants will produce electricity at $65 per megawatt-hour by the mid-2020s. By comparison, onshore wind and solar have reached a levelized cost of energy of $50 per megawatt-hour.[23] However, with China leading the way in SMR deployment, it is likely that costs will come down rapidly and make SMRs a competitive source of renewable energy.

Furthermore, SMRs received a shot in the arm in February 2018 with the FUTURE Act—part of the US's Bipartisan Budget Act of 2018. This will provide tax credits of up to $18 per megawatt-hour for electricity produced by nuclear plants. However, the program has a cap of six gigawatts of extra national-nuclear capacity, beyond which the credits won't be offered (the US currently has a nuclear power capacity of 99.4 gigawatts of electricity).

Since a large amount of the energy and heat produced is destined for residential and commercial buildings, it's worth looking at the energy-efficiency opportunities in these structures. Heating and lighting of buildings account for about 10 percent of global greenhouse-gas emissions. Retrofitting existing buildings with energy-efficient lighting, heating, and air-conditioning equipment—as well as power-management systems that minimize the use of energy when spaces are not being used—can lead to 30–50 percent energy savings. Furthermore, financing for the capital investment required for the retrofits is available from global companies such as Sustainable Development Capital. Since the equipment installed during a typical building retrofit, such as LED lights and motion sensors, is quite tried and tested, financers like Sustainable Development Capital can be reliably paid back in a few years by the building owners from the savings in their energy bills.

In buildings that are being newly constructed, the possibilities for energy efficiency are even greater through better building design. Simple measures such as orienting the long side of a building to face the direction of the midday sun can keep buildings warmer in cool climates. In hotter countries, the opposite approach of orienting the narrow face of the building to the direction of the sun can help to keep buildings cooler. Narrow spaces between buildings also help in hot climates, since buildings provide each other with shade. Regardless of climate, smaller windows are a good idea. They lead to lower heat loss on cold days and avoid a greenhouse effect on sunny ones. Improved insulation of walls, roofs, and floors, as well as weather-stripped doors and triple-pane windows also bring all-weather benefits by reducing heating and cooling costs.

It makes sense that the OneNYC plan features building efficiency as one of its main pillars. It is one of the few ways to make a quick difference in the fight against climate change. And as urbanization gives rise to thousands of hectares of new cityscape in the coming decades, local authorities would do well to implement sustainable-building standards as a way to make quick headway in the SDC.

Transportation

Transport is the second-biggest source of carbon emissions. The majority of transport fuel is still fossil-fuel based. Passenger cars and trucks account for over 80 percent of greenhouse gas emissions from the transportation sector.[24] Despite all the hype about electric vehicles (EVs), the global electric-car stock was only 3.1 million in 2017[25]—just 0.2 percent of the total amount of passenger light-duty vehicles in circulation.[26] However, sales are growing at a fast pace, with 54 percent year-on-year growth in 2017. The IEA predicts that we'll have a global stock of 130 million EVs by 2030. Furthermore, it believes that 30 percent of new car sales could be electric by 2030 and has launched the EV 30@30 campaign to help reach this goal.

Yet, even this pace of EV deployment is unlikely to be enough to keep temperature rises below 2°C. There must be a much more aggressive move towards public transport and smart mobility. Here, the trends are reasonably encouraging. Bank of America estimates[27] we've likely reached peak car stocks in many developed markets, as consumers shift from prioritizing ownership to access on demand.

We're gradually shifting towards the world of Mobility as a Service (MaaS), where individuals own fewer cars and instead purchase Mobility as a Service. Value generation will move away from manufacturers and single-mode transport providers (such as railway or bus companies) and shift to aggregate-service providers that offer access to the best transport option for a particular journey. According to the Center for Automotive Research, car ownership will remain the preferred option for people who need to travel longer distances regularly and require a great deal of flexibility. Most other transit requirements will be better provisioned by some form of asset-sharing option—whether it be a shared bicycle, a ride-hailing car service, or mass transit. Sooner or later, MaaS will transform the entire transport industry.

The smart-mobility industry, consisting of on-demand mobility and data-driven services, is expected to add $1.5 trillion in extra revenue to the car industry by 2030, which is over 40 percent the value of car-industry sales today ($3.5 trillion).[28] Seeing the writing on the wall, car manufacturers are making their own bets to secure a piece of the MaaS market. For example, in February 2019, car-making giants BMW and Daimler announced a $1.1 billion investment into a joint urban-mobility business.

Manufacturing and Construction

Manufacturing, construction, and industrial processes are roughly comparable to transport in their contribution to carbon emissions. Almost half of the CO_2 released by the industrial sector comes from the production of only four commodities: ammonia (used in fertilizers), ethylene (used for making plastics), steel, and cement.[29] Assuming that demand for cars, plastics, buildings, and infrastructure continues to rise according to current projections,[30] all four commodities will need to be produced through much less carbon-intensive processes or the emitted CO_2 will need to be captured.

Technological solutions that are close to commercial viability exist in all four cases. But, as with wind and solar power in the past, political support and the right incentives are required to scale up deployment and bring down the costs until these technologies become commercially attractive options in their own right.

Let's look at steel and cement to understand some of the challenges to the broader adoption of cleaner industrial processes. Interestingly, China's adoption of such new green processes will be crucial, since it produces and uses these materials more than any other country.

Steel production has a huge carbon footprint because it is generally made using a blast furnace in which carbon (coke) is added to reduce iron oxide and produce molten iron and CO_2. There is a better, although not carbon-neutral, alternative: direct-reduced iron (DRI). In DRI, natural gas instead of coke is typically used to reduce the iron ore. Sponge iron is produced, which can then be used to make steel via an electric-arc furnace. In a major trial, Swedish company HYBRIT—a JV between steel producer SSAB, state-owned iron-ore producer LKAB, and Vattenfall, a state-owned power company—is using a carbon-free form of DRI. To eliminate carbon emissions, HYBRIT will use hydrogen produced using renewable energy as the reduction agent instead of natural gas. HYBRIT's arc furnace will also use clean energy.

Unfortunately, HYBRIT's technology—and others like it—will not reach commercial scale for at least another decade, unless incentives and investments are made available to accelerate their deployment and bring down their cost. Massive strategic investments in China helped to bring down the costs of wind and solar power through widespread installations, but it is unlikely that the rising superpower will devote the same resources to champion "green" steel initiatives. Over the past decade, China has shored up its steel-making capacity with many new coke-fired plants. Perhaps China and other large steel-producers could develop carbon capture and storage (CCS) as a medium-term solution for decarbonizing the industry.

Cement—the world's most-used material—also poses a tricky challenge. The vast majority of the world's demand is met by the Portland cement process, in which carbon is emitted in the production of clinker, a crucial ingredient in cement mixture. Clinker is made by heating ground limestone to over 1,600°C in a kiln, causing a chemical reaction that yields calcium oxide and CO_2. The power to grind the material and the energy needed to heat the kiln can also produce significant CO_2 emissions.

Many companies are making advances in clinker substitutes. American start-up Solidia has developed a special carbonatable calcium silicate clinker (CCSC) technology, which reduces overall CO_2 emissions by 70 percent. UK-based Novacem has developed ultra-low carbon cement based on magnesium instead of calcium. Novacem's cement could even be net carbon-negative, since the cement continues to absorb CO_2 as it hardens after mixing with water.

These measures have yet to take off, since high-clinker Portland cement is still the certified building standard in most jurisdictions. However, many countries are experimenting with new forms of cement in buildings and infrastructure. In particular, China is spending more than any other country on R&D in new cement-production techniques.[31] If it can deploy a large-scale, cost-effective solution domestically, it may provide a path for the rest of the world to follow. However, since existing plants have long life spans—up to fifty years[32]—conversion to widespread "green" cement production is a multi-decade proposition. Once again, a more practical medium-term solution may be carbon capture and storage.

Playing with Fire

As we have seen, solutions are emerging to help decarbonize the world's infrastructure and industry, but many challenges stand in the way of broad adoption. On our current course, it will probably take about two decades to overcome the intermittency problem of wind and solar power and make meaningful progress in the uptake of EVs and the introduction of low-carbon industrial processes for basic materials like steel and cement. In the meantime, CO_2 production continues to rise, not fall, and there will be some inertia before we move off the "business as usual" trajectory painted by Fuss, Lamb, Callaghan, et al. in Figure 7-1.

Inertia in Hydrocarbon Industries

The major oil and gas companies are betting on this inertia by continuing to ramp up exploration and production in anticipation that demand will continue to rise. By 2025, ExxonMobil expects to double its capital investments in exploration and refining to $200 billion, while increasing its oil and gas production by 25 percent. In fact, the company expects that the industry will be growing production at a faster rate in 2025 than it is today!

But it is not all plain sailing for the oil and gas industries. They face a fourfold threat that is boxing them in to a business model that relies on fewer hydrocarbons. The first is a growing public outcry around the world. Citizens are becoming much more vocal about the failure to tackle climate change, pushing for net-zero emissions as soon as possible. I'll go into more details on these protest movements later in the book. But suffice to say, changing public opinion will place increasing pressure on legislators and oil companies.

Second, investors are starting to cool on fossil fuels. This is driven partly by public opposition but also by expectations that government will regulate fossil-fuel extraction more going forward, and that some oil assets could become "stranded".

Some investors are already divesting from oil and gas companies. At the time of writing, Go Fossil Free, an industry watchdog, reported that 1,100 institutional investors had pledged to divest over $11 trillion from coal, oil, and gas assets.[33] Investors are also becoming more activist on corporate boards of fossil-fuel companies, pushing them to address carbon emissions more aggressively.

Third, fossil fuel companies are coming under heightened pressure from litigation from a movement reminiscent of the huge civil-litigation case in 1998 by forty-six states and the District of Columbia against America's four biggest tobacco companies. As of mid-2019, eight US cities, five counties, and one state are suing fossil-fuel companies that sell products that contribute to global warming. They hope to match the success of the litigation against tobacco companies, which forced them to stop advertising to youth, to limit lobbying, and to fund anti-smoking campaigns.

Fourth, hydrocarbon companies expect there to be a carbon tax in the future. Some countries such as the UK, Finland, and Ireland, as well as the Canadian state of British Columbia, have already introduced carbon taxes. A bipartisan bill to tax carbon emissions in the US was introduced in September 2019,[34] and seventy companies, including PepsiCo, Johnson & Johnson, Tesla, and General Mills, are lobbying lawmakers to adopt such a policy. In recognition of the way the wind is blowing, even ExxonMobil is advocating for a carbon tax in an effort to try and influence its extent and therefore manage risk. Tellingly, the company says it will support a tax in exchange for immunity for lawsuits such as those being filed by US cities.[35]

For all these reasons, analysts at JP Morgan think fossil-fuel companies are facing a "trilemma" of lower revenue growth from oil and gas sources, increasing pressure by government and society to transition to lower-carbon-intensive energy, and the need to still return cash to shareholders.

As Christyan Malek, head of EMEA oil and gas research remarked, "The industry has gotten to a point where they can no longer pay lip service, they have to spend dollars [on diversifying into renewable energy production]. But they've got to do that whilst giving back cash to shareholders, as well as supporting the bread and butter business. To do all three is very difficult, and that is why we think the sector's risk-reward is, at best, challenged."

Negative-Emissions Technologies

Hopefully, these headwinds will steer oil and gas companies and other hydrocarbon producers in a more renewable direction. But even if that were the case, and even if governments introduced legislation to reach carbon neutrality by 2040 or sooner, it's unlikely that it would be feasible without a significant contribution form large-scale carbon capture and storage (CCS) and negative-emissions technologies.

Let's review the relative merits of these negative-emissions technologies as they stand today (see Figure 7-2). The first method, direct air capture, absorbs carbon from the air and stores it underground. Its great advantage is that it doesn't need to be located near a power-generation or industrial facility where CO_2 is produced. It may be the closest thing to a panacea, but currently the costs are sky high and the technology is not commercially scalable.

FIGURE 7-2: OVERVIEW OF NEGATIVE-EMISSIONS TECHNOLOGIES[36]

Negative-emissions Technology	Annual Capture Capacity (billions of metric tons of CO_2)	Cost (\$/metric ton of CO_2)
Direct Air Capture	0.5–5	200–600
Bioenergy with Carbon Capture and Storage (BECCS)	0.5–5	100–200
Biochar	0.5–2	90–120
Enhanced Weathering	2–4	50–200
Afforestation & Reforestation	0.5–3.6	5–50

The second technology, which seems to be closer to commercial viability, is bioenergy with carbon capture and storage (BECCS). BECCS involves burning biomass to generate heat and power and then injecting the CO_2 into rocky formations deep underground. As we saw earlier, bioenergy must be accompanied by sustainable-forestry practices to ensure that space for bio-crops does not come at the expense of forests. In addition, the types of rocks where carbon can be sequestered are not evenly distributed around the world. We'd need to build infrastructure or supply chains to move CO_2 from where it is produced to where it can be stored—investments with their own carbon footprints. Over the years, analysts have also cautioned that CO_2 could be released back in the atmosphere through leaks. However, recent studies, such as one carried out by researchers at Princeton University, suggest that this is a relatively low risk.[37]

Another option being discussed is biochar. This involves the burning of biomass in the absence of oxygen. When added to soil, it can increase the amount of carbon the ground can store. However, it consumes a vast amount of wood, and if that is not grown sustainably, it could inadvertently harm the climate.

Enhanced weathering, meanwhile, involves mining and using minerals that react with and capture CO_2. But it's small-scale at the moment, so its full potential is unknown.

These technologies are mostly at an early stage of development and are too expensive for commercial deployment at present. However, legislation like the FUTURE Act will help to incentivize progress. The act provides twelve-year tax credits for the construction of a new fossil-fuel power plant or carbon-dioxide-producing industrial plant that incorporates CCS by 2024. Under the act, companies will also be paid up to $35 per metric ton of CO_2 if the CO_2 is reused (for example, for pushing out oil from depleted fields), and up to $50 for carbon buried underground and stored. These incentives would meet at least a quarter of the current cost of BECCS or enhanced weathering, and almost one-half the cost of biochar.

In a promising development, analysis released in Science in July 2019 suggests afforestation could be the most promising method of carbon capture and storage. Scientists at the Swiss Federal Institute of Technology in Zurich analyzed almost 80,000 satellite-photo measurements of tree cover across the globe and combined them with huge global databases on soil and climate conditions to assess where trees could be planted in areas that were not already urban or used by agriculture. Their research predicts that if 0.9 billion hectares of the right species of trees are planted in the right soil types across the globe, forests could capture 205 gigatons of CO_2 in the next forty to one hundred years. This equates to two-thirds of all the CO_2 we have emitted since the Industrial Revolution.[38]

Tom Crowther, a professor of global-ecosystem ecology who led the research, estimates that it would cost the world $300 billion to plant 0.9 billion hectares. However, it would take fifty to one hundred years for the full effects to be felt, which means that it would vital for the world to remain focused on other nearer-term options for reducing current emissions, which we've already discussed.

Although there are many technological, funding, and deployment challenges in decarbonizing the economy, it seems that the public will to speed up change is growing in strength. Without this welcome sense of urgency, I fear we could be playing with fire. There is much we do not understand about the world's climate and ecology. Further greenhouse-gas emissions could trigger runaway second-order effects that accelerate global warming beyond current projections.

First, the permanent melting of glaciers could dramatically increase the level of floods, monsoons, typhoons, cyclones, tsunamis, hurricanes, destruction of coral reefs, and destruction of coastlines. Measurements show that sea temperatures have been rising steadily since the 1950s, and climate models have long forecast that warmer oceans cause more intense storms.

Second, in the past decade methane levels in the atmosphere have shot up. Although methane stays in the atmosphere for less time than CO_2 (a decade or so, compared to centuries), its warming effect is twenty-five times that of CO_2. Scientists are unsure why concentrations of the gas have increased so dramatically, but one theory is that it is a knock-on effect from the thawing of northern tundra in and around the Arctic Circle—experiments prove a large amount of methane is found beneath the surface. Another is that methanogens that break down organic matter and emit methane have been growing in number as tropical wetlands have gotten wetter and warmer.[39]

Third, a hotter planet leads to more forest fires like the ones that ravaged the Amazon, Australia, and California in 2019. This is a double whammy, since burning forests release vast amounts of CO_2 and also leave fewer trees to photosynthesize CO_2 from the atmosphere.

The social and political knock-on effects of climate change could also be very destabilizing. The prospects of tens of millions of "climate refugees" as well as the potential for increased conflict over scarce resources such as water are quite chilling to imagine.

Carbon Taxes

An important jolt that would help to speed up the transition to a carbon-neutral future would be to put a higher price on carbon. There are two ways in which this could be done: putting a tax on each ton of CO_2 produced, or issuing pollution permits to companies, which can then trade the permits on an open market. The first—a carbon tax—is widely recognized to be the better option.

Carbon permits—also known as cap-and-trade schemes—have not had the effects their architects wanted. The EU, some US states, and China all have a form of carbon permits, which tend to be focused on a narrow band of carbon-producing industries like power, oil refining, and steel and cement making.

Yet such schemes raise less revenue and are less effective in reducing emissions. A study by the IMF's Ian Parry, Victor Mylonas, and Nate Vernon suggests carbon taxes raise twice as much as cap-and-trade schemes and cut about 50 percent more emissions. They suggest a tax of $70 per ton of CO_2 by 2030 would raise the equivalent of 1–2.5 percent of GDP among G20 economies—public revenue that would go a long way to achieving the SDC. According to researchers from the Potsdam Institute and the Mercator Institute, if India replaced fuel subsidies with carbon taxes consistent with the Paris Agreement, it would raise 95 percent of the amount it needs to invest in infrastructure and public services to meet the SDGs. And in Sweden, where a carbon tax has been in operation since 1991, and currently stands around $108 per ton of CO_2, it has encouraged strong growth in power generation from non-hydrocarbon sources such as hydro and nuclear.[40]

Although public concern about the detrimental impacts of climate change are increasing, there is probably some work to be done in making high carbon taxes acceptable to a broader segment of the population and business community. After all, a high carbon tax is likely to pass through into higher prices for a wide range of consumer products. To increase support for such a tax, some of the monies raised may need to be given back to citizens in the form of lower personal-income tax—particularly to lower-income earners. Additionally, in the absence of global alignment on carbon taxes, countries introducing high carbon taxes may need to place tariffs on dirty imports and tax credits for clean exports to gain support from the business community, which might otherwise have to compete with foreign competitors from countries without carbon-reduction incentives.[41]

Adapting to Water Scarcity

Although 70 percent of the Earth's surface is covered by water, 97.5 percent of that is seawater, and a further 1.75 percent is frozen in glaciers, the poles, and permafrost. It is only the remaining 0.75 percent that is available as freshwater easily accessible for human use. Another complication is that this narrow sliver of freshwater is very unevenly distributed relative to the major centers of population. Nine countries—the United States, Canada, Colombia, Brazil, the Democratic Republic of Congo, Russia, India, China, and Indonesia[42]—hold about half of the world's freshwater supplies and account for about half of the world's population. But zooming in further, we find that China and India account for a third of the world's population yet possess only a tenth of its freshwater. Moreover, the US and some regions experiencing the world's fastest population growth, such as South Asia and the Middle East, are the most water-stressed.

Switching to the demand side, 70 percent of global freshwater withdrawals are used directly in agriculture, 20 percent to wash, process, and prepare food from field to fork, and 10 percent for municipal and industrial needs.[43] As a result, reforming water usage in the food-value chain will be an essential part of any water-management strategy—especially in many emerging economies where agriculture is particularly water-intensive.

When it comes to managing fresh water, there are many technological solutions that can reduce the amount of water used to grow crops and

184

minimize leakage in municipal supplies. However, the biggest gains in water conservation—especially in water-stressed areas—are likely to come from encouraging smarter consumption of this precious resource. In most of the world, the problem is that water is treated as a "free resource," which leads to waste and overuse.

Let's look at what can be done to adapt to water scarcity. I will first explore some technologies and water-management practices that can increase the efficiency of water usage, before looking at how the total consumption of water can be reined in.

Efficiencies in Using Water

Agricultural Efficiencies

Since agriculture uses the vast majority of freshwater, efforts to reduce water usage in irrigation are essential. In this area, various technologies have also come to the fore that can help to improve the efficiency of water usage.

Drip-irrigation, first championed by the Israeli firm Netafim, is one such technology. Instead of flooding agricultural fields with water and fertilizer, 50 percent of which is wasted, drip-irrigation works by dripping small amounts of both directly onto a plant, saving 25–75 percent of water compared to traditional methods, according to Netafim. It says its method achieves 95–97 percent efficiency in delivering water to crops for the photosynthetic process. This not only saves a large amount of water but also increases crop yields dramatically.

But the high cost of drip-irrigation limits its use to cash crops such as sugarcane and soybean. The capital investment and management required is also usually beyond the means of small-farm owners. This is a significant shortcoming, since over 70 percent of the world's farms are less than one hectare.[44]

A potentially revolutionary idea that would require much less water is indoor farming, which, if required, can be arranged into vertical structures to reduce land use. The idea is particularly catching on in Singapore, the Netherlands, and the US for growing vegetables. An exciting company I have worked with recently is Empire State Greenhouses (ESG), which plans to produce fifty types of organic crops in a renewably powered, eighty-acre facility under development in Cobleskill, New York. Using vertical growing towers fitted with LED "grow lights," it offers 24/7, year-round, indoor growing conditions that allow three to five-times more crops to be produced per year, compared with conventional farming methods. ESG's hydroponic method—that is, growing plants without soil—also uses much less water. According to Louis Ferro, ESG's Chairman, the Cobleskill facility will be 95 percent water-efficient.

Indoor farming is very commercially attractive because it achieves higher crop yields with low energy and water costs. It also increases the geographic and seasonal flexibility of food production, since indoor growing can take place in any climatic region, at any time of year, close to consumers concentrated in large urban centers.

Indoor farming also provides benefits from the standpoint of transportation costs and national food security. Just three counties, two in California and one in Arizona, account for 99 percent of the US's supply of salad greens, according to ESG. However, these counties are 2,500–3,000 miles from the Northeast, which is one of the main centers of demand. These Western counties are all highly vulnerable to problems such as drought and field contamination. For example, Arizona lettuce crops recently suffered an outbreak of E. coli due to cattle manure contaminating water used for irrigation. Local indoor production near urban centers such as the Northeast of the US would help to increase resilience in the food supply chain of the US—and elsewhere—as well as reducing transport costs.

Municipal Efficiencies

On a municipal level, one of the biggest sources of water loss is leakage in water pipes. In Delhi it's been reported that over 50 percent of water is "non-revenue," meaning it is either stolen or lost in leaks. In Hanoi, the figure is 44 percent. Even in the developed world it is high, with rates of 40 percent in Montreal and 28 percent in London.[45]

Often, as in London, leaks are the result of old infrastructure that needs upgrading. New technology involving sensors and smart valves can be installed to send signals that pinpoint where leaks are occurring and help to optimize maintenance schedules. Another opportunity for efficiency in water use is the treatment and reuse of wastewater. Singapore and Israel are again leaders in this area. Israel treats and reuses 86 percent of its water, primarily for agricultural use. Singapore meets 30 percent of its water needs by treating wastewater and produces three times as much water this way than is available in its local catchment.[46]

Desalination

Many are excited by the opportunities of desalination of seawater as an answer to our water scarcity worries. Currently, there are almost 16,000

plants in operation worldwide, producing 95 million cubic meters of desalinated water a day.[47] Almost half the production of desalinated water occurs
in the Middle East and North Africa, with Saudi Arabia and the United Arab
Emirates having the largest market shares (15.5 percent and 10.1 percent,
respectively).

However, the high capital cost and energy intensity of desalination make
it the most expensive way to produce water. For example, the SOREK plant
in Israel—one of the largest desalination plants in the world, responsible
for meeting 20 percent of Israel's municipal-water needs—required a total
capital investment of $400 million and is powered by seventy megawatts
of natural-gas-generated electricity.[48] On average, energy consumption
for surface freshwater treatment is approximately 0.6 kWh/m^3, whereas
the least energy-intensive desalination plants require 3 kWh/m^3.[49] To date,
this is why desalination has been restricted to rich, water-stressed countries with abundant energy reserves, such as the Gulf region. But this mode
of water production creates a sizeable carbon footprint. In Abu Dhabi, for
example, desalination contributes to more than 22 percent of the Emirate's
CO_2 emissions.[50]

To reduce the cost and increase the sustainability of desalination, there
have been several small-scale pilots in the Middle East, India, and Spain to
power desalination plants with renewable-energy sources, such as concentrated solar power (CSP). CSP hasn't been used at large scale to date because
of its inherent intermittency problem. However, as the cost of battery
storage decreases, the broad deployment of more affordable and sustainable
desalination capacity becomes a viable option.

Reducing Water Consumption

The technological solutions that I have described so far certainly have a
role to play, but a key priority must simply be to reduce water consumption through appropriate incentives and policies. Reminding consumers of
the scarcity—and therefore value—of water is essential. According to Siemens's Green City Index, Amsterdam consumes the least amount of water
among developed cities. At 146 liters per person per day, it uses roughly
half of the global average of 288 liters per person per day, and about a
quarter of the average of US and Canadian cities, which stands at 590 liters
per person per day.[51]

Amsterdam's success in reducing water and energy consumption
is due in large part to its investment in educating the public on sustainability issues. For example, the city turned a major shopping street called

Utrechtsestraat—also known to locals as "Climate Street"—into a zone where sustainability projects are showcased and tested, before the best ones are rolled out across the city. This form of awareness-building resulted in the adoption of a smart meter, which is now used in many Dutch households.[52]

Amsterdam has also introduced a pricing system for water so that it is viewed as a valuable resource rather than a free commodity. Most houses are fitted with water meters, and the city charges a differentiated rate depending on the time of day—rather like electricity prices, which are more expensive during peak times. According to Waternet, the city's water company, the mere act of installing meters and charging for water reduced household water consumption by 10–15 percent.

To reach its star status as the world's most water-efficient city, Amsterdam has also implemented many of the other solutions outlined above. It is the best-performing city in Europe in terms of municipal water leakage, losing just 3.5 percent of water, compared with the European average of 22.6 percent.[53] It has also enacted measures to encourage more water-efficient toilets and household appliances like dishwashers and washing machines.

Another substantial impact on water consumption can be derived from more thoughtful eating habits. As I already mentioned, 90 percent of the world's freshwater is used in the food-value chain. As a result, it's worth considering the broader environmental benefits of dietary changes. For example, meat generally uses much more water than crops—it takes 1,847 gallons of water to produce a pound of beef, whereas a mere twenty-six gallons of water will yield a pound of tomatoes. Since the production of meat, particularly beef, is also a big source of greenhouse-gas emissions, we are likely to see attempts to control meat consumption appearing more frequently in policy agendas. Recall that it already features in the OneNYC plan.

One approach could be to require food manufacturers and retailers to provide more information on the natural-resource footprint of their products. Just as nutritional labels inform people about how much of their daily recommended intake of saturated fat, sugar, or sodium a product contains, perhaps the labels could also tell consumers how much of their "personal-resource budget" went into producing the product. Greater public disclosure of carbon emissions and the use of water and other resources would probably drive businesses to minimize their environmental footprint as a point of product differentiation, as well as empowering citizens to make smarter decisions.

Towards a Circular Economy?

Now that we have reviewed some key actions needed to meet the climate change and environmental aspects of the SDC, it is encouraging to note that the OneNYC plan includes many of them. Transitioning to green power, retrofitting buildings to higher energy-efficiency standards, and reducing waste and increasing recycling are very laudable, specific interventions. Although water scarcity does not feature directly in the OneNYC plan, I am hopeful that it will soon move up the list of policy priorities.

But the big question is whether or not initiatives like those in the OneNYC plan—even if adopted globally—will be enough to keep average temperature rise to below 2°C. While it would certainly go a long way, full-scale implementation of New York City's current proposals will take about twenty years. So, for that period, CO_2 levels would still continue to rise—or only fall slightly. In other words, even a Global Green New Deal would fall short.

So, what else is required? It seems that NYC's Green New Deal falls short of addressing the elephant in the room. Can we decouple economic activity and consumption from the use of finite natural resources? Proponents of a concept called the "circular economy," such as the Ellen MacArthur Foundation, believe that this decoupling is not only possible, but also essential for humanity's future prosperity.

The Foundation defines the circular economy as having three main elements. First, it believes that waste and pollution in our production processes must be designed out—products should not be "made to be made again." Second, it advocates keeping products and materials in use through repair, reuse, remanufacturing, or recycling. Third, it encourages returning materials like organic food-waste, cotton, and woods back into the natural system through processes such as composting and anaerobic digestion.

Moving from a "take-make-waste" model to a circular economy has obvious advantages for bringing our resource footprint from 1.7 Earths back down to sustainable levels. However, unlike many of the specific solutions we have reviewed in this chapter, such as renewable-energy sources, embracing a circular economy involves an entire overhaul of our production systems, our attitudes, and our daily habits. As shown in Amsterdam's approach to water conservation, system-wide solutions are required. These include investments in specific technological measures such as wastewater treatment and municipal leakage-detection systems, but most of the impact comes from public education and awareness-building, as well as incentives such as higher prices on water to reduce consumption.

But the key question is how can the circular economy paradigm be extended to other important sectors without affecting our overall economic well-being? If we produce fewer goods—for example, by wasting less food, using more reusable packaging, repairing and reusing clothing, and sharing cars and buildings with Uber and Airbnb—how do we continue to keep the economy growing and creating new jobs? After all, consumption is a major driver of our economies. In the US and UK, consumption accounts for 68 percent and 66 percent of GDP, respectively; in most of the EU it is above 50 percent, and in India it is almost at 60 percent.[54]

The answer is probably that the circular economy will shift the balance of consumption away from physical materials and physical assets towards services and experiences. We may be getting a glimpse into this future world through nascent business models such as MaaS. Widespread adoption of MaaS may well reduce the number of vehicles being manufactured and sold, but it is likely to unlock demand for mobility, which may previously have been too difficult by public transport or too expensive through car ownership. These additional trips will add to economic activity as a paid service. As the new model evolves, it's likely that additional services will be offered that go beyond point-to-point transit. Perhaps they will include concierge solutions to take your children to school, little league, and ballet lessons. Or maybe your elderly relatives can live at home instead of an assisted-living community, availing of delivery services, home health-visits, and concierge-assisted trips to visit you. It is possible that your business would save money by contracting a flexible mobility solution to take your reps from client to client, instead of offering them a company car or reimbursing for their mileage. Mobility will probably integrate with other industries such as leisure and tourism, offering packaged experiences such as going to cultural shows and holiday destinations, in which door-to-door mobility is woven into the experience. With the rise of autonomous vehicles, the range of services and experiences that clever entrepreneurs will dream up can only multiply.

But what about jobs? In the short to medium term, the seven million US autoworkers and almost four million professional drivers[55] are right to be worried about their employment, since the number of vehicles being produced may gradually shrink and autonomous vehicles may reduce the need for drivers. However, with fewer vehicles on the road, each one will work up much greater mileage, increasing the need for workers in fleet management, maintenance, and repairs. Service jobs may also mushroom in areas such as concierges for school runs, assistance for elderly mobility and provision of home health services (UberHealth is already tapping into these pockets of demand), and personalized tour guides. In order to analyze consumer- and business-travel patterns and serve up the exact mobility offering to a given passenger or business, there may be many new jobs for data scientists, software engineers, digital marketers and corporate sales-people. The new operating system and digital infrastructure required to operate autonomous connected cars will generate tech jobs for computer scientists, network engineers, and cyber-security professionals. And let's not forget the economic benefits that MaaS might bring if it helps workers in isolated neighborhoods to access job-rich parts of a city.

Other industries could also be ripe for servicization in the circular economy. Fast fashion is one possible candidate. Typically, we only use 20 percent of our clothing on a regular basis,[56] and we often buy expensive clothes that we only wear on a few occasions. Rent the Runway, a company based in New York City, is helping to change the relationship consumers have with their clothes. It allows consumers to rent clothes for three to four days and has ten million members using its app.

If the recent global public outcry about single-use plastics is a gauge of increasing social and environmental consciousness, I suspect business models such as Rent the Runway are likely to catch on. For example, in the UK, an estimated one hundred grocery stores purporting to be zero-waste have opened in the past two years. Supermarkets are being forced to follow suit. Iceland, one of the UK's biggest supermarket chains, has vowed to eliminate plastic packaging on its own brand products by 2023.[57]

In India, thousands of dabbawalas—literally meaning "ones who carry the box"[58]—deliver freshly prepared lunches in "tiffin" boxes (steel containers, each with four to five compartments) to office workers every day. The tiffin boxes are collected at the end of the day and used repeatedly, saving mountains of plastic each day. So efficient is the system, Harvard Business School graded it "Six Sigma," meaning dabbawalas make fewer than 3.4 mistakes per million transactions.[59] The system has been in existence for years in Mumbai, but it provides an excellent example of how well the circular economy can function.

Although still in its infancy, the circular economy paradigm is beginning to influence many sectors. The shift will certainly be accelerated by changes in policies, such as bans on single-use plastic packaging. The States of New York, California, and Hawaii, along with thirty-two countries, have announced single-use plastic bag bans, and twenty-seven countries have introduced bans on other forms of single-use plastics such as plates, cups, or straws.[60] As circular business models scale up, we may be able to address the scourge of overconsumption and alleviate some pressure from the planet's man-made climate crisis.

Crucially, the upending of whole sectors will require new labor skills. It will be part of a wider transformation of the role of humans in the 21st century economy, which I shall address in the next chapter.

CHAPTER 8

HUMANS

"Useless People" on UBI, or Ten Billion Innovators

In Silicon Valley, the ground zero of American high-tech innovation culture, an idea is being discussed in corporate boardrooms and trendy coffee shops by those who are inclined toward public policy and big ideas. Universal Basic Income—or UBI as it's often abbreviated by its advocates—is seen as a potential solution to many of modern society's social and economic ills.

While the philosophical underpinnings of UBI are debated endlessly, the actual mechanics are implemented in a remarkably simple way: create a universal right for individuals to receive money from the government without any requirement to do work or meet any other eligibility test.[1]

Why should governments want to give away piles of free money to their citizens? The key concern is that the rapidly accelerating pace of technological change is making work more automated and efficient, and a broad and deep array of jobs will be eliminated in the coming years as a consequence. UBI is intended to soften the blow to workers by providing a cash safety-net for those whose jobs will be displaced by the changes that new technology will inevitably carry in its wake.

The author and philosopher Professor Yuval Harari, who is himself an ardent supporter of UBI, has even gone so far as to say that automation may displace a "useless class" of "unnecessary people" from the workforce who will need to be supported by UBI—and that such individuals might turn to drugs and video games[2] in the absence of more productive employment or interests.

Silicon Valley's tech innovators have created incredible technological innovation—but innovation isn't just about technology: the development challenges the world faces must be solved more holistically. You only need to recall our discussion in chapter 2 about the social innovation that was pivotal in sustaining the great civilizations of our past to appreciate that the truly great challenges the world faces are not simply technical problems to be optimized or solved, but fundamentally complex social challenges that must be rethought from the ground up.

Although UBI is plagued with potential unintended consequences— notably, the risk of disempowering the millions of workers it pledges to assist in its implementation—there is an important kernel of truth behind the philosophy. Innovation that increases efficiency and productivity, which is a great deal of what innovation does, has the unavoidable side effect of replacing jobs by its very definition. Fewer hours of labor input are required to produce the same (or better) results as output. The net result of this increasing efficiency is more unemployed workers throughout the economy, lower wages for those workers, or both.

The key exception to this grim rule of efficiency is redeploying those labor hours on fulfilling new demand—creating goods and services that people want, but which did not exist before. This is Christensen's paradigm of market-creating innovation, which I profiled in chapter 6. Throughout most of the 20th century, as technology eliminated obsolete jobs, new demands arose as the menu of goods and services on offer expanded, and new jobs were created in the process.

But is there something fundamentally different about previous waves of technological disruption and the one that could be brought on by the rise of intelligent machines? Some argue that this time it could be different. Past leaps forward in technology, such as the steam engine and electrification, enabled the mechanization of human labor in relatively narrow ways. Machines increased workers' strength and made procedural work faster and easier to replicate. But the mechanical equipment installed in factories required precise guidance and setup from human workers to operate them and to monitor the quality of their output. And so, vast numbers of jobs were created to operate these machines in order to meet the latent demand that mass production had unlocked.

More recently, the introduction of computer software, spreadsheets, and databases allowed repetitive business tasks to be performed more efficiently. Developing and updating these new tools employed a good number of skilled computer programmers, and to integrate the technology into companies' business processes required armies of project managers and business analysts as well.

But now, as machines become more intelligent, the work of operators may simply be absorbed by the machines themselves. Intelligent machines aren't simply getting faster, they're using increasingly sophisticated machine-learning algorithms to crunch through vast datasets in order to learn how to perform tasks better. Moreover, robotics is increasingly being powered by machines with sophisticated sensorimotor systems that can monitor and adapt to the real world, interact intelligently to calibrate their own processes, and programmatically improve the quality and efficiency of their output. In short, the possibility now exists that people will—to an ever-greater extent—be removed from the work processes that once relied on their human intelligence and guidance.

So how will we move forward? It should be clear by now that the notion of sedating a "useless class" of people on UBI is diametrically opposite to the spirit of this book, and it is not my favored solution. Rather than giving up on millions of "unnecessary" people, I will focus in this chapter on how we must invest in the ten billion people who will inhabit this planet by 2050 to transform them into ten billion innovators. Indeed, to solve the significant problems the world collectively faces, it will be essential to unleash this vast pool of creative talent.

We must also expand the concept of what it means to be an innovator to be more inclusive. Innovators cannot be thought of as being limited to a narrow group of technological elites—innovators must permeate a truly expansive segment of the population, taking on challenges that intelligent machines simply cannot address.

The most salient of these challenges are often related to the antiquated social, political, and economic systems that we have inherited, but have done little to update. The democratic system of governance dates from the ancient Greeks. The oldest vestiges of our legal system date from the Romans. Our education system is a slight upgrade from the Victorian Era. And our healthcare system isn't much newer, with the basic infrastructure developed as part of a social-welfare system around World War II. It's unlikely that such systems can be dramatically improved merely by analyzing past data. This type of fundamental innovation must be done through novel, clean-sheet, strategic thinking—by humans, striving to create a better world for themselves and for future generations.

Moravec's Paradox—A Paradox No Longer?

This is not the first time that scholars and theorists have predicted that the next round of technological innovation would create an efficiency revolution across the world's economy, reducing the need for human work. Even the august economist John Maynard Keynes,[3,4] prophesied that the society of his grandchildren's generation would enjoy a fifteen-hour work week. Since no society is currently enjoying such a glut of leisure time, why should we believe the theorists this time around?

To answer this question, let's start by looking back to changes to the workplace over the last forty years. One of the most striking transformations over this period is how the ubiquity of the computer has changed the structure of the way work is organized. Many of the jobs we once took for granted—such as pools of typists, technicians who developed photographic prints, travel agents, bank tellers, and office clerks—have disappeared entirely. Many of these jobs were not of the low-wage manual kind, but rather middle-skilled professions, which required some education and relatively sophisticated technical skills. In fact, manual jobs such as construction workers, short-order cooks, and hairdressers have survived the ever-expanding onslaught from the computer quite well until now.

This unequal distribution of job elimination was presaged by a theory known as "Moravec's Paradox." The paradox was developed by computer scientist Hans Moravec, in cooperation with Rodney Brooks and Marvin Minsky. The theory states that cognitive activities, such as computations and logical operations, require far less computing power than sensorimotor skills like balance and vision, which use up huge resources to accurately compute.

In other words, the logic required to locate a customer's bank account, check on their available balance and other details such as overdraft or withdrawal limits, and to dispense a desired amount of cash, can easily be done by a very basic computer. But the computational resources to enable a robot to crack and egg and fry it in a pan are immense.

Moravec framed the key idea very well in his 1988 book Mind Children: "Encoded in the large, highly evolved sensory and motor portions of the human brain is a billion years of experience about the nature of the world and how to survive in it." In a similar vein, he continued: "The deliberate process we call reasoning is, I believe, the thinnest veneer of human thought, effective only because it is supported by this much older and much more powerful, though usually unconscious, sensorimotor knowledge."

That millions of years of evolution from the earliest microbes to modern humans allows us to comprehend, manipulate, perceive, and move through our environment without even being conscious of the immense computational powers that allow us to perform these amazing feats.

Conversely, the symbolic reasoning that's based in the human neocortex,[5] which is the analytic basis of machine computation, is an extremely recent phenomenon and therefore is less developed than the vast stores of sensorimotor knowledge animals have accreted across countless millennia.

In an interview with PBS's Nova in 1997, Hans Moravec captured the paradox brilliantly with an illuminating example: "I make a connection between nervous systems and computer power that involves the retina of the vertebrate eye. The human eye has four layers of cells which detect boundaries of light and dark and motion. The 'results' are sent at the rate of ten results per second down each of those millions of fibers. It takes about a hundred computer instructions to do a single edge motion detection. So you've got a million times ten per second, times a hundred instructions; that's equivalent to a billion calculations per second in the retina. That is a thousand times as much computer power as we had for most of the history of robotics and artificial intelligence (AI). So, we were working with one-thousandth the power of the retina, or roughly what you might find in an insect."

However, since the late 1990s, computing power has continued to increase at an exponential rate, in accordance with Moore's law. Gordon Moore, a cofounder of Intel, made the prediction in 1965 that computing power would double approximately every two years for the next decade. As it turned out, Moore's prediction was too conservative: his "law" has held up for over half a century. As a result, we have much more computing power today than was at Moravec's disposal twenty years ago.

These vast increases in computing power are the essential ingredient that has enabled the coming age of AI and robotics. As AI continues to automate cognitive work and take on progressively higher-order, data-driven decision making, the next generation of robotics, fueled by computer vision and natural language processing, threatens to turn Moravec's Paradox on its head. It is precisely these new developments that will enable the automation of many forms of dexterous manufacturing and service work.

Artificial Intelligence

Artificial intelligence uses massive computing power to analyze enormous datasets, which are now available due to the digitization of much of our world. This data is collected from a bewildering array of sources: clicks on social media, online purchases, sensors in our ubiquitous smartphones, data from smart appliances and smart cars, and bio-signals captured from wearable connected devices.

Once captured, AI can recognize patterns buried deep within these datasets—which humans would have neither the time nor the analytic horsepower to detect—and use them to aid scientific inquiry, business decision-making, and a myriad of other uses.

The business applications of AI have become so ubiquitous that you probably take many of them for granted already. For example, in the financial-services world, AI is the complex algorithmic-trading engine at hedge funds, or on a simpler scale, the robo-advisor that helps retail investors plan for their retirements at a lower cost than they could get from a traditional broker. When you buy products on Amazon or another online retailer, the algorithm that suggests additional products for you to buy based on your past purchases[6] is generated by AI. Similarly, the recommendation you receive from Spotify and Netflix for additional music or movies comes from AI.[7] And, of course, whenever you Google something, the search engine technology is based on AI,[8] which Alphabet is now using as a beachhead to develop ever-more-sophisticated and complex neural networks. Finally, Facebook is now using a new AI system called Rosetta to help solve a challenge that bedevils the virtual worlds that we collectively inhabit—hate speech on social-media networks.[9]

Another important domain where AI stands to make immense contributions is in scientific research. Automation will allow researchers to test millions—perhaps even billions—of combinations of ideas in laboratories to amazing effect. In the process, scientists and engineers will be able to create novel products and open up new markets. Recently, Northwestern University set out to make new types of metallic glass, which were stronger and less stiff than either metal or glass alone, and which could be used in applications such as smartphone screens and spacecraft. The researchers used AI to generate ideas for creating metal-glass hybrids. The excerpt below from *The Verge* explains the scientists' method.

The AI method they used is similar to the ways people learn a new language, says study co-author Apurva Mehta, a scientist at Stanford University's

SLAC National Accelerator Laboratory. One way to learn a language is to sit down and memorize all the rules of grammar. 'But another way of learning is just by experience and listening to someone else talk,' says Mehta. **Their approach was a combination.** *First, the researchers looked through published papers to find as much data as possible on how different types of metallic glasses have been made. Next, they fed these 'rules of grammar' into a machine-learning algorithm. The algorithm then learned to make its own predictions of which combination of elements would create a new form of metallic glass—similar to how someone can improve their French by going to France instead of endlessly memorizing conjugation charts. Mehta's team then tested the system's suggestions in lab experiments.*[10]

The process wasn't perfect, since the algorithm's suggestions for some ratios of elements were off, but the scientists still gained useful insights from their AI method, which helped them to find new metallic glasses. And performing more experiments will only make the algorithm smarter over time.

Robotics

Vastly faster computing, combined with the exponential cost-decreases in computer memory and sensor technology, has enabled huge improvements in natural-language processing, computer vision, and robotic dexterity. As a result, speech, vision, and fine motor skills may soon come into the reach of robots within a matter of years.

Perhaps the most obvious example of our progress is the automation of factory and warehouse work. Amazon, headed by one of the world's richest men, has invested extensively in this technology. To distribute its merchandise more efficiently to its end customers, Amazon has built product-fulfillment centers that are larger than a million square feet, or roughly the size of twenty-three football fields combined, and that are stocked with literally millions of products.[11] These centers are staffed by swarms of robots that coordinate their activity "like a marching army of ants," according to the company's chief technologist, Tye Brady.

Amazon's robots are powered by AI. Unlike the robots of yesteryear that were built to perform repetitive tasks on factory floors, Amazon's new generation of robots is adaptive and reactive to its surroundings, meaning the robots are able to change their goals based on the circumstances in which they find themselves. As a result, Amazon's robots are capable of employing self-adaptive AI to generate efficiency under the challenges and changing circumstances of dynamic real-world conditions. But when asked recently whether robots present a risk to human jobs, Brady responded with sanguine reassurance: "The more robots we add to our fulfillment centers, the more jobs we're creating."

Robotic technologies are making inroads in a much broader range of areas than just the factory or warehouse floor. In hospitals and nursing homes, robots are delivering medications, bringing meals to patients, and transporting specimens to laboratories.[12] In the relatively near future, new applications will expand to helping patients to get out of bed or into a wheelchair.[13] But what of the human acceptance of robots performing medical procedures on them? When researchers at Embry-Riddle Aeronautical University in Florida asked people how they felt about the idea of robotic dentists performing common procedures on them, "32 percent of the survey's participants were opposed to teeth cleaning or whitening by a robot at the normal price charged by a human dentist, but 83 percent said they'd be willing if offered a 50 percent discount."[14] So, it turns out that we would prefer the human touch in jobs where there is currently a social dimension, but we would switch to robots for a lower cost, not to mention for other advantages such as the avoidance of negative outcomes caused by human error.

Robots powered by sophisticated AI are also entering other manually dexterous fields, such as preparing food for human customers in restaurants. In Boston, Massachusetts, for example, four former MIT students teamed with the famed French chef and restaurateur Daniel Boulud to create a cafe called Spyce.[15,16] At Spyce, a fully automated kitchen equipped with rotating woks cooks a dozen Latin, Asian, and Mediterranean-style dishes for the hip, urban clientele. Orders are taken digitally on iPod-style screens mounted to the countertops, which are then prepared in three minutes or less. Perhaps most impressive, the starting price for every entree at Spyce is just $7.50.

Humans Complementing Intelligent Machines

As AI and automation technologies continue to evolve, machines will fully substitute for humans in hundreds of millions of jobs. While some jobs will be highly resistant to takeover by robots, there will also be an entirely new class of work that will be performed by humans complementing and coaching intelligent machines. This is closely analogous to the massive amounts of jobs that were created in prior periods of technological revolution—when armies of workers were required to operate industrial machines, or swathes of IT-services jobs were created to work with computer software.

What will the dynamic look like this time around as humans complement intelligent machines? A likely answer to this question is illustrated with a powerful anecdote about humans, intelligent machines, and chess, presented by Brynjolfsson and McAfee in their seminal book The Second Machine Age. Following the defeat of world chess champion Garry Kasparov by the IBM computer Deep Blue in 1997, it seemed likely that machines were to triumph over humans in logical pursuits, chess being the ultimate test of rapid logical reasoning. However, as Brynjolfsson and McAfee point out, an intelligent machine has been shown to be even more powerful when it works together with a human.

Reflecting on freestyle chess tournaments, Kasparov noted the winner was not a human or a supercomputer, but a couple of amateur American chess players using three regular PCs at the same time. "Their skill at manipulating and 'coaching' their computers to look very deeply into positions effectively counteracted the superior chess understanding of their grandmaster opponents and the greater computational power of other participants...Human strategic guidance combined with the tactical acuity of a computer was overwhelming." This insight tells us a lot about future job potential. Note how Kasparov refers to the humans' "skill at manipulating and 'coaching' their computers." This sort of human-machine interaction augurs high-paying jobs in the future.

Another dimension of humans working together with AI and robotics is how it can help to bring the collective and cumulative wisdom of human experience to every instance a task is performed. Let's take an area of healthcare innovation I have been exploring in recent years: robotic surgery. Unlike the name may suggest, robotic surgery isn't performed entirely by autonomous robots—at least, not yet. Rather, it uses robotics technology to assist and augment human surgeons to enhance their ability to visualize a surgical site, plan the surgery, and improve their physical dexterity and precision during the surgery itself.

The techniques for robotic surgery vary with the application but often include 3D visualization of the patient, typically created using CAT scans or MRI imaging or with the use of miniaturized probes, sensors, and instruments. While the technologies for assisting robotic surgery remain quite expensive at this relatively early stage of development, the data suggests that these tools can reduce such key metrics as hospital readmission rates and improve long-term patient outcomes.

These improved outcomes are already impressive, but many in the field believe that more profound advantages lie ahead. Robotic surgery has the potential to act as the top of a massive data-gathering funnel—where anonymized data and images of procedures, how they were conducted, and information on the outcomes can be captured.

Once this type of data-gathering architecture is in place, the medical profession would have a truly global pool of case histories. Surgeons around the world could use the best practices gleaned from thousands of cases to assist them in their planning and decision-making process. Instead of being limited to their own experiences, or the experiences of physically co-located colleagues with whom they can confer in person, every surgeon with access to the system could have a level of knowledge that would exceed today's most experienced specialist. Cost reductions would likely ensue as procedures would become more standardized and be performed by less-experienced practitioners—all culminating in complex surgical procedures becoming more affordable and accessible. While such a vision may sound as though it's a dream of a distant future, leading medical companies are very active in researching ways to make it a reality.

Jobs in the Crosshairs

As a consequence of the developments we've already explored, AI and robotic technologies threaten both white-collar and blue-collar jobs throughout the global economy. McKinsey, the strategic consultancy, estimates that the loss of 800 million jobs is possible by 2030 on a global basis. The strategy the McKinsey employed in its study was to examine the tasks involved in each type of job as they are defined today, and to ask the question, "What proportion of these tasks could be done by a robot using technology that already exists today?"

Although this number may seem alarmingly high, it is probably a significant underestimate of the true rate of potential job loss. McKinsey's study is based on tasks that can be automated with existing technology today. However, the potential use cases that new technology can serve up are evolving extremely fast. Moreover, McKinsey's analysis did not consider approaching existing work in completely new ways. Most productivity gains, and therefore job losses, come from combining technology and reorganization of the way work is done to make it more compatible with automation—a process called Business Process Enhancement. Additionally, McKinsey did not consider the downstream, knock-on effects of other technological developments within the global economy. Recall the relatively simple example, which I introduced in chapter 7: Mobility as a

Service. If MaaS becomes the dominant paradigm for transportation, it is quite likely that auto-manufacturing jobs may be lost as the demand for cars declines due to decreased personal ownership. But as I alluded to in the previous chapter, it is quite likely that any automotive-manufacturing jobs that might be lost are likely to be made up by a host of technology and service jobs.

So, how will creative destruction reshape the map of human work in the coming decades? If more than 800 million jobs could be lost, which job types will be most affected? And crucially, what jobs will spring up in their place?

One approach to answering this question is to characterize the type of work that will be most susceptible to automation by intelligent machines and then to map those characteristics to various categories of jobs. A notable example of the technique was adopted by the American-Taiwanese venture capitalist Kai-Fu Lee's classification of jobs in his book AI Superpowers, which I have adapted in what follows.

According to Lee, human work that is most at risk from AI and robotics technology shares the following four characteristics. First, this work is routine, meaning that it is largely rules-based and requires relatively little creative-thinking.[17] Second, it is low-dexterity, meaning the work requires relatively little fine-motor acuity or sophisticated decision-making. Third, the work is asocial and doesn't require high levels of interpersonal skills. Fourth, the work takes place in highly structured environments, which are relatively predictable in terms of the inputs received and the tasks that must be performed there.

Stratifying jobs according to these characteristics would indicate that a first tier of jobs that are most at immediate risk would include those that are routine, low-dexterity, asocial, and set in structured environments. Examples would be bank tellers, fast-food preparers, truck drivers, garment-factory workers, and so on.

Similarly, a second tier of jobs would be those that are gradually under threat. These would include jobs that are routine, require low dexterity, or are set in a structured environment but require a high level of human interaction. Such jobs may include café waiters, bartenders, and general-practitioner physicians. As illustrated by the survey on robotic dentists, social acceptance of robots performing these jobs will increase as costs go down and trust is established. This second tier would also encompass jobs that are relatively asocial but require some creative thinking in a somewhat unstructured environment. Examples of such jobs might be IT technicians, general surgeons, and some forms of analysts.

After reviewing jobs that are now in the crosshairs from the great progress made by AI and robotics technology, we come to the jobs that will be growth areas, even as these automation technologies continue their march forward. The jobs that follow are least at risk because they have creative and strategic elements, require high manual or intellectual dexterity, and are situated in unstructured environments that require human judgment.

As always, these jobs will be abundant in areas of innovation—particularly Christensen's variety of market-creating innovation. Given the magnitude of the initiatives involved, another vast area of job creation will stem from the Sustainable Development Challenge (SDC). Many of these jobs will contain long-term design and social-interaction elements. In order to better understand these job opportunities, it's important to revisit the three main categories of the SDC that we covered in chapter 5: basic provisioning, cleaning up infrastructure and industry, and human-capacity building.

First, basic provisioning, which ensures that citizens have their fundamental needs met, will create millions of jobs in developing countries as citizens at the very bottom of the pyramid are—hopefully—"graduated" out of poverty into gainful employment in burgeoning private-enterprises. As social safety nets are improved, there will be increased opportunities in areas such as social work and development trainers in graduation programs. Education and healthcare will be two of the largest sources of new jobs according to McKinsey, who predict that fifty to eighty-five million jobs will be created in healthcare and aging, and fifty to ninety million in informal work such as childcare, early-childhood education, cleaning, cooking, and gardening.

As aging becomes an increasing concern, these jobs will become critical to increasing the productivity of the working-age population as well as creating opportunities for the elderly to lead independent lifestyles and participate in economic activity for longer. To support the working-age population, a full complement of jobs such as childcare, career coaches, cooking, cleaning, and fertility services are needed to help workers juggle family commitments and make empowering career decisions. Childcare, which is often prohibitively expensive, is essential to empowering the female workforce, especially in emerging markets. At the opposite end of the age spectrum, elder-care jobs, such as home caretakers, physical therapists, and cooks are becoming more critical. Healthcare employment will also rise, with a notable spike in psychiatric care to combat the rising epidemic of mental health afflicting the world.

The second key area is sustainable infrastructure and industry, which must be reformed and expanded around the world. This area includes creating modern smart-cities, decarbonization of industry, renewable energy and water security, as well as circular economy and waste-reduction initiatives. The world appears to be poised on the cusp of an intelligent urban-design revolution. Many global cities—including Seoul, Boston, New York City, Oslo, Bogota, and others—are redefining their core municipal operations to be "smart" and sustainable. That will create vast numbers of jobs in fields such as environmental-resource management, Internet of Things, civil engineering, and more. As 2.4 billion people are projected to join the global population between 2015 and 2050—with 1.3 billion in Africa alone[18]—the need to massively expand existing cities and build entirely new ones will only grow more urgent. As the need to build smart cities expands, it will create enormous demand for a vast array of urban planners, architects specializing in sustainable designs, skilled construction-workers, network engineers, and developmental-finance personnel.

In the next few decades, construction will begin on many more massive, pre-planned urban areas, such as Malaysia's Iskandar, which aims to be the next Shenzhen, the Chinese city that sprung up next to Hong Kong and grew from a fishing village in the 1970s to a city of over twelve million people today. The Malaysian sovereign fund, Khazanah Nasional, estimated the total investment required for Iskandar over twenty years to be $87 billion, but the total figure will be much higher. Saudi Arabia's plan to build the NEOM mega-city, which it says will be entirely powered by renewable energy, will be backed by $500 billion from the Saudi government and its investment fund, as well as other investors. China is planning to build a city three times the size (in area terms) of New York City or Singapore. By reflecting on the scope of such initiatives, one can begin to get a sense of the scale of the demand for workers to design, build, and administer such colossal projects.

Additionally, new services will be required to support urbanization on such an immense scale. Water-conservation technology will, of necessity, become a growth field, as will waste management and recycling. Due to the threat posed by climate change, it's critical to develop—and then deploy at scale—greener ways to produce steel and cement, such as with the processes we reviewed in the previous chapter. Green raw materials will be essential to the coming building boom, and their design and fabrication will create many productive and well-paid jobs. In a similar vein, new smart-cities will require clean energy and smart grids to power them, as well as supplemental carbon-capture technology to minimize the impact of the legacy of burning fossil fuels—all of which will create innovation and job growth in those sectors.

Finally, human-capacity building—including professional and vocational training, apprenticeships, and programs for lifelong learning—is absolutely essential to ensure competitiveness in a globalized, AI and robotics world. Human-capacity building increases worker productivity and creates a bulwark against displacement by intelligent machines. While aiding workers to be more resilient and productive in nearly every sector of the economy, human-capacity building also creates a range of new jobs for teachers, tutors, coaches, educational consultants, and the entrepreneurs who create and develop online courses and training programs, which will almost certainly be a growth industry in the decades to come.

A serious effort to meet the SDC will result in a panoply of new jobs, as well as generating significant social capital. However, these jobs also can—and must—be infused with innovation, leveraging intelligent machines. Without technology-enabled productivity improvements in jobs such as healthcare, education, construction, and many others mentioned above, the costs of meeting the SDC will be prohibitive and the wages for these roles may stagnate.

How We Shape Humans, Shapes Our Economy

The calculus of job creation and destruction that I have just presented should trigger neither alarm nor complacency. Unlike some commentators, I don't believe that it is inevitable that technology will displace workers so rapidly that we will be faced with crippling mass-unemployment. Nor do I think that we are assured to create more jobs than are destroyed, as has been the case in previous episodes when new technologies have revolutionized the entire economy. Instead, I believe that in the 21st century, economies will be shaped by how they set up their model of human development. Let's explore why this might be the case.

When we think about how technology can improve the productivity of an economy, it's natural to think great technological progress that has a broad impact across many sectors will cause the overall productivity growth-rate of an economy to accelerate.

As Lord Adair Turner explained in his lecture at Johns Hopkins University in 2018, this is not necessarily the case.[19] Under certain circumstances, even when there is very high productivity-growth in some sectors of the economy, the productivity growth of the overall economy can actually decline.

How is such a thing possible? Typically, if "dynamic" sectors of an economy experience great improvements in labor productivity, wages for workers in those sectors tend to rise. However, higher wages will not necessarily raise prices in these sectors, because labor-productivity improvements will allow firms to automate work, shed workers, and produce the goods and services at lower costs.

What happens to the displaced workers? If there aren't enough dynamic, growing sectors in the economy to absorb the workers being displaced, they are likely to slip into stagnant sectors with lower productivity-growth. Displacement is likely to become a path to lower wages and diminished prospects for wage growth in the future. Perhaps even more tragically, if displaced workers do not have an avenue to retrain themselves in up-to-date skills, they may not be able to fill high-paying jobs that are available in emerging, dynamic sectors. If those dynamic sectors become starved of qualified workers, while displaced workers continue to slide into more stagnant sectors, Turner pointed out that productivity decline for the overall economy could be the result.

To illustrate Turner's argument with a historical example, let me take you back to the town of Newport, Rhode Island, during the Gilded Age. The Gilded Age was a period of booming American industrialization and economic expansion between the end of post-Civil War Reconstruction and the beginning of the Progressive Era of social reform. During this era, America's industrialist robber-barons, the oligarchs of their day, accumulated and concentrated wealth at a scale the world has seldom seen, excepting the fatal decadence of royal courts and the recent cohort of tech magnates.

During this period, which corresponds roughly with the Victorian Era in Britain and the Belle Époque in France, the uncontested destination for summering for the American robber-baron class was Newport, Rhode Island. In late 19th-century Newport, conspicuous consumption was the order of the day: the captains of American industry built lavish mansions, then furnished them with large complements of domestic staff—butlers, cooks, landscape gardeners, chauffeurs—and employed merchants and retainers, from dressmakers and tailors to crews and sailors for their seaborne yachts, which they launched from Brenton Cove into Narragansett Bay.

Newport, flush with huge sums of money at its peak, was a magnet for displaced workers from cities looking to find employment at well-paying service jobs. But, as the demand for these jobs increased, the productivity of the jobs remained stubbornly constant. Cooks and butlers could only perform a relatively constant amount of work in a given amount of time, especially since domestic appliances were still quite primitive and limited. While these service workers were earning reasonable wages, they were not improving their skills and employability in the economy overall.

For a time, their wages rose as wages in the dynamic industrial sectors rose. But eventually, the rising wages and growing costs of managing these estates became too much for even ultra-wealthy robber-baron families to continue to foot the bill. Many of the estates became "white elephants," and the jobs servicing them disappeared from the stagnating economy.[20]

Ultimately, Newport became a marble mausoleum, locked in its Gilded Age past. Without dynamic sectors, technically skilled workers, or a university to pull it forward into the future, Newport gradually became a tourist haven. In many ways Newport, Rhode Island, was fortunate. The incredible mansions built there by turn-of-the-century plutocrats still constitute a worldwide attraction—and some have been converted into universities. The naval base, situated there since Civil War times, has provided another steady form of government employment. Many other smaller, less grand, less strategically important locations in the country have fared far worse.

The lessons learned from Newport are stern. If people are not infused with the skills and motivation to be innovative and entrepreneurial, if they are not provided opportunities to retrain themselves throughout their career to find work in the new dynamic sectors, it is all too likely that they will slide into more stagnant parts of the economy.

At the opposite end of the spectrum from the Newport economy are ICE hubs. As you will recall from chapter 5, ICE stands for Innovative, Connected, and Entrepreneurial, and we will discuss the pivotal role of ICE hubs in Empowering Local Communities in part III of the book. For now, we will only describe their essential characteristics to show how they adopt an entirely different approach to human development—one which results in much more prosperous outcomes.

ICE hubs share several key principles in common. They are crucibles of R&D and innovation which incubate streams of products and services. They are also characterized by "networked governance," which brings together diverse stakeholders from business, the public sector, and civil society to address local problems or to develop capabilities in specific industries. Crucially, ICE hubs are well connected to external pools of talent, capital, and ideas, which helps drive innovation. And finally, they are full of entrepreneurs who create new markets and multitudes of new jobs in the process. To fill these employment opportunities, ICE hubs typically encourage displaced workers to re-skill themselves through publicly funded and employer-sponsored programs.

It's not just developed countries that must transform their struggling deindustrialized communities into ICE hubs. The transformation will be required in developing countries as well. The world has grown accustomed to China—and before it, South Korea and Japan—gaining a foothold in manufacturing sectors with low-cost labor, using it as a springboard into higher-value industries. It has become a model that many countries have tried to emulate.

However, in the near future, it's not clear that a large population of low-cost workers will remain as powerful an advantage. With the rise of automation, developed markets are once again becoming more attractive for manufacturing. The key driver of this new competitive advantage is the high penetration of robotics, as well as high-skilled labor available in developed countries to amplify the power of technology.

One striking example of how automation has already begun to shift global supply chains is the manufacturing-innovation story unfolding at Nike. The athletic footwear and apparel powerhouse has been working with the high-tech manufacturing company Flex since 2015, with the goal of integrating greater automation into its labor-intensive shoemaking process.

Because of greater automation, Nike is now in the process of moving more of its manufacturing capacity to North America. This new strategy marks a significant shift from Nike's decades-long policy of making shoes in low-cost Asian countries—and it has the potential to cause substantial disruption to its nearly half-a-million line workers in fifteen countries, as well as the more than one million employees working in Nike's contracted factories in forty-two countries around the world. Analysts at Citibank estimate that by using Flex's processes to produce the Nike 2017 Air Max shoe, the cost of labor will be reduced by half, and materials costs will decline by a fifth, creating a 12.5 percent increase in gross margins for the shoe company.[21]

Adidas is also making significant strides in automation: the German shoe giant's new, automated "Speedfactories," which are located in the US and Germany, can produce shoes in five hours—compared with the several weeks of manufacturing time it takes to fabricate the shoes using its traditional supply chains in Asia.[22]

These automation trends do not bode well for countries in South Asia, the Middle East, and Africa, with their huge youth bulges of future workers and immense job-creation needs. The International Labour Organization (ILO) predicts that 56 percent of employment in the low-cost East Asian economies of Cambodia, Indonesia, the Philippines, Thailand, and Vietnam is at risk of being automated over the next two decades, with clothing and footwear manufacturing jobs most at risk.[23] The situation in Africa, Central Asia, and parts of South Asia is equally acute. With current demographic trends, India needs to create ten to twelve million new jobs each year to keep unemployment and underemployment in check. Even with GDP growth in the 6–7 percent range, recent job creation remains far short of that goal.[24]

So it seems that in all kinds of countries, how we develop human capital is fundamental to shaping our economy.

Learning for Life and Lifelong Learning

An economy that is geared to generate innovators and entrepreneurs will drive productivity in existing sectors as well as generate a plethora of new market-opportunities. Workers displaced by automation will find high-paying work in new fields, often occupying roles that may not have existed even a few years before. The rocket fuel for this type of ICE economy is a workforce full of people who are energized by learning, thrive on creative challenges, and are motivated to solve real-world problems.

Let's explore what kind of a model is required to develop a pipeline of such creative workers and to support them through a lifetime of learning, experimentation, entrepreneurship, and frequent transition.

Creating Lifelong Learners

In the 21st-century economy, where humans must be ICE-adaptable and constantly strive to create new sources of value, our goal should be to raise curious, self-directed learners who possess a true passion for open-ended inquiry and problem solving—learning for life.

Unfortunately, the world has become obsessed with testing and grading, which runs directly counter to these goals. Trapped in a system that seems to incentivize regurgitating information, students avoid taking risks due to a quite rational fear of failure. These students inevitably choose subjects that are the least challenging or simply refuse to engage with knowledge outside the narrow subject-matter that's required for their exams.

Moreover, excessive grading encourages learning by rote instead of critical thinking. Grades have become a goal in and of themselves, rather than a waypoint on the path to intellectual development and workforce readiness. Our grade-based system also ignores the other skills that are so vital to succeed in life—such as collaboration, verbal communication, leadership, emotional intelligence, and creativity. Furthermore, grading is a wholly inadequate way of coaching someone to improve their performance. If a student receives a bad grade, they are told by society that they're bad at that subject and maybe should give up on pursuing it entirely—whereas a different approach with greater personalized feedback and attention might have helped them to achieve much more.

What we need most is a different educational model: a model that harnesses humanity's natural curiosity and rewards the self-directed pursuit of knowledge and its application to solving real-world problems. When compared with our current grade-based model, the Montessori style of education, pioneered by Italian doctor Maria Montessori during the early 20th century, seems far ahead of its time and much more appropriate to the needs of our current economy and society. Montessori's system has been taken up most notably in North America, though she first began her work in Italy, before fleeing to the Netherlands because of the rise of fascism. She later spent time India, where she is alleged to have taught many teachers her approach.

The Montessori method emphasizes independence, responsibility, self-discipline, leadership, initiative, and a lifetime love of learning. Montessori's guiding philosophy was, "The greatest sign of success for a teacher is to be able to say, 'The children are now working as if I did not exist.'" Montessori believed that if students were allowed to pursue self-directed learning, they would develop a joy of learning which would stand them in good stead throughout life.

Perhaps the defining characteristic of Montessori schools is that teachers function as guides who "follow the student," in order to figure out how they wish to learn. Such an approach allows students to see the big picture and to take ownership of their own education. Also, classes are of mixed age-groups, which encourages older students to be mentors and younger ones to see where their own learning is leading.

Many of the rock stars of the tech world in the US attended Montessori schools in their youth, including the founders of Google, Larry Page and Sergey Brin; the CEO of Amazon, Jeff Bezos; and the founder of Wikipedia, Jimmy Wales. Indeed, Page and Brin have put the secret to their success down to attending Montessori nursery schools, where "not following order and rules, being self-motivated, questioning what's going on in the world, and doing things a bit differently" set them up well for life, according to Page.

Of course, not every child can become a billionaire tech-titan—but imbuing students with the essential characteristics of critical thinking and self-directed learning will set them up to succeed in the lifelong pursuit of learning and practical problem-solving.

At present, Montessori-style education is overwhelmingly found at the kindergarten and primary school level, but there are no obvious reasons why the Montessori principles cannot be integrated into secondary and higher education as well. It's crucial to inculcate into students the motivation to learn, improve, and innovate—and to do so at a very early age. Without this foundation of innate curiosity, the best lifelong-learning programs in the world are not likely to succeed to their full potential.

To see how Montessori principles might work in higher education, let's look at a project that exemplifies the theme. Recently, I was introduced by Peter Raymond, a friend and New York City-based entrepreneur, to the University of Denver's Project X-ITE, an innovation hub for entrepreneurial endeavors. One of the events organized by this cross-disciplinary initiative was an "Open Innovation" summit whose goal was to create a plan for transforming the university into a next-generation "smart" campus. The summit brought together students, faculty, and staff with experts in the latest thinking in architecture, design, building technology, AI, and much more. The 300 participants divided into small groups to solve challenges on transportation, energy, communication, food and water distribution, and many other aspects of campus infrastructure.

Initially, the teams discussed the nature of the challenges facing the university. Next, they were exposed to the latest ideas for solving these problems by the experts in attendance. Finally, teams worked together to develop their short- and long-term recommendations, which were recorded for the university to use in its transition to a smart campus.

What was remarkable about the summit was that such a large, participative exercise could integrate such a diverse array of views and opinions to generate a very specific open-source playbook of recommendations in the course of a day. The project's organizers managed to inspire belief in the participants that everyone was part of something far larger than themselves. Each group's ideas were debated, and no strict hierarchy or arbitrary rules were allowed to stifle the collective creativity. Of course, not every learning experience needs to be on this scale, but it's important to infuse the emphasis on systems-thinking, collaborative problem solving, and community engagement into the curriculum.

It's encouraging to see the importance of these skills—as well as the fingerprints of the Montessori philosophy—percolating into modern management thinking. Sanjay Rajagopalan, head of research and design at Infosys, emphasizes the importance of "learning velocity"—the speed it takes to go from a question to an idea. Similarly, Eric Schmidt, the Executive Chairman of Alphabet, the holding company behind Google, says their recruitment efforts focus on bringing "learning animals" into their organization. Recently, there's also been much discussion of "agile" workplaces, a term which is used to describe "a variety of approaches to organizing work that emphasize small, self-managed, multidisciplinary teams with end-to-end control of product development, service delivery, and solving other business problems; rapid cycles of activity known as sprints; and a test-and-iterate approach to performing work."[25] The agile concept began as a software-development methodology, but has since been deployed more broadly into other sectors of the economy.

What all these examples illustrate, is the growing importance of behavioral qualities such as emotional intelligence, collaboration, and the desire for continuous learning over so-called technical "hard skills." While hard skills will remain very valuable, learning agility and "human" qualities will be essential in the future workplace.

Activating Displaced Workers

Even if early education can create a generation of "learning animals" equipped for the ICE economy, they will require continued support on their lifelong learning journey and in navigating numerous career transitions. But in the coming decades, when vast populations of workers may be rendered unemployed by intelligent machines, we will need a robust system to retrain displaced workers for new jobs that ICE economies will offer.

Highly successful worker-training programs from the past may offer some useful lessons in designing our future model. The Servicemen's Readjustment Act of 1944—more commonly known as the GI Bill—is one such example. The act was created after lobbying from veterans' groups, such as the American Legion and the Veterans of Foreign Wars (VFW). The lobbying groups drove a hard bargain and managed to secure meaningful benefits for veterans: payments to attend high school, college, or a vocational school; low-cost mortgages to purchase housing; low-interest-rate loans to start businesses; and one year of unemployment compensation. The bill was passed by a US Congress eager to avoid the social unrest of the 1920s and 1930s, which stemmed from discontentment about WWI veterans' benefits.

Though the GI Bill is now widely regarded as a public-policy home run, it's far less commonly known that the bill was subject to much heated debate at the time. President Roosevelt, in fact, wanted the act to apply only to economically disadvantaged veterans, and for college tuition funding to be granted only to applicants who were top scorers on an exam. By 1956, almost eight million GIs had used the act's education benefits and over two million had attended universities or colleges. The GI Bill was a major driver of competitiveness for the US economy. Provisions from the act were also made available to veterans of the US wars in Vietnam and Korea.

The principle behind the GI Bill—aiding people displaced from the workforce to regain a foothold in a high-value position—could be applied to displaced workers who have been negatively impacted by technological advances. Countries such as Denmark, Germany, and Singapore are at the early stages of enacting public policies that create these types of benefits. Most nations, unfortunately, have done little to design any lifelong-learning provisions whatsoever.

As with many other facets of the new economy, the city-state of Singapore is ahead of the pack in creating an environment of lifelong learning. In a symbol of just how seriously the government takes the issue, the city-state has mobilized its Ministries of Finance, Education, and Trade and Industry to pursue lifelong learning goals—and in so doing has recognized the importance of the initiative to its future economic competitiveness.

Singapore's Committee on the Future Economy (CFE), co-chaired by the Finance, Education, and Trade and Industry Ministries, spent more than a year in 2016–17 studying the requirements that would lead Singapore to compete in the future global economy. One specific recommendation that emerged from the CFE was the directive that educational institutions provide more "modular" training programs, such as short courses and targeted certifications, to ensure they matched job market needs.

Singapore has also made it easy for its citizens to chart their own professional and educational pathways by providing a one-stop career and learning portal, which is managed by SkillsFuture, a statutory board under the Ministry of Education. The portal offers information and tools to search for training programs that will broaden and deepen their skills. Financial support to pay for the training courses comes via the SkillsFuture Credit scheme, which offers direct-education subsidies of approximately $370[26] for any citizen over twenty-five who wishes to take a pre-approved course. The government will also provide periodic "top-ups"[27] so that learners can accumulate credit. In 2016, 18,000 courses were available. The courses were accessed by 126,000 Singaporeans over the course of the year.[28] The scheme also incentivizes employers to offer training to their workers. Companies are eligible for subsidies ranging from 50 to 90 percent of course fees for approved courses, with SMEs falling into the 90 percent bracket.

Denmark also has a highly advanced system for assisting its displaced workers. Its famous "flexicurity" program was established to help the Danish economy implement the benefits of both labor-market flexibility and labor-market security. Part of Denmark's approach is the Active Labor Market Policies (ALMP), which was implemented more than twenty-five years ago. Under the ALMP system, workers must attend training programs to receive unemployment benefits from the state. The programs have been shown to have an overall positive effect on both employment and earning potential for displaced workers in Denmark.[29]

Denmark also has a tripartite system, similar to the model maintained in Germany, where employers, governments, and unions are brought together to tackle specific labor issues. For example, in March 2018 the Danish government, the Danish Confederation of Trade Unions, and the Confederation of Danish Employers concluded an agreement which confirmed €120 million in funding for continuous adult-learning. Funds were earmarked to help workers that wanted to upgrade qualifications within their field or gain new skills to enter a different field. The allowance paid to participants while attending courses was also increased from 80 to 100 percent of unemployment benefits.[30]

In addition to these safeguards, Denmark also has what it calls the National Skills Anticipation System, which provides Danes information on 850 occupations, including a sector-by-sector assessment of future needs, employer surveys, and a public sector skill-forecast based on supply-and-demand metrics.

Alas, in most countries the framework for lifelong learning and human development has not yet evolved as far as in Denmark. Indeed, most countries apportion the vast majority of their adult-education spending to university programs. For example, in the US, annual government spending on students in non-college adult education represents about one percent of the spending on students studying at university![31] And according to the independent "Inquiry into the Future for Lifelong Learning"[32] in the UK, 86 percent of the annual £55 billion investment in adult education by government, employers, and individuals is focused on the 18–24 age cohort (see Figure 8-1).

If we are going to get serious about lifelong learning, a more balanced allocation of resources seems to be warranted across age cohorts. A proposal that points in the right direction has recently been put forward by the UK's Liberal Democrat Party. Under their scheme, every UK citizen over 18 would gain access to a "Personal Education and Skills Account" (PESA).[33] The government would make three contributions of £3,000 each to PESAs at ages twenty-five, forty, and fifty-five. This would amount to a six-fold increase in its current £1.5 billion spending on training for those over twenty-five. Workers and their employers would also be able to make tax-free contributions to PESAs, with the government adding 20 percent on top. PESA funds could be used to pay for education and training courses delivered through accredited providers and workers would also receive career guidance sessions to help meet a career goal.

And where could the public funds for lifelong learning programs like PESAs come from? In countries like the US and the UK, there seems to be an obvious opportunity to re-allocate spending from traditional undergraduate university programs whose costs have skyrocketed—saddling students with excessive debt and placing a large toll on the public purse. Moreover,

FIGURE 8-1: ANNUAL SPEND ON LEARNING BY AGE COHORT IN THE UK

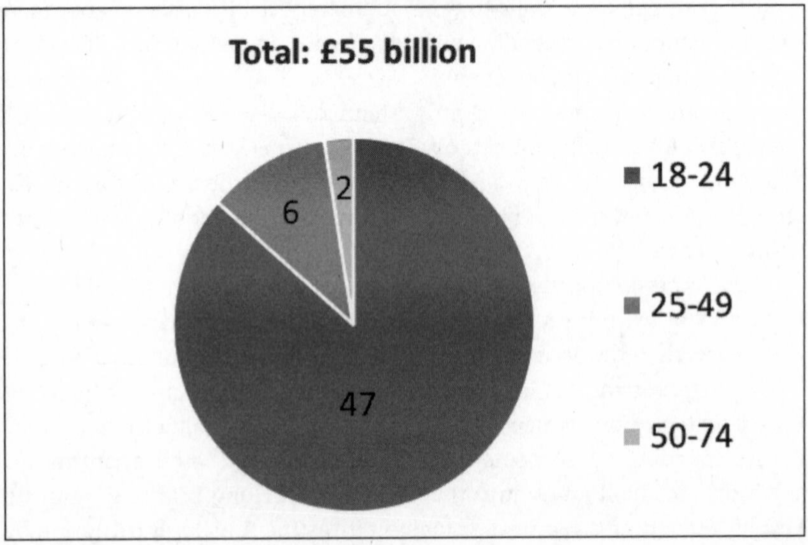

Total: £55 billion

- 18-24
- 25-49
- 50-74

2
6
47

the practical employment value of these expensive qualifications is increasingly being called into question. According to Gallup, between 2015 and 2019, the proportion of Americans who had a great deal or quite a lot of confidence in higher education fell from 57 percent to 48 percent.[34] And in a poll conducted by Ipsos MORI for the Sutton Trust, only 65 percent of those sixteen and younger in the UK think it is important to go to university, compared with 86 percent in 2013.[35] It seems that the public trust in universities is falling fast.

To remain relevant, universities and technical colleges will need to re-invent themselves. In his book, A New U,[36] education critic Ryan Craig argues that institutions of higher education should provide faster and cheaper "last mile programs", bearing strong connections to employers, and focusing on developing technical and job skills that land high-demand, high-wage jobs as a direct outcome. The resulting savings in traditional tertiary education would free up public funds to be re-deployed on lifelong learning programs.

The Magnitude of Change

To achieve a lifelong human development model similar to the model I have outlined, most countries will need to overhaul their current education and job training system. Let's look at the US as an all-too-typical example to illustrate the magnitude of change required.

In a world where human development is increasingly important for growth and preserving the human role in economic activity, it seems tragic that the United States appears to be mired in a crisis in every aspect of its education and skill-building model. The OECD's Program for the International Assessment of Adult Competencies (PIAAC) has shown that the US has underperformed its developed-nation peers in all measures—literacy, quantitative, and problem solving in a technology-rich environment.[37]

The OECD's Program for International Student Assessment (PISA) also ranks countries based on the performance of a sample of fifteen-year-old students on standardized tests in reading, mathematics, and science. While an imperfect measure, the 2015 PISA rankings (the latest available) showed American youngsters ranking 40/72 in math, 24/71 in science, and 24/72 in reading.[38] A 2018 study by Hays showed that 90 percent of employers surveyed said skills shortages were having a negative effect on their productivity, staff turnover, and employee satisfaction, while 73 percent say there is a skills shortage in their industry, with construction and pharmaceuticals particularly effected.[39]

What has led to this woeful state of affairs in American education? The first factor to examine is the overall decline in school funding. In US high schools, total education funding fell by 4 percent in real terms per student over 2010–14, even as the economy grew. This compares with an increase of 5 percent in overall education spending across the other thirty-five OECD countries.[40]

Another contributing factor is that teacher motivation, which has been strongly tied to student attainment, is one of the lowest among developed countries. US teachers have a heavier workload and lower pay than most of their OECD counterparts. American teachers spend around 1,000 hours teaching per year, compared with 600 hours in Japan and 550 in South Korea. In the latter two countries, teachers often specialize in one course, such as algebra, and teach only a few classes a day.

To make matters worse, teacher pay in the United States has been declining in real terms—the average US teacher made 1.6 percent less in 2016–17 compared with 1999–2000. Meanwhile, teachers in Arizona, Colorado, Indiana, Michigan, and North Carolina have experienced double-digit declines in pay. As compensation has declined, so has the social status of the occupation relative to other countries. Between rising workloads, falling pay, and an overall drop in morale, it's not at all surprising that teachers are leaving the profession in droves.[41]

Shifting attention to university education, the challenge here appears to be the sheer financial barriers to access. The cost of attending university in the US has skyrocketed over the last thirty years—as has student debt. During the 1987–88 academic year, US students at public universities paid an average of $3,190 for a single year's tuition in a four-year program, with prices indexed to 2017 levels. In 2017, the average cost for a similar program had risen to $9,970—representing an increase of 213 percent. A driving factor behind this dramatic increase was states reducing their overall spending on education—but the situation isn't much better at private schools. At a private nonprofit US college, the average cost of tuition in 1988 was $15,160 in 2017 dollars; during the 2017–18 school year, those costs had spiked to $34,740—nearly a 120 percent increase.[42]

Moreover, the total amount of student debt in the US tripled in ten years, soaring from $363 billion in 2005 to more than $1.2 trillion in 2015. This increase in total student loan indebtedness reflects more students attending college, as well as a higher proportion of students taking out loans and higher average per-student borrowing amounts than in the past.

In 2004, the average student loan indebtedness was $15,651—but by 2013 that indebtedness had risen to $25,000.

Opportunities for adult education outside multi-year programs in colleges and universities also leave a great deal to be desired. Public funding for adult learning was cut by 21 percent between 2001 and 2017.[43] Nevertheless, in 2014 Congress did pass the Workforce Innovation and Opportunity Act (WIOA) to modernize programs that help the long-term unemployed find jobs, retrain displaced workers for new careers, up-skill incumbent workers, engage disconnected youth in school or work, and provide adults with basic literacy services. Each year, roughly twenty million Americans receive assistance through such programs.[44]

Despite its rhetoric on jobs, the Trump administration's stance on life-long learning is murky at best. The administration proposed a 21 percent cut in funding to the Department of Labor (DOL) in the 2018 budget[45] (which was ultimately blocked by Congress) and it also wants to cut the DOL's funding by 10 percent[46] in the 2020 budget. Cuts of this magnitude would likely result in cuts to programs like Job Corps, which provides job training to disadvantaged youth. Notwithstanding these proposed amendments to the DOL budget, it seems that Trump is a big supporter of adult apprenticeships. For example, his administration, in the summer of 2017, announced efforts to establish industry-recognized apprenticeship programs (IRAPs). And in August 2018, the DOL announced $150 million in funding to support fifteen to thirty apprenticeship partnerships between institutions of higher education and national industry associations.[47]

And what of mid-career mobility? Ironically, the prolonged cuts to adult education have coincided with creeping growth in excessive and non-transferrable certifications to qualify for professions—most of which must be self-funded. A study by the Brookings Institute[48] found that occupational licensing has spread to cover 30 percent of the US workforce, up from 5 percent in the 1950s. Of course, licensure of many professions makes sense. Doctors, lawyers, and electricians require mandatory certifications to ensure your house doesn't go up in flames from faulty wiring, and to prevent incorrect medical diagnoses and shoddy legal advice. Similarly, we would like our barbers, cosmetologists, and manicurists to be qualified and certified to ensure that improperly sterilized hairdressing and cosmetology instruments do not lead to the spread of conditions such as conjunctivitis, folliculitis, and even blood-borne pathogens like hepatitis.

But quite often, the licensing requirements have become too costly, lengthy, and non-transferable. For example, Michigan requires 1,460 days of education and training for someone to become an athletic trainer. In Nevada, a person who wants to be a travel guide must perform 733 days of training and spend $1,500 for a license.[49] Not only do certifications discourage people from taking up new careers and stifle job creation, they also prevent people from moving across state lines, since certificates are generally state-specific. If a worker is displaced from their job due to automation, they may find it hard to move to another state because licensure proves to be a barrier to mobility for the worker or their spouse. One of the great strengths of the US labor market has always been its flexibility, including both the ease of movement from one occupation to another and the ability to move across state lines in the US's vast geography. Excessive licensure, however, is now stifling this flexibility.

Against this dismal portrait, organic change is afoot in the US. Disillusionment with traditional university programs is leading millennials and Generation Z to increasingly look for new alternatives such as online micro-courses, especially for newer careers without licensure restrictions, and employers are ramping up training relevant to new job requirements—both of which are a very positive sign for the US labor market.

However, the overall model for human development in the US—as in most other countries—needs to be transformed before it can support people to become lifelong learners and innovators. To make this possible, we as a society need to acknowledge the increased level of investment required to help workers make multiple professional transitions during their career. These investments must begin in early education to create self-directed, resilient learners. But they must also include apprenticeships, ongoing support for education and skills-development, and financial allowances to help displaced workers and their families bridge the transitional periods between career moves.

CHAPTER 9

LONG-TERM PROVISIONING

Divine Intervention

When faced with the Great Trust Crisis and the existential threats posed by the Sustainable Development Challenge (SDC), the sheer magnitude, complexity, and urgency of the problems the world faces can feel overwhelming to us all.

Against such odds, the forces of progress must unite to avert a dystopian future and to promote a more prosperous destiny for the planet. But are there any specific movements that could push us over the tipping point towards positive change?

Curiously, just before the Great Trust Crisis became apparent, a countervailing movement began to stir that could become such a force of positive change. During the summer of 2015, the Vatican made an extraordinary departure from its past policy: Pope Francis issued an encyclical—a letter to all bishops in the church—stating that "technology based on the use of highly polluting fossil fuels...needs to be progressively replaced without delay."[1]

This exhortation, however, posed an immediate dilemma: How could the church reconcile the position stated in the pope's encyclical, while allowing Catholic organizations to hold positions in funds that were invested in coal companies, hydraulic fracking, and oil stocks?

Over the past decade, I have worked with many investment clients and partners on "impact investments"—deploying capital on projects that could achieve progress in one or more areas of the SDC while also generating a financial return. However, the pope's encyclical and the implications that flow from it struck me as something potentially very different—nothing less than the seed of a worldwide movement to steer capital toward sustainable development investments on a vast scale.

The initial results, thus far, are quite impressive: in just four years, faith-based investment organizations and other large investors around the world have issued policies to divest $11 trillion in hydrocarbon assets from their holdings—a significant increase from $52 billion just four years earlier.[2] Furthermore, a recent study[3] showed that a higher percentage of faith-based organizations are divesting their hydrocarbon assets than any other type of investor. This movement includes an incredibly diverse array of religious groups: the World Council of Churches, the Unitarians, the Lutherans, the Islamic Society of North America, Japanese Buddhist temples, and the Diocese of Assisi.

Following the example of their faith-based counterparts, a broader community of investors have followed suit and contributed their economic and social power to the cause. When measured by assets, the insurance industry, including European giants Axa and Allianz, lead the pack with commitments to divest $3 trillion in assets. Colleges and university endowments, from Edinburgh to Sydney to Honolulu, have also joined the charge, including half the UK's institutions of higher education. Sovereign wealth funds and pension funds are also important players in the divestment process.

The strategy has even been embraced by celebrities from Leonardo DiCaprio to Barack Obama. Even the Rockefeller family, heirs to the world's first great oil fortune, has pledged to divest hydrocarbon holdings from its family charities.

But are the twin engines of investor pressure and high-profile celebrity endorsements enough to drive real-world change? There is some evidence to suggest that they are, in fact, getting results. Peabody Energy, the world's largest coal company, cited the hydrocarbon-divestment movement's negative impact on its ability to raise capital as one of its challenges during its 2016 bankruptcy announcement. More broadly, an October 2018 Goldman Sachs report argued that the divestment movement has been a key driver of the coal industry's near 60-percent derating between 2013–18.[4]

While the pressure on the oil and gas industry continues to build, it has not yet succeeded in reducing production volumes at the major oil companies. But as we discussed in chapter 7, oil and gas firms face a "trilemma"—the need to grow revenue from traditional oil and gas operations, reduce carbon footprint, and generate returns for shareholders all at the same time. This, perhaps, is one of the main reasons why oil and gas companies are lobbying in favor of a $30-per-ton carbon tax in the US—hoping that it will help with public perception and quell the mounting pressure from lawsuits for environmental damage.

Undoubtedly, there are still many powerful lobbies around the world that point out the short-term or intermediate-term benefits of hydrocarbons: export revenues and the energy independence derived from shale gas in the US, job creation from coal mining in India, and the sheer energy demand required to power Chinese growth. But if the pace of hydrocarbon divestment continues at its current rate, then perhaps the diversification to renewable forms of energy generation will accelerate to a pace needed to keep global temperature increases below the critical 2°C threshold.

Moreover, if the weight of private capital can be mobilized to drive funding to other important aspects of the SDC, perhaps the sustainable-investing movement is the talisman we need to fulfill the numerous initiatives outlined in part II of this book.

In this chapter, we will explore the magnitude of investment needed to meet the SDC, before exploring various fiscal and financial avenues—including sustainable investing—to supply the required capital.

The Cost of Faustian Bargains

In the last few chapters, we've reviewed the main initiatives required to address the SDC—a reflection of the actions required to mitigate the cumulative effects of the Faustian bargains we have struck in the past. Of course, estimating the total cost of these initiatives is not a simple calculation given the complexity of the issues we face.

Nevertheless, based on the most credible, publicly available sources, I believe that a conservative estimate of the incremental unfunded investment required to meet the SDC is approximately $5 trillion dollars per year until at least 2030, and probably well beyond. This estimate is composed of the following components, each of which I have discussed earlier in the book.

First, graduating to a sustainable livelihood the 650 million people currently suffering from extreme poverty globally, will require about $65 billion per year over at least ten years. As we saw in chapter 6, we arrive at this figure by assuming the graduation cost per person to be about $1,000 based on costs observed in previous studies such as by Banerjee et al.[5]

Second, as we also learned in chapter 6, McKinsey suggest we need to invest $1.4–1.6 trillion each year to build affordable housing for an estimated 440 million households globally over at least the next decade.

Third, according to the IMF, we need to invest $1.2 trillion more annually on education and healthcare to reach the SDG goals related to these two areas in developing countries up to 2030. My analysis suggests that out of this figure, $670 billion needs to be spent on education and $530 billion on health. Recall, I've assumed that no additional funding will be devoted to healthcare and education in developed countries, where the IMF estimates that there is potentially overspending and room for greater efficiency.

Fourth, increasing the fertility rate in aging economies and raising female participation in the workforce in youth-bulge nations will require most countries to increase the amount they currently spend on childcare from below 0.5 percent to 1 percent of GDP. This amounts to about $400 billion globally on an annual basis.

Fifth, according to the United Nations Conference on Trade and Development (UNCTAD), we need to spend $1.2 trillion more each year on economic infrastructure (power, transport, telecommunications, water and sanitation) if developing countries are to meet UN targets relating to enhanced infrastructure.

Sixth, UNCTAD also estimates that we must spend approximately an additional $600 billion annually on climate change mitigation and adaption in developing countries. This figure includes investments in renewable-energy generation as well as research and deployment of other climate-friendly technologies. It also encompasses investments to adapt to the impact of climate change in agriculture, water management, coastal protection, and so on.[6]

Although a staggering figure, I believe that the estimated $5 trillion annual investment requirement to address the SDC is a conservative assessment. For example, the figure for graduating citizens from poverty only covers the extreme poor and excludes the millions that live in impoverished conditions just above this extremely deprived segment. Similarly, the $670 billion in extra funding needed for education in the developing world includes some spending on lifelong learning, but it probably does not go far enough to ensure youth bulges are harnessed to their full effect. The UN's Sustainable Development Goal on education, which the IMF's figure is based on, vaguely calls to "substantially increase the number of youth and adults who have relevant skills, including technical and vocational skills, for employment, decent jobs and entrepreneurship."[7] Any additional investments required to support lifelong learning in developed countries has not been accounted for at all. Furthermore, the estimate does not include the sizeable extra provisions that we will have to make for elder care in aging societies—at least for a few decades until declining fertility rates can be reversed and manageable dependency ratios restored.

Other omissions from this total figure include investments in economic infrastructure required in advanced economies, many of which need to spend much more on infrastructure than they have budgeted. As we saw in chapter 6, according to the American Society of Civil Engineers (ASCE), the US has a $2 trillion infrastructure-funding gap up to 2025, and this gaping hole will likely persist beyond the arbitrary end point of their review. Advanced countries will also need to make large investments into climate change mitigation and adaption, which are also not included in the estimates above. Furthermore, while difficult to predict and quantify, the increased risks of climate-related refugees and conflict are also not accounted for in these estimates.

Finally, the IMF's and UNCTAD's estimates include the strong assumption that developing countries will invest as efficiently as high performing nations do today—an unlikely outcome, since it would require a leap in institutional quality that is not feasible in most cases before 2030.[8]

Not only is the bill for the world's cumulative Faustian bargains very large, it is already past due. The scope and magnitude of the challenges we now face make it very clear that the risk of time lost to inaction will be unacceptably high. Looking ahead, the UN predicts that there will be forty-three megacities with populations above ten million people by 2030.[9] If such development does not occur in a sustainable way, the world will be saddled with another generation of energy-inefficient buildings and hydrocarbon-based power plants that will add to carbon emissions for decades to come.

So how will we fund the $5 trillion in additional annual investment required to meet the SDC? To put the figure into perspective, it accounts for about 6 percent of total global GDP, which is hovering just over $80 trillion, and about one-fifth of the global tax base, which is about $25 trillion.

To fund these investments completely out of public money would require a 20 percent increase in taxes or a commensurate increase in the efficiency of public spending—both of which seem unrealistic in the timeframes mentioned above. Since raising taxes isn't the solution, let's turn our attention to public and private pools of assets and wealth.

Where Else to Look?

If taxes cannot fill the funding gap for the SDC in the near to medium term, let's take stock of the world's wealth so we can identify where else we might find sources of capital. Figure 9-1 lays out a full picture of global pools of public and private wealth.

FIGURE 9-1: STOCK OF GLOBAL WEALTH ($ TRILLION)

PUBLIC	PRIVATE
Central bank reserves: 13[10]	Pension funds: 43[11]
Public commercial assets: 75[12]	Insurance companies: 34[13]
Sovereign Funds: 7.5[14]	Investable assets: 122[15]
Public total: 96	**Private total: 199**
Grand total: 295	

If we remove central bank reserves from our consideration because these pools of capital are reserved for short-term liquidity purposes and cannot be used for longer-term SDC initiatives, we are left with over $280 trillion—most of which is private wealth, to the tune of about $200 trillion. This is very encouraging, because if a very small proportion of this capital could be annually steered into SDC initiatives, most of the funding gap would be closed. Now let's look more closely at each component of wealth to see what specific roles each might play.

Public Wealth

Public Commercial Assets

As mentioned in chapter 3, Detter and Fölster estimate that public commercial-assets such as real estate, buildings, land, and state-owned enterprises could account for $75 trillion in value.[16] The remarkable thing is that most countries lack centralized accounting of what assets the state actually owns.

If they knew what assets they held, states could manage them in a professional way and generate higher rates of return.

Detter and Fölster point to the example of Jernhusen, a publicly owned Swedish property developer, which manages a $1.8 billion real estate portfolio in and around the railway stations of the three largest Swedish cities: Stockholm, Gothenburg, and Malmö. With an independent board and a stated aim of value maximization, Jernhusen has achieved impressive returns on equity—17 percent in 2015, for example—and has invested $1.4 billion in transport-related infrastructure since its founding in 2001.[17] It stumps up cash for projects that will benefit the whole country. One of its major recent development projects was the Station Stockholm City, which has greatly improved long-distance and commuter rail traffic through Stockholm, by freeing up space at Stockholm's Central Station.

When the assets such as Station Stockholm City mature in value, they can be partially or fully sold, thereby filling public coffers. Alternatively, they can simply generate higher yields for the government, providing a steady source of public revenue to spend on policy objectives.

As Detter and Fölster point out, just a one percent average increase in annual yield on these $75 trillion pool of global assets would yield $750 billion in public revenues—this would go a long way to plugging the funding gap for the SDC.

Sovereign Funds

Sovereign funds—pools of public wealth that are invested through a professionally managed fund—are often in the news. Some are very large individual investors. Norges Bank, which manages the Government Pension Fund of Norway, has a market value of over one trillion US dollars. It has invested in over 9,000 companies, and on average, it owns a 1.4 percent share of all the world's listed companies.[18]

Yet, despite their individual heft, the collective wealth of sovereign funds is around $7.5 trillion—a relatively small amount compared to the other pools of capital in Figure 9-1.

Nevertheless, I think sovereign funds deserve attention because they can help with one of the biggest problems most governments face in meeting the SDC: the need to fund large investments over multiple time-horizons with the single tool of the annual fiscal budget.

The annual budget is a time-tested means of paying for repeated, predictable public services—the running costs of the country, if you will. The budget makes sure that schools, hospitals, law-enforcement units, courts, military, roads, and other services and infrastructure continue to run—and that public workers are paid.

But there are many situations where an annual budgetary process falls short. One example is an economic downturn or shock, such as a poor harvest in an agrarian economy, or a destructive climatic event, or a full-blown financial crisis like the one in 2007–8. Shocks like these usually lead to key projects, like building a port, being put on hold, and public services being curtailed because tax revenues plummet and cuts to the budget need to be made.

With the annual budget as the only source of funds, it can also be difficult for governments to plan and commit to a medium-term economic development strategy. Short-term spending priorities often win out over longer-term development needs due to immediate political pressures, like winning elections. In addition, political winds (and with them, ruling parties) change, blowing away development plans from the budget.

Moreover, it is practically impossible to make sure an annual budget covers very long-term liabilities like healthcare costs for an aging population or a climate change-induced catastrophe. As these costs become real, they choke spending in other areas, or the government is forced to push the burden onto citizens—such as increasing healthcare co-pays—ultimately leading to stagnation of the economy and the decline in the quality of public services.

So, we need to find an apolitical funding-and-development solution that is insulated from such political machinations. Specifically, we need bodies that are accountable to, but independent from, political parties to carry out these long-term investment and development programs. Sovereign funds of different forms—operating at a national or at a regional or local level—can play such a function.

Many sovereign funds in operation today—for example, Norges Bank, the Abu Dhabi Investment Authority, and the Alaska Permanent Fund Corporation—receive their funds from surplus public revenues related to the oil and gas industry or other commodities. But resource-poor countries like Singapore have shown that a country doesn't need natural resources in order to establish sovereign funds from public surpluses. In the future, it's conceivable that countries could set up sovereign funds with capital from a wide variety of sources: resource taxes (such as a carbon tax); wealth taxes on real estate, capital gains, or estates; or taxes on other highly profitable sectors benefiting from excess market power, such as Big Tech.

In the future, nations—and even devolved regions within a country—might also consider establishing a set of funds to cover investment and intervention needs over multiple time horizons (see Figure 9-2). Let's look at how this might work.

FIGURE 9-2: SOVEREIGN FUNDS SPANNING MULTIPLE HORIZONS

Timeframe of Impact	Type of Vehicle	Description	Example
Very short-term (Days/Months)	· Liquidity facilities · Stabilization funds · Resilience funds	Very liquid investments that can be quickly mobilized to address a crisis such as an economic shock or natural disaster	Chilean Stabilization Fund
Medium-term (5–10 years)	· Domestic Development Funds · PPPs	Strategic investments (usually domestic) targeting both above-market financial returns and specific socioeconomic impact (e.g., population health, infrastructure)	Mubadala Khazanah
Long-term (10+ years)	· Pension Funds · Sovereign Wealth Funds · 'Trust' Funds*	Long-term investments in a diversified portfolio of assets (large component tends to be foreign) with the goal of capital appreciation to address very long-term liabilities such as aging population	ADIA Norges Bank GIC Singapore Australian Future Fund

* Trust Funds are long-term funds set up for a specific purpose (for example, environmental remediation following a mining project).

Very Short-Term: Stabilization Fund

If an economy is subject to big swings due to factors such as commodity price fluctuations or frequent natural disasters, surplus public capital could be held in various types of "stabilization" or "resilience funds" to mitigate wild swings in public expenditure that would otherwise occur. The capital in such funds are usually invested in short-term liquid assets so that they can be quickly drawn down to provide much-needed resources in a crisis. For example, Chile uses its stabilization fund to prevent the interruption of public services in years when the price of copper falls dramatically and puts a major dent in public revenues. Indonesia and the Philippines have started down the path of creating "resilience funds," which, given their propensity for natural disasters, is both prudent and ultimately the kind of move that will save lives and preserve livelihoods.

Medium-Term: Sovereign Development Fund

Sovereign Development Funds can play two important roles over the medium term: 1) domestic development, and 2) providing leadership on global SDC initiatives.

To date, most sovereign funds have **not** been set up with domestic development mandates—instead they have been tasked with investing overseas for stabilization purposes or to grow pools of capital for future generations.

However, as longer-term domestic development priorities expand, governments are setting up dedicated Sovereign Development Funds (SDFs) to support national economic-development goals. Where such initiatives have been successful, SDFs have coordinated their investments through the national fiscal framework and have focused on capacity-building investments that would have been too large, too long-term, or too early-stage for the private sector. For example, corporations rarely invest in basic scientific research, greenfield-infrastructure development, or the incubation of new clusters. As a result, SDF initiatives have often focused in such areas, taking on challenges such as promoting early-stage innovation, developing social infrastructure, deepening financial markets, and seeding capital-intensive industrial clusters.

The Nigerian Sovereign Investment Authority (NSIA), funded by Nigeria's vast oil wealth, is doing exactly this. Nigeria's government raked in $33 billion from oil exports in 2017[19]—more than the entire GDP of eighty-nine countries. Yet Nigeria is still in the bottom third of countries by GDP per capita (PPP), despite its resource wealth. Such resource bounty and simultaneous poverty are sadly a common phenomenon in emerging economies. Seven of the top ten countries by natural resource wealth are emerging economies and, of the top thirty countries which rely most on natural resources for their GDP, over half are in the bottom quarter of poorest countries.

The reason is the well-known "resource curse." Poor governance allows corrupt rulers to siphon off profits for their own benefit, and large volumes of exports lead to a currency appreciation that leaves other sectors of the economy uncompetitive in international markets. Furthermore, if too much resource-related capital is released into the domestic economy, it can push up the value of local assets, such as real estate, and price out local residents.[20]

These tragic outcomes only exacerbate the enormous economic-development challenges weighing on these nations. Nigeria's population is exploding at a time when automation and AI threaten to make job creation more difficult. Colossal public health and educational investments will be required to transform Nigeria's youth bulge into a demographic dividend.

NSIA is showing it can be part of a solution. For example, it is investing in a trans-Nigerian gas pipeline to Kano state in the north of the country. This will provide a reliable source of energy to an area ravaged by deforestation because of the burning of firewood for energy by local residents with few other choices. The fund hopes that reliable energy will be a catalyst for economic activity and will help to defuse disaffection among the people in the Kano region, which helps fuel movements such as Boko Haram. It also hopes that with better economic prospects, fewer people will attempt the risky migration out of the country.

Turning to other examples of SDFs, Abu Dhabi's Mubadala Investment Company has been pivotal in creating new industries in the Emirates, such as aluminium smelting, aircraft-parts manufacturing, and private healthcare. Khazanah Nasional, the SDF of Malaysia, has been instrumental in developing the special economic zone of Iskandar. Dubbed "Malaysia's Shenzhen," it will form part of an integrated production-and-services base with Singapore, offering cheaper costs to manufacture than in the city-state. The project had already attracted over $25 billion in overseas investment as of March 2018.[21]

SDFs can also play a critical role in pooling together global sustainable-development funds geared towards incubating and catalyzing innovative solutions to some of our biggest global challenges. There could be funds targeted at R&D into new green technologies, pilot projects like green cement, or large-scale deployment of battery storage and smart grids globally. These would especially target developing countries, where funds are limited.

Cooperation between SDFs will be important to ensure maximum success in tackling the SDC. It would be wasteful for sovereign funds to compete on developing battery storage, for example. Instead, international coordination between funds could pool together more capital via co-investments from various countries. This would allow funds to share risk and ensure that technological breakthroughs are diffused more rapidly across different geographies.

Long-Term: Sovereign Wealth Funds

The last piece of the puzzle is how to deal with distant, long-term challenges several decades away, like climate change or the needs of an aging population. To be prepared for such challenges, countries should set aside pools of surplus capital and invest them into projects that give them a steady long-term return.

Such "future generation" funds are exemplified by entities such as the Abu Dhabi Investment Authority, the Australian Future Fund, and the Alaska Permanent Fund. These funds invest overseas because they want to access a full set of global opportunities to maximize returns and diversify risk, and they do not want to drive up asset prices at home. More such funds are needed, so that nations are as resilient as possible in their public finances.

Private Wealth

When you tally the numbers, the inescapable conclusion is that neither public revenues nor public wealth alone can solve the SDC. The total amount of taxes collected globally ($25 trillion per year), and the pool of capital held in Sovereign Wealth Funds ($7.5 trillion) are dwarfed by global private wealth—currently standing at about $200 trillion and growing at the rate of $8 trillion per year.[22]

In order to successfully finance the SDC, we must create the proper incentives to steer private capital into the funding gap. The solution, in short, must be a capitalist one.

We've already begun to see the beginnings of such a solution in the form of investments with "ESG characteristics." ESG, which stands for "Environmental, Social, and Governance," is a framework for sustainable investing, which seeks to generate market returns while serving a greater good.

The Power of Private Capital

Let's first look at the scale of global private wealth, how it's distributed, and why it holds so much promise for helping to fund the SDC. In 2017, total global personal wealth reached approximately $200 trillion, which is two-and-a-half times the size of global GDP. Just over $120 trillion of this total global-wealth pool is held in "investable assets" such as listed equities, bonds, commodities, and investment funds. In other words, private citizens have direct control over how this capital is invested and can chose to channel it to stocks of companies that operate in ESG-compliant ways or investment funds that invest sustainably. These private investors, additionally, also have the option of disinvesting from companies that engage in carbon-intensive businesses or other poor business practices, such as exploitative labor standards or the failure to meet other key human-rights goals.

The remaining $80 trillion of personal-wealth assets are managed by large institutions, such as insurance companies and pension funds. These organizations have tremendous power to advocate for improved corporate practices through greater board-activism, since collectively, they own significant shares in most listed big-cap companies. They also have the necessary clout to lobby governments for regulatory or policy changes that improve the overall system and incentivize good corporate behavior.

Looking through the lens of geography, residents of North America hold 40 percent of the total roughly $200 trillion pool of global personal wealth, followed by residents of Europe, who own 22 percent, and finally Asia, whose residents own 18 percent. These proportions are likely to shift in the coming years, since Asia is growing its pool of wealth at a staggering rate of almost 20 percent per year. The magnitude of personal wealth is more than enough for each of these regions to fund its own SDC requirements quite comfortably. The only region where this is not the case is Africa, which only has $1.6 trillion in total private wealth.[23] As a result, Africa must attract additional investment from abroad to have a significant impact on its SDC priorities.

Based on this worldwide review of private capital, it should be clear that mobilizing this vast resource could readily fund the requirements of the SDC. In fact, merely the $8 trillion by which global wealth is increasing each year—representing an annualized growth rate of 4 percent—is enough to fund the full SDC requirement of $5 trillion, as discussed earlier in the chapter. In other words, if we keep our current investments unchanged, and only allocate our new, additional wealth towards SDC initiatives, we will have enough capital to fund them in their entirety.

Of course, a much bigger impact on sustainability would come about if private investors did shift a significant proportion of their current investments to more sustainable companies and assets. The knock-on effects on market pricing would have a profound effect on promoting investment with stronger ESG characteristics, for example, by increasing the cost of capital for oil companies and reducing it for clean technology companies. In a nutshell, this game-changing shift in private capital is what the sustainable investment movement could help to achieve.

The Momentum Behind Sustainable Investing

Before we look at the momentum gathering behind sustainable investing, let's review the various investment approaches that are lumped under this umbrella—all of which have two goals in common: deliver a positive socio-economic impact and generate a market rate of financial return—or better. Sustainable investment strategies break down into three broad categories: direct impact, exclusion strategies, and ESG integration.

In direct-impact strategies, investments are made into specific companies or projects that have the potential to achieve significant direct impact. The investments themselves vary widely but tend to focus on areas like agriculture, off-grid solar power, education, healthcare, and financial inclusion in developing countries. In developed markets, the emphasis tends to be on projects that help lower-income communities by providing affordable housing, food supply to poor neighborhoods, healthcare centers, and access to financial services.

Numerous impact-investing funds, such as Acumen and Bamboo Capital Partners are active in these types of projects in developing countries. Impact funds are also taking off in richer countries. For example, the Impact America Fund (IAF) is investing in scalable technology-solutions that focus on underserved communities. The fund makes it a point to invest in entrepreneurs with experience within these communities: most of the fund's portfolio companies have founders who are women or people of color. In many cases, the portfolio companies themselves are also dedicated to empowering minority-owned businesses. One of IAF's portfolio companies, ConnXus, is a cloud-based SaaS platform that connects procurement professionals with a database of 1.7 million minority, woman, veteran, and LGBT-owned vendors. By making it easier for large corporations to contract with diverse vendors, ConnXus ultimately helps drive the expansion of minority- and female-owned companies.

A 2017 survey conducted by the Global Impact Investing Network (the GIIN, pronounced like the drink) found that in 2016, more than 200 self-identified impact investors, such as IAF, made nearly 8,000 investments worth more than $22 billion in the US alone.

Direct-impact investments also include green and social-impact bonds—a new, rapidly growing form of fixed-income vehicles that are used to fund projects with specific sustainability goals. Perhaps the best-known promoter of these vehicles is the World Bank, which raised more than $13 billion in more than 150 different green bonds in twenty currencies during the ten-year period between 2008 and 2018.[24] These financial instruments barely existed a decade ago but had grown to half a trillion dollars in cumulative bond issuances by 2018.[25] Social-impact bonds function the same way as green bonds but target specific social-impact goals rather than environmental goals.

Exclusion strategies actively avoid investing in unsustainable corporate securities or assets. Some investors "tilt" their portfolios away from unsustainable investments without avoiding them entirely. Disinvestments from tobacco and hydrocarbon companies were early examples of this strategy.

ESG-integration strategies factor sustainability considerations into the process of selecting investments that are expected to generate above-market financial return. While the overall meaning of ESG is generally well understood, there is still not a common standard for what specific metrics should be used to determine whether a company has a positive impact. Even less know-how exists on how to relate such impact metrics to financial performance.

Before going any further, it's probably worth distinguishing sustainable investing from philanthropy, which involves donating money to projects or causes that aim to deliver a positive impact to society—but without the expectation of any financial return. One well-known example of a philanthropic organization is the Bill & Melinda Gates Foundation, which has an endowment valued at $42.3 billion. Through donations and grants, the Foundation seeks to support innovative projects, primarily in the areas of poverty, healthcare, and education. Its healthcare budget alone exceeds that of the World Health Organization (WHO). Other examples of philanthropic investment include the Stichting INGKA Foundation founded by the Swedish billionaire Ingvar Kamprad, who founded the global giant IKEA. The foundation has assets worth in excess of $30 billion. In recent years, Stichting INGKA has targeted its investments towards aiding refugees and children in the developing world.

Over the last decade, sustainable investing has moved from the fringes of the investment world into the mainstream. For example, the United Nations-backed Principles for Responsible Investment (UNPRI), an organization created in 2006 to promote approaches to sustainable investing, has grown from a founding group of nineteen institutional investor signatories to over 2,000 signatories with a total of $80 trillion assets under management.[26]

It is also a growing trend, particularly among women and the younger millennial generation, to select investment managers who can deliver both competitive returns and positive societal outcomes. This increased interest in ESG topics is evident in even the most retail-oriented corners of the financial world. For example, Yahoo Finance, the most visited finance-news website in the United States,[27] recently added functionality that allows users to track the sustainability scores of thousands of publicly traded companies.

Reflecting the wave of interest in sustainable investing, the US-based Forum for Sustainable and Responsible Investment (USSIF) reported that US-domiciled assets under management using sustainable investing strategies grew from just under $9 trillion at the beginning of 2016 to $12 trillion at the beginning of 2018—an increase of nearly 40 percent.[28] If these data are to be believed, more than 25 percent of all US-domiciled assets are invested with some aspect of sustainability in mind.

Furthermore, the USSIF report seems to indicate that investors have begun to engage in more direct dialogue on ESG issues with the companies they invest in. The report states that forty-nine institutional asset owners and eighty-eight money managers—with total assets under management of over $10 trillion combined—reported engaging with companies about ESG issues. These numbers are rising. For example, the number of money managers who stated they engaged with companies on such issues has increased more than 40 percent over a two-year period, according to the report.[29]

But are these eye-popping figures for the size of sustainably invested assets credible? Unfortunately, there is ample evidence to suggest that many sustainable investment products are subject to "greenwashing"—a marketing gimmick whereby asset managers add a thin veneer of ESG scoring to their products to attract potential investors. The Dow Jones Sustainability Europe Index, for example, includes British American Tobacco. And Vanguard's Socially Responsible Investing European Stock Fund includes Royal Dutch Shell.

Since there are no clear standards or fiduciary requirements for companies to report on the ESG impact they actually achieve, asset managers often rely on ESG scores provided by various rating agencies in order to construct their investment products. However, since a consistent model is yet to be defined about what metrics should be used to construct sustainability ratings, many weak, check-box-style indicators are currently in use. For example, a common ESG metric is a yes-or-no answer to the question: "Does your company have a gender-equality policy?" Obviously, this may have little correlation with whether the company has a balanced gender-ratio or pay parity.

Unsurprisingly, a recent report suggests that correlations between ESG ratings from different providers may be as low as 30–40 percent.[30] On a similar note, a Wall Street Journal article highlighted how Tesla can simultaneously rank in the top, middle, and bottom of all carmakers worldwide based on environmental issues, depending on which ESG ratings provider you use.[31] Disconcertingly, there are also anecdotal reports from asset managers suggesting that corporate frauds—such as the Volkswagen emissions scandal—would not be detected by standard ESG screening tools currently in use.[32]

In my view, there are three serious barriers holding back progress in sustainable investing. First, there is an overall lack of clarity around the definition of sustainable investment. Without a clear nomenclature and standard criteria to delineate the different types of sustainable investing strategies, it is confusing for investors to understand what they are investing in and for industry associations to tabulate the magnitude of funds flowing into each category. Second, there is a lack of consistency in how sustainability metrics are defined by various ESG ratings providers and even less research on how strong those metrics are as indicators of socioeconomic impact. And third, we need a consistent and pragmatic standard for how companies should report their ESG impact so that the non-financial returns can be used as a consideration for investment—just like their financial returns are. These barriers must be overcome if private capital is to play the leading role in meeting the SDC, and if the sustainable investing movement is to deliver its full impact.

Universal Owners

To increase the significance and impact of sustainable investing, and to overcome the challenges already described, we need strong leadership. As I've already noted, there's a great deal of bombast about sustainable investing in the global asset-management industry. Much of it is merely marketing speak aimed at proliferating investment products and growing assets under management. So, amidst all the distracting PR noise, who can we turn to for a credible viewpoint on ESG matters?

International institutions such as the United Nations Principles for Responsible Investing group (UN PRI) certainly have a role to play in developing common sustainable investing standards and practices. Indeed, the UNPRI is working with its signatory organizations to do just that. However, leadership must ultimately come from the top investment organizations themselves, and I believe we can apply four criteria to identify those whose perspectives are most credible on sustainable investing matters.

The first criterion for credibility is that the investor's financial goals must align closely with a sustainable and optimized world order. That would already narrow it down to a small group of long-term investors who are so big that they own a broad sampling of the entire global market. Second, the vast majority of the investor's investments should be passive, so that it benefits when the returns of the overall market increase. This criterion excludes hedge funds or highly active managers, who generate returns by taking bets on specific investment ideas. Third, the investor should be subject to limited political influence. Fourth, and finally, the investor should both have strong investment capabilities to design robust ESG investment frameworks and the global influence to drive the change.

Do such investors exist? While no investor perfectly satisfies all the criteria listed above, some come quite close. In the field of finance, such investors are referred to as **Universal Owners**. The challenges of Universal Owners are unique, because they have vast and diversified investment portfolio with exposure to the entire global market. Even if some of their portfolio companies were able to increase profits through unsustainable practices, such as scrimping on worker training and health benefits or not adopting energy efficient practices, it is likely that other companies in the investor's portfolio would adversely affected by these actions due to skilled labor shortages, higher taxes, or higher energy prices. In short, universal owners benefit when the entire system is improved and when their portfolio companies adhere to sustainable practices.

Japan's Government Pension Investment Fund (GPIF) fulfills many of the criteria of the Universal Owner. The fund manages the pensions of Japan's public workers—an enormous domestic savings-account of nearly $1.5 trillion.[33] In 2017, GPIF announced that approximately 10 percent of its equity portfolio—or ¥1 trillion ($8.9 billion)—would be invested in ESG indices, representing an uplift from the 3 percent already invested in ESG.[34]

Some of the characteristics of GPIF's investment are worth examining in detail, since they serve as a broader metaphor for the way a Universal Owner might participate in ESG initiatives. Both of GPIF's new environmental-equity indices over-weight companies with high carbon-efficiency and that disclose the quantity of their carbon emissions.[35] Additionally, both indices over-weight and under-weight their amount of ownership in companies in varying industries depending on the level of damage to the environment that each company creates relative to its peers in the space.

GPIF is also partnering with MSCI (Morgan Stanley Capital International) on the Japan Empowering Women Index. The index will be composed of companies whose gender initiatives have been verified by MSCI to encourage female participation in the workforce. GPIF was part of the initial selection when the MSCI Empowering Women Index was begun in 2017. Additionally, GPIF has begun a dialogue with the companies it invests in, both domestically in Japan and internationally, to ensure that women are better represented in senior management roles.

Finally, GPIF is working with the World Bank Group on promoting green, social, and sustainability bonds.[36] GPIF is investing in the bonds issued by World Bank and the International Finance Corporation. The initial investments by GPIF in the new sustainability bonds exceeded the equivalent of half a billion US dollars. GPIF officials said that, in the future, they plan to consider ESG investments across asset classes.

BlackRock, a US-based, private-sector investor with over $6.5 trillion under management,[37] also bears some of the characteristics of a Universal Owner. With such a massive and largely-passive portfolio, BlackRock is exposed to the global financial system—which means the franchise benefits when the entire system is enhanced. Perhaps this is why BlackRock's CEO, Larry Fink, has become increasingly focused on sustainability topics in his annual letters to the CEOs of companies that BlackRock has invested in. For example, in his 2019 letter, Fink wrote:

> *Purpose is not the sole pursuit of profits but the animating force for achieving them. Profits are in no way inconsistent with purpose—in fact, profits and purpose are inextricably linked* [his emphasis]. *Profits are essential if a company is to effectively serve all of its stakeholders over time— not only shareholders, but also employees, customers, and communities. Similarly, when a company truly understands and expresses its purpose, it*

functions with the focus and strategic discipline that drive long-term profit-
ability. Purpose unifies management, employees, and communities. It drives
ethical behavior and creates an essential check on actions that go against the
best interests of stakeholders. Purpose guides culture, provides a framework
for consistent decision-making, and, ultimately, helps sustain long-term
financial returns for the shareholders of your company.[38]

In this excerpt, Fink encourages the CEOs of BlackRock's portfolio companies to serve all its stakeholders—an important aspect of sustainable business practice, and in contrast with the current shareholder-centric paradigm.

Between engagement forums and standards bodies such as the UNPRI, and universal owners such as Japan's Government Pension Investment Fund, there is ample cause for optimism about making progress towards establishing a common framework for ESG and sustainable investing products. This would be a positive step—not just for citizens who are eager to invest in a sustainable way, but also for the betterment of society and the planet.

PART III

EMPOWERING LOCAL COMMUNITIES

CHAPTER 10

LOCAL DEVELOPMENT

The Bangalore Miracle

Located in its more isolated southern tip, Bangalore was never one of the major cities of the Indian subcontinent—it did not have the power and status of Delhi, Mumbai, Kolkata, or Chennai. When feudal lord Kempe Gowda founded the city in 1537, his mother gave him two instructions: "Build lakes, plant trees." This quite literally laid the foundations of Bangalore's reputation as a sleepy but pleasant city for much of the 20th century—prized by pensioners for its all-round pleasant temperatures, as well as its natural beauty.

Fast-forward to 2019 when Bangalore was named the most dynamic city in the world by JLL City Momentum Index,[1] topping even Silicon Valley on this metric. It is an essential base for any serious global Big Tech company or venture-capital fund. Bangalore has come a long way. The city (along with Hyderabad and Chennai) is set to see the fastest GDP growth among all Indian cities up to 2030.[2] Bangalore's technology industry now adds more than 200,000 jobs a year, provides employment to nearly ten million people,[3] and makes up 40 percent of India's IT industry. Most of these jobs are much higher paid than average incomes in urban areas across India. More broadly, India's technology industry, which has risen on the back of Bangalore's success, accounts for almost $85 billion in annual exports and places India as the world's leading exporter of Information and Communications Technology (ICT), according to the Global Innovation Index.[4]

How did Bangalore go from a feudal backwater to a superstar tech city in India—a country which ranks 122nd out of 187 for income per-capita? It is a story that can be understood by taking the perspective of bold community builders who shared a common vision of Bangalore as a global tech capital. They forged strong partnerships between government, research institutes, and entrepreneurs and also made extremely good use of Bangalore's factor advantages: cheap land and low-cost, well-educated labor. If Bangalore could reach these heights within the Indian context, it must tell us that world-class innovation has the potential to take root almost anywhere on Earth.

It all started in the 1970s with a man called R. K. Baliga. He had studied at the Indian Institute of Science in Bangalore, one of India's most prestigious universities, before working in the US for General Electric as a test engineer. His experience in the US had a profound effect on him. He dreamed of making his native Bangalore into the Silicon Valley of India—an ambition that was met with derision in India and the US alike. But Baliga was not deterred by the naysayers. He won the support of the Chief Minister of Karnataka to establish "Electronic City" on a 332-acre plot of land next to a couple of villages on the outskirts of Bangalore.

It is hard to exaggerate how big an achievement this was for Baliga—one that owed a lot to the foresight of the chief minister. India was deeply bureaucratic in the 1970s, making business creation extremely difficult. Moreover, obtaining land was (and remains) notoriously difficult because most land is owned by smallholder farmers, and politicians are loath to lose votes by upsetting them.

Electronic City was officially established by Karnataka State Electronics Development Corporation (Keonics), a promotion agency for the electronics industry, of which Baliga was the chairman. Keonics would play a pivotal role in attracting Western technology companies like Hewlett Packard and Siemens to Bangalore. It also spurred the growth of Indian tech titans such as Wipro and Infosys.

Bangalore first pierced the international consciousness in 1989 when a General Electric representative travelled to India on a mission to sell airplanes. The Indian government asked him to set up an office in the country as a favor. GE collaborated with Wipro to establish a base in Bangalore, thereby bringing international attention to a city most foreigners had never heard of.

As Electronic City was getting going, Bangalore benefitted from a transformational change. By the 1990s, India was beginning to remove the shackles of its highly restrictive economy. Along with the rollout of the internet in India, its liberalization drive would help turbocharge the technology ecosystem in Bangalore.

This is where some bold entrepreneurship came into play, especially by a man named Raman Roy. He saw an opportunity to use the internet to connect to markets on the other side of the world. It would herald a new phenomenon in international commerce: business process outsourcing (BPO). His business model used the IT-savvy, English-speaking talent in Bangalore for the benefit of clients thousands of miles away. Roy went on to set up call centers for both American Express and General Electric in the 1990s and other first-mover Western companies that outsourced to Bangalore, like British Airways, Swissair, and Texas Instruments.

Today, the wider city hosts major global technology companies such as Google, Amazon, and Apple, as well as the headquarters of countless homegrown giants. But Bangalore's prowess goes far beyond BPO. Of the top ten global IT services companies, half are Indian. The city also has deep expertise in computer-chip design, systems software, and telecommunications (such as satellite technology). The technology industry has spilled over into adjacent sectors—a key characteristic of highly successful economic hubs. For example, Shell, the energy company, has one of its three R&D centers in Bangalore, the others being in Amsterdam and Houston.

Having grown to India's third-largest city, with ten million inhabitants, Bangalore's success has radiated great optimism. The Karnataka state government wants to generate 20,000 more start-ups in sectors like biotechnology, IT, tourism, and agricultural technology by 2020. It has established a fund in order to lure entrepreneurs from across India to meet this goal. Meanwhile, the federal government plans to fund up to fifty worthy start-ups nationwide in 2018–19 with grants of $150,000 each and is funding five incubation hubs on the Karnataka coast.

If such an economic miracle could happen in Bangalore, why couldn't it happen anywhere? In this chapter, we will build on the paradigms of Inclusive Governance and Investing With Purpose to show how local communities can take control of their own economic development in an increasingly interconnected world.

The Global-Local Pendulum

Bangalore, New York, London, Dubai, and Singapore—along with cities that sprouted in China's special economic zones (SEZs)—are iconic examples of what I call innovative, connected, and entrepreneurial (ICE) hubs. ICE hubs thrived on the globalization wave from the 1980s up to the Global Financial Crisis of 2007–8. In emerging economies, cities like Bangalore and the Chinese SEZs exploited their lower labor costs and other factor advantages to gain footholds in specific sectors in which they built up increasing specialization. Meanwhile, Western hubs benefitted from the ensuing trade and global connectivity by facilitating access to their large markets with financial, logistics, and information services.

We will recall from chapter 1 that Washington Consensus policies urged countries to open up to new global customer markets and suppliers. According to this policy doctrine, countries would make themselves attractive to foreign investment and trade by lowering taxes and deregulating markets.

But what the Washington Consensus didn't properly appreciate was the need to complement its focus on openness with commensurate investments in concrete strategies to build up local capabilities. The aftermath of the Global Financial Crisis shook confidence in globalization, as it became clear that many localities in the West—especially cities, towns, and rural areas previously dependent on manufacturing—were struggling to recover and risked being left behind entirely.

Recognizing the growing populist sentiment in marginalized communities and the mounting backlash against globalization, some prominent theorists have suggested that it's time that the pendulum swung back to focus on local communities. Bruce Katz and Jeremy Nowak refer to this movement as "New Localism" in their 2018 book The New Localism: How Cities Can Thrive in the Age of Populism.[5] In their view, bipartisan gridlock at the national level combined with constrained federal budgets have hindered progress on the key challenges of the day: widening inequality, the need for more high-paying jobs, low productivity, environmental sustainability, and urban regeneration.

In response, they believe that cities should be empowered to take the lead in rejuvenating the economy. Katz and Nowak point to several examples, such as the former steel city of Pittsburgh, Pennsylvania, as success stories that illustrate their paradigm. Once a major steel-producing town, Pittsburgh has pulled itself out of the doldrums of deindustrialization and reinvented itself as an emerging technology hub, by employing a model that bears strong resemblance to the case of Bangalore.

Pittsburgh's rejuvenation story began in March 1979, when a reactor at Three Mile Island Nuclear Generating Station experienced a cooling malfunction and partial meltdown of its reactor core. Carnegie Mellon's Robotics Institute, recently established thanks to a $3 million grant from manufacturing giant Westinghouse Electric Corporation, responded to the crisis by building remote-controlled robots that could investigate the wreckage of the nuclear reactor and help to develop a mitigation plan. At the time, robotics seemed liked mere science fiction. Yet to meet the challenge of the nuclear plant cleanup, the roboticists transformed "the stationary robot used for repetitive tasks into a new class of technology and application: robots on wheels outfitted with cameras, lights, radiation detectors, vacuums, scoops, scrapers, drills, and a high-pressure spray nozzle."[6]

The roboticists gradually created an entirely new market, small at first, that eventually led to self-driving vehicles today. By 1986, mobile robots made in Pittsburgh were deployed to monitor active volcanoes in Alaska, to search for meteorites in Antarctica, and to sweep for buried hazards across large areas in Nevada. In 1996, the National Robotics Engineering Center (NREC) was founded within Carnegie Mellon's Robotics Institute.

With this start, agglomeration effects took hold, and Pittsburgh's robotics industry continued to grow throughout the early 2000s. Pittsburgh is now known as "Roboburgh" due to its robotics prowess. Dozens of companies have formed, thousands of jobs have been created, and capital has flooded in. For example, the accelerator Innovation Works has invested $72 million to seed fund 300 local companies since 1999, which have gone on to raise $1.8 billion in follow-up funding. Carnegie Robotics, a spin-off of the NREC, was founded in 2010 to commercialize and productize the NREC's research prowess. Employment in robotics grew 300 percent from 2011–16, the vast majority being highly paid.

A key ingredient underpinning Pittsburgh's success is what Katz and Nowak refer to as "networked governance"[7]—using innovation and multi-stakeholder networks to tackle "complex urban challenges such as economic opportunity, climate change, and infrastructure."[8] Pittsburgh's benefited from an "extended and concerted focus on robotics by Carnegie Mellon researchers, local entrepreneurs, philanthropic investors, and city policymakers."[9] In 1985, a group called Strategy 21 was established between the City of Pittsburgh, Allegheny County, Carnegie Mellon, and the University of Pittsburgh, in close collaboration with philanthropies and business leaders.[10] The collective was focused on diversifying the economy after the collapse of the steel industry and rapid depopulation of the city. It focused on achieving four goals: winning the federal competition for the Software Engineering Institute at Carnegie Mellon, obtaining one of the five federally funded supercomputers, advocating for a new airport terminal, and creating the NREC. Strategy 21 succeeded in achieving all four of its objectives.

By putting itself on the map, Pittsburgh benefited from a flow of national and international capital, as well as some of the best entrepreneurial talent from around the globe. Originally, a small trickle of migrants was attracted by Westinghouse's need for engineers; now, a wave of migrants has been lured by work in Carnegie Mellon, the University of Pittsburgh, and the University of Pittsburgh Medical Center. Pittsburgh has also invested heavily in STEM training for its local workers, to power its new technology-driven economy.

Katz and Nowak, as well as theorists of a similar bent like Michael Porter[11] and Richard Florida, all focus on the formation of large agglomerations as the inevitable—and desirable—outcome in modern economic development. But as we have already seen, although cities and mega-clusters may create great prosperity, this can also come with significant side effects. In Bangalore, 25–35 percent of the population now lives in slums, because many people have been lured to the city due to its economic growth but have become priced out of proper housing.[12] The city is also choked by some of the worst traffic jams anywhere in the world, as public infrastructure struggles to keep up. Anybody that's been to San Francisco knows how challenging the housing and homelessness problems there have become. Indeed, due to its unaffordability, San Francisco is no longer regarded as one of the top twenty most dynamic cities globally.[13] Rather than value creation being concentrated in cities—which contributes to the negative side effects we see in places like Bangalore and San Francisco—it would surely be better if other localities also were centers of prosperity.

So the question becomes whether local development miracles can take root in small towns and rural areas. If so, is this the answer to the challenge of rejuvenating deindustrialized towns in the American heartland, or the North of England, the Italian Mezzogiorno, and all the other local communities left behind in the rush to globalize? To answer these questions, let's pay another visit to Germany.

In chapter 4, we discovered that Germany has an abundance of prosperous small towns and is a role model of Inclusive Governance. Two key ingredients of Germany's success are its highly devolved system of governance and its deep network of local-business funding. The country is divided into sixteen states and over 400 districts, each of which can set local policy and gather local taxes. In fact, over 50 percent of German taxes are raised at the subnational level. This is comparable with the US, where 44 percent of taxes are collected sub-nationally, but much higher than the UK, where only 6 percent of taxes are collected by local government.[14] In addition to strong public finances at the local level, Germany's 400 local savings-banks—or Sparkassen—work closely with local government to channel funds into local businesses. The Sparkassen are noncommercial, public-sector entities whose controlling owners are municipalities or districts. Usually they are chaired by a local politician. Funded by Sparkassen, Germany's Mittelstand firms—small and medium-sized businesses with typically less than €50 million in annual revenues—have always engaged the local community as important stakeholders. For example, Mittelstand companies regularly partner with local vocational schools to offer apprenticeships and employment to local youth. In short, small-town Germany has enjoyed a tight nexus between local business, government, and civil society for many decades.

Mittelstand companies are highly skilled at incremental innovations, often in relatively unloved—some may say "boring"—niches of the global economy. BHS Corrugated, a company that produces machinery for producing corrugated cardboard, has perfected such innovations. The company's CEO spends about a quarter of his time travelling the world to understand what his customers want. In the EU and US, there is high demand for high-performance machines with lots of settings. Meanwhile, customers in Asia and Africa prefer slower but cheaper machines. Therefore, the company has developed different machines for different markets to cater to these needs.[15] This is just one example of the thousands of small innovations that have helped to sustain local Mittelstand in small towns that rarely grab the limelight. In the wake of AI and automation, perhaps the model of innovation will have to evolve from the incremental to the market-creating variety, but the broad model of local decision-making and collaboration will continue to be a source of strength.

ICE Hubs

Fundamentally, I don't see a big difference in the formula for successful local development between a small German town and big cities like Bangalore and Pittsburgh. They are all places that have, to a large extent, laid a foundation of Inclusive Governance and invested with purpose in sustainable development. But these local economic miracles also have a distinctive signature—they have all emerged from hubs that unleashed innovation, connectedness, and entrepreneurship (ICE). Let's look at each of these three elements in turn.

Innovation: ICE Hubs are Market-Creating Factories

ICE hubs have a participative culture of solving specific societal, environmental, or economic challenges—and in the process, creating new markets that employ thousands of people, like the BPO industry in Bangalore. They are also adept at evolving to new opportunities, such as AI in the case of Pittsburgh or biotech in the case of Singapore. Innovative, knowledge-intensive new sectors offering high-paying jobs are magnets for youth, who typically arrive in the locality to work at a university, corporation, or start-up that is advancing the field, and often end up starting entrepreneurial ventures of their own.

ICE hubs also take careful account of their locality's factor advantages, weaving them into the fabric of the new markets they create. Bangalore capitalized on its availability of land to build Electronic City and the many business parks and research centers that followed. It made use of its pools of lower-cost, well-educated technology-talent from the Indian Institute of Science and the Indian Institute of Technology. Its favorable climate was also an important factor in attracting creative workers and their families to live and work in the city.

Connectedness: ICE Hubs are Nodes for Capital, Talent, and Ideas

On a local level, ICE hubs are beacons of networked governance in which the private sector, universities and research organizations, and local government operate in close partnership. A prerequisite of this is devolution—a key element of Inclusive Governance. The local government has real power to grow business ecosystems by raising local taxes, zoning and developing land, funding infrastructure, nurturing start-ups, and so on. As Katz has remarked, "Networked governance is really a form of participatory democracy. Our vision of city power extends beyond traditional governmental power, to market and city power. What is happening among many of the stakeholders is a kind of co-governing that is evidence-driven, data-rich, and outcome-oriented."[16]

ICE hubs rally around a shared development vision that all the stakeholders are bought into. Pittsburgh catapulted itself to success through the Strategy 21 collective, Bangalore through Keonics, and Singapore has done it numerous times through a variety of governmental bodies. More recent vision statements include New York City's OneNYC 2050 plan and Stockholm's Vision 2040, both of which have a low-carbon economy at their center.

Critical to innovation and entrepreneurship are the serendipitous collisions and networking between entrepreneurs, venture capitalists, NGOs and foundations, researchers, and government officials. ICE hubs are buzzing with meet-up groups, hack-a-thons, co-working spaces, and conferences that foster these connections and enable the exchange of ideas and the shaping of new business models.

On a global level, ICE hubs attract capital, talent, and IP because they have made themselves jurisdictions that are easy to do business in and that are also well connected to capital markets. They are highly attractive locations for investment because so many new companies are created in them every year. Bangalore creates around 1,200 tech start-ups annually.[17]

Knowledge workers flock to ICE hubs because they are physically attractive places to live. Some hubs like Bangalore are lucky to have excellent climates and natural beauty. But cities can't rest on their laurels, and Bangalore's traffic and unaffordability are forcing talented Indians to consider other, less clogged cities. ICE hubs have to work hard to remain attractive place to live.

They have excellent transport connections within their locality and to other parts of their region, country, and the world. Dubai is one of the best-connected cities in the world for shipping and aviation. It has used this as a springboard to become a global hub in logistics (sea and air), retail, tourism, and hospitality, and a regional hub for financial services and corporate headquarters.

Hubs also put themselves on the map through winning marketing strategies, such as conferences and sporting events. Abu Dhabi hosts the Abu Dhabi Grand Prix, Mubadala World Tennis Championships, CNN Middle East's HQ, and the HQ of the International Renewable Energy Association.

Entrepreneurship: ICE Hubs Celebrate Entrepreneurship

ICE hubs are places where entrepreneurs thrive. Through their educational institutions—from schools, to universities, to adult-education centers—they incubate lifelong learners who go on to help start businesses or launch new products and are serial problem-solvers. Schools teach risk-taking, self-reliance, problem solving, and creativity, and they encourage pupils to be ambitious. These are among the attitudes that studies show millennials and Generation Z—born from the mid-1990s onwards—are already displaying to a larger extent than previous generations.[18]

Society in Bangalore was conservative in the 1980s and 1990s. The idea that someone would turn down a job with an established business to set up their own was frowned upon. Now, all that has changed. Stories like Sharath Babu's have become modern folklore. Babu came from a slum-dwelling family whose main source of income was the steamed rice-cakes his mother sold from a pavement shack. However, he made his way to IIM Ahmedabad (part of a network of management schools that equal Harvard in prestige in India), but turned down a plum job with a multinational that would have paid off all his debts to set up his own company. With just $30 in seed capital, he went on to found FoodKing, which delivers food to urban professionals, and had a turnover of over £1.2 million in 2018.[19] Bangalore's IIM now offers entrepreneurship as an elective. In a setup becoming typical of pro-entrepreneurship localities, it has also partnered with global chipmaker Intel on the "Next Big Idea" to identify forty business plans whose creators will receive intense mentorship and introductions to venture-capital funds. ICE hubs attract many such sources of investment capital for local development, innovation, and entrepreneurship.

Beyond Cities

Towns and rural areas have become the ground zero of populism in many countries, reflecting a deep dissatisfaction with the status quo. For example, two-thirds of US rural and small-town voters voted for President Trump, while 55 percent of rural voters in Britain voted for Brexit.[20] Despite decades of urbanization, these areas still account for a large chunk of these countries' and others' populations. According to Gallup, only about one-third of Americans live in big cities, while almost 40 percent live in towns or rural areas.[21]

Connected Towns

Of course, not all towns and rural areas are the same. The segments of these communities showing the greatest signs of revitalization are "connected towns"—typically larger settlements within two- or three-hours' reach of a major city via good transportation links. While they have their own independent economies, connected towns benefit greatly from the proximity to customers, specialized talent, and professional services in the nearby city. In addition, connected towns often act as local-business and trading hubs for an ecosystem of other smaller towns and rural communities in the vicinity.

A good example of a connected town that is reshaping itself into an ICE hub is Bournemouth. A seaside town located two hours from London with a population of 180,000 people, Bournemouth had become a haven for pensioners who were drawn to its good weather, tranquil surroundings, and seven miles of pristine, sandy beaches. In some districts of the urban area, the median age had been pushing seventy.[22]

But in the past decade, something special has been happening in Bournemouth. It is now one of only two boroughs in the UK where the population is getting younger. As we saw in chapter 6, a young workforce is vital for economic growth and vitality. So how did an aging resort town become one of the biggest youth-magnets in the country?

Central to Bournemouth's revival has been its thriving digital economy, the fastest growing in the UK, according to a study published in 2015.[23] The town particularly excels in digital marketing and is also well known for its stable of visual-effects firms. Overall, the creative-tech sector generates almost £400 million in revenues and employs more than 7,500 residents.[24] Bournemouth is also the European headquarters for cybersecurity solutions multinational ESET and the European technology-and-operation hub for JP Morgan.

As with Bangalore, Pittsburgh, and so many other ICE hubs, universities have played a key role in powering Bournemouth's economic turnaround. Since 1989 Bournemouth University has housed the UK's National Centre for Computer Animation (NCCA), which is regarded as one of the world's leading institutions for computer graphics. Notably, a steady stream of graduates from the NCCA has gone on to achieve success in the visual-effects industry—NCCA graduates worked on all five films nominated for the 2018 Oscars in the category of visual effects: Blade Runner 2049; Guardians of the Galaxy Vol. 2; Kong: Skull Island; Star Wars: The Last Jedi; and War for the Planet of the Apes.[25]

Arts University Bournemouth has also played a significant role in spurring the digital-technology industry. With funding from the regional-development agency, the university launched an incubator in the early 2000s. Run by local visionary Matt Desmier, the incubator launched seventy-five businesses in four years, with a 95 percent survival rate.[26] In 2019 the university is also opening an Innovation Studio, which will support digital startups through mentorship and access to the university's extensive facilities. The studio was funded by the Dorset Local Enterprise Partnership

(LEP)—a voluntary partnership between the regional authorities and businesses to help determine local economic priorities and lead economic development and job creation. LEPs were set up by the British government in 2011, and when used well, offer a good framework for networked governance.

To build on its connections with the creative media and technology sectors in London, Bournemouth has worked hard to build its reputation for digital innovation on the global stage. Since 2012, Bournemouth University has run the BFX Festival for special effects. BFX started off as a student competition to identify the next wave of talent in visual effects and animation and has morphed into an international conference, bringing together leaders in the visual effects, animation, visualization, and computer-games industries. A natural connector, Matt Desmier from the Arts University incubator also organized a series of annual "Silicon Beach" festivals to put Bournemouth's creative-media capabilities on the map.

Small-Town Manufacturing

So far, we've seen how cities and larger, connected towns can steer a course to a prosperous future. However, a significant part of the population lives in smaller towns and rural areas like Selma, Alabama, population 19,000, where half of all households earn less than $25,000 a year, or Beckley, West Virginia, where more than one in five residents live below the poverty line.[27] The list of such American communities could go on and on. A similar problem exists in other Western nations: the seaside and northern towns of the UK (most have not done as well as Bournemouth), the rapidly aging towns of Southern Europe, and the poorer towns of Eastern Germany.

But when we look at smaller towns that are doing well—like German towns hosting Mittelstand companies, or towns like Newton, Iowa, which is a wind-power manufacturing hub, or Columbus, Indiana, which is the headquarters of engine manufacturer Cummins—a common thread seems to be the presence of some form of specialized, advanced manufacturing that generates an abundance of high-paying jobs. Even though manufacturing jobs have ebbed away from small towns in the US due to off-shoring or automation, the manufacturing sector is still a larger employer in these communities than agriculture, mining, forestry, and fishing combined.[28] Higher-value manufacturing that relies heavily on R&D and design may have a key role to play in reviving small towns and rural areas in the future. Dorset, the county where Bournemouth is located, provides an interesting example of how a region can build up a diverse, advanced manufacturing-and-engineering sector worth about £1.4 billion in gross-value-added (GVA) as of 2019, employing 25,000 people,[29] and covering a range of sectors such as aerospace, defense, and marine technologies.

The Dorset coast between the towns of Poole and Christchurch form a marine technology-and-services cluster. Sunseeker International, a global manufacturer of luxury yachts, does all its manufacturing across seven production plants in the area and is seeing its strongest-ever order book. In partnership with the UK's Royal National Lifeboat Institution, which is headquartered in Poole, Sunseeker invests heavily into R&D on composite materials used in the marine industry. Making use of the spillovers in this knowledge-intensive sector, companies like Norco GRP and Finnish multinational Wärtsilä apply composite technology to tidal-power generation and other renewable-energy solutions.

Dorset also sits on the edge of an aerospace cluster in the southwest of the UK that is one of the largest in Europe.[30] Defense manufacturer Cobham, a company in the FSTE 250 Index, is located five miles north of the town. It is a market leader in aerial refueling, military-vehicle intercom systems, and satellite, radio, and wireless mobile-connectivity products. BAE Systems, one of the largest defense manufacturers in the world, also has three sites across Dorset.

The Dorset LEP has a highly ambitious plan to double the size of Dorset's economy, create 80,000 new jobs, and increase productivity by 55 percent over the next twenty years. To enable this ambitious growth plan, Dorset has plans to expand Bournemouth's international airport and improve road networks in the region. It must also continue to drive innovation, draw in top creative talent, and forge connections with global markets.

Rural Awakening

Dorset appears to be a region on its way to ICE-hub status by taking advantage of opportunities in the digital and advanced-manufacturing sectors. But what about rural areas that are far from big cities and may be dependent on agricultural and extractive sectors? Here, there are fewer clear models of success, perhaps because the ICE-hub model has not yet been tried in these areas yet. However, I believe that rural economies could be reawakened with new opportunities arising in food and agriculture industry and a variety of "green" manufacturing businesses. Since there are few clear-cut examples to date, let me illustrate the possibilities through an imaginary case study. Taking inspiration from one of my favorite authors—the late Gabriel García Márquez, the great literary genius of magical realism—let's see how a fictional rural town (which I will call Gabriel) could transform itself into an ICE hub of the modern green-economy.

Gabriel, population 7,000, is located in the Appalachian Mountains of West Virginia and is within a few hours' drive from Washington, DC, Baltimore, and Pittsburgh. It is the main town of Gabriel County, and was until recently the site of two underground coalmines owned by Century Coal, which also owns other mines in the Appalachia region. The two coalmines employ over 600 people in the county, and many more jobs are indirectly dependent on the mines in the area.

Unfortunately for the residents of Gabriel, coal is no longer competitive. By 2018, three-quarters of coal produced in the US was more expensive as a source of energy than solar or renewables.[31] The number of active coal mines decreased by more than half between 2008 and 2016, with most of the closures occurring in the Appalachia region.[32] Century Coal put off closing its Gabriel mines and zig-zagged in statements about their future. But in January 2020, the company finally announces that it can no longer keep them open.

The decision is devastating for the local community. As Gabriel's mines were already scaling down operations in the years preceding the official closure, the town's population had already been in decline. While the median age of the town's population was thirty-five in 1990, it had risen to forty-three by 2018, and over a quarter of residents were over sixty-five. Most young people had already moved to nearby big cities, and the median wage had also fallen precipitously. Reflecting on the impact of mine closures on local communities, the son of a mineworker from another coal mining town comments: "[Mining leaves] these massive swathes of just total obliteration of these mountains that you've called home and your family has called home for generations. It's just a complete erasure of that identity, and it is a violation of who you are as a person."[33]

However, Gabriel is not like the other towns in how it responds to this crisis. Bill Rainmaker, a senior vice-president (SVP) at Century Coal who is a Gabriel resident, recommends that Century Coal rezone the land to take advantage of federal government carbon-offset credit for reforestation—part of the US effort to meet commitments it made under the Paris Agreement. Gabriel County agrees and goes even further by providing sales-tax exemptions under a scheme that incentivizes the redevelopment of brownfield sites. Soon Century Coal is filling in land and planting trees.

Rainmaker has other ideas too. He persuades the board of Century Coal to install a solar farm on the land, taking advantage of the federal government's solar tax-credit, which allows commercial entities to deduct 22 percent of the cost of installation from their federal taxes.[34] After a relatively easy setup, the solar farm is soon connected to the grid and supplies residents of Gabriel Country with cheaper electricity than before. Rainmaker's next venture is more novel—he wants to use the rest of the available land above the mines to start a hydroponic indoor-farming facility.

Rainmaker succeeds in persuading Century Coal's board to back this venture. He even persuades them to make him the SVP of a new subsidiary, which subsumes all of Century Coal's assets in Gabriel. The new company is named Appalachia Greens in reference to the lettuce, herbs, and salad greens the indoor farming facility produces. Rainmaker's bet is that because Gabriel is much closer to big urban centers of the Northeast than Arizona or California, where 99 percent of these vegetables are sourced, it will be able to capture a slice of the regional market. There's a strong consumer trend to buy local produce, and the low shipping cost from Appalachia relative to the Western states makes Appalachia Greens' produce comparatively cheaper.

The company employs experts from other indoor-farming clusters, as well as some of the former mining employees who had used their lifelong learning accounts to take micro-courses in indoor farming maintenance, management, logistics, and marketing. The facility is up and running by 2021, creating even more jobs to pluck, package, and process the vegetables. One year into operations, the company boasts sixty employees, many of them former mining staff.

As the hydroponic facility gets going, the marketing department hatches a plan to supply produce in personalized, reusable boxes, directly to households and workplaces, instead of selling exclusively through distributors. The business is a resounding success with customers, who are excited about the reduction in wasteful packaging. Appalachia Greens charges a premium on its direct-delivery service and increases its profit margins. By 2023 the company grows to ninety employees, as more specialized logistics, marketing, and factory floor workers are hired.

Flush with the success of its circular business model, Appalachia Greens decides to branch out into wine and cider making. The region has a favorable environment for classic wines like Riesling and Pinot Noir due to its cool climate. By 2025 Appalachia Greens employs 200 people in its various business units. Artisanal wine and fruit drinks are bottled at a small bottling facility in the town and sent to neighboring towns and a few hipster bars in the big cities. The bottling and indoor farming facilities benefit from cheap energy produced by the solar farm.

Tapping into a consumer demand for fortified products, Appalachia Greens soon begins fortifying its beverages with nutrients, using the knowledge it has gained in its hydroponic business unit. The immense popularity of the new brand of "nutra-drinks" attracts the attention of researchers from the University of Maryland's Department of Nutrition and Food Science, who start visiting Appalachia Greens to learn about the new techniques. They begin carrying out joint research projects with the company, and after a while, these projects become a modular option for students in the department.

Gradually, Gabriel makes a name for itself in the metro areas of DC, Baltimore, and Pittsburgh as a place where nature meets green enterprise. Devotees of the Appalachia Greens brand visit to taste local produce and enjoy the area's lakes and hiking trails. By 2030, Bill Rainmaker and Jennifer Miller, a government official of Gabriel County, begin to discuss the next wave of growth opportunities for the region. Miller has studied economic development at a local technical-college and is keen to help the county prosper. Rainmaker and Miller reckon they can build on the area's growing tourist traffic to develop hospitality and outdoor-recreation businesses. Gabriel sits by a beautiful mountain lake, but the waterfront and marina have been in a poor state for years. An unused coal-drop yard near the waterfront scars the landscape, but Rainmaker and Miller believe there is great potential if it is cleaned up.

The county partners with Appalachia Greens and other local businesses to create the Gabriel Development Corporation (GDC). GDC's first mission is to redevelop the waterfront area. It works with the council to rezone the land for commercial property development, before approaching investors who are excited by the county's growing tourist traffic. The development corporation soon publishes the Gabriel Vision 2040—a ten-year development plan that envisions the town as a renowned center for agricultural innovation, health and nutrition, and sustainable lifestyle, where the population grows to 25,000 and the median wage rises by 30 percent.

Within a few years, the marina redevelopment is completed, and a resort-hotel complex is up and running. The GDC also funds the construction of a new apartment block on brownfield land adjacent to the hotel complex to provide housing for the increasing number of graduate and PhD students studying in Gabriel. To cater to the students and tourists, coffee shops, bars, and restaurants pop up around the marina and a new downtown quarter is born. Meanwhile, the resort opens a spa that offers "healthy-living" retreats that specialize in designing "micronutrient" dietary programs personalized to each guest's health profile.

The health spa partners with NutraGabriel, a spin-off venture of Appalachia Greens' fortified-drinks division, which has conducted years of research on creating the optimal diet—down to the micro-nutrient level—based on the analysis of a vast array of genetic, tissue, and microbiome data on individuals. At the health spa, visitors provide a variety of bio-samples and undergo various tests to "feed" NutraGabriel's AI-driven dietary-design models. Visitors have the option to subscribe to a service that will deliver freshly prepared meals, adhering to their personal "micronutrient" dietary plans, to their workplace or residence. NutraGabriel works with Appalachia Greens' food-delivery and fortified-drinks divisions to operationalize this service.

NutraGabriel's meteoric success creates a battery of high-paid jobs for data scientists and marketing analysts, drawing in hundreds of young workers to the area. It also attracts the attention of UHealth, the country's largest health insurer, which takes a 20 percent equity stake in the company. UHealth sees great potential in NutraGabriel's banks of bio-data and its capabilities in diet modification. The insurer offers the service to its members in the expectation that improved diets will reduce the incidence of chronic diseases, and thereby reduce average healthcare costs per patient.

By 2040, Gabriel is completely transformed from the dying coal town it was just twenty years earlier. Although this imaginary example makes some assumptions about future technologies, regulatory incentives, and consumer attitudes, I believe it paints a plausible path for rural development that harnesses the power of innovation, connection and entrepreneurship. Gabriel progressively innovates to create new markets and promotes entrepreneurial ventures within a framework of networked governance. It makes itself an attractive place to live and visit through the sustainable development of its natural assets. And it connects itself to capital, talent, and IP by forging relationships with universities and attracting the attention of investors.

ICE Communities in a Turbulent World

Powerful global trends and events can severely test the resilience of even the strongest ICE communities. While Pittsburgh, Bangalore, Dorset, and Gabriel may have many of the right elements in place, they are not immune to international currents.

In Bournemouth and Dorset's case, the overriding concern is Brexit. Although a weaker pound has made some companies' exports more competitive, the prospect of Brexit is already dampening business confidence and holding back investment. Outpost VFX, one of the growing visual-effects companies in Bournemouth, has decided to open an office in Barcelona rather than expand in Britain. JP Morgan's technology-and-operations center could leave the town in a no-deal Brexit scenario.[35] Bournemouth University, which has been a magnet for international talent, has also reported for the first time that some of its faculty openings had no applications from EU candidates.[36]

The trade war raging between the US and China is having wide ripple effects on ICE communities throughout the world. From a small fishing village in the 1970s, Shenzhen has risen to international stardom as one of China's wealthiest cities and home to tens of thousands of manufacturers making components for a wide range of products. But today it is a city in crisis. US tariffs slapped on Chinese imports such on USB cables have made it very difficult for Chinese exports to stay competitive. Combined with rising rents and wage bills, many manufacturers have moved to places like Vietnam or India—or are expecting to go bust.[37]

In the next chapter, I will look at how cracks in the global structures of trade and cooperation have contributed to the tensions behind developments such as Brexit and the US-China trade war. While global connectivity is an essential driver in the growth of ICE hubs, unless global norms engender some form of a level playing field, faith in that connectivity can start to crumble.

CHAPTER 11

REFORMING GLOBALIZATION

Backlash Against Globalization

2019 will be remembered as a year when the march of globalization was dealt several body blows. Although the benefits of the past three decades of globalization have not been evenly distributed, the solution is hardly to choke off trade altogether. Under its newly elected Prime Minister Boris Johnson, the UK government is strongly committed to leaving the European Union's economic structures. Meanwhile, 2019 saw President Trump continuing to escalate his trade war with China by progressively ratcheting up tariffs on imports. Although a Phase One Trade Agreement seems on the cards, there is much left to resolve between the two nations.[1] How rapidly the sentiment has shifted away from free trade and global integration!

As I explained in the previous chapter, the key to local prosperity lies in sparking the dynamo of private enterprise in ICE hubs, which are connected to each other by the global flows of goods, services, capital, talent, and ideas. Throughout history, whenever we have choked off this "lifeblood," local economies have suffered. In late 18th century England, the Corn Laws, which put steep import-duties on cereal grains, were introduced to keep grain prices high and protect domestic producers. However, the restrictions on grain imports led to soaring prices and brought about widespread malnourishment as bread became unaffordable for average cit-izens. Two hundred years later, the mere prospect of Brexit is hurting the British economically, with capital spending down by 11 percent on average across firms and productivity down by 2–5 percent as a result of the refer-endum, according to Bank of England research.[2] And the US-China trade war has deeply wounded Shenzhen's manufacturers, US farmers, and a host of US and Chinese companies. For example, John Deere has announced that it will cut tractor production by one-fifth at two of its North Ameri-can factories,[3] potentially putting at risk the livelihoods of communities like Waterloo in Iowa (population: 70,000).

These are worrying developments, not just for countless towns in UK, China, and the US, but also for trading hubs across the world. Germany, whose Mittelstand hubs rely heavily on international trade, has been flirt-ing with recession due to the knock-on effects of the US-China trade war on its economy. Why have the UK and the US taken actions that are stir-ring up the international order, and what does it mean for the prosperity of ICE hubs? In this chapter, I will first explore the benefits of regional trade and cooperation blocs like the EU, before looking at the reasons why the British people chose to give them up in favor of regaining more national sovereignty. I will then turn our attention to the flaws in the global trading system that sparked the US-China trade war, before examining how these festering issues could be addressed.

Regional Power Blocs

The decades following World War II and leading up to the Global Finan-cial Crisis marked one the most intense periods of trade liberalization ever to happen. In 1994, the conclusion of the Uruguay Round of trade negoti-ations transformed the General Agreement on Tariffs and Trade (GATT), which had underpinned international trade since the end of World War II, into the World Trade Organization (WTO) that we know today. It was the largest trade negotiation ever undertaken, and it covered everything from "toothbrushes to pleasure boats, from banking to telecommunications, from the genes of wild rice to AIDS treatments." There have been incre-mental changes to the WTO since the Uruguay Round, such as lifting tariffs on IT products.[4] The Doha Round of negotiations began in 2001 but has remained deadlocked due to disagreements between developed nations and developing ones over the former's use of agricultural subsidies.

Layered on top of the WTO regime (and GATT before it), numerous regional economic-cooperation groups like the EU, NAFTA, and ASEAN have formed over the years. These regional groups reduce tariffs, harmonize regulations beyond the requirements of the WTO, and give each member-nation access to the much bigger regional market. This can be particularly beneficial for small and medium-sized countries, which is why fifty-four of the African Union's fifty-five countries signed up to the African Continental Free Trade Agreement (AfCFTA) in 2019. The agreement aims to reduce 90 percent of tariffs and create a single market with the free movement of goods and services.

Regionalization also creates the opportunity to integrate capital markets, thereby expanding the channels for wealth from savers to reach corporate and government investments. The EU, having already issued a common currency in 1999, is now attempting to establish a capital-markets union by harmonizing regulations between its members. This move will broaden access to capital for countries striving to meet the dual imperative of the Sustainable Development Challenge and the growth of local ICE hubs.

Since the Global Financial Crisis, the overall level of trade has continued to grow, but its growth rate has slowed down, and it has become more regional in nature. From 2000–12, the share of trade in goods between countries in the same region declined from 51 to 45 percent. However, since then, the trend has gone in reverse, and the proportion of intraregional trade has grown. This partly reflects the fading significance of offshore, low-cost manufacturing. Only 18 percent of the trade in goods is now based on labor-cost arbitrage—defined as exports from economies where GDP per capita is one-fifth of the importing economy.[5] Other factors, such as availability of skilled labor, proximity to customers, the ability to deploy high-tech automation, and the quality of infrastructure, are now significant determinants for companies deciding where to locate production. These trends strengthen the case for production closer to home and increase the significance of regional economic unions even further.

Membership in a regional economic union also allows a country to project more influence on the global stage than it could individually. To illustrate this point, let's look ahead to the world as it is likely to be in two or three decades. On our present course, four players will be the dominant economic powers: China, the US, the EU, and India. Together, they will account for about 66 percent of global GDP in 2050 (see Figure 10-1).[6]

In market exchange-rate terms, China's economy is expected to surpass the US by 2030.[7] So, the US will no longer be top dog, but it will still be twice as rich as China on a per-capita basis by 2050. Strikingly, India's economy will grow from being about one-seventh of the US' in 2020, to a little less than one-third in 2050. Germany, which I'll use as a proxy for the EU, will remain close to US levels of income per capita.[8]

As Figure 10-1 shows, no other country—not even Japan, Brazil, or the Russian Federation—will come close to the big four in terms of economic weight. Of course, none of the EU's member nations on their own would be considered on a par with the other three economic superpowers. However, as part of the EU, their collective policy decisions reverberate around the world in what has been called the "Brussels effect."[9] For example, once the EU enacted the General Data Protection Regulation (GDPR), virtually all multinationals had to abide by the regulations because they could not afford to give up access to hundreds of millions of middle-class consumers living across the union. However, the EU often fails to operationalize its economic power, like the US and China do. As economics commentator Martin Sandbu writes in the Financial Times, "A similar power is Europe's for the taking. What it must find is the will to use it."[10] But the fact remains, merely by enacting regulations, the EU makes its power felt globally.

Looking forward, unless the former Soviet states and countries in Africa, Latin America, the Middle East, and Asia (excluding China and India) can collectivize their economic power into strong regional economic unions such as the EU—or unless they align themselves closely with the big four—they will have diminishing influence on international affairs.

Given the growing importance of regional economic unions, it is unlikely that leaving the EU will be positive for Britain's long-term economic prosperity. Let's take a look at the plight of Britain's automotive industry to illustrate this point. After a torrid period in the 1970s, Britain's automotive industry experienced a renaissance in the 1980s when Japanese carmakers such as Honda and Nissan were lured to the UK because of its access to Europe's single market. With a base in Britain, these manufacturers could sell to hundreds of millions of the world's richest consumers and source parts without any tariffs or checks at borders.

FIGURE 10-1: SHARE OF THE WORLD ECONOMY IN 2050[11]

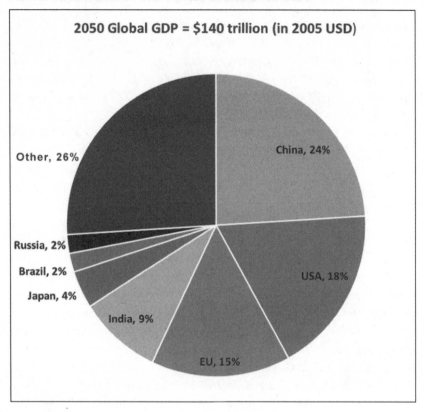

2050 Global GDP = $140 trillion (in 2005 USD)

China, 24%

Other, 26%

Russia, 2%

Brazil, 2%

Japan, 4%

India, 9%

EU, 15%

USA, 18%

Since the prospect of Brexit has threatened this entire paradigm, investment in the British automotive industry since the referendum has fallen off a cliff, declining by 80 percent. Production volumes are down 9 percent and production forecasts by 17 percent.[12] Honda is closing its Swindon plant in southern England, and Nissan has announced that it will divert production from its Sunderland plant in the northeast of the country.[13] Not only will these communities lose thousands of high-paying manufacturing jobs, the local concentration of automotive manufacturing know-how will gradually ebb away. Indeed, a white paper from Oxford University's Saïd Business School estimates that the UK could lose 35 percent of its production volume in the next decade if it leaves the EU without a special deal and trades only on WTO terms.

Rodrik's Trilemma and the Future of the Nation-State

Given the growing benefits of regional economic unions, how can we explain Britain's decision to leave the EU? Brexit polling data seemed to suggest that the single biggest reason that people voted for Brexit was "that decisions about the UK should be taken in the UK."[14] In effect, voters appeared to eschew economic integration with the EU in favor of greater sovereignty over the UK's affairs.

This sentiment is an example of a broader set of trade-offs that Harvard economist Dani Rodrik has termed a "trilemma," in which "we cannot have hyper-globalization, democracy, and national self-determination all at once."[15] Rodrik believes that countries can fully achieve at most two at any given time—they must choose.[16]

The first option is to embrace globalization and make the sovereign decision to enter into trade and cooperation agreements. But in doing so, a country takes away the democratic decision-making power of its citizens to change the rules of those cooperation agreements. Many of those powers are ceded to the governance bodies of a regional economic union or a global trade organization. Over the last thirty years, much of the world has selected this option and plunged headlong into global economic integration. However, as I explained in chapter 2, although the net-total benefit of global trade has been positive, it has not been shared equally. Certain emerging markets—particularly China—have benefited tremendously from global economic integration, whereas many communities in the West have lost out, leaving behind great swathes of marginalized citizens.

Worse still, when countries fall on hard times, membership in regional economic unions or global trading agreements limits the levers they can use to cushion the impact. For example, they can't apply export subsidies, put up capital controls, or raise tariffs on imports—at least, they're not supposed to. In the eurozone, countries also can't allow their currency to fluctuate freely in response to economic shocks or change their interest rates independently. It's worth noting that none of these levers are likely to improve the long-term real productivity or competitiveness of a nation, but in some cases, they could provide short-term relief.

Rodrik's second option is that nation-states sign up to a limited version of global economic integration, so a country preserves more national sovereignty and democratic control over how goods, services, capital, and people flow across its borders, as well as over its monetary policy and currency.

However, in this option, we lose some of the benefits of global integration that are critical for growing and maintaining trade.

In the third option, countries could give up national self-determination entirely and go for a global democracy aligned with global markets where we all get to vote on the rules. The last option seems a long way off—being hard enough to achieve among mostly like-minded EU-states—[17]and therefore doesn't seem realistic for this discussion.

Introduced over a decade ago, Rodrik's trilemma has aged well. It has highlighted genuine tensions between globalization, sovereignty, and democracy, and has even prompted many to question the future of the nation-state. To a greater or lesser extent, all countries will feel the pressure to reap the benefits of economic integration and will be forced to cede some powers to supranational governance bodies. But I believe that a nation-state can do much more to alleviate these tensions, and in the process, it can re-define its role in the 21st century.

Let's use Britain as an example to unpack how nation-states could be more effective in bridging global and local interests. If we dig below the surface, we find that, although many Britons expressed sovereignty as a reason to vote Leave, some of the deeper reasons had little to do with the EU. The think tank UK in a Changing EU and the Joseph Rowntree Foundation found that people in the towns that voted most heavily to leave had three overriding priorities: first, provide young people who did not want to go to university with jobs and training; second, help low-paid adults gain new skills; third, nurture local businesses and revive high streets.[18]

Due to a combination of misperceptions and misinformation, many Britons in these communities came to believe that the EU was to blame for their problems. They perceived the government to be spending more on the EU than their local priorities. But in reality, the UK's transfers to the EU represent about one-third of 1 percent of UK GDP and less than 1 percent of UK public spending.[19] Some blamed immigrants from Europe for taking jobs (mostly low-paid), when the bigger problem was that too few high-paying jobs were being created. In fact, many of the concerns expressed by Leave voters had little to do with the EU and could be traced back to domestic policy failings, particularly a lack of investment in public services and local economic development in the austerity years following the Global Financial Crisis.

In other words, to ease some of the tensions of Rodrik's trilemma, Britain could have played its role as a nation-state more effectively by adhering more closely to the three key tenets of this book. First, nation-states must do the hard work of Empowering Local Communities to bring about their own economic success stories. By devolving power downwards, a nation-state becomes more democratic because citizens gain more control over the decisions that affect them. In most cases, this will more than compensate for the decision-making rights ceded to supranational governance bodies. And as marginalized communities give way to local economic miracles, people feel a greater sense of shared prosperity.

Second, a nation-state should Invest With Purpose to address the SDC. Development goals might include provisions for carbon neutrality, infrastructure renewal, employment creation, and the provision of lifelong learning—all backed up by investment commitments and incentives for the private sector to participate. By creating the conditions that result in a more resilient economy, the nation-state can help to mitigate risks that arise from globalization.

Third, a nation-state must be the champion and guarantor of Inclusive Governance, ensuring that it cascades down to subnational levels of government. By offering a cohesive social contract and upholding inclusive constitutions, nation-states can go a long way to minimizing the number of marginalized citizens who feel they do not gain from the benefits of globalization as much as others in society.

Of course, improved nationhood is not the cure for all globalization issues. For Britain and other countries, frictionless borders with neighboring countries and the inequities in the global trading system do present real challenges and will be the subject of the rest of the chapter.

Reforming the Rules of Trade

As we have seen, the backlash against globalization is fueled by millions of citizens, especially from middle-class and lower-income segments of the population in the West, who feel their interests have not been served by increased global integration. The WTO agreements forged twenty-five years ago did not create a level playing field, and they are also in need of an update to keep up with a changing world economy.

But there are reasons for tempered optimism. Despite the strategic tensions between the US and China, the four big blocs—especially the US, China, and the EU—appear to be converging economically. As a result, their interests are also converging in some key areas, even if they themselves don't admit it publicly. These growing shared interests may provide a window of opportunity to update the rules of global economic cooperation so that they boost prosperity in more communities. In particular I see opportunity in key areas such as subsidies, digital trade, labor standards, IP, and sustainability which I will cover in the pages ahead. I am fully aware that there are also other crucial global issues such as international security, migration flows, and the spread of disease. But for the purposes of this book, I will focus on these economic aspects of globalization.

As China and India become more developed, they will need to find new ways to raise their productivity, since basic industrialization and export-led growth will have run their course. At present, China heavily subsidizes its huge and inefficient state-owned enterprises and is subject to countervailing duties and anti-dumping measures enacted by the other big powers. However, there are signs that China's leaders' approach to trade is evolving. They have pledged to end market-distorting subsidies and become fully compliant with the relevant WTO rules. However, it is unclear how they would prove this, as it is believed China itself does not keep a tally of all its massive subsidies.[20] China has also proposed to curb the ability of its local governments to force tech transfer from foreign companies.[21]

In terms of labor, as China moves up the value chain, "Made in China" will no longer mean "cheap." By 2016, Chinese hourly wages were almost on a par with Portugal and were above those of Brazil and Mexico.[22] A qualified engineer with a few years' experience typically earns €3,000 per month in China, not far behind the €5,000 earned by their German counterpart.[23] In the decade prior to 2017, Chinese wages grew at a rate of over 10 percent per annum and are expected to continue rising. Thus, wage gaps between China, the EU, and the US will only narrow in the decades to come. A similar, albeit slower, convergence will occur between India and the other big blocs. As a result, China and India should have less incentive to compete on the basis of low labor costs—both in terms of wages and poor working conditions.

Regarding innovation, we're used to the US and Europe dominating the stage. But the big blocs are also converging on this dimension at an accelerating rate. Between 2008 and 2017, Chinese IP only generated $12.2 billion from the sale of overseas licenses, compared with $128.4 billion generated by the US. Yet $4.8 billion of Chinese IP earnings were earned in 2017 alone, showing the rapid growth of its innovation capacity. Although India was still far behind the US and China in patent applications to the UN's World Intellectual Property Organization (WIPO) in 2018—the US made 56,142; China 53,345; Germany 19,883; and India just 2,013—India registered the fasted growth in applications with an increase of 27 percent.[24] The Global Innovation Index (GII)—a joint project between WIPO, INSEAD, and

Cornell University—ranked India the eighty-first most innovative country globally in 2015, but India's position has since shot up to fifty-second.[25]

China's legal norms on IP have long been a bugbear of Western companies, which have suffered from stolen IP. However, China's posture on IP standards is likely to evolve, since it will want to protect the barrage of IP-intensive products that it will bring to the global markets. Already, patent litigations in China (mostly among Chinese firms) are rising significantly. In 2016 Chinese courts heard ten times the number of IP-related litigations as the US.[26] And in response to the growing demand, China has created specialized IP courts in Beijing, Shanghai, and Guangzhou. Since the creation of the courts, injunctions are increasingly being used by China's legal system in order to protect IP rights.[27]

Finally, there are signs of convergence among the big blocs in their approach to sustainability. Although President Trump pulled the US out of the Paris Agreement on climate change, it's unlikely that the US will remain outside international efforts to tackle climate change once he has left office, as two-thirds of Americans support action on it.[28] Furthermore, despite the federal level withdrawal, twenty-four US states are committed to meeting the goals of the Paris Agreement.[29] The EU leads the world in climate change action. China and India—two of the most polluted countries on Earth—are also taking climate change very seriously as they face an increasing backlash from citizens concerned about the environment. Unlike the US, they are still committed to the Paris Agreement.

Leveling the Playing Field

As I write, the US-China trade war seems to be reaching a Phase One Agreement, with China agreeing to buy an additional $200 billion worth of US goods over two years. But deep-seated tensions remain. Indeed, the international trading regime's problems go beyond the trade war between the world's two biggest economic powers that currently dominates the headlines. In the short period between December 2017 and April 2019, governments imposed trade distortions affecting over $1.15 trillion[30] (or more than 5 percent) of total merchandise trade.[31] The vast majority of these barriers were put up by other G20 countries besides the US or China.[32] This reflects the overall lack of faith in the global trading regime.

Notwithstanding the sledgehammer approach to world trade under President Trump, the US is right to complain that China hasn't committed to a level playing field in world trade. The US and other powers like the EU and Japan have three main grievances with China, all of which arise because of weaknesses in the WTO's rules. The US also believes the WTO's dispute mechanism is biased.

The first grievance is that China ignores WTO rules sanctioning state subsidies. China subsidizes its industry with vast sums of cheap credit channeled through state-owned companies such as banks, as well as with direct investments from the state, which it doesn't disclose.[33] This allows Chinese companies to mass-produce products, price them at lower rates than other countries can manage, and dump them on world markets. For example, Chinese solar-panel producers have rapidly grown to a position of market leadership by benefitting from this model.[34] Specifically, the industry has benefitted from "free or low-cost loans, tax rebates, research grants, cheap land, energy subsidies and technological, infrastructure and personnel support," and "sometimes even straight-up cash."[35]

Under WTO rules, public bodies cannot support private enterprises through such mechanisms.

But the problem lies in the WTO's definition of what constitutes a "public body," which it says are agencies that perform "governmental functions," meaning they "regulate, restrain, supervise or control the conduct of private citizens."[36] When the rules were written, the WTO assumed that economies would all become Western-style market economies, where there is a fairly clear distinction between the public and private sector. However, in quasi-market economies like China's, the definition is harder to maintain, as there is some ambiguity as to whether state-owned enterprises perform governmental functions. Also, the WTO relies on self-reporting of subsidies. China delays and sometimes even refuses to notify the WTO about its subsidies,[37] and the WTO has little power to enforce compliance.

To be clear, China is not the only trading power that uses subsidies. For example, the EU spends over one-third[38] of its budget on supporting its agricultural sector under the Common Agricultural Policy (CAP)—although it technically abides by the rules.[39] The CAP is also extremely wasteful—resources could be spent elsewhere, such as on stoking innovation, and they offer an unfair advantage to EU producers. Agricultural subsidies were on the agenda for the Doha Round but proved too contentious for an agreement to be reached.

Another major grievance is China's rules on forced tech-transfer. To access the Chinese market, foreign firms in high-tech industries such as automotive, electronics, pharmaceuticals, and advanced chemicals, are required to form joint ventures (JVs) with Chinese companies and to transfer technology to the Chinese JV partner.[40] Once the technology is captured by the Chinese JV partner, it can end up competing with the foreign investor.[41] Some companies, such as in the chemicals and pharmaceuticals industries, have also been forced to disclose trade secrets to the Chinese government in exchange for licensing and other regulatory approvals.[42] These requirements breach the legal commitments not to require technology transfers from foreign firms China made when it joined the WTO in 2001.[43] The WTO has failed to prevent China from breaching these commitments.

A third bone of contention is the preferential treatment China receives by being classified as a developing country, such as its right to uphold higher barriers to entry into its market compared with developed countries.[44] The WTO's classification system is self-defining, and China continues to class itself as developing. Arguably, this should now change, given China's economic advances.

Finally, the US complains that the WTO's appellate body, a tribunal of judges that decides on WTO rulings, has been biased against it. Specifically, the US argues the appellate body repeatedly rules against America's use of anti-dumping and anti-subsidy duties for imports, which it thinks are priced unfairly low.[45] It is another area where the WTO needs reform.

Although the US and China still seem far apart in their trade negotiations, hopefully initiatives such as the Ottawa Group—a group of countries including Australia, Brazil, Canada, Chile, the European Union, Japan, Kenya, South Korea, Mexico, New Zealand, Norway, Singapore, and Switzerland, which want to reform the WTO by agreeing to new rules on subsidies and tech transfer—will help bring China and the US to the table for a constructive dialogue.

New Rules for Digital Trade

The second area where the international trading regime desperately needs reform is in digital trade. Again, the tension between the state-centered Chinese model and the market economies of the West is evident. Beijing is wary of efforts by a group of seventy countries led by Singapore, Australia, and Japan, which wants to create a set of global rules to regulate e-commerce and cross-border data flows and has sought to water down such proposals.[46]

China has a fundamentally different approach to regulating the internet. It exerts much more control over companies than in the West, and there are far fewer restrictions against companies or the government collecting personal information on citizens. It is also very reluctant to allow the cross-border transfer of Chinese data. As a result, those in favor of a free and open global internet fear the world is moving towards a "splinternet," where state-controlled countries like China, Russia, Turkey, and their economic allies are cut off from the rest.

For its part, the US is keen to cement its dominance over global internet commerce. As President Obama said of EU investigations into US tech companies, "We have owned the Internet. Our companies have created it, expanded it, perfected it in ways that they can't compete. And oftentimes what is portrayed as high-minded positions on issues sometimes is just designed to carve out some of their commercial interests." Under the influence of the growing political power of Big Tech from Silicon Valley, the US has pursued a "digital-trade agenda" in its recent trade negotiations that promotes cross-border data flows with minimal restrictions, strong intellectual-property rights, and the opening up of government procurement to foreign tech companies.[47]

While the elements of this digital-trade agenda may seem reasonable, they should in no way dilute protections on personal data, as we discussed in chapter 4. For example, it has been reported that Facebook lobbied against what it saw as "overly restrictive" GDPR legislation,[48] and both Facebook and Google are against California's similar legislation.[49] Given the importance of the digital economy to prosperity in the 21st century, competition authorities need to account for the importance of companies' ownership of personal data as a way in which they can abuse market power. This applies not just to the US, but also to China's digital giants such as Alibaba and Tencent.

Another salient digital-trade issue is cross-border data flows, where a battle is raging between jurisdictions that insist data must be stored locally and not taken out of the country, like China, and those that are in favor of data moving around the globe—such as Japan, the EU, and the US.[50]

Governments are concerned their companies' valuable IP could be stolen by competitors in other countries, that criminals can hide data, that their citizens' personal data will be abused, or that hostile countries or non-state actors will be able to use data against them. However, there is a significant risk that if digital trade suffers as a result of onerous rules, then ICE hubs lose out on a tremendous innovation opportunity because they cannot access valuable data.

In response to the polarized argument on data flows, Japan's Prime Minister Shinzō Abe has called for a middle path: "data free flow with trust" (DFFT). Abe believes that if states build confidence that cross-border data flows are secure—and therefore, that personal data and IP are protected—we

273

can obtain buy-in from them to increase flows. This chimes with the EU's push for GDPR to be a universal standard globally so that consumers' personal data is not abused.[51]

An influential US-based think tank, the Information Technology and Innovation Foundation (ITIF), has outlined some broad measures on how to achieve DFFT. First, it proposes that countries adopt policies that allow them to block data flows involving illegal distribution of unlicensed content. Second, it believes countries should support independent encryption technology to allow the secure flow of data. The ITIF rightly pushes back against recent efforts by Australia, China, and the UK to mandate tech firms to install back doors into ICT products and services for governments. A window provided to one stakeholder weakens overall security because it provides an opening for others, such as hackers. Third, instead of countries telling companies where they can store or process data, the ITIF thinks they should instead focus on holding companies accountable for managing the data they collect, regardless of where it's stored. Fourth, the ITIF calls for new international standards such as a "Geneva Convention on the Status of Data," which give national governments the confidence that they can gain access to domestic data stored in other nations.[52] It looks like an uphill battle at present, but eventually the major economies may see the benefit to international rules on data transparency, settling questions of jurisdiction and cross-border data requests from law enforcement.

Labor Standards

In the rush to globalize, labor considerations in trade deals have often received short shrift, and we've missed an important lever to improve global labor conditions and create a more level playing field for labor competition across countries.

Simply enshrining labor standards in domestic law, especially in developing countries, has often not been enough to improve working conditions to the extent required. For example, the OECD ranks China as a leader on employment-protection laws, but this masks the problem that these laws are often not enforced, and that they do not apply to tens of millions of rural migrants without a hukou passport, who are employed informally without a contract. [53,54]

The situation can be even more perilous in countries such as Bangladesh and Thailand. In 2013 the Rana Plaza building in the Bangladeshi capital of Dhaka, home to several garment factories producing clothes for well-known Western brands, collapsed, killing 1,134 people. And in Thailand, an investigation by the Associated Press and The Guardian newspaper revealed that the country's aquaculture industry relies heavily on forced labor.[55]

Working conditions could be better protected through trade agreements, by raising minimum labor standards and empowering corporations, trade unions, and NGOs to challenge governments that allow them to be violated. For example, the International Labor Organization (ILO) has proposed a Universal Labor Guarantee, which calls for fundamental rights such as an "adequate living wage," limits on working hours, and health-and-safety protection in the workplace.[56] Currently, the WTO rules only permit states to raise claims against other states for the violation of human rights in labor practices. An important step forward would be to empower corporations, trade unions, and labor-rights groups to sue foreign governments for compensation if local practices violate human-rights standards or commitments made in trade agreements.

Legislation governing cross-border supply chains in major trading countries can also have positive ripple effects for global labor. For example, the UK's 2015 Modern Slavery Act holds businesses responsible for human-rights abuses for companies in their supply chain. In response to the new law, UK investors representing $3 trillion in assets have put pressure on governments globally to tighten health-and-safety measures, give trade unions more power, and improve working conditions overall.[57] Alignment on such laws by some of the biggest developed economies could have a very positive impact, not only improving the welfare of workers globally, but also preventing unfair competition from pulling jobs out of developed countries.

Innovation: Incentive vs. Access

In America, a twelve-week treatment for Hepatitis C using Harvoni, a drug from Gilead Sciences, costs $94,500. This puts the drug far out reach of 85 percent of Americans with Hepatitis C, who are unable to afford the treatment.[58] In fact, one-quarter of Americans are unable to fill prescriptions due to high prices, and Americans continue to suffer the highest prescription-drug costs of anywhere in the world.[59]

In India, patients also struggle to gain access to the latest medicines, but for a diametrically opposite reason. India has weak enforcement of IP protections for drugs and medical products, which leads to circulation of unlicensed "copies" of patent-protected products that may be of questionable quality.[60] Since India imports the majority of its medicines, devices, diagnostics, patient aids, and monitoring tools, manufacturers are reluctant to launch products in the country until several years after their introduction into better-regulated markets. Clearly, this limits the access Indian patients have to high-quality, innovative products.[61]

In both countries, patients are needlessly suffering. In the US, patent protection is arguably too strong. A study by the University of California Hastings College of the Law, covering drugs that were awarded with patents between 2005 and 2015, found that 78 percent of new patents were issued for drugs that featured only incremental, non-innovative modifications to pre-existing IP.[62] In India, weak IP rules disincentivize businesses and researchers from innovating because they fear their inventions will be illegally copied. India has one of the lowest rates of investment in scientific research globally, at just 0.8 percent of GDP, and it makes relatively few scientific breakthroughs in healthcare.[63]

The lesson to be drawn from the US and Indian examples is that a balance must be struck between spurring innovation through IP protection and lowering the cost of accessing IP to an affordable level. Sadly, stories such as the pricing of Harvoni are eroding public faith in IP rules, and opposition is mounting from a plethora of countries, NGOs, international think-tanks, branches of the UN, and even the influential Nobel Prize-winning economists Joseph Stiglitz and Paul Krugman.[64]

But we should be careful not to "throw the baby out with the bathwater." Instead of scrapping international IP rules entirely, they should be reformed, and "excesses" in cases like the US pharmaceuticals industry should be addressed. Just like rules on the trade in goods, global agreements on IP standards haven't changed since the Uruguay Round. Back then, WTO members did agree to the Trade-Related Aspects of Intellectual Property Rights (TRIPS), which were supposed to protect IP from being copied. But like the definition of subsidies, there has been a significant ambiguity surrounding TRIPS because individual nations have some degree of freedom to determine when they can use "compulsory licenses"—licenses to use patented inventions without the patent holder's consent in various circumstances, such as a public-health interest.[65]

Large developing countries like Brazil, South Africa, and India are pushing back on existing TRIPS rules. India wants TRIPS to be the maximum ceiling for IP protection and thinks that countries should be prohibited from implementing more extensive restrictions. Some UN agencies, such as UNCTAD and the United Nations Development Programme (UNDP), have even advised developing countries on how to work around TRIPS.[66] A degree of relaxation on IP rules does seems necessary, but as India's economy becomes more innovative and converges with the US, EU, and China, it should also consider the future benefits of preserving a robust IP-protection framework at the global level.

Since broad agreement on TRIPS seems unlikely in the near future, a more fruitful short-term approach may be to explore ways to reduce the cost of accessing IP, especially for poorer countries. One approach may be for governments to coordinate their procurement of IP-intensive products from large corporations benefitting from overly protective IP rules. In 2016, twelve Latin American countries banded together to jointly procure Zika virus prevention and treatment drugs in order to secure supply and achieve lower drug prices. Such procurement deals are common among European countries and could be applied more often among developing nations, strengthening the case for regional economic-cooperation groups, such as AfCFTA. There is also no reason why procurement deals should be limited to medicines. They could be expanded to other sectors to help developing countries obtain valuable technology.

In the digital age, another way to reduce the cost of IP is to make access to some data free through the digital commons. McKinsey estimates that better-quality open data could unlock $3.2 trillion to $5.4 trillion globally for education, transportation, consumer products, electricity, oil and gas, healthcare, and consumer finance.[67]

One low-hanging fruit is the huge amount of data held by governments. It's promising that sixty-two countries have already signed up to the Open Data Charter principles, which call for data to be open by default, usable, and comparable.[68] However, most signatories are failing to live up to these principles and to reap the benefits of open data, according to the Open Data Barometer.[69]

Privacy concerns often stand in the way of making data, especially personal data, more openly available. The UK's National Health Service (NHS) admirably launched the Care.data project in 2013 to bring together primary-care-center patient data and hospital-episode statistics in order to support research and plan services. Use of patient data required patients' consent, but the program was forced to close after three years because too many patients—more than one million—opted out of the scheme.[70]

I noted in chapter 4 that social-media companies should have a legal obligation to keep their users safe. This would help engender more confidence in their data being used for beneficial purposes. Another more global measure could be the creation of data trusts, as proposed by the Open Data Institute.[71] Under this model, control over data-sharing would be given to an independent third party, which would be legally bound to ensure the data was used for a defined purpose and that confidentiality was maintained. Patient data trusts, for example, could enable people with rare medical conditions to donate their bio-data for research, helping to reduce the cost of developing innovative new drugs.[72] Trusts could be established transnationally to reap the benefits of very large data-pools. Already, international initiatives like the Global Partnership for Sustainable Development Data and DataKind are spearheading the use of private-sector data to tackle global, social, and humanitarian challenges.[73] Citizens can play an active role in establishing more organizations like these to spur the innovation called for by the SDC.

But perhaps the best way to mitigate the tense debate on incentivizing IP development versus enabling IP access is to help poorer nations increase their ability to generate more IP themselves. In fact, embedding provisions to support developing nations in building up their innovation capacity in a future TRIPS agreement may help to achieve the alignment that is currently elusive.

How could such a model work? Many poorer countries and regions lack the resources and capital to jump-start an innovation ecosystem. To get over this hurdle, Stephen Ezell and Nigel Cory at ITIF point to the example of the Established Program to Stimulate Competitive Research (EPSCoR), a body set up by the US Congress within the National Science Foundation (NSF) in 1978 to address the lack of federal R&D funding in poor-performing states for innovation. EPSCoR has helped to spur innovation across the US, by providing assistance in building up local scientific-research capabilities to states that historically received less R&D funding. Over time, these states became better placed to win federal-research grants. Ezell and Cory propose that a global form of EPSCoR should be established to fund research and build up innovation-capacity in developing countries that respect IP rules but are struggling to get their innovation clusters up and running. They also highlight WIPO's technical-assistance portfolio as a vehicle to channel funding for capacity-building in developing countries. Currently Australia, China, France, Italy, Japan, Mexico, Portugal, Korea, and Spain provide funding for the portfolio, but the US and China are notably absent.[74]

Public investment in innovation, whether funded by domestic governments or international bodies like WIPO, would probably have the multiplier effect of crowding in private capital from investors and corporations. For example, the big technology companies and venture funds are already setting down roots in the emerging innovation-hubs of the developing world—places like Lagos in Nigeria, Nairobi in Kenya, and Hyderabad in India. Some companies have made it a key part of their corporate social-responsibility (CSR) programs to help build up innovation infrastructure in poorer countries. For example, Cisco's CSR group provides smart-city equipment to developing-country cities and funds training in IT skills through its CISCO Networking Academy. In the city of Vijayawada in India, it has helped create the "Golden Mile," with free Wi-Fi, smart sensors that help manage traffic, air-quality sensors, CCTV, and an integrated e-governance platform for the local government.[75] Programs like this spur innovation in places like India, as well as creating more demand for Cisco's products and developing a pipeline of future workers.

Commitment to Sustainability

We won't get very far in promoting sustainability—especially tackling climate change—without broad international cooperation. Specifically, we need global alignment around how much natural resource we use—for example, through carbon-emission targets or daily water-usage goals—and on how to influence the pricing of these resources—for example, through carbon taxes. In addition, global capital pools will be needed to help poorer countries make the clean-technology investments required.

Sustainability is an area where citizen power is already beginning to bring about significant change. Consider the impact of the school strikes led by Swedish teenage activist Greta Thunberg, through which school kids are demanding 100 percent clean energy and greater action against climate change. A climate strike on November 30, 2018, took place in more than one hundred countries, involving over 50,000 school students.[76] Since then, pupils have taken part in school strikes on Fridays in what's become known as FridaysForFuture. Following the school strikes and various other protests around the EU, Germany, the UK, and France all committed to achieve net-zero carbon emissions by 2050. Norway has committed to do so by 2030. Eighteen EU countries now support net-zero carbon emissions by 2050. It seems that other EU member countries will move to this target after some haggling with the Central European states that are currently resisting.

In addition to binding emissions targets, national guidelines on individual resource usage would go a long way towards empowering citizens to take greater ownership for their contribution to tackling climate change. Of course, this would have to be accompanied by corporate disclosures on the carbon footprint and resource intensity of products and services to enable citizens to make informed purchasing decisions.

When it comes to increasing the effective price of carbon, there are some promising developments afoot. For example, some Republicans are proposing a US carbon tax that would levy charges on domestic industries and imports which are carbon-intensive, and redistribute the revenues to ordinary Americans. The EU doesn't appear to be fully going down the carbon tax road yet, but it is setting a higher price for carbon in its cap-and-trade system. The price tripled to about €25 per metric ton in July 2019, compared with the beginning of 2018. Analysis by commodity-market analysts CRU suggests prices could reach €40 per metric ton by 2028. Like in the US, the EU is also considering a carbon tax on imports.[77]

China has been experimenting with a cap-and-trade system since 2011, with pilots in numerous cities including Shanghai and Shenzhen, and plans to introduce the system nationwide in 2020. As the world's biggest carbon emitter, China contributes over 25 percent of global emissions compared to the US's 14 percent[78]—although the US's contribution is much higher in per-capita terms. Policy action in both countries will have an important effect on climate change in the years to come.

Poorer countries such as India are investing billions into sustainability projects that are commercially viable, like solar farms, but are wary of signing up to commitments that slow down their ability to industrialize and catch up economically. That is why it's so important to build up the international pools of capital dedicated to the SDC, and to grow the market for financing mechanisms, such as green bonds, which can support large-scale investments in sustainable infrastructure.

Strategic Struggles

As the four big economic blocs converge, I have argued that their shared interests are likely to grow in the areas of trade, labor, IP, and sustainability. Hopefully, this provides a window of opportunity to reform the international system now, so that it works in the best interests of the whole planet in the decades to come. But an improved world order cannot be taken for granted, and we should not naïvely think it will happen. Indeed it could get worse, as several major risks stand in the way.

First, the short-term gains from protectionism and strategic rivalry will always compete with the benefits of acting out of shared interests. There will always be a temptation for governments to shore up dying industries to avoid job losses and win votes. President Trump's protection of the US coal industry is a case in point. Nations are also tempted to protect emerging industries in the hope of nurturing domestic companies that go on to be global market leaders, as China has done with its solar photovoltaic (PV) manufacturing industry. Although these transgressions are generally unproductive in the long-run because they suck resources into unproductive sectors or provoke retaliatory actions such as countervailing duties, they will be difficult to stamp out entirely and will probably need to be tolerated.

Furthermore, governments will restrict foreign direct-investment for national-security reasons. In fact, there has recently been a tightening of foreign-investment laws among some Western powers. For example, Germany now includes media in its definition of critical sectors, which must undergo investment screening by the German government before foreign investments into German companies can be made.[79] Recently, the US prohibited Chinese company Huawei from installing 5G technology in the US because it thinks it might hand power to China over strategic US infrastructure.

The second risk is that international dialogue and cooperation break down as strategic rivalries or military conflicts become toxic. For example, the rhetoric surrounding the current US-China trade war does not bode well for agreements on some of the global reforms outlined earlier in this chapter. Some commentators even believe that we are entering a Cold War between the US and China, as views in the US harden and China seeks to set up parallel international structures.[80] According to political scientist Bruno Maçães, author of Belt and Road: A Chinese World Order, the BRI is not simply a way for China to project its economic and political power but a blueprint for a future global economic system.[81] Meanwhile, President Trump seems to be intent on getting his way on pet grievances, such his perception that other countries have "taken advantage"[82] of the US, even if it means tearing down the current international order. As the two superpowers pull in these different directions, we get further away from a constructive dialogue on reforming the international system.

The third risk is the attitudes of people themselves. In this chapter, I have advocated for stronger nationhood, regional cooperation, and improvements in the international system of trade. If done well, these changes will support local efforts for achieving prosperity, rather than detracting from them. However, it will always be tempting for populist forces to rail against greater integration. I would encourage such voices to take a hard look at whether their country's problems are truly the result of the membership of a regional- or global-cooperation group, or whether they are caused by domestic-policy failings such as the lack of investment in local development and public services.

CHAPTER 12

CONCLUSION: THE CITIZEN'S GUIDE

People Power

For ten days in April 2019, parts of London were forced to a standstill by the "Extinction Rebellion," a protest movement seeking to highlight the climate disaster and calling for net-zero carbon emissions by 2025. Protestors blocked traffic at famous London landmarks, including Oxford Circus, Marble Arch, and Waterloo Bridge. They glued themselves to the entrance of the London Stock Exchange, sat on top of trains on London's light railway, and chained themselves to the house of Jeremy Corbyn, leader of the government's opposition. They staged "die-ins" at high-profile locations to draw attention to what they see as the risk of human and ecological extinction from climate change.

The Extinction Rebellion protestors were derided by some UK government figures at the time, and there's no doubt they caused damage to property and disrupted the lives of ordinary Londoners. But their alarm with the state of the planet struck a chord with the British public. Within a couple of months, Prime Minister Theresa May announced the UK's commitment to net-zero carbon emissions by 2050. Although this was well short of the Extinction Rebellion's target of 2025, carbon neutrality by 2050 is now a formal national mandate, and one which the government would not have committed to without the protests.

In 2019, protests have proliferated on a variety of issues concerning political, economic, and civil justice. In June, up to two million[1] people marched through Hong Kong to demand the city's government drop a bill that would allow Hong Kong citizens convicted of serious crimes to be extradited to Mainland China. Carrie Lam, the chief executive of Hong Kong, held firm at first, saying she would not scrap the bill. However, after days of swelling demonstrations, she was forced to back down—and even after doing so, protests have continued unabated. During October in Lebanon, a million or more people[2] (in a country of six million) took to the streets to protest the government's plans to tax WhatsApp calls. The protesters forced the resignation of the Prime Minister Saad Hariri, but that appears unlikely to quell their fervor. Their deeper grievance is Lebanon's kleptocratic political system and its economic malaise. And earlier in the year, Washington saw the third annual Women's March—a protest inaugurated in January 2017, a day after Donald Trump was sworn in as president. The 2017 march was the largest protest in American history with 3.3 million to 5.6 million participating. The event has become an annual occurrence, with another large march in 2018 and smaller but significant one in 2019. No longer are millions of women prepared to put up with the myriad of injustices they face in society.

Popular action is rising all over the world, and it's reaffirming that people-power matters. But as demonstrated by the melee of movements above, people are agitating for a disparate range of causes. However, to address the big challenges of our time, we need a common vision which unites rather than deepens polarization.

Throughout this book, I've invited you explore these challenges, by taking the diverse perspectives of a marginalized citizen, a development investor, and a community builder. Whatever your political tribe, I hope our discussion has helped to crystallize a common framework for thinking about the key choices that can make a positive difference.

This framework, or Citizen's Guide, revolves around three themes:

- **Advancing Inclusive Governance** to win back the public trust
- **Investing With Purpose** to address the long-term, Sustainable Development Challenge (SDC)
- **Empowering Local Communities** to become innovative, connected, entrepreneurial (ICE) hubs in a globalizing world.

Let's now review the key ideas that make up the Citizen's Guide, and how it can help us to make choices for building a more prosperous society.

Advancing Inclusive Governance

In part 1 of the book we learned how to recognize and decode a Faustian bargain—a dangerous brand of false promise which typically offers a short-term benefit, like a tax windfall, but comes with a much bigger long-term cost to society, such as a lack of long-term public investment.

As voters, I believe it is critical to denounce divisive politics and rally behind political leaders who reject Faustian bargains and offer Inclusive Governance. Central to this paradigm are cohesive social contracts which promote political participation, civil liberties, and socioeconomic mobility for the entire population. Such social contracts must be upheld by inclusive laws and institutions, which are resilient to "capture" by a ruler or by special interests, and they must be buttressed by a political culture that encourages respectful dialogue between differing points of view.

Cohesive social contracts include all parts of the population in the national narrative. They devolve power to subnational levels so that local communities can take control of their social and economic destiny. They promote the growth of a prosperous middle-class by championing entre-preneurial private-enterprise—the job-creation dynamo of any economy. And they build a bridge to economic opportunity for all citizens by invest-ing in the enablers of socioeconomic mobility.

Bold political leaders are not afraid to clarify the social contract they plan to deliver by declaring a long-term vision for their country or local-ity. We've already seen numerous examples of this at the city level: New York City's OneNYC 2050 plan emphasizes environmental sustainability; Abu Dhabi Vision 2030 focuses on building a diversified economy with an expanded private sector, stronger capital-markets, and significant invest-ment in human-capital development; Stockholm's Vision 2040 adds social inclusion and robust democracy as key priorities.

Upholding cohesive social contracts requires a robust system of law and institutions, starting with an inclusive constitution and an electoral system in which each vote counts. "First past the post" electoral systems, whose problems have been compounded by frequent gerrymandering, have repeatedly elected leaders without majority support in countries such as the UK and the US. As voters, we cannot assume that electoral processes will continue to remain robust without constant vigilance—we need to chal-lenge their deficiencies in order to build stronger democracies.

Another aspect of inclusion involves maintaining the balance between workers and asset owners. We need tougher action from anti-trust authorities to restore market competition and combat rent-seeking behavior by large corporations and asset owners. In most countries, the tax code could also be revised to be more pro-worker, for example, by offering tax-breaks for training and development. Employees must be more actively engaged in corporate governance and regain representation on company boards. And to make our cities more affordable places to live and work for lower-income families and small businesses, local governments must be given "up-zoning" powers to develop job-rich or transit-rich areas, or those with high-quality schooling.

In the digital age, we also must call for new legislation and institutions to restore faith in the news and in digital-media platforms. GDPR legislation in the EU and similar moves in California represent a good start, but we need to explore measures that confer fiducial responsibility on companies to safeguard personal data and prevent the spread of fake news.

Investing With Purpose

In 2016, the UN announced the Sustainable Development Goals (SDGs), a broad set of imperatives for addressing the world's critical challenges. Critics rightly question whether their sprawling scope detracts from their practical application. Others point to some of their obvious omissions, such as the lack of an explicit focus on managing population and demographics.

Notwithstanding their flaws, the SDGs reflect the world's enormous under-investment in building an inclusive society that operates within the limits of its natural resources. In this book, I narrow the focus to key initiatives in three discrete investable areas: 1) basic provisioning, 2) cleaning up industry and infrastructure, and 3) building up human capacity. Collectively, I refer to these initiatives as the Sustainable Development Challenge, which I outlined in chapter 5.

Triangulating between various analyses produced by UNCTAD, the IMF, McKinsey Global Institute, and many other studies, I conservatively estimate the investment gap for meeting the SDC to be about $5 trillion every year for several decades. Since the global tax base is approximately $25 trillion, we would need an average tax increase of 20 percent to cover the investment gap. Growing public levies by this magnitude would clearly be unachievable, not to mention a significant dampener on economic growth.

Some of the investment gap could be closed by spending the taxes we already raise much more efficiently—particularly in the case of health-care and education in some developed countries. For example, healthcare spending above $1,000 per capita seems to have little incremental effect on health and well-being, as measured by Disability-Adjusted Life Years. Bearing this in mind, does it make sense to spend five-times that amount in Germany or ten-times as much in the United States?

As taxpaying citizens, wouldn't it be more sensible to advocate for a much lower-cost "universal" healthcare system that provides free, high-quality, basic healthcare to all citizens—as well as elective treatments at a more affordable cost.

As parents and students, our goal should be to populate the world with ten billion innovators by 2050. To achieve this, we need to work actively with schools and policymakers to ensure that the precious resources being ploughed into our schooling system will produce agile, lifelong learners who can provide human "value-add" in an AI-augmented workplace.

And as many millennials are already doing, we should reevaluate whether the exorbitant cost of an undergraduate university degree is worth the debt and financial stress that it brings to students and parents alike. Would it be more pragmatic to invest the same resources into shorter degrees or an entrepreneurial venture, while continue a lifelong practice of personal development through more bite-sized, just-in-time forms of learning?

In most other areas of the SDC, additional funds will be required to fill the investment gap, and the public purse simply will not be able to keep up. Instead, the reallocation of a small fraction of global private wealth—which stands at $200 trillion, and which is growing by $8 trillion per year—would easily meet the needs of the SDC.

As investors, more of us are exploring sustainable investing opportunities, which help to reallocate more private capital to SDC initiatives. Since the pope issued an encyclical in 2015 ordering the Catholic Church to divest its hydrocarbon assets, over 1,000 large institutional investors have followed suit and withdrawn a total of $11 trillion[3] from the hydrocarbon-fuels industry. Similar momentum seems to be growing among retail investors. The Forum for Sustainable and Responsible Investment (USSIF), an NGO that tracks sustainable investments, reported that 25 percent of US assets under management, or $12 trillion, had been invested in funds or projects with a sustainable objective as of 2018.[4]

While this figure is encouraging, we are sorely in need of a standard framework to measure and report environmental, social, and governance (ESG) impact in order to ensure that our capital is achieving our desired sustainability goals. This is an area where leaders of Universal Owners—the largest investors with exposure to the entire market—can step up to provide a sustainable-investing framework that will drive measurable socioeconomic impact.

Specific areas of the SDC which need significant investment are combating poverty, building infrastructure, and increasing the provision of childcare. Leaders of development banks and Sovereign Wealth Funds could lead the charge by raising a $1 trillion Graduation Fund to eradicate extreme poverty in developing nations and address pockets of debilitating poverty in more advanced economies. Large institutional investors also play a critical role in developing economic projects like power plants, roads, and ports, as well as supporting the incubation and scale-up of critical technology platforms that contribute to the decarbonization of industry and infrastructure, such as battery storage, carbon capture and sequestration, and decarbonized processes for manufacturing fertilizers, plastics, steel, and cement. The growing market for green and social-impact bonds will also help with these types of projects.

As consumers, we make purchasing decisions worth $55 trillion globally every year. Shifts in global consumption patterns can profoundly advance the objectives of the SDC. The worldwide movement towards Mobility-as-a-Service, the impetus to buy energy from renewable sources, the gathering momentum for ethically sourced garments, and the adoption of alternatives to animal proteins in our diet are all encouraging indicators of the growing sentiment to embrace a more sustainable future. However, to transform people's good intentions into greater impact, we need much better standards and information to guide our purchasing and investment decisions. Imagine products being required to audit production-and-distribution processes in order to disclose carbon footprint, water intensity, and forestry impact on their label. What if we could also compare these figures against a global standard for our "personal resource budget"—rather like we look at the recommended dietary allowance (RDA) on food packaging?

As innovators and entrepreneurs, we have unlimited scope to dream up market-creating innovations that solve some of the world's biggest challenges in an affordable way. For example, CEOs of innovative corporations can have a big impact on ending poverty or fighting climate change by developing solutions like BBOXX, which is providing people in Africa with off-grid, solar-powered electricity, along with phone-charging, radio, and TV products all at low cost.

As community residents, our self-defeating NIMBY attitudes remain quite entrenched. Opposition to new real estate and infrastructure in our local neighborhoods is doing untold, long-term damage to the economy by reducing the land available for affordable housing and transportation links in major cities. In the long-term, this starves our businesses of workers and makes it harder for young people to start families, leading to an aging society. But since the impact of NIMBY-ism can take decades to boomerang back, many of us don't give it a second thought until it's too late.

As employers, we also have a significant role to play in the SDC. Leading companies have long realized that investing in their people makes good business sense because it allows them to attract top talent, even in tight labor markets. They offer their workforce apprenticeships and frequent training. They work hard to engage women and close the gender pay-gap. And they also implement family-friendly policies such as flexible working arrangements, reasonable paid-leave for new parents, and subsidized access to affordable childcare. But these inclusive practices go far beyond good business strategy, particularly in aging societies. Partly as a result of such policies, which the government mandated and helped to fund, Germany has been able to push up its fertility rate from 1.3 to 1.6 over the past two decades.

Empowering Local Communities

Localism works best when greater powers are devolved to communities, empowering them to raise local taxes and make critical investment decisions that help to create ICE hubs, which in turn draw in talent, businesses, and outside investment.

City mayors play a pivotal role in engaging businesses, investors, universities, and residents to develop a long-term development vision—recall the examples of the OneNYC plan or Stockholm Vision 2040. With buy-in to a common plan, supported by capable urban planning, zoning, and development by well-governed local government—urban economic "miracles" become possible. By creating a business-friendly environment as well as an affordable and attractive place to live, cities like Pittsburgh in the US and Dubai in the UAE have put themselves on the map as growing economic powerhouses.

Business leaders, whose companies feed off the infrastructure and the supply of talent in ICE hubs, can give back to the ecosystem by providing well-paid jobs and a commitment to ongoing professional development. They can partner with schools and universities to prepare young people for the workplace through internships and apprenticeships. They can also encourage innovation and entrepreneurship by sponsoring local R&D and providing mentorship for and investment into start-ups.

As teachers and parents, we play a pivotal role in engaging youth to equip them with the learning agility required for the future workplace, as well as the values and judgment needed for good citizenship. What better way to develop these skills in young people than by engaging them in the solving of local, real-world problems, in partnership with businesses, local government, and NGOs?

ICE hubs thrive on connectivity with ideas, customers, and capital from around the world. We can all perform a useful service by following Matt Desmier's example to create forums—online and real world—to connect our communities with others with common social and economic priorities.

However, connectivity must come in the context of a "fair" international framework for trade. As the WTO approaches its twenty-fifth anniversary, international governance is in need of a major reboot. Many issues such as subsidization by state-controlled governments, digital trade, labor standards, and IP must be addressed as the interests of the major economic powers of the future—US, EU, China, and India—increasingly converge.

Powering Prosperity

In the course of my lifetime, a tiny blip in human history, I have been moved by several watershed moments that marked momentous change: the fall of the Berlin Wall in 1989, the end of apartheid in 1994, the first legalization of same-sex marriage by the Netherlands in 2000, and the Paris Agreement on climate change in 2016. These dramatic achievements can all be traced back to the courageous leadership of citizens who were able to rally humanity to raise the high-water mark of freedom.

After many decades of ascent in the post-World War II era, we are again at such a watershed moment, when the hard-earned freedoms of political participation, civil liberties, and socioeconomic mobility have all fallen into decline. To escape the Great Trust Crisis that has resulted, we as citizens in our various roles in society must make choices that put the world back on a positive trajectory—choices that are laid out in this Citizen's Guide.

The alternatives are truly disquieting. Britain could become the Disunited Kingdom as it crashes out of the EU. Populist governments could persist in divisive politics and take a bulldozer to international cooperation. The Chinese government could tighten control over its populace even further. And climate change could escalate to an extinction-level threat. These are all very real possibilities that could result from apathy and inaction.

To avoid these—and many other troubling outcomes—it's time to cast aside differences and to focus on our shared interests in order to make the big changes that are required. In this book, I have laid out a Citizen's Guide for Advancing Inclusive Governance, Investing With Purpose, and Empowering Local Communities. Now it's over to you—it's your turn to make a difference. At this pivotal time in history, I leave with you a simple but thought-provoking question: what choices will you make to power prosperity in the 21st century?

ACKNOWLEDGMENTS

This book has been a long time in development, and it owes much to my family, colleagues, and friends, who have helped to carry me along through the adventure. The love and support of my wife, Priyanka, and my two sons, Kabir and Raphael, have inspired and motivated me to complete this long project. It was with Priyanka's encouragement that the project was born, and she has been an invaluable thought-partner and a constructive voice throughout. Her contributions have helped to breathe passion into the key messages, and she has brought the project back on track whenever it was at risk of veering off course. Without my family's patience and sacrifice, this book would certainly have not been possible.

There have been many collaborators who have helped to shape and develop the content of the book. First and foremost, my deepest thanks go to Matthias Lomas, my senior editor and researcher, and co-writer for the project, whose ideas have significantly helped to challenge and clarify my own in all aspects of the book, and whose tireless support has been a pivotal contribution. I am particularly indebted to his critical thinking on the major sustainability, macroeconomic, and policy topics in the book.

I am very grateful to my publisher at Post Hill Press, David Bernstein. David's counsel on framing the key arguments and connecting with my audience has left an indelible mark on the book. My friends and colleagues, Ash Bennington and Mike Moran, have provided excellent editorial steering, helping to structure the narrative and enliven the story telling. Their decades of experience in financial journalism and political risk have also helped to enrich my perspectives in these important areas.

It would be impossible to write a book of this scope without the detailed input of a series of global experts. For many years, Rachel Ziemba has been my anchor and go-to person for all things pertaining to macroeconomics, development economics, and real assets. The book is indebted to her boundless knowledge on these topics and her insightful critique on many of the key ideas. Rachel has also been very generous in giving her time to review many iterations of the manuscript and to enhance its analytical rigor. On matters of financial markets and institutional investing, Gina Sanchez has been a tireless thought-partner. Her passion and knowledge of sustainable investing and ESG have helped to inform many of the key arguments in the book. Similarly, on environmental sustainability and climate change topics, Shelley Goldberg has provided excellent analysis on the latest trends, technologies, and market development.

Writing this book has been an enlightening experience, and I owe a deep debt of gratitude to all the people who have helped me to learn and grow throughout the journey.

ENDNOTES

Chapter 1

1   Daniel Dunford and Ashley Kirk, "How Right or Wrong Were the Polls About the EU Referendum?," *The Telegraph*, June 27, 2016, https://www.telegraph.co.uk/news/2016/06/24/eu-referendum-how-right-or-wrong-were-the-polls/.

2   Heather Stewart, Rowena Mason, and Rajeev Syal, "David Cameron Resigns after UK Votes to Leave European Union," *The Guardian*, June 24, 2016, https://www.theguardian.com/politics/2016/jun/24/david-cameron-resigns-after-uk-votes-to-leave-european-union.

3   Michael Mackenzie and Eric Platt, "How Global Markets Are Reacting to UK's Brexit Vote," *Financial Times*, June 24, 2016, https://www.ft.com/content/50436fde-39bb-11e6-9a05-82a9b15a8ee7.

4   Jamie McGeever and Patrick Graham, "UK Markets Shudder after Brexit Vote, Sterling Hits 31-Year Low," *Reuters*, June 23, 2016, https://www.reuters.com/article/us-britain-eu-markets/uk-markets-shudder-after-brexit-vote-sterling-hits-31-year-low-idUSKCN0Z92MA.

5   Jake Cordell Cordell, "Taking Stock: 12 Charts Showing the First Three Months of Brexit in the Financial Markets," *City A.M.*, September 23, 2016, https://www.cityam.com/taking-stock-first-three-months-brexit-financial-markets/.

6   "Gross Domestic Product (GDP) Year-on-Year Growth in the United Kingdom (UK) from 2000 to 2018," Statista, https://www.statista.com/statistics/281734/gdp-growth-in-the-united-kingdom-uk/.

7   "Death by a Thousand Cuts," University of Oxford website, April 10, 2019, https://www.sbs.ox.ac.uk/news/death-thousand-cuts.

8   "AstraZeneca Will Keep UK Investment Freeze if No Brexit Clarity," *Reuters*, October 15, 2018, https://uk.reuters.com/article/uk-britain-eu-astrazeneca/astrazeneca-will-keep-uk-investment-freeze-if-no-brexit-clarity-idUKKCN1MP1Q9.

9   Tim Worstall, "Brit PM David Cameron Says Brexit Would Be Economic Self-Harm," *Forbes*, June 3, 2016, https://www.forbes.com/sites/timworstall/2016/06/03/brit-pm-david-cameron-says-brexit-would-be-economic-self-harm/.

10 "Toby Helm and James Tapper, "Resentful in Redcar: 'We Made the Finest Steel in the World—Now We Make Lattes,'" *The Guardian, February 3, 2018*, https://www.theguardian.com/politics/2018/feb/03/brexit-redcar-bracknell-steel.

11 "Public Trust in Government," Pew Research Center, April 11, 2019, https://www.people-press.org/2019/04/11/public-trust-in-government-1958-2019/.

12 "Mubadala makes a $15bn commitment to the Softbank Vision Fund," Press Release, Mubadala Development Company, May 20, 2017, https://www.mubadala.com/en/news/mubadala-makes-15bn-commitment-softbank-vision-fund.

13 Erin Durkin, "New York City to Amazon: Drop Dead," *The Guardian*, November 14, 2018, https://www.theguardian.com/technology/2018/nov/14/amazon-hq2-new-york-protest-queens-long-island-city.

14 Ezra Klein, "Greece's Debt Crisis, Explained in Charts and Maps," Vox, https://www.vox.com/2015/7/1/8871509/greece-charts.

15 Martin Wolf, "Greek Economy Shows Promising Signs of Growth," *Financial Times*, May 19, 2019, https://www.ft.com/content/b42ee1ac-4a27-11e9-bde6-79eaea5acb64.

16 "Greek Unemployment Drops to Lowest Since June 2011," RTÉ, https://www.rte.ie/news/business/2019/0711/1061516-greek-jobless-figures/.

Chapter 2

1 "2017 Edelman Trust Barometer," Daniel J. Edelman Holdings, Inc, January 21, 2017, https://www.edelman.com/research/2017-edelman-trust-barometer.

2 "The Five Capitals," Forum for the Future, https://www.forumforthefuture.org/the-five-capitals.

3 Oliver Morley, "UK Government—Did We Rule the Empire with 4,000 Civil Servants?," *National Archives* (blog), August 1, 2012, https://blog.nationalarchives.gov.uk/blog/uk-government-did-we-rule-the-empire-with-4000-civil-servants/.

4 Shubhra Chakrabarti and Utsa Patnaik, eds., *Agrarian and Other Histories: Essays for Binay Bhushan Chaudhuri* (New York: Columbia University Press, 2018).

5 Samuel P. Huntington, *The Third Wave: Democratization in the Late Twentieth Century* (Norman: University of Oklahoma Press, 1993).

6 "About Polity," Center for Systemic Peace, http://www.systemicpeace.org/polityproject.html.

7 "The Revolutionary Nature of Growth," *Economics and Strategy Research* (June 2011), http://www.fastestbillion.com/res/Research/Revolutionary_growth-220611.pdf.

8 Anna Lührmann et al., "State of the World 2017: Autocratization and Exclusion?," *Democratization* 25, no. 8 (2018), https://www.tandfonline.com/doi/full/10.1080/1351034 7.2018.1479693.

9 "Democracy in Retreat: Freedom in the World 2019," Freedom House website, https://freedomhouse.org/report/freedom-world/freedom-world-2019/democracy-in-retreat.

10 David Lubin, "The New Macroeconomics of Populism," Chatham House website, https://www.chathamhouse.org/expert/comment/new-macroeconomics-populism#.

11 Daniel Treisman, ed., *The New Autocracy: Information, Politics, and Policy in Putin's Russia* (Washington: Brookings Institution Press, 2018), http://willzuzak.ca/cl/bookreview/Treisman2018NewAutocracyRussia.pdf.

12 Ibid.

13 Ibid. As Ella Paneyakh and Dina Rosenberg point out in their analysis, Russia's courts are not wholly corrupt.

14 Tonia E. Ries, David M. Bersoff, Ph.D., Sarah Adkins, Cody Armstrong, Jamis Bruening, "2018 Edelman Trust Barometer Global Report," Edelman, January 21, 2018, https://www.slideshare.net/EdelmanInsights/2017-edelman-trust-barometer-global-results-71035413; https://www.edelman.com/sites/g/files/aatuss191/files/2018-10/2018_Edelman_Trust_Barometer_Global_Report_FEB.pdf; https://www.edelman.com/sites/g/files/aatuss191/files/2019-02/2019_Edelman_Trust_Barometer_Global_Report.pdf.

15 "2018 Edelman Trust Barometer," Daniel J. Edelman Holdings, Inc, January 21, 2018, https://www.edelman.com/research/2017-edelman-trust-barometer.

16 Manès Weisskircher, "Austria's Right-Wing Government at Six Months: What's the Record So Far?," London School of Economics and Political Science (blog), https://blogs.lse.ac.uk/europpblog/2018/06/18/austrias-right-wing-government-at-six-months-whats-the-record-so-far/.

17 Natasha Lomas, "Cambridge Analytica's Parent Pleads Guilty to Breaking UK Data Law," Tech Crunch, January 9, 2019, https://techcrunch.com/2019/01/09/cambridge-analyticas-parent-pleads-guilty-to-breaking-uk-data-law/.

18 See: Marshall Allen, "Health Insurers are Vacuuming up Consumer Data That Could Be Used to Raise Rates," Health Leaders, July 17, 2018, https://www.healthleadersmedia.com/finance/health-insurers-are-vacuuming-consumer-data-could-be-used-raise-rates.

19 April Glaser, "What We Know About How Russia's Internet Research Agency Meddled in the 2016 Election," Slate, February 16, 2018, https://slate.com/technology/2018/02/what-we-know-about-the-internet-research-agency-and-how-it-meddled-in-the-2016-election.html.

20 Peter Kafka, "An Astonishing Number of People Believe Pizzagate, the Facebook-Fueled Clinton Sex Ring Conspiracy Story, Could Be True," Vox, December 9, 2016, https://www.vox.com/2016/12/9/13898328/pizzagate-poll-trump-voters-clinton-facebook-fake-news.

21 Bryson Masse, "There Are Now 8,000 Fake Science 'Journals' Worldwide, Researchers Say," VICE, September 6, 2017, https://motherboard.vice.com/en_us/article/xwwb8n/there-are-now-8000-fake-science-journals-worldwide-researchers-say.

22 Christopher Shiel, "Piketty's Political Economy," Journal of Australian Political Economy 74, http://media.wix.com/ugd/b629ee_2d2a62b529e847e89942d5a3d3a58580.pdf.

23 Ibid.

24 Lakner, Christoph and Milanovic, Branko, Global Income Distribution: From the Fall of the Berlin Wall to the Great Recession (December 1, 2013). World Bank Policy Research Working Paper No. 6719. Available at SSRN: https://ssrn.com/abstract=2366598.

25 Soutik Biswas, "Inequality in India Can Be Seen from Outer Space," BBC.com, May 27, 2018, https://www.bbc.co.uk/news/world-asia-india-44193144.

26 "The Gap Between India's Richer and Poorer States Is Widening," The Economist, September 2, 2017, https://www.economist.com/finance-and-economics/2017/09/02/the-gap-between-indias-richer-and-poorer-states-is-widening.

27 Jonathan Haskel and Stian Westlake, Capitalism Without Capital, (Princeton University Press November 28, 2017), 86.

28 Interview, "Milton Friedman Responds," Chemtech (February 1974), 72.

29 James Reda, "How Stock Buybacks Can Affect Executive Compensation," CLS Blue Sky Blog, August 3, 2018, http://clsbluesky.law.columbia.edu/2018/08/03/how-stock-buybacks-can-affect-executive-compensation/.

30 Map from Tanvi Misra, "How Cities Are Divided by Income, Mapped," CityLab, February 27, 2018, https://www.citylab.com/equity/2018/02/how-cities-are-divided-by-income-in-3-maps/553898/. Original visualization from "Mapping Incomes," ESRI, http://storymaps.esri.com/stories/2018/mapping-incomes/index.html.

31 "Temple Bar District," http://nws.eurocities.eu/MediaShell/media/Dublin_Temple%20bar_28102015.pdf.

32 Nick Routley, "These Charts Show the Extreme Concentration of Global Wealth," World Economic Forum website, January 7, 2019, https://www.weforum.org/agenda/2019/01/visualizing-the-extreme-concentration-of-global-wealth.

33 Andrew Henderson, "How to Avoid Estate Taxes: 17 Countries with No Death Tax," Nomad Capitalist, https://nomadcapitalist.com/2018/05/17/how-to-avoid-estate-taxes/.

34 "The Basics of US Estate and UK Inheritance Tax," Buzzacott, https://www.buzzacott. co.uk/insights/the-basics-of-us-estate-and-uk-inheritance-tax.

35 Emmie Martin, "Here's How Much Housing Prices Have Skyrocketed over the Last 50 Years," CNBC website, June 23, 2017, https://www.cnbc.com/2017/06/23/how-much-housing-prices-have-risen-since-1940.html.

36 Tara Golshan, "Trump Said He Wouldn't Cut Medicaid, Social Security, and Medicare," Vox, March 12, 2019, https://www.vox.com/policy-and-politics/2019/3/12/18260271/trump-medicaid-social-security-medicare-budget-cuts.

37 Sarah O'Brien, "Fed Survey Shows 40 Percent of Adults Still Can't Cover a $400 Emergency Expense," CNBC.com, May 22, 2018, https://www.cnbc.com/2018/05/22/fed-survey-40-percent-of-adults-cant-cover-400-emergency-expense.html.

38 Larry Fink, "Purpose and Profit," BlackRock website, https://www.blackrock.com/corporate/investor-relations/larry-fink-ceo-letter.

Chapter 3

1 Larry Rohter, "Real Deal on 'Joe the Plumber' Reveals New Slant," *New York Times*, October 16, 2008, https://www.nytimes.com/2008/10/17/us/politics/17joe.html.

2 "Meet Joe Plumber/Obama Talks to Joe Plumber (FULL VIDEO)," YouTube, https://www.youtube.com/watch?v=BRPbCSSXyp0.

3 Jake Tapper, "'Spread the Wealth'?," ABC News (blog), October 14, 2008, https://web.archive.org/web/20081026174223/http://blogs.abcnews.com/politicalpunch/2008/10/spread-the-weal.html; and Beth Fouhy, "McCain, Obama Get Tough, Personal in Final Debate," AP, https://web.archive.org/web/20081021004119/http://ap.google.com/article/ALeqM5ha9qKZFKzFvH74G3c5PxRG_lHRIAD93RC8FG0.

4 "'Joe the Plumber' Takes Center Stage in Presidential Debate," YouTube, October 17, 2008, https://www.youtube.com/watch?v=29i5lGF5Glw.

5 Ibid.

6 "Public Trust in Government: 1958–2019," Pew Research Center, April 11, 2019, https://www.people-press.org/2019/04/11/public-trust-in-government-1958-2019/.

7 Carroll Doherty, "Key Findings on Americans' Views of the U.S. Political System and Democracy," Pew Research Center, April 26, 2018, https://www.pewresearch.org/fact-tank/2018/04/26/key-findings-on-americans-views-of-the-u-s-political-system-and-democracy/.

8 Ronald Inglehart, "The Age of Insecurity: Can Democracy Save Itself?," *Foreign Affairs*, May/June 2018, https://www.foreignaffairs.com/articles/2018-04-16/age-insecurity.

9 See for example Joseph Stiglitz's arguments regarding the balanced-budget multiplier in *The Price of Inequality* (New York: W.W. Norton, 2012).

10 As reported by the BBC: Tim Harford, "The iPhone at 10: How the Smartphone Became So Smart," BBC.com, December 26, 2016, https://www.bbc.co.uk/news/business-38320198.

11 "Revenue Statistics 2018: Tax Revenue Trends in the OECD," OECD, 2018, https://www.oecd.org/tax/tax-policy/revenue-statistics-highlights-brochure.pdf.

12 Ibid.

13 Lisa Rapaport, "U.S. Health Spending Twice Other Countries' with Worse Results," *Reuters*, March 13, 2018, https://uk.reuters.com/article/us-health-spending/u-s-health-spending-twice-other-countries-with-worse-results-idUKKCN1GP2YN.

14 "Revenue Statistics 2018: Tax Revenue Trends in the OECD," OECD, 2018, https://www.oecd.org/tax/tax-policy/revenue-statistics-highlights-brochure.pdf.

15 Ibid.

16 "Great Leap Forward: Chinese History," Encyclopædia *Britannica*, https://www.britannica.com/event/Great-Leap-Forward.

17 Edward Tse, *The China Strategy* (New York: Basic Books, 2012), 93–95.

18 Ibid, 62.

19 "Will China's Belt and Road Initiative Outdo the Marshall Plan?," *The Economist*, March 8, 2018, https://www.economist.com/finance-and-economics/2018/03/08/will-chinas-belt-and-road-initiative-outdo-the-marshall-plan.

20 Frank Tang and Sidney Leng, "China's tax cuts were meant to boost its slowing economy, but will they end up hurting debt-ridden regions?" *South China Morning Post*, April 11, 2019, https://www.scmp.com/economy/china-economy/article/3005670/chinas-tax-cuts-were-meant-boost-its-slowing-economy-will; Chengdu, "The story of China's economy as told through the world's biggest building," *The Economist*, February 23, 2019, https://www.economist.com/essay/2019/02/23/the-story-of-chinas-economy-as-told-through-the-worlds-biggest-building.

21 Zheng Yangpeng and Sandy Li, "Chinese Developers under Pressure as Key Funding Source Dries up," *South China Morning Post*, June 9, 2018, https://www.scmp.com/business/banking-finance/article/2149890/chinese-developers-under-pressure-key-funding-source-dries.

22 Tania Branigan, "China's welfare system: difficult, inflexible and blatantly unfair?" *The Guardian*, April 23, 2013, https://www.theguardian.com/global-development/2013/apr/23/china-welfare-system-inflexible-unfair. Conversion to US dollars from Chinese yuan made on 07/12/19.

23 Tania Branigan, "China's welfare system: difficult, inflexible and blatantly unfair?" *The Guardian*, April 23, 2013, https://www.theguardian.com/global-development/2013/apr/23/china-welfare-system-inflexible-unfair.

24 "Xi Jinping's Turn away from the Market Puts Chinese Growth at Risk," *Financial Times*, https://www.ft.com/content/3e37af94-17f8-11e9-b191-175523b59d1d.

25 "China's Private Sector Faces an Advance by the State," *The Economist*, December 8, 2018, https://www.economist.com/business/2018/12/08/chinas-private-sector-faces-an-advance-by-the-state.

26 Tom Mitchell, Xinning Liu, and Gabriel Wildau, "China's private sector struggles for funding as growth slows," *Financial Times*, January 21, 2019, https://www.ft.com/content/56771148-1d1c-11e9-b126-46fc3ad87c65.

27 "What China Talks about When It Talks about Stimulus," *The Economist*, November 15, 2018, https://www.economist.com/finance-and-economics/2018/11/15/what-china-talks-about-when-it-talks-about-stimulus.

28 United Nations, "#Envision2030: 17 goals to transform the world for persons with disabilities, Department of Economic and Social Affairs: Disability, September 2015, https://www.un.org/development/desa/disabilities/envision2030.html.

29 "The Constitution: Amendments 11–27," National Archives website, https://www.archives.gov/founding-docs/amendments-11-27.

30 Ibid.

31 "Declaration of Independence: A Transcription," National Archives website, https://www.archives.gov/founding-docs/declaration-transcript.

32 Ganesh Sitaraman, *The Crisis of the Middle-Class Constitution* (New York: Knopf Doubleday, 2017), https://billmoyers.com/story/book-excerpt-the-crisis-of-the-middle-class-constitution/.

33 Ibid.

34 "The Public Wealth of Nations: Unlocking the Value of Global Public Assets," Citi website, https://www.citivelocity.com/citigps/public-wealth-nations/.

35 As highlighted by Dag Detter and Stefan Fölster in *The Public Wealth of Nations* (London: Palgrave MacMillan, 2015).

36 Noah Smith, "Private Prisons Are a Failed Experiment," *Bloomberg*, April 1, 2019, https://www.bloomberg.com/opinion/articles/2019-04-01/u-s-private-prisons-are-a-failed-government-experiment.

37 Michael Poyker and Christian Dippel, "Do Private Prisons Affect Criminal Sentencing?" (paper, UCLA, June 19), 2019, https://www.anderson.ucla.edu/faculty_pages/christian.dippel/privateprisons_sentencing.pdf.

38 Anita Mukherjee, "Impacts of Private Prison Contracting on Inmate Time Served and Recidivism," SSRN, June 6, 2019, https://papers.ssrn.com/sol3/papers.cfm?abstract_id=2523238.

39 Nicola Slawson, "The Public Services You Didn't Know Were Run by Charities," *The Guardian*, May 20, 2016, https://www.theguardian.com/voluntary-sector-network/2016/may/20/10-public-services-run-charities.

40 Gardiner Harris, "Medical Charities Once Advised on Coping with a Disease. Now They Try to Cure It," *New York Times*, October 31, 2016, https://www.nytimes.com/2016/11/06/giving/medical-charities-once-advised-on-coping-with-a-disease-now-they-try-to-cure-it.html.

41 G. Hardin, "The Tragedy of the Commons," *Nature* 162 (1968), 1243–1248.

42 Valentina Romei, "Governments Fail to Capitalise on Swaths of Open Data," *Financial Times*, October 31, 2018, https://www.ft.com/content/f8e9c2ea-b29b-11e8-87e0-d84e0d934341.

43 Patrick Gillespie, "Trump Budget Proposes 40% Cut to Job Training Programs," CNN.com, May 24, 2017, https://money.cnn.com/2017/05/24/news/economy/trump-budget-job-training-programs/index.html.

44 "US Election 2016: Trump Says Election 'Rigged at Polling Places,'" BBC.com, October 17, 2016, https://www.bbc.co.uk/news/election-us-2016-37673797.

45 David A. Graham, "Democracy, Interrupted," *The Atlantic*, January 13, 2019, https://www.theatlantic.com/politics/archive/2019/01/trump-continues-to-attack-rigged-elections/580030/.

46 Doha Madani, "'I Think I'd Take It': Trump Says He'd Accept Dirt on an Opponent from a Foreign Government," NBCNews.com, https://www.nbcnews.com/politics/donald-trump/i-think-i-d-take-it-trump-says-he-d-n1017031.

47 "Robert Mueller to Testify before Congress on July 17," *Financial Times*, https://www.ft.com/content/579f26f2-97b3-11e9-9573-ee5cbb98ed36.

Chapter 4

1 Erik J. Zurcher, *Turkey: A Modern History* (London: I.B. Tauris, 1994).

2 Michael J. Abramowitz, "Democracy in Crisis," Freedom House, https://freedomhouse.org/report/freedom-world/freedom-world-2018.

3 "Turkey's Last Big Independent Media Firm is Snapped up by a Regime Ally," *The Economist*, March 27, 2018, https://www.economist.com/europe/2018/03/27/turkeys-last-big-independent-media-firm-is-snapped-up-by-a-regime-ally.

4 "Basic Law for the Federal Republic of Germany," *Bundesamt für Justiz*, https://www.gesetze-im-internet.de/englisch_gg/englisch_gg.html.

5 Scott Casleton, "It's Time for Liberals to Get over Citizens United," Vox, May 7, 2018, https://www.vox.com/the-big-idea/2018/5/7/17325486/citizens-united-money-politics-dark-money-vouchers-primaries.

6 Ben W. Heineman Jr, "Super PACs: The WMDs of Campaign Finance," *The Atlantic*, January 6, 2012, https://www.theatlantic.com/politics/archive/2012/01/super-pacs-the-wmds-of-campaign-finance/250961/.

7 Laura McCamy, "Companies Donate Millions to Political Causes to Have a Say in the Government—Here are 10 That Have Given the Most in 2018," *Business Insider*, October 13, 2018, https://www.businessinsider.com/companies-are-influencing-politics-by-donating-millions-to-politicians-2018-9?r=US&IR=T.

8 Ibid.

9 Dorothee Allain-Dupré, "State of Play: Subnational Public Finances in the EU and 'Making Fiscal Decentralisation Work,'" OCDE, https://cor.europa.eu/en/events/Documents/ECON/2018.11.12-Presentation-by-Dorothée-Allain-Dupré-OECD.pdf.

10 "Germany Federal Country," OECD.org, https://www.oecd.org/regional/regional-policy/profile-Germnay.pdf.

11 "Lost a Fortune, Seeking a Role," *The Economist*, January 8, 2015, https://www.economist.com/finance-and-economics/2015/01/08/lost-a-fortune-seeking-a-role.

12 "Income Inequality," OECD.org, https://data.oecd.org/inequality/income-inequality.htm.

13 "Germany's Social Mobility among Poorest Worse than in the United States—OECD," June 15, 2018, https://www.dw.com/en/germanys-social-mobility-among-poorest-worse-than-in-the-united-states-oecd/a-44245702.

14 "The German School System," IamExpat, https://www.iamexpat.de/education/primary-secondary-education/german-school-system.

15 "Why Singapore Gives Top Priority to Fighting Income Inequality," *The Straits Times*, February 6, 2018, https://www.straitstimes.com/opinion/why-spore-gives-top-priority-to-fighting-income-inequality.

16 "Corruption Perceptions Index 2018," Transparency International, https://www.transparency.org/cpi2018.

17 "Rule of Law Index 2019," World Justice Project, https://worldjusticeproject.org/sites/default/files/documents/WJP_RuleofLawIndex_2019_Website_reduced.pdf.

18 Ibid.

19 See: Tessa Wong, "Singapore Fake News Law Policies Chats and Online Platforms," BBC.com, May 9, 2019, https://www.bbc.co.uk/news/world-asia-48196985; and Peter Guest, "Singapore Says It's Fighting 'Fake News.' Journalists See a Ruse," *The Atlantic*, July 19, 2019, https://www.theatlantic.com/international/archive/2019/07/singapore-press-freedom/592039/.

20 Ibid.

21 Ibid.

22 Yuen Sin, "Parliament: Inequality Not So Bad in Singapore, but Cracks Showing in Social Mobility, Says Ong Ye Kung," *Straits Times*, May 15, 2018, https://www.straitstimes.com/politics/parliament-inequality-not-so-bad-in-singapore-but-cracks-showing-in-social-mobility-ong-ye.

23 Marissa Lee, "Young and Not so Upwardly Mobile," *Business Times*, July 20, 2019, https://www.businesstimes.com.sg/brunch/young-and-not-so-upwardly-mobile.

24 Glenn Phelps and Steve Crabtree, "Worldwide, Median Household Income about $10,000," Gallup.com, December 16, 2003, https://news.gallup.com/poll/166211/worldwide-median-household-income-000.aspx.

25 Goh Chor Boon and S. Gopinathan, "The Development of Education in Singapore Since 1965" (background paper, Asia Education Study Tour for African Policy Makers, June 18–30, 2006), https://pdfs.semanticscholar.org/c528/f7851df53fc7ac210eaec0a8042946f43663.pdf.

26 Ibid.

27 Ibid.

28 Jacqueline Woo, "Tanjong Pagar Terminal: An Icon of the Port of Singapore," *Straits Times*, August 14, 2017, https://www.straitstimes.com/business/an-icon-of-the-port-of-singapore.

29   Jean-Claude Muller, "Singapore Biopolis Fifteen Years Later," BtoBioInnovation, http://
     btobioinnovation.com/singapore-biopolis/; approximate figure, Singaporean dollars
     converted into US dollars using historical conversion found here: https://www.xe.com/
     currencytables/?from=USD&date=2019-09-23.

30   Ibid, approximate based on 2006 exchange rates (from www.xe.com as above).

31   "Doing Business 2019: Training for Reform" (flagship report, World Bank Group), http://
     www.doingbusiness.org/content/dam/doingBusiness/country/s/singapore/SGP.pdf.

32   Luthfi T. Dzulfikar, "A Better Research Funding Model for Indonesia: Learn-
     ing from Singapore," The Conversation, August 22, 2019, http://theconversation.
     com/a-better-research-funding-model-for-indonesia-learning-from-singapore-121770.

33   "GIC Private Limited: Singapore," IFSWF website, https://www.ifswf.org/
     member-profiles/government-singapore-investment-corporation

34   "Big Tech Faces Competition and Privacy Concerns in Brussels," The Economist, March
     23, 2019, https://www.economist.com/briefing/2019/03/23/big-tech-faces-competition
     -and-privacy-concerns-in-brussels.

35   "Tech Giants Face New Threats from the Government and Regulators," The Economist,
     March 14, 2019, https://www.economist.com/united-states/2019/03/14/tech-giants-face
     -new-threats-from-the-government-and-regulators.

36   "Board-Level Presentation," Worker-Participation.eu, https://www.worker-participation.
     eu/National-Industrial-Relations/Across-Europe/Board-level-Representation2.

37   Joseph E. Stiglitz, "America Has a Monopoly Problem—And It's Huge," The Nation,
     October 23, 2017, https://www.thenation.com/article/america-has-a-monopoly-problem
     -and-its-huge/.

38   Ibid.

39   "Big Tech Faces Competition and Privacy Concerns in Brussels," The Economist, March
     23, 2019, https://www.economist.com/briefing/2019/03/23/big-tech-faces-competition
     -and-privacy-concerns-in-brussels.

40   Ben Casselman, "A Start-up Slump Is a Drag on the Economy. Big Business May Be to
     Blame," New York Times, September 20, 2017, https://www.nytimes.com/2017/09/20/
     business/economy/startup-business.html.

41   Peter Corning, "Stakeholder Capitalism: An Idea Whose Time Has Come Again," ISCS
     website, https://complexsystems.org/410/stakeholder-capitalism-an-idea-whose-time
     -has-come-again/.

42   Robert J. Rhee, "A Legal Theory of Shareholder Primacy," Harvard Law School Forum on
     Corporate Governance and Financial Regulation (blog), April 11, 2017, https://corpgov.
     law.harvard.edu/2017/04/11/a-legal-theory-of-shareholder-primacy/.

43   Lenore M. Palladino, "Ending Shareholder Primacy in Corporate Governance" (working
     paper, Roosevelt Institute, February 8, 2019), http://rooseveltinstitute.org/wp-content/
     uploads/2019/02/RI_EndingShareholderPrimacy_workingpaper_201902-1.pdf.

44   Alberto Chilosi and Mirella Damiani, "Stakeholders vs. Shareholders in Corporate Gover-
     nance," Munich Personal RePEc Archive, March 20, 2017, https://www.researchgate.net/
     publication/24113035_Stakeholders_vs_Shareholders_in_Corporate_Governance, 40.

45   "Unilever's Sustainable Living Plan Continues to Fuel Growth," Unilever website,
     October 5, 2018, https://www.unilever.com/news/press-releases/2018/unilevers-sustain-
     able-living-plan-continues-to-fuel-growth.html

46   "Paul Polman, Unilever's Advocate of Kinder Capitalism, Steps down with Tarnished
     Legacy," The Independent (UK), November 29, 2018, https://www.independent.co.uk/
     news/business/comment/paul-polman-unilever-kinder-capitalism-stakeholder-capital-
     ism-kraft-foods-london-rotterdamn-a8658851.html.

47 Phil Oakley, "Unilever—A Share for All Seasons?," *Investors Chronicle*, January 9, 2019, https://www.investorschronicle.co.uk/comment/2019/01/09/unilever-a-share-for-all-seasons/.

48 "ESG & Corporate Financial Performance: Mapping the Global Landscape" (investment document, Global Research Institute, December 2015), https://institutional.dws.com/content/_media/K15090_Academic_Insights_UK_EMEA_RZ_Online_151201_Final_(2).pdf.

49 "15th Annual Demographia International Housing Affordability Survey: 2019," http://www.demographia.com/dhi.pdf, 12.

50 Robin King et al., "Confronting the Urban Housing Crisis in the Global South: Adequate, Secure, and Affordable Housing," World Resources Institute, July 2017, https://www.wri.org/publication/towards-more-equal-city-confronting-urban-housing-crisis-global-south.

51 "Revenue Statistics 2018: Tax Revenue Trends in the OECD," OECD, https://www.oecd.org/tax/tax-policy/revenue-statistics-highlights-brochure.pdf, 8.

52 "Britain Unveils a Plan to Regulate Online Content, *The Economist*, April 11, 2019, https://www.economist.com/britain/2019/04/11/britain-unveils-a-plan-to-regulate-online-content.

53 Max Roser and Esteban Ortiz-Ospina, "Global Extreme Poverty," Our World in Data, March 27, 2017, https://ourworldindata.org/extreme-poverty.

Chapter 5

1 Zahra Ahmad, "Flint Again Most Impoverished City in the Nation, New Census Data Shows," MLive, https://www.mlive.com/news/flint/2018/09/more_than_half_of_flints_child.html.

2 Figures from "World Population Growth," Our World in Data, https://ourworldindata.org/world-population-growth. Licensed under CC-BY by the author Max Roser.

3 Figures from "Natural Population Growth, 2015," Our World in Data, https://ourworldindata.org/grapher/natural-population-growth. Licensed under CC-BY.

Chapter 6

1 Maxwell Suuk, "Ghana's Battle with Deforestation," *Deutsche Welle*, https://www.dw.com/en/ghanas-battle-with-deforestation/a-18507509.

2 "Districts of Ghana," http://www.statoids.com/ygh.html; and "Savelugu-Nanton Hospital Patients Share Wards with Dead Bodies," Joy Online, November 29, 2017, https://www.myjoyonline.com/news/2017/November-29th/savelugu-nanton-hospital-patients-share-wards-with-dead-bodies.php.

3 Ibid.

4 Ibid.

5 Various sources: Samuel Duodu, "Northern Region Records Increasing Population Growth," Graphic Online, July 16, 2018, https://www.graphic.com.gh/news/general-news/northen-region-records-increasing-population-growth.html; "Fertile Poverty: Northern Ghana's High Birth Rate," Polity.org, July 21, 2011, https://www.polity.org.za/article/fertile-poverty-northern-ghanas-high-birth-rate-2011-07-21; and "Ghana—Total Fertility Rate," Knoema, https://knoema.com/atlas/Ghana/topics/Demographics/Fertility/Fertility-rate.

6 Tomomi Tanaka, Camille Nuamah, and Michael Geiger, "Ghana's Challenges: Widening Regional Inequality and Natural Resource Depreciation," World Bank (blog), December 14, 2018, https://blogs.worldbank.org/africacan/ghanas-challenges-widening-regional-inequality-and-natural-resource-depreciation.

7 Ibid.

8 "The Number of People in Extreme Poverty—Including Projections to 2030," Our World in Data, https://ourworldindata.org/uploads/2019/04/Extreme-Poverty-projection-by-the-World-Bank-to-2030.png.

9 As reported in: Ana Swanson, "Does Foreign Aid Always Help the Poor?," World Economic Forum, October 23,2015, https://www.weforum.org/agenda/2015/10/does-foreign-aid-always-help-the-poor/.

10 Ibid.

11 "Development Aid Drops in 2018, Especially to Neediest Countries," OECD, http://www.oecd.org/newsroom/development-aid-drops-in-2018-especially-to-neediest-countries.htm.

12 Steve Radelet, "Angus Deaton, His Nobel Prize, and Foreign Aid," Brookings (blog), October 20, 2015, https://www.brookings.edu/blog/future-development/2015/10/20/angus-deaton-his-nobel-prize-and-foreign-aid/.

13 "Aid to the Rescue," The Economist, August 14, 2014, https://www.economist.com/finance-and-economics/2014/08/14/aid-to-the-rescue.

14 Jeff Stein, "The U.N. Says 18.5 Million Americans Are in 'Extreme Poverty.' Trump's Team Says Just 250,000 Are," Washington Post, June 25, 2018, https://www.washingtonpost.com/news/wonk/wp/2018/06/25/trump-team-rebukes-u-n-saying-it-overestimates-extreme-poverty-in-america-by-18-million-people/?utm_term=.3957328116a2.

15 Hugo Bachega, "Homeless in US: A Deepening Crisis on the Streets of America," BBC.com, October 8, 2018, https://www.bbc.co.uk/news/world-us-canada-45442596.

16 Lifted from Abhijit Banerjee et al., "A Multifaceted Program Causes Lasting Progress for the Very Poor: Evidence from Six Countries," Science 348, no. 6236 (May 15, 2015), https://science.sciencemag.org/content/348/6236/1260799?sso=1&sso_redirect_count=1&oauth-code=cf1cef44-ac7d-4dc4-8387-2e02f0ed0855.

17 Abhijit Banerjee et al., "Graduating the Ultra-Poor in Ghana," Abdul Latif Jameel Poverty Action Lab, https://www.povertyactionlab.org/evaluation/graduating-ultra-poor-ghana.

18 Abhijit Banerjee et al., "A Multifaceted Program Causes Lasting Progress for the Very Poor: Evidence from Six Countries," Science 348, no. 6236 (May 15, 2015), https://science.sciencemag.org/content/348/6236/1260799?sso=1&sso_redirect_count=2&oauth-code=cf1cef44-ac7d-4dc4-8387-2e02f0ed0855&oauth-code=a352dff5-372b-4b1f-b9fb-711f46da9acb, NB: the authors use 5 percent "social discount rate."

19 Ibid.

20 BBOXX Locations, https://www.bboxx.co.uk/global-locations/.

21 "The Solar Revolution" (BBOXX company brochure, 2014), http://www.bboxx.co.uk/wp-content/uploads/2014/10/NEW-COMPANY-BROCHURE-website.pdf.

22 Stella Dawson, "Why Does M-PESA Lift Kenyans out of Poverty?," CGAP (blog), January 18, 2017, https://www.cgap.org/blog/why-does-m-pesa-lift-kenyans-out-poverty.

23 Thorsten Beck, "How Mobile Money is Driving Economic Growth," World Economic Forum website, September 15, 2015, https://www.weforum.org/agenda/2015/09/how-mobile-money-is-driving-economic-growth/.

24 Tavneet Suri and William Jack, "The Long-Run Poverty and Gender Impacts of Mobile Money," Science 354, no. 6317 (December 8, 2016), http://www.findevgateway.org/sites/default/files/publication_files/new_jack_and_suri_paper_1.pdf.

25 Ibid.

26 Clayton M. Christensen, Efosa Ojomo, and Karen Dillon, The Prosperity Paradox: How Innovation Can Lift Nations Out of Poverty (New York: Harper Business, 2019), 270.

27 Ibid, 271–273.

28 Ibid, 272.

29 A purely hypothetical example.

30 "Slum Almanac 2015-2016," UN Habitat for a Better Urban Future, https://unhabitat.org/slum-almanac-2015-2016/.

31 Robin King et al., "Confronting the Urban Housing Crisis in the Global South: Adequate, Secure, and Affordable Housing," World Resources Institute, July 2017, https://www.wri.org/publication/towards-more-equal-city-confronting-urban-housing-crisis-global-south.

32 Andre Tartar and Wei Lu, "These Cities Make NYC Housing Look Dirt Cheap," *Bloomberg*, October 19, 2017, https://www.bloomberg.com/news/articles/2017-10-19/these-cities-make-nyc-housing-look-dirt-cheap?utm_content=graphics&utm_campaign=socialflow-organic&utm_source=twitter&utm_medium=social&cmpid%3D=social-flow-twitter-graphics.

33 "15th Annual Demographia International Housing Affordability Survey: 2019," http://www.demographia.com/dhi.pdf.

34 "Why 'Affordable Housing' in Africa Is Rarely Affordable," *The Economist*, September 7, 2017, https://www.economist.com/the-economist-explains/2017/09/07/why-affordable-housing-in-africa-is-rarely-affordable.

35 Ibid.

36 Richard Hyams, "Redefining the Green Belt to Tackle the UK's Housing Crisis," PBC Today, February 4, 2019, https://www.pbctoday.co.uk/news/planning-construction-news/redefining-green-belt-housing-crisis/51988/; and "A Rebellion against House-Building Spells Trouble for the Tories," *The Economist*, August 17, 2019, https://www.economist.com/britain/2019/08/17/a-rebellion-against-house-building-spells-trouble-for-the-tories.

37 "A Rebellion against House-Building Spells Trouble for the Tories," *The Economist*, August 17, 2019, https://www.economist.com/britain/2019/08/17/a-rebellion-against-house-building-spells-trouble-for-the-tories.

38 "The Democratic Coalition Is Split over Housing Costs in Cities," *The Economist*, April 17, 2019, https://www.economist.com/united-states/2019/04/17/the-democratic-coalition-is-split-over-housing-costs-in-cities.

39 "Rent Controls Are Back in Vogue. Can They Make London Affordable?," *The Economist*, February 2, 2019, https://www.economist.com/britain/2019/02/02/rent-controls-are-back-in-vogue-can-they-make-london-affordable.

40 Ibid.

41 "The Democratic Coalition Is Split over Housing Costs in Cities," *The Economist*, April 17, 2019, https://www.economist.com/united-states/2019/04/17/the-democratic-coalition-is-split-over-housing-costs-in-cities.

42 "House Building in England," FullFact.org, March 22, 2018, https://fullfact.org/economy/house-building-england/; see also UK population stats here: "Overview of the UK Population," Office for National Statistics website, https://www.ons.gov.uk/peoplepopulationandcommunity/populationandmigration/populationestimates/articles/overviewoftheukpopulation/mar2017; and local government housing construction over time: Matthew Weaver, "How Did the Crisis in UK Social Housing Happen?," *The Guardian*, October 4, 2017, https://www.theguardian.com/society/2017/oct/04/how-did-the-crisis-in-uk-social-housing-happen.

43 Zoie Matthew, "Here's what You Need to Know about Controversial Housing Bill SB 50 (Updated)," *Los Angeles Magazine*, May 16, 2019, https://www.lamag.com/citythinkblog/sb-50-explainer/.

44 "Energy Access Database," IEA website, https://www.iea.org/energyaccess/database/.

45 Hanna Ritchie and Max Roser, "Water Use and Stress," Our World in Data, July 2018, https://ourworldindata.org/water-use-sanitation.

46 Ibid, latest available figures.

47 "Energy Access Outlook 2017," IEA website, October 19, 2017, https://www.iea.org/access2017/.

48 "ICT trends in the LDCs," ITU website, https://www.itu.int/en/ITU-D/LDCs/Pages/ICT-Facts-and-Figures-2017.aspx. Low income countries defined as $1,025 gross national income and below.

49 "Global Mobility Report 2017: Tracking Sector Performance," Sustainable Mobility for All, 48, https://openknowledge.worldbank.org/bitstream/handle/10986/28542/120500.pdf?sequence=6.

50 "America's Infrastructure Scores a D+," 2017 Infrastructure Report Card website, https://www.infrastructurereportcard.org/.

51 Arne Holst, "Smartphone Penetration Rate as Share of the Population in the United States from 2010 to 2021," Statista, August 21, 2019, https://www.statista.com/statistics/201183/forecast-of-smartphone-penetration-in-the-us/.

52 "Internet/Broadband Fact Sheet," Pew Research Center, June 12, 2019, https://www.pewinternet.org/fact-sheet/internet-broadband/.

53 "A Blueprint for Addressing the Global Affordable Housing Challenge" (executive summary, McKinsey Global Institute, October 2014), https://www.mckinsey.com/~/media/McKinsey/Featured%20Insights/Urbanization/Tackling%20the%20worlds%20affordable%20housing%20challenge/MGI_Affordable_housing_Executive%20summary_October%202014.ashx.

54 "World Investment Report 2014" (report, UNCTAD, 2014), 142, https://unctad.org/en/PublicationsLibrary/wir2014_en.pdf.

55 SDGs 6, 7, 9, 11, see "Sustainable Development Goals," UN website, https://sustainabledevelopment.un.org/?menu=1300. In UNCTAD's analysis, economic infrastructure includes power, transport, telecommunications, water and sanitation.

56 "World Investment Report 2014" (report, UNCTAD, 2014), 142, https://unctad.org/en/PublicationsLibrary/wir2014_en.pdf.

57 Water.org, https://water.org/.

58 Max Roser and Esteban Ortiz-Ospina, "Global Rise of Education," Our World in Data, https://ourworldindata.org/global-rise-of-education.

59 Ibid.

60 Milton Ezrati, "Closing the Skills Gap," City Journal, July 31, 2018, https://www.city-journal.org/html/closing-skills-gap-16083.html.

61 Dana Burde and Leigh L. Linden, "Bringing Education to Afghan Girls: A Randomized Controlled Trial of Village-Based Schools," American Economic Journal: Applied Economist 5, no. 3 (2013), http://www.leighlinden.com/Afghanistan_Girls_Ed.pdf.

62 Harounan Kazianga et al., "The Effects of 'Girl-Friendly' Shools: Evidence from the BRIGHT School Construction Program in Burkina Faso," IZA Discussion Papers 6574 (2012), https://www.econstor.eu/bitstream/10419/58766/1/716270242.pdf.

63 "Shanghai Poverty Conference: Case Study Summary," Worldbank, http://web.worldbank.org/archive/website00819C/WEB/PDF/CASE_-62.PDF.

64 Ibid.

65 Abhijit V. Banerjee and Esther Duflo, Poor Economics (New York, NY, PublicAffairs, April 26, 2011), 89.

66 Esther Duflo, Pascaline Dupas, and Michael Kremer, "The Impact of Free Secondary Education: Experimental Evidence from Ghana," Poverty Action, February 9, 2017, https://www.poverty-action.org/sites/default/files/publications/DDK_GhanaScholarships.pdf.

67 See for example "Missed Opportunities: The High Cost of Not Educating Girls," The World Bank, July 11, 2018, https://www.worldbank.org/en/topic/education/publication/missed-opportunities-the-high-cost-of-not-educating-girls.

68 Max Roser, "Fertility Rate," Our World in Data, December 2, 2017, https://ourworldin-data.org/fertility-rate#empowerment-of-women.

69 Ibid.

70 The IMF calculates developing countries must spend $1.2 trillion more each year to reach well-performing countries' standards in education and healthcare, but to the author's knowledge it has not made the split between the two (education and healthcare) publicly available. Developing economies currently spend around 13 percent of government expenditure on education on average, according to the UN Education for All (EFA) commission, found here: https://en.unesco.org/gem-report/report/2015/education-all-2000-2015-achievements-and-challenges. EFA sets a 20 percent goal for governments to spend on education to reach the standards of well-performing countries. Thus they need to increase expenditure by 7 percent of government expenditure on average. When compared with the 5.5 percent increase required for developing countries spending on healthcare (see footnote 74), the 1.2 trillion additional expenditure recommended by the IMF, can be apportioned as $670 billion for education and $530 billion for healthcare. IMF report: https://www.imf.org/en/Publications/Staff-Discussion-Notes/Issues/2019/01/18/Fiscal-Policy-and-Development-Human-Social-and-Physical-Invest-ments-for-the-SDGs-46444.

71 "It's Wrong to See Surgery as an Expensive Luxury," The Economist, April 26, 2018, https://www.economist.com/special-report/2018/04/26/it-is-wrong-to-see-surgery-as-an-expensive-luxury.

72 "Universal Health Care, Worldwide, Is Within Reach," The Economist, April 26, 2018, https://www.economist.com/leaders/2018/04/26/universal-health-care-worldwide-is-within-reach, and original source can be found here: https://www.thelancet.com/action/showPdf?pii=S0140-6736%2813%2962105-4.

73 Figures from "Burden of Disease," Our World in Data, https://ourworldindata.org/bur-den-of-disease. Licensed by Max Roser and Hannah Ritchie (2019).

74 "More and Wiser Health-Care Spending Could Save Millions of Lives," The Economist, April 26, 2018, https://www.economist.com/special-report/2018/04/26/more-and-wiser-health-care-spending-could-save-millions-of-lives.

75 Olga Khazan, "Americans Are Dying Even Younger," The Atlantic, November 29, 2018, https://www.theatlantic.com/health/archive/2018/11/us-life-expectancy-keeps-falling/576664/.

76 Figures from "Burden of Disease," Our World in Data, https://ourworldindata.org/bur-den-of-disease. Licensed by Max Roser and Hannah Ritchie (2019).

77 Currently, developing economies spend approximately 9.5 percent of government expenditure on healthcare on average, according to a weighted average of WHO data found here: Ke Xu et al., "Public Spending on Health: A Closer Look at Global Trends" (report, World Health Organization, 2018), https://apps.who.int/iris/bitstream/handle/10665/276728/WHO-HIS-HGF-HF-WorkingPaper-18.3-eng.pdf?ua=1. The WHO's Abuja Agreement established 15 percent of GDP government spending as the goal to reach well-performing countries' level on healthcare. Thus, developing countries need to increase government expenditure by 5.5 percent on average.

78 Vitor Gaspar et al., "Fiscal Policy and Development: Human, Social, and Physical Investments for the SDGs" (staff discussion notes no. 19/03, International Monetary Fund, January 23, 2019), https://www.imf.org/en/Publications/Staff-Discussion-Notes/Issues/2019/01/18/Fiscal-Policy-and-Development-Human-Social-and-Physical-Invest-ments-for-the-SDGs-46444.

79 Kevin Sullivan, "Saudi Arabia's Riches Conceal a Growing Problem of Poverty," *The Guardian*, January 1, 2013, https://www.theguardian.com/world/2013/jan/01/saudi -arabia-riyadh-poverty-inequality.

80 Elizabeth Dickinson, "Can Saudi Arabia's Young Prince Wean the Welfare State?," *Foreign Policy*, June 5, 2017, https://foreignpolicy.com/2017/06/05/is-saudi-arabias-massive- economy-reform-coming-off-the-rails-mohammed-bin-salman/.

81 "Saudi Youth Unemployment Declines by 6% in 2018," *Saudi Gazette*, April 16, 2019, http://saudigazette.com.sa/article/563562/SAUDI-ARABIA/Saudi-youth-unemployment -declines-by-6-in-2018.

82 "Public Sector as a Share of Paid Employment," World Bank Group, https://dataviz. worldbank.org/t/DECDG/views/wwbiTABLEAU-2/Dashboard1?iframeSizedToWin- dow=true&:embed=y&:showAppBanner=false&:display_count=no&:showVizHome=no.

83 "What's Holding Back the Private Sector in Mena?," https://www.eib.org/attachments/ efs/econ_mena_enterprise_survey_en.pdf.

84 Ibid.

85 Linda N. Edwards, "The Status of Women in Japan: Has the Equal Employment Oppor- tunity Law Made a Difference?," *Journal of Asian Economics* 5, no. 2 (1994), 235, http:// www.bristol.ac.uk/poverty/ESRCJSPS/downloads/research/japan/6%20Japan-Poverty, %20Inequality%20and%20Social%20Exclusion%20(Gender)/Articles%20(Japan%20 Gender)/English/Edwards,%20L.%20N.%20(1994)%20The%20Status%20of%20 Women%20in%20Japan.pdf.

86 Jay Shambaugh, Ryan Nunn, and Becca Portman, "Lessons from the Rise of Women's Labor Force Participation in Japan," *Brookings*, November 1, 2017, https://www.brook- ings.edu/research/lessons-from-the-rise-of-womens-labor-force-participation-in-japan/.

87 Mitsuru Obe, "Five Things to Know about Japan's Revised Immigration Law," *Asian Review*, April 1, 2019, https://asia.nikkei.com/Spotlight/Japan-immigration/Five-things -to-know-about-Japan-s-revised-immigration-law.

88 Kenichi Yamada, "South Korea Fertility Rate at New Lows, Dipping Below 1.0 Threshold," *Nikkei Asian Review*, February 28, 2019, https://asia.nikkei.com/Economy/South-Korea -fertility-rate-at-new-lows-dipping-below-1.0-threshold.

89 Troy Stangarone, "North Korea Can't Solve South Korea's Demographic Crisis," *The Diplomat*, October 17, 2019, https://thediplomat.com/2018/11/north-korea-cant-solve -south-koreas-demographic-crisis/.

90 Kazuo Yamaguchi, "Japan's Gender Gap," *Inter Press Service*, March 27, 2019, http://www. ipsnews.net/2019/03/japans-gender-gap/.

91 Hyojeong Kim, "A Long Way to Go for Gender Equality in South Korea," *Huffington Post*, November 20, 2015, https://www.huffingtonpost.ca/girls-twenty/gender-equality-south -korea_b_8523302.html.

92 Gilles Pison, "Which Countries Have the Most Immigrants?," World Economic Forum, March 13, 2019, https://www.weforum.org/agenda/2019/03/which-countries-have-the -most-immigrants-51048ff1f9.

93 "German Birth Rate Surges to Highest Level in over Four Decades," *The Local*, March 28, 2018, https://www.thelocal.de/20180328/german-birth-rate-surges-to-highest-level -in-over-four-decades.

94 "OECD Family Database," OECD, http://www.oecd.org/els/family/database.htm.

95 "Gender Wage Gap," OECD, https://data.oecd.org/earnwage/gender-wage-gap.htm.

96 Housing Prices, OECD, https://data.oecd.org/price/housing-prices.htm.

97 "OECD Family Database," OECD, http://www.oecd.org/els/family/database.htm.

98 Roughly 0.5 percent of global GDP: https://data.worldbank.org/indicator/ny.gdp.mktp.cd.

Chapter 7

1 Stephen Leahy, "Cities Emit 60% More Carbon Than Thought," *National Geographic*, March 6, 2018, https://news.nationalgeographic.com/2018/03/city-consumption-greenhouse-gases-carbon-c40-spd/.

2 Maya Miller, "Here's How Much Cities Contribute to the World's Carbon Footprint," *Scientific American*, June 27, 1928, https://www.scientificamerican.com/article/heres-how-much-cities-contribute-to-the-worlds-carbon-footprint/.

3 Michael J. Coren, "Humans have depleted the Earth's natural resources with five months still to go in 2018," *Quartz*, August 1, 2018, https://qz.com/1345205/humans-have-depleted-the-earths-natural-resources-with-five-months-still-to-go-in-2018/.

4 Data obtained from the calculator feature on: https://www.footprintnetwork.org/.

5 Arvind Subramanian, "India is right to resist the west's carbon imperialism," *Financial Times*, November 26, 2015, https://www.ft.com/content/0805bac2-937d-11e5-bd82-c1fb87bef7af.

6 "The Insect Apocalypse is Not Here but There Are Reasons for Concern," *The Economist*, March 21, 2019, https://www.economist.com/science-and-technology/2019/03/21/the-insect-apocalypse-is-not-here-but-there-are-reasons-for-concern.

7 "A Brief History of Climate Change," BBC.com, September 20, 2013, https://www.bbc.co.uk/news/science-environment-15874560.

8 Michael Le Page, "Was Kyoto Climate Deal a Success? Figures Reveal Mixed Results," *New Scientist*, June 14, 2016, https://www.newscientist.com/article/2093579-was-kyoto-climate-deal-a-success-figures-reveal-mixed-results/.

9 Helen Briggs, "What Is in the Paris Climate Agreement?," BBC.com, May 31, 2017, https://www.bbc.co.uk/news/science-environment-35073297, and "Paris Climate Agreement Q&A," Center for Climate and Energy Solutions website, https://www.c2es.org/content/paris-climate-agreement-qa/.

10 "Mapped: How Climate Change Affects Extreme Weather around the World," *Climate Brief*, March 11, 2019, https://www.carbonbrief.org/mapped-how-climate-change-affects-extreme-weather-around-the-world.

11 "Weather, Climate & Catastrophe Insight" (annual report, AON, 2018), http://thoughtleadership.aonbenfield.com/Documents/20190122-ab-if-annual-weather-climate-report-2018.pdf.

12 David Roberts, "This Graphic Explains Why 2 Degrees of Global Warming Will Be Way Worse Than 1.5," Vox, October 7, 2018, https://www.vox.com/energy-and-environment/2018/1/19/16908402/global-warming-2-degrees-climate-change.

13 Josh Holder, Niko Kommenda, and Jonathan Watts, "The Three Degree World: The Cities That Will Be Drowned by Global Warming," *The Guardian*, November 3, 2017, https://www.theguardian.com/cities/ng-interactive/2017/nov/03/three-degree-world-cities-drowned-global-warming.

14 Sabine Fuss et al., "Negative Emissions—Part 2: Costs, Potentials, and Side Effects," *Environmental Research Letters* 13 (2018), https://iopscience.iop.org/article/10.1088/1748-9326/aabf9f/pdf.

15 Ibid.

16 "Our Work," Center for Climate and Energy Solutions website, https://www.c2es.org/our-work/.

17 Faith Birol, "Renewables 2018: Market Analysis and Forecast from 2018 to 2023," IEA website, https://www.iea.org/renewables2018/.

18 Kimmo Tiilikainen and Fatih Birol, "Modern Bioenergy Is Critical to Meeting Global Climate Change Goals," *Climate Home News*,

November 10, 2018, https://www.climatechangenews.com/2018/10/11/
modern-bioenergy-critical-meeting-global-climate-change-goals/.

19 "Power Generation Costs," IRENA website, https://www.irena.org/costs/Power-
Generation-Costs.

20 Sheng Zhou et al., "Roles of Wind and Solar Energy in China's Power Sector: Implications of Intermittency Constraints," *Applied Energy* 213 (March 2018), https://www.
sciencedirect.com/science/article/pii/S0306261918300230.

21 Veronika Henze, "Energy Storage is a $620 Billion Investment Opportunity to 2040,"
BloombergNEF, November 6, 2018, https://about.bnef.com/blog/energy-storage-620
-billion-investment-opportunity-2040/.

22 David Stevens and Jasmine Chung, "Energy Storage Developments in the Last
Twelve Months, Lexology, August 7, 2018, https://www.lexology.com/library/detail.
aspx?g=7327e6ff-a819-43f5-9b7e-6dd4c98f17bf.

23 LCEO is an economic assessment of the average total cost to build and operate a
power-generating asset over its lifetime divided by the total energy output of the asset
over that lifetime. See: Jason Deign, "Small Modular Nuclear Reactors Will Soon Face a
Moment of Reckoning," *Green Tech Media*, May 14, 2018, https://www.greentechmedia.
com/articles/read/small-modular-nuclear-reactors-moment-of-reckoning#gs.8bsog1.

24 "Fast Facts on Transportation Greenhouse Gas Emissions," EPA website, https://www.
epa.gov/greenvehicles/fast-facts-transportation-greenhouse-gas-emissions, statistics as
the US used as an indication.

25 Tom DiChristopher, "Electric vehicles will grow from 3 million to 125 million by 2030,
International Energy Agency forecasts," CNBC, May 30, 2018, https://www.cnbc.
com/2018/05/30/electric-vehicles-will-grow-from-3-million-to-125-million-by-2030-iea.
html.

26 Cornie Huizenga, "New CEM Campaign Aims for Goal of 30% New Electric Vehicle Sales
by 2030," IEA website, June 8, 2017, https://www.iea.org/newsroom/news/2017/june/
new-cem-campaign-aims-for-goal-of-30-new-electric-vehicle-sales-by-2030.html.

27 Graham Rapier, "BANK OF AMERICA: We've reached 'peak car,'" *Business Insider*, June
15, 2017, https://www.businessinsider.com/bank-of-america-weve-reached-peak-
car-2017-6?
r=US&IR=T.

28 Paul Gao et al., "Disruptive Trends That Will Transform the Auto Industry," McKinsey
& Company website, January 2016, https://www.mckinsey.com/industries/automo-
tive-and-assembly/our-insights/disruptive-trends-that-will-transform-the-auto
-industry.

29 Arnout de Pee et al., "Decarbonization of Industrial Sectors: The Next Frontier" (report,
McKinsey & Company, June 2018), 13, https://www.mckinsey.com/~/media/mckinsey/
business%20functions/sustainability/our%20insights/how%20industry%20can%20
move%20toward%20a%20low%20carbon%20future/decarbonization-of-industrial-sec-
tors-the-next-frontier.ashx.

30 "How to Get the Carbon out of Industry," *The Economist*, November 29, 2018, https://
www.economist.com/technology-quarterly/2018/12/01/how-to-get-the-carbon
-out-of-industry.

31 Ibid.

32 Arnout de Pee et al., "Decarbonization of Industrial Sectors: The Next Frontier" (report,
McKinsey & Company, June 2018), 22.

33 "1,000+ Divestment Commitments," GoFossilFree, https://gofossilfree.org/divestment/
commitments/.

34   Miranda Green, "GOP Congressman Introduces Bipartisan Carbon Tax Bill," *The Hill*, September 26, 2019, https://thehill.com/policy/energy-environment/463269-gop -congressman-introduces-bi-partisan-carbon-tax-bill.

35   Umair Irfan, "Exxon Is Lobbying for a Carbon Tax. There Is, Obviously, a Catch," Vox, October 18, 2018, https://www.vox.com/2018/10/18/17983866/climate-change-exxon -carbon-tax-lawsuit.

36   Figures from Akshat Rathi, "The Ultimate Guide to Negative-Emission Technologies," *Quartz*, October 8, 2018, https://qz.com/1416481/the-ultimate-guide-to-negative -emission-technologies/.

37   Hang Deng, Jeffrey M. Bielicki, Michael Oppenheimer, Jeffrey P. Fitts, Catherine A. Peters, "Leakage risks of geologic CO_2 storage and the impacts on the global energy system and climate change mitigation," Springer Link, July 26, 2017, https://link. springer.com/article/10.1007/s10584-017-2035-8.

38   Mark Fischetti, "Massive Forest Restoration Could Greatly Slow Global Warming," *Scientific American*, July 4, 2019, https://www.scientificamerican.com/article/ massive-forest-restoration-could-greatly-slow-global-warming/?sfns=mo.

39   "Scientists Struggle to Explain a Worrying Rise in Atmospheric Methane," *The Economist*, April 28, 2018, https://www.economist.com/science-and-technology/2018/04/28/ scientists-struggle-to-explain-a-worrying-rise-in-atmospheric-methane.

40   "How to Design Carbon Taxes," *The Economist*, August 18, 2018, https://www.economist. com/finance-and-economics/2018/08/18/how-to-design-carbon-taxes.

41   Ibid.

42   Shanna Freeman, "How Water Works," *How Stuff Works*, https://science.howstuffworks. com/environmental/earth/geophysics/h2o1.htm#targetText=But%20freshwater%20 isn't%20evenly,Business%20Council%20for%20Sustainable%20Development%5D.

43   Tariq Khokhar, "Chart: Globally, 70% of Freshwater is Used for Agriculture," World Bank (blog), March 22, 2017, https://blogs.worldbank.org/opendata/chart-globally-70-fresh-water-used-agriculture#targetText=In%20most%20regions%20of%20the,percent%20 increase%20in%20water%20withdrawals.

44   Sarah K. Lowder, Jakob Skoet, and Terri Raney, "The Number, Size, and Distribution of Farms, Smallholder Farms, and Family Farms Worldwide," *World Development* 87 (November 2016), https://www.sciencedirect.com/science/article/pii/ S0305750X15002703#f0020.

45   "The Best Way to Solve the World's Water Woes Is to Use Less of It," *The Economist*, February 28, 2019, https://www.economist.com/special-report/2019/02/28/the-best-way-to -solve-the-worlds-water-woes-is-to-use-less-of-it.

46   "Manufactured Water Can Supplement the Natural Stuff, but Never Replace It," *The Economist*, February 28, 2019, https://www.economist.com/special-report/2019/02/28/ manufactured-water-can-supplement-the-natural-stuff-but-never-replace-it.

47   Ibid.

48   Hedy Cohen, "Sorek Power Plant Starts Operating," *Globes*, July 12, 2016, https://en. globes.co.il/en/article-sorek-power-plant-starts-operating-1001139055.

49   "Desalination Powered by Renewable Energy," *Water Scarcity Atlas*, https://waterscarci-tyatlas.org/desalination-powered-by-renewable-energy/.

50   Tom Freyberg, "Desalination + Renewables: A Long Engagement without the Wedding?," *WaterWorld*, March 1, 2018, https://www.waterworld.com/articles/wwi/print/volume-33 /issue-2/technology-case-studies/desalination-renewables-a-long-engagement-with-out-the-wedding.html.

51   Siemens, "Green City Index," Accessed 2017, https://www.siemens.com/entry/cc/fea-tures/greencityindex_international/all/en/pdf/gci_report_summary.pdf.

52 "Climate Street," *Amsterdam Smart City*, https://amsterdamsmartcity.com/projects/climate-street.

53 "Climate Street," *Amsterdam Smart City*, https://amsterdamsmartcity.com/projects/climate-street.

54 "Household Spending," OECD, https://data.oecd.org/hha/household-spending.htm.

55 Burt Rea et al., "Making the Future of Mobility Work: How the New Transportation Ecosystem Could Reshape Jobs and Employment," *Deloitte Review* 21 (July 31, 2017), https://www2.deloitte.com/insights/us/en/deloitte-review/issue-21/transportation-ecosystem-future-of-mobility-reshaping-work.html. The number of professional drivers is likely to be higher as it doesn't include the part-time and contract workers for ride-hailing and other services.

56 "The True Cost of Fast Fashion," *The Economist*, https://films.economist.com/infashion/#true-cost-of-fast-fashion.

57 Stephen Moss, "The Zero-Waste Revolution: How a New Wave of Shops Could End Excess Packaging," *The Guardian*, April 21, 2019, https://www.theguardian.com/environment/2019/apr/21/the-zero-waste-revolution-how-a-new-wave-of-shops-could-end-excess-packaging.

58 Edd Gent, "The Unsurpassed 125-Year-Old Network That Feeds Mumbai," BBC.com, January 15, 2017, http://www.bbc.com/future/story/20170114-the-125-year-old-network-that-keeps-mumbai-going.

59 Ibid.

60 Mike Blake, "Most Countries Are Taking the Threat of Plastic Pollution Seriously. According to a UN Report, 127 Countries Had Implemented Some Type of Policy Regulating Plastic Bags by July 2018," *Business Insider*, April 3, 2019, https://www.businessinsider.com/plastic-bans-around-the-world-2019-4?r=US&IR=T#most-countries-are-taking-the-threat-of-plastic-pollution-seriously-according-to-a-un-report-127-countries-had-implemented-some-type-of-policy-regulating-plastic-bags-by-july-2018-1.

Chapter 8

1 "What is the Freedom Dividend?," Yang2020 website, https://www.yang2020.com/what-is-ubi/.

2 Ibid.

3 Bryan Lufkin, "Just How Short Could We Make the Working Week?," BBC.com, August 28, 2018, http://www.bbc.com/capital/story/20180828-just-how-short-could-we-make-the-workweek.

4 John Maynard Keynes, "Economic Possibilities for our Grandchildren," Yale website, http://www.econ.yale.edu/smith/econ116a/keynes1.pdf.

5 Pasko Rakic, "Evolution of the Neocortex: Perspective from Developmental Biology," *Nature Reviews Neuroscience* 10 (October 10, 2009), https://www.ncbi.nlm.nih.gov/pmc/articles/PMC2913577/.

6 Blake Morgan, "How Amazon Has Reorganized around Artificial Intelligence and Machine Learning," *Forbes*, July 16, 2018, https://www.forbes.com/sites/blakemorgan/2018/07/16/how-amazon-has-re-organized-around-artificial-intelligence-and-machine-learning/#4852fd3c7361.

7 Robert Safian, "5 Lessons of the AI Imperative, from Netflix to Spotify," *Fast Company*, September 11, 2018, https://www.fastcompany.com/90234726/5-lessons-of-the-ai-imperative-from-netflix-to-spotify.

8   Craig B. Karl, "AI Is Transforming Google Search. The Rest of the Web Is Next," *Wired*, February 4, 2016, https://www.wired.com/2016/02/ai-is-changing-the-technology -behind-google-searches/.

9   Richard Nieva, "Facebook's New Rosetta AI System Helps Detect Hate Speech," CNET, September 11, 2018, https://www.cnet.com/news/facebooks-new-rosetta-ai-system-helps -detect-hate-speech/.

10 Angela Chen, "How AI Is Helping Us Discover Materials Faster Than Ever," *The Verge*, April 25, 2018, https://www.theverge.com/2018/4/25/17275270/artificial-intelligence -materials-science-computation.

11 "Meet the Robots at Amazon," YouTube, May 16, 2018, https://www.youtube.com/ watch?v=HSA5Bq-1fU4.

12 Mattie Milner and Stephen Rice, "Robots Are Coming to a Hospital Near You," Fast Company, May 11, 2019, https://www.fastcompany.com/90345453/robots-are-coming -to-a-hospital-near-you.

13 Trevor Mogg, "Meet Robear, a Japanese Robot Nurse with the Face of a Bear," Digital Trends, February 26, 2015, https://www.digitaltrends.com/cool-tech/riken-robear/.

14 Kimberly Holland, "Are You OK with Having a Robot Dentist?," Healthline, march 27, 2018, https://www.healthline.com/health-news/are-you-ok-with-a-robot-dentist#1.

15 Meredith Somers, "Spyce Restaurant Opens with Robotic Kitchen Ready to Serve," MIT Sloan website, May 4, 2018, https://mitsloan.mit.edu/ideas-made-to-matter/ spyce-restaurant-opens-robotic-kitchen-ready-to-serve.

16 Spyce Food Co., Site by JSGD, 2019, https://www.spyce.com/.

17 Josh Zumbrun, "Is your Job 'Routine'? If So, It's Probably Disappearing," *Wall Street Journal*, April 8 2015, https://blogs.wsj.com/economics/2015/04/08/is-your-job-routine -if-so-its-probably-disappearing/.

18 "World Population Prospects 2019," United Nations website, https://esa.un.org/unpd/ wpp/Publications/Files/Key_Findings_WPP_2015.pdf.

19 Adair Turner, "Capitalism in the age of robots: work, income and wealth in the 21st-cen- tury," Institute for New Economic Thinking, May 2018, https://www.ineteconomics.org/ research/research-papers/capitalism-in-the-age-of-robots-work-income-and-wealth -in-the-21st-century.

20 "World Population Prospects 2019," United Nations website, https://www.curbed.com/ 2017/9/28/16375440/gilded-age-mansion-museum-vanderbilt-newport.

21 Jennifer Bissell-Linsk, "Nike's focus on robotics threatens Asia's low-cost workforce," *Financial Times*, October 22, 2017, https://www.ft.com/content/585866fc-a841-11e7-ab55 -27219df83c97.

22 Ibid

23 Ibid

24 Jeffrey Gettleman and Hari Kumar, "India's Leader is Accused of Hiding Unemploy- ment Data Before Vote," *The New York Times*, January 31, 2019, https://www.nytimes. com/2019/01/31/world/asia/india-unemployment-rate.html.

25 Yves Morieux, "Bringing Managers back to Work," BCG, October 4, 2018 https://www. bcg.com/publications/2018/bringing-managers-back-to-work.aspx?utm_medium=E- mail&utm_source=201810Agile&utm_campaign=201810_Agile_OUTREACH_NONE_ GLOBAL&utm_usertoken=9bbb4dfa91412d7f39a2a09fb3a0a9098c29fdfa&redir=true.

26 SkillsFuture Credit, https://www.skillsfuture.sg/Credit. Using June 24, 2019, exchange rate with US dollars.

27 The Singaporean government has not yet decided when and says it will depend on "overall take-up rate, the Government's current fiscal position and the overall training participation rate of Singaporeans." See: https://www.myskillsfuture.sg/content/portal/ en/header/faqs/skillsfuture-credit.html

28 "TODAY Online—S'poreans Use SkillsFuture Credit Mostly for ICT Courses," Ministry of Communications and Information website, January 8, 2017, https://www.gov.sg/news/content/today-online-sporeans-use-skillsfuture-credit-mostly-for-ict-courses.

29 Svend Jespersen et al., "Costs and Benefits of Danish Active Labor Market Programs" (paper, Economic Policy Research Unit, University of Copenhagen, July 2004), http://web.econ.ku.dk/jrm/%D8kPolE04/JespersenMunchSkipper.pdf.

30 Carsten Jorgensen, "Denmark: Social Partners Welcome New Tripartite Agreement on Adult and Continuing Education," Eurofound, March 6, 2018, https://www.eurofound.europa.eu/publications/article/2018/denmark-social-partners-welcome-new-tripartite-agreement-on-adult-and-continuing-education.

31 "Fast Facts: Expenditures," National Center for Education Statistics, Accessed November 1, 2019, https://nces.ed.gov/fastfacts/display.asp?id=75.

32 Data from: Tom Schuller and David Watson, "Learning through Life" (report, Inquiry into the Future for Lifelong Learning, 2009), http://www.learningandwork.org.uk.grid-hosted.co.uk/wp-content/uploads/2017/01/Learning-Through-Life-Summary.pdf.

33 Rajay Naik, David Barrett, Stephen Evans, David Hughes, Rt Hon Sir Simon Hughes, Shakira Martin, Dame Ruth Silver, Ruth Spellman, Matthew Taylor, John Widdowson, "Personal Education Skills and Accounts: Recommendations from the Independent Commission on Lifelong Learning," March 2019, https://assets.nationbuilder.com/libdems/pages/44888/attachments/original/1552911710/Lifelong_Learning_Commission_-_PESA_Report_-_FINAL.pdf?1552911710&_ga=2.216036626.543076955.1552912369-1754857485.1510675649.

34 Jeffrey M. Jones, "Confidence in Higher Education Down Since 2015," Gallup, October 9, 2018, https://news.gallup.com/opinion/gallup/242441/confidence-higher-education-down-2015.aspx?g_source=link_newsv9&g_campaign=item_248492&g_medium=copy.

35 Richard Adams, "Young people more sceptical of need to go to university, poll finds," *The Guardian*, August 14, 2019, https://www.theguardian.com/education/2019/aug/15/young-people-more-sceptical-of-need-to-go-to-university-poll-finds.

36 Ryan Craig, *A New U: Faster + Cheaper Alternatives to College*, BenBella Books, September 11, 2018, https://www.amazon.com/Ryan-Craig/e/B00SE3443E?ref_=dbs_p_ebk_r00_abau_000000.

37 "About PIACC," OECD, http://www.oecd.org/skills/piaac/.

38 "What Is PISA?," OECD, https://www.oecd.org/pisa/.

39 "Hays Survey Shows Sklils Shortage Will Challenge US Employers' Ambitious Growth Plans," Hays website, https://www.hays.com/press-releases/hays-survey-shows-skills-shortage-will-challenge-us-employers'-ambitious-growth-plans-2104620.

40 "Education at a Glance," OECD, https://www.oecd-ilibrary.org/education/education-at-a-glance-2017_eag-2017-en.

41 Valerie Strauss, "Where Have All the Teachers Gone?," *Washington Post*, September 18, 2017, https://www.washingtonpost.com/news/answer-sheet/wp/2017/09/18/where-have-all-the-teachers-gone/?utm_term=.a6201f442432.

42 Emmie Martin, "Here's How Much More Expensive It Is for You to Go to College Than It Was for Your Parents," CNBC.com, November 29, 2017, https://www.cnbc.com/2017/11/29/how-much-college-tuition-has-increased-from-1988-to-2018.html.

43 "Invest in America's Workforce: We Can't Compete if We Cut," National Skills Coalition website, https://www.nationalskillscoalition.org/resources/publications/file/We-Cant-Compete-if-We-Cut-1.pdf.

44 Angela Hanks, "President Trump's Budget Breaks His Promises to Workers—Again," Center for American Progress, March 17, 2017, https://www.americanprogress.org/issues/economy/news/2017/03/17/428535/president-trumps-budget-breaks-promises-workers/.

45 Angela Hanks, "President Trump's Budget Breaks His Promises to Workers—Again," Center for American Progress, March 17, 2017, https://www.americanprogress.org/issues/economy/news/2017/03/17/428535/president-trumps-budget-breaks-promises-workers/.

46 Kate Rabinowitz and Kevin Uhrmacher, "What Trump Proposed in His 2020 Budget," *Washington Post*, March 12, 2019, https://www.washingtonpost.com/graphics/2019/politics/trump-budget-2020/?utm_term=.a298db53ed56.

47 "US Department of Labor: Employment and Training Administration," https://www.doleta.gov/grants/docs/FOA-ETA-18-08.pdf

48 Brad Hershbein, David Boddy, and Melissa S. Kearney, "Nearly 30 Percent of Workers in the US Need a License to Perform Their Job: It Is Time to Examine Occupational Licensing Practices," Brookings, January 27, 2015, https://www.brookings.edu/blog/up-front/2015/01/27/nearly-30-percent-of-workers-in-the-u-s-need-a-license-to-perform-their-job-it-is-time-to-examine-occupational-licensing-practices/.

49 Ibid.

Chapter 9

1 Franciscus Jorge Mario Bergoglio 13.III.2013, "Encyclical Letter *LAudato Si* of the Holy Father Francis on Care for Our Common Home" (Vatican Press, *Libreria Editrice Vaticana*), 122, http://w2.vatican.va/content/francesco/en/encyclicals/documents/papa-francesco_20150524_enciclica-laudato-si.html.

2 "Global Disinvestment Tops $11 Trillion Mark," *Business Weekly*, October 19, 2019, https://www.ebusinessweekly.co.zw/global-disinvestment-tops-11-trillion-mark/.

3 "The Global Fossil Fuel Divestment and Clean Energy Investment Movement" (report, Arabella Advisors, 2018), https://www.arabellaadvisors.com/wp-content/uploads/2018/09/Global-Divestment-Report-2018.pdf.

4 Michele Della Vigna et al., "Re-Imagining Big Oils" (report, Goldman Sachs, November 1, 2018), https://www.goldmansachs.com/insights/pages/reports/re-imagining-big-oils-f/re-imagining-big-oils-report-pdf.pdf.

5 Abhijit Banerjee et al., "A Multifaceted Program Causes Lasting Progress for the Very Poor: Evidence from Six Countries," *Science* 348, no. 6236 (May 15, 2015), https://science.sciencemag.org/content/348/6236/1260799?sso=1&sso_redirect_count=2&oauth-code=cf1cef44-ac7d-4dc4-8387-2e02f0ed0855&oauth-code=a352dff5-372b-4b1f-b9fb-711f46da9acb, NB: the authors use 5 percent "social discount rate."

6 "World Investment Report 2014" (report, UNCTAD, 2014), 142, https://unctad.org/en/PublicationsLibrary/wir2014_en.pdf.

7 "Sustainable Development Goal 4," UN sustainable development website, https://sustainabledevelopment.un.org/sdg4.

8 UNCTAD is silent on this point.

9 "68% of the world population projected to live in urban areas by 2050, says UN," United Nations: Department of Economic and Social Affairs, May 16, 2018, https://www.un.org/development/desa/en/news/population/2018-revision-of-world-urbanization-prospects.html.

10 Dag Detter and Stefan Fölster, *The Public Wealth of Nations: How Management of Public Assets Can Boost or Bust Economic Growth*, (London: Palgrave Macmillan, 2015).

11 "Global Pension Assets Study – 2018, Willis Towers Watson, February 5, 2018,https://www.willistowerswatson.com/en-CA/insights/2018/02/global-pension-assets-study-2018. As per the Willis Towers Watson report, in 2018 total pension assets for the 22 major pension markets globally reached $41.355 billion. Based on author's experience, the global total is likely to be approximately $43 billion.

12   Dag Detter and Stefan Fölster, *The Public Wealth of Nations: How Management of Public Assets Can Boost or Bust Economic Growth*, (London: Palgrave Macmillan, 2015).

13   "Total Assets of Insurance Companies Worldwide from 2002 to 2017," Statista, https://www.statista.com/statistics/421217/assets-of-global-insurance-companies/.

14   Claire Milhench, "Global Sovereign Fund Assets Jump to $7.45 Trillion—Preqin," *Reuters*, April 12, 2018, https://uk.reuters.com/article/uk-global-swf-assets/global-sovereign-fund-assets-jump-to-7-45-trillion-preqin-idUKKBN1HJ28P.

15   Anna Zakrzewski et al., "Global Wealth 2018: Seizing the Analytics Advantage" (paper, Boston Consulting Group, June 2018), https://www.bcg.com/publications/2018/global-wealth-seizing-analytics-advantage.aspx.

16   Dag Detter et al., "The Public Wealth of Nations: Unlocking the Value of Global Public Assets," Citigroup website, June 2015, https://www.citivelocity.com/citigps/public-wealth-nations/.

17   Dag Detter and Stefan Fölster, *The Public Wealth of Cities: How To Unlock Hidden Assets To Boost Growth and Prosperity*, (Washington, D.C.: Brookings Institution Press, 2017).

18   "The Fund's Market Value," Norges Bank website, https://www.nbim.no/.

19   Daniel Workman, "Crude Oil Exports by Country," World's Top Exports, October 7, 2019, http://www.worldstopexports.com/worlds-top-oil-exports-country/.

20   Indranil Ghosh, "Transforming Emerging Economies with Sovereign Development Funds," Emerging Market Views, February 13, 2019, https://em-views.com/transforming-emerging-economies-with-sovereign-development-funds.

21   "Iskandar Malaysia Records Committed Investments of RM302b," The Star Online, October 9, 2019, https://www.thestar.com.my/business/business-news/2019/10/09/iskandar-malaysia-records-committed-investments-of-rm302b.

22   Anna Zakrzewski et al., "Global Wealth 2018: Seizing the Analytics Advantage" (paper, Boston Consulting Group, June 2018), https://www.bcg.com/publications/2018/global-wealth-seizing-analytics-advantage.aspx.

23   Ibid.

24   "10 Years of Green Bonds: Creating the Blueprint for Sustainability Across Capital Markets," The World Bank, March 18, 2019, https://www.worldbank.org/en/news/immersive-story/2019/03/18/10-years-of-green-bonds-creating-the-blueprint-for-sustainability-across-capital-markets.

25   Ibid.

26   "About the PRI," Principles for Responsible Investment, PRI Association, https://www.unpri.org/pri/about-the-pri.

27   "Most Popular Personal Finance Websites in the United States as of July 2019, Based on Monthly Visits (in Millions)," Statista, https://www.statista.com/statistics/203953/us-market-shares-of-selected-print-imedia-websites/.

28   "Report on US Sustainable, Responsible and Impact Investing Trends 2018," US SIF Foundation, 2018, https://www.ussif.org/files/Trends/Trends%202018%20executive%20summary%20FINAL.pdf.

29   Ibid.

30   Jassmyn Goh, "Selectors in the Dark on ESG Criteria," Expert Investor Europe, October 24, 2018, https://expertinvestoreurope.com/blind-mans-buff-on-esg/

31   James Mackintosh, "Is Tesla or Exxon More Sustainable? It Depends Whom You Ask" *Wall Street Journal*, September 17, 2018. https://www.wsj.com/articles/is-tesla-or-exxon-more-sustainable-it-depends-whom-you-ask-1537199931

32   "Analysis: Is ESG a Scam?," Huddleston Jones, August 30, 2017, https://huddlestonjones.com/2017/08/30/analysis-is-esg-a-scam/.

33 "Japan's GPIF to Allow Increased Investment in Foreign Bonds – Nikkei," *Reuters UK Financials*, September 30, 2019, https://uk.reuters.com/article/japan-gpif-debt/japans-gpif-to-allow-increased-investment-in-foreign-bonds-nikkei-idUKL3N26L2U0.

34 Junko Fujita and Takashi Umekawa, "Japan's GPIF Expects to Rais ESG Allocations to 10 Percent: FTSE Russell CEO," *Reuters Business News*, July 14, 2017, https://www.reuters.com/article/us-japan-gpif-esg/japans-gpif-expects-to-raise-esg-allocations-to-10-per-cent-ftse-russell-ceo-idUSKBN19Z11Y.

35 "GPIF Selected Global Environmental Stock Indices" Paper, Government Pension Investment Fund, September 25, 2018, https://www.gpif.go.jp/en/topics/GPIF%20Selected%20Global%20Environmental%20Stock%20Indices.pdf.

36 "Asia's Progress on ESG is Glacially Slow but Attitudes Are Changing," *Financial Times*, https://www.ft.com/content/c6264b0f-e326-37fa-b398-70ff5b1dee7f.

37 Paul R. La Monica, "BlackRock Has $6.5 Trillion in Assets Under Management," CNN Business, April 16, 2019, https://edition.cnn.com/business/live-news/stock-market-news-today-041619/h_87176fe34b84c40986b061ac0e0715b9.

38 Larry Fink, "Larry Fink's 2019 Letter to CEOs" (letter, BlackRock, 2019), https://www.blackrock.com/corporate/investor-relations/larry-fink-ceo-letter.

Chapter 10

1   "JLL City Momentum Index 2019: Bengaluru World's Most Dynamic City, Hyderabad Ranked Second," JLL website, January 17, 2019, https://www.jll.co.in/en/newsroom/jll-city-momentum-index-2019-bengaluru-worlds-most-dynamic-city.

2   Fransua Vytautas Razvadauskas, "Cities of the Future: Fastest Growing 'Megacities to Be' Are in India," Euromonitor International Market Research Blog, January 25, 2017, https://blog.euromonitor.com/2017/01/cities-of-the-future-fastest-growing-megacities-to-be-are-in-india.html.

3   Shilpa Kannan, "Bangalore: India's IT Hub Readies for the Digital Future," BBC.com, September 3, 2013, https://www.bbc.com/news/technology-23931499.

4   Catarina Walsh, "India Is on the Rise—but It Already Leads the World in These Sectors," World Economic Forum website, September 29, 2017, https://www.weforum.org/agenda/2017/09/indias-rising-sectors/.

5   Bruce J. Katz and Jeremy Nowak, *The New Localism: How Cities Can Thrive in the Age of Populism* (Washington, DC: Brookings Institution Press, 2018).

6   Ibid, 62.

7   Ibid.

8   Eric Jaffe, "The Power of 'Networked Governance' to Solve City Problems," Medium, January 11, 2018, https://medium.com/sidewalk-talk/the-power-of-networked-governance-to-solve-city-problems-dffc93df8abd.

9   Ibid.

10 Bruce J. Katz and Jeremy Nowak, *The New Localism: How Cities Can Thrive in the Age of Populism* (Washington, DC: Brookings Institution Press, 2018), 77

11 Michael E. Porter, "Clusters and the New Economics of Competition," *Harvard Business Review* (November 1998), https://hbr.org/1998/11/clusters-and-the-new-economics-of-competition.

12 Shiva Kumar, "Slums Increasing in Bangalore," *Times of India*, August 21, 2013, https://timesofindia.indiatimes.com/city/bengaluru/Slums-increasing-in-Bangalore/articleshow/21962048.cms.

13 Ananya Bhattacharya, "Bangalore Tops a New List of World's Fastest-Changing Cities," Quartz India, January 17, 2017, https://qz.com/india/887292/bangalore-tops-a-new-list-of-the-worlds-fastest-changing-cities/.

14   "Global Revenue Statistics Database," OECD, October 21, 2019, https://stats.oecd.org/ Index.aspx?DataSetCode=RS_GBL.

15   Cathrin Schaer, "Secrets of German SME Success Revealed," *Handelsblatt Today*, February 3, 2018, https://www.handelsblatt.com/today/companies/mittelstand-secrets -of-german-sme-success-revealed/23580982. html?ticket=ST-24755329-0dgbLQntDfchvA19KVVx-ap1.

16   Richard Florida, "Can a 'New Localism' Help Cities Transcend Gridlock?," CityLab, January 23, 2018, https://www.citylab.com/equity/2018/01/can-a-new-localism-help -cities-transcend-gridlock/551219/.

17   Akshaya Sokan, "Why Bengaluru Is the Silicon Valley for AI Startups in India," *Analytics India*, February 26, 2019, https://www.analyticsindiamag.com/why-bengaluru-is-the -silicon-valley-for-ai-startups-in-india/.

18   For example, this study shows the entrepreneurial mindset of American millennials: "America's Voice on Small Business" (paper, America's SBDC and the Center for Gen- erational Kinetics, May 2017), https://americassbdc.org/wp-content/uploads/2017/05/ White-Paper-GenStudy-6-1-2017.pdf.

19   "Sharath Babu, "Founder & CEO of Food King at Beyond Management Initiative Session," PaGaLGuY, December 5, 2018, https://www.pagalguy.com/articles/sharath-ba- bu-founder-ceo-of-food-king-at-beyond-management-initiative-session-liba-chennai.

20   Andy Beckett, "From Trump to Brexit, Power Has Leaked from Cities to the Countryside," *The Guardian*, December 12, 2016, https://www.theguardian.com/ commentisfree/2016/dec/12/trump-brexit-cities-countryside-rural-voters.

21   Frank Newport, "Americans Big on Idea of Living in the Country," Gallup, December 7, 2018, https://news.gallup.com/poll/245249/americans-big-idea-living-country.aspx

22   Sean Coughlan, "The town thronged with old people," BBC News, May 9, 2014, https:// www.bbc.co.uk/news/magazine-27066299.

23   Tech Nation report: "Digital Sector in Bournemouth Is Worth 7,500 Jobs and 340m in Turnover," Daily Echo, May 18, 2018, https://www.bournemouthecho.co.uk/news /16234357.digital-sector-in-bournemouth-is-worth-7500-jobs-and-340m-in-turnover/.

24   "Bournemouth: Jobs in Digital Tech up 25% from 2014 to 2017," Tech Nation, https:// technation.io/insights/report-2018/bournemouth/.

25   "BU Graduates Attend 90th Academy Awards, Bournemouth University website, January 24, 2018, https://www.bournemouth.ac.uk/news/2018-01-24/bu-graduates-attend-90th -academy-awards.

26   Matt Desmier, interview with the author, May 9, 2019.

27   Samuel Stebbins, "These Are the Poorest Cities in Every State in the US," *USA Today*, May 7, 2019, https://eu.usatoday.com/story/money/2019/05/07/poorest-cities-in-every -state-in-the-us/39431283/.

28   Eduardo Porter, "The Hard Truths of Trying to 'Save' the Rural Economy," *New York Times*, December 14, 2018, https://www.nytimes.com/interactive/2018/12/14/opinion/ rural-america-trump-decline.html.

29   Dorset EMC, https://www.dorsetemc.com/#targetText=Engineering%20and%20Manu facturing%20in%20Dorset,have%20potential%20for%20further%20growth. Currency conversion used: https://www.xe.com/currencyconverter/convert/?Amount=800%2C 000%2C000&From=GBP&To=USD.

30   "Dorset Local Enterprise Partnership (LEP)," Dorset website, https://dorsetlep.co.uk/ invest-in-dorset/key-sectors/advanced-engineering-and-manufacturing/.

31   Eric Gimon et al., "The Coal Cost Crossover: Economic Viability of Existing Coal Com- pared to New Local Wind and Solar Resources" (paper, Energy Innovation, March 2019),

https://energyinnovation.org/wp-content/uploads/2019/03/Coal-Cost-Crossover_
Energy-Innovation_VCE_FINAL.pdf.

32 "Today in Energy," US Energy Information Administration website, January 30, 2019,
    https://www.eia.gov/todayinenergy/detail.php?id=38172.

33 Mark Olalde, "What Happens to the Land after Coal Mines Close?," Desmog, March 25,
    2018, https://www.desmogblog.com/2018/03/25/what-happens-land-after-coal-mines
    -close.

34 Josh Smith, "Your Guide to the Solar Tax Credit in 2019," MarketWatch, February 27,
    2019, https://www.marketwatch.com/story/your-guide-to-the-solar-tax-credit-2019
    -02-27.

35 Jill Ward, "This Pro-Brexit Seaside Town Is Starting to Fret," *Bloomberg Businessweek*,
    August 16, 2018, https://www.bloomberg.com/news/articles/2018-08-16/this-british
    -seaside-town-is-dreading-brexit; see also: Darren Slade, "JP Morgan 'Could Leave
    Bournemouth' under No-Deal Brexit, Says MP," Daily Echo, January 23, 2019, https://
    www.bournemouthecho.co.uk/news/17374901.jp-morgan-could-leave-bournemouth
    -under-no-deal-brexit-says-mp/.

36 Jill Ward, "This Pro-Brexit Seaside Town Is Starting to Fret," *Bloomberg Businessweek*,
    August 16, 2018, https://www.bloomberg.com/news/articles/2018-08-16/this-british
    -seaside-town-is-dreading-brexit.

37 Xie Yu, "Perfect Storm of Trade War, higher Costs Threatens Survival of China's Small
    Export Businesses," *South China Morning Post*, September 14, 2018, https://www.scmp.
    com/economy/china-economy/article/2164115/perfect-storm-trade-war-higher-costs
    -threatens-survival-chinas.

Chapter 11

1 Kirsten Korosec, "Trump Adds Tariffs to $550 Billion of Chinese Imports in Trade
   War Reprisal," Tech Crunch, August 23, 2019, https://techcrunch.com/2019/08/23/
   trump-adds-tariffs-to-550-billion-of-chinese-imports-in-trade-war-reprisal/?guc-
   counter=1&guce_referrer_us=aHR0cHM6Ly93d3cuZ29vZ2xlLmNvbS8&guce_refer-
   rer_cs=40qgnH8brAjyJSUD_nyq_A.

2 "Brexit Has Cut UK Productivity by up to 5%, Says BoE," *Financial Times*, https://www.
   ft.com/content/8ab44f8c-cb2e-11e9-af46-b09e8bfe60c0.

3 Rajesh Kumar Singh, "Farm Equipment Maker Deere's Dealers Reel from Trade War, Bad
   Weather," *Reuters UK*, August 9, 2019, https://uk.reuters.com/article/us-deere-dealers
   -sales/farm-equipment-maker-deeres-dealers-reel-from-trade-war-bad-weather
   -idUKKCN1UZ21F.

4 "IT Tariffs Slashed in Biggest WTO Deal Since 1996," *Financial Times*, https://www.
   ft.com/content/af1b755e-a41c-11e5-8218-6b8ff73aae15.

5 As defined in "Globalization in Transition: The Future of Trade and Value Chains"
   (report, McKinsey & Company, January 2019), https://www.mckinsey.com/featured
   -insights/innovation-and-growth/globalization-in-transition-the-future-of-trade
   -and-value-chains.

6 "Global Europe 2050" (report, European Commission, 2012), 63, https://ec.europa.eu/
   research/social-sciences/pdf/policy_reviews/global-europe-2050-report_en.pdf. This
   assumes the UK remains as a member of the EU. The UK represented about 15% of the
   EU's economy in 2018.

7 George Magnus, "China Is Speeding Ahead but the Brakes May Well Change Things
   Sharply," *The Times* (London), June 25, 2019, https://www.thetimes.co.uk/article/
   china-is-speeding-ahead-but-the-brakes-may-well-change-things-sharply-756gl2mpt.

8   "The World in 2050," PWC, https://www.pwc.com/gx/en/issues/economy/the-world-in -2050.html.

9   "Europe Must Find Its Will to Power," *Financial Times*, https://www.ft.com/ content/4aaba4bc-91c2-11e9-aea1-2b1d33ac3271

10 Ibid.

11 "Global Europe 2050" (report, European Commission, 2012), https://ec.europa.eu/ research/social-sciences/pdf/policy_reviews/global-europe-2050-report_en.pdf.

12 Matthias Holweg, "Death by a Thousand Cuts," University of Oxford, April 10, 2019, https://www.sbs.ox.ac.uk/sites/default/files/2019-04/Strategic%20outlook%20for% 20UK%20auto%20sector_white%20paper_09%20April%202019.pdf.

13 Ibid.

14 Lord Ashcroft, "How the United Kingdom Voted on Thursday…and Why," Lord Ashcroft Polls, June 24, 2016, https://lordashcroftpolls.com/2016/06/how-the-united-kingdom -voted-and-why/.

15 Dani Rodrik, *The Globalization Paradox: Democracy and the Future of the World Economy.* New York and London: W.W. Norton; 2011.

16 "The Inescapable Trilemma of the World Economy," Dani Rodrik's Weblog, June 27, 2007 https://rodrik.typepad.com/dani_rodriks_weblog/2007/06/the-inescapable.html.

17 Ibid.

18 Joseph Rowntree Foundation, "What Do People Want from Brexit?: JRF and UK in a Changing Europe," (York, United Kingdom: Joseph Rowntree Foundation, July 2019), https://www.comresglobal.com/wp-content/uploads/2019/07/ComRes_JRF-and-UKan dEU_What-People-Want-From-Brexit-Report.pdf.

19 Hugo Dixon, "The EU Budget," InFacts, https://infacts.org/briefings/eu-budget/.

20 Michael Martina and David Lawder, "Exclusive: China Offers to End Market-Distorting Subsidies but Won't Say How," *Reuters*, February 14, 2019, https://www.reuters.com/ article/us-usa-trade-china-subsidies-exclusive/exclusive-china-offers-to-end-market -distorting-subsidies-but-wont-say-how-idUSKCN1Q32X6.

21 Gabriel Wildau, "China Drafts Law to Ban Forced Tech Transfer from Foreign Partners," *Financial Times*, December 24, 2008, https://www.ft.com/content/90cd02ba-0739 -11e9-9fe8-acdb36967cfc.

22 Sophia Yan, "'Made in China' Isn't So Cheap Anymore, and That Could Spell Headache for Beijing," CNBC, February 27, 2017, https://www.cnbc.com/2017/02/27/chinese-wag es-rise-made-in-china-isnt-so-cheap-anymore.html; and Tim Worstall, "Chinese Wages Are Showing Paul Krugman Is Right Once Again," *Forbes*, March 1, 2017, https://www. forbes.com/sites/timworstall/2017/03/01/chinese-wages-are-showing -paul-krugman-is-right-once-again/#78deeab93fea.

23 Sha Hua, "German Firms Face Staffing Woes as Chinese Labor Costs Skyrocket," *Handelsblatt Today*, August 13, 2018, https://www.handelsblatt.com/today/ companies/not-so-cheap-german-firms-face-staffing-woes-as-chinese-labor-costs-sky- rocket/23583006.html?ticket=ST-765271-SSQGljaQy9dpOmjJqwzs-ap1.

24 D. Ravi Kanth, "India Posts Highest Growth in Patent Applications in 2018," *Mint* (India), March 20, 2019, https://www.livemint.com/politics/policy/india-posts-highest-growth- in-patent-applications-in-2018-1553021506627.html.

25 "Global Innovation Index 2019," Global Innovation Index website, https://www.globalin- novationindex.org/Home.

26 Jason Zukus, "How China Is Emerging as a Leader in Global Innovation and IP Rights," *The Diplomat*, July 7, 2017, https://thediplomat.com/2017/07/how-china-is-emerging-as- a-leader-in-global-innovation-and-ip-rights/, China 2014 figures.

27 Kirwin Lee and Daniel Chew, "Key Aspects and Changes to China's new Regulations on Interim Injunctions in IP Cases," Haseltine Lake Kempner, March 28, 2019, https://www.haseltinelake.com/media-centre/news/2019/march/key-aspects-and-changes-to-china%E2%80%99s-new-regulations-on-interim-injunctions-in-ip-cases.

28 John Harwood, "Most Americans Want Action on Climate Change. Republicans Are the Exception: Poll," CNBC, December 17, 2018, https://www.cnbc.com/2018/12/17/americans-want-action-on-climate-change-republicans-are-the-exception-poll.html.

29 "Led and Supported by," United States Climate Alliance website, https://www.usclimatealliance.org/about-us.

30 Simon J. Evenett and Johannes Fritz, "Jaw Jaw Not War War: Prioritising WTO Reform Options," Global Trade Alert website, June 12, 2019, https://www.globaltradealert.org/reports/47.

31 Figure from UNCTAD: "Growth of Global Goods Exports to Reach 10.4% in 2018," UNCTAD website, December 5, 2018, https://unctad.org/en/pages/newsdetails.aspx?OriginalVersionID=1943.

32 Simon J. Evenett and Johannes Fritz, "Jaw Jaw Not War War: Prioritising WTO Reform Options," Global Trade Alert website, June 12, 2019, https://www.globaltradealert.org/reports/47.

33 Michael Martina and David Lawder, "Exclusive: China Offers to End Market-Distorting Subsidies but Won't Say How," *Reuters*, February 14, 2019, https://www.reuters.com/article/us-usa-trade-china-subsidies-exclusive/exclusive-china-offers-to-end-market-distorting-subsidies-but-wont-say-how-idUSKCN1Q32X6.

34 "Two Proposals for WTO Reform," *Financial Times*, https://www.ft.com/content/34d7c5d0-98c5-11e9-8cfb-30c211dcd229.

35 Chen Gang, "China's Solar PV Manufacturing and Subsidies from the Perspective of State Capitalism," *Copenhagen Journal of Asian Studies* 33, no. 1 (2015), https://rauli.cbs.dk/index.php/cjas/article/view/4813/5239.

36 As per the appellate body's definition quoted in: Gregory Messenger, "The Pubic–Private Distinction at the World Trade Organization: Fundamental Challenges to Determining the Meaning of 'Public Body,'" *International Journal of Constitutional Law* 15, no. 1 (January 2017), 60–83, https://academic.oup.com/icon/article/15/1/60/3068317/.

37 Michael Martina and David Lawder, "Exclusive: China Offers to End Market-Distorting Subsidies but Won't Say How," *Reuters*, February 14, 2019, https://www.reuters.com/article/us-usa-trade-china-subsidies-exclusive/exclusive-china-offers-to-end-market-distorting-subsidies-but-wont-say-how-idUSKCN1Q32X6.

38 Nicolas Moes, "EU Budget, Common Agricultural Policy and Regional Policy—En Route to Reform?," Bruegel (blog), February 22, 2018, https://bruegel.org/2018/02/eu-budget-common-agricultural-policy-and-regional-policy-en-route-to-reform/.

39 "WTO Agreement on Agriculture," European Parliament website, http://www.europarl.europa.eu/factsheets/en/sheet/111/wto-agreement-on-agriculture; however the EU did agree to aim to phase out export subsidies for agriculture in 2001 at the beginning of the Doha Round, although it took until 2015 for it finally to agree to definitively phase them out, see: Alan Matthews, "The EU Has Finally Agreed to Eliminate Export Subsidies...Three Cheers!," Cap Reform, November 25, 2015, http://capreform.eu/the-eu-has-finally-agreed-to-eliminate-export-subsidies-three-cheers/.

40 Kun Jiang et al., "China's Joint Venture Policy and the International Transfer of Technology," Vox China, February 6, 2019, http://voxchina.org/show-3-115.html.

41 "China Drafts Law to Ban Forced Tech Transfer from Foreign Partners," *Financial Times*, https://www.ft.com/content/90cd02ba-0739-11e9-9fe8-acdb36967cfc.

42 Jane Cai, "Is the US Right to Cry Foul about Forced Technology Transfer to Do Business in China—And What Is Beijing's Position?," *South China Morning Post*, January 10, 2019, https://www.scmp.com/news/china/diplomacy/article/2181528/us-right-cry-foul-about-forced-technology-transfer-do-business.

43 "EU Steps up WTO Action against China's Forced Technology Transfers," European Commission website, December 20, 2018, http://trade.ec.europa.eu/doclib/press/index.cfm?id=1963.

44 Amanda Lee, "China Refuses to Give up 'Developing Country' Status at WTO Despite US Demands," *South China Morning Post*, April 6, 2019, https://www.scmp.com/economy/china-economy/article/3004873/china-refuses-give-developing-country-status-wto-despite-us.

45 "WTO Suffers Collateral Damage from Trump and China," *Financial Times*, https://www.ft.com/content/45c6967c-d143-11e8-a9f2-7574db66bcd5.

46 "Nations Move to Avoid Global Ecommerce 'Splinternet,'" *Financial Times*, https://www.ft.com/content/3a8b7458-1fe5-11e9-b2f7-97e4dbd3580d.

47 Shamel Azmeh and Christopher Foster, "The TPP and the Digital Trade Agenda: Digital Industrial Policy and Silicon Valley's Influence on New Trade Agreements" (working paper, Department of International Development, London School of Economics and Political Science, January 2016), http://www.lse.ac.uk/international-development/Assets/Documents/PDFs/Working-Papers/WP175.pdf.

48 Carole Cadwalladr and Duncan Campbell, "Revealed: Facebook's Global Lobbying against Data Privacy Laws," *The Guardian*, March 2, 2019, https://www.theguardian.com/technology/2019/mar/02/facebook-global-lobbying-campaign-against-data-privacy-laws-invest-ment.

49 Chris Middleton, "DGPR USA: Why Tech Industry No Lobbying against Consumer Privacy," Internet of Business, August 29, 2018, https://internetofbusiness.com/gdpr-usa-is-tech-industry-lobbying-against-consumer-interests/.

50 Nigel Cory, Robert D. Atkinson, and Daniel Castro, "Principles and Policies for 'Data Free Flow with Trust,'" Information Technology & Innovation Foundation website, May 27, 2019, https://itif.org/publications/2019/05/27/principles-and-policies-data-free-flow-trust.

51 Ibid.

52 Ibid.

53 "China's Labour Law Is No Use to Those Who Need It Most," *The Economist*, August 17, 2017, https://www.economist.com/china/2017/08/17/chinas-labour-law-is-no-use-to-those-who-need-it-most.

54 Tom Hancock, "China's migrant workers feel pinch as Beijing pulls back on wages," *Financial Times*, September 3, 2017, https://www.ft.com/content/0383433e-8ca0-11e7-a352-e46f43c5825d.

55 Margie Mason et al., "Shrimp Sold by Global Supermarkets Is Peeled by Slave Labourers in Thailand," *The Guardian*, December 14, 2015, https://www.theguardian.com/global-development/2015/dec/14/shrimp-sold-by-global-supermarkets-is-peeled-by-slave-labourers-in-thailand.

56 Guy Ryder and Richard Samans, "Toward People-Centered Growth," Project Syndicate, June 13, 2019. https://www.project-syndicate.org/commentary/labor-markets-government-investment-three-priorities-by-guy-ryder-and-richard-samans-2019-06.

57 Tom Hancock, "China's migrant workers feel pinch as Beijing pulls back on wages," *Financial Times*, September 3, 2017, https://www.ft.com/content/c73b5b1e-0ba4-11e6-b0f1-61f222853ff3.

58   Tahir Amin, "The Problem with High Drug Prices Isn't 'Foreign Freeloading,' It's the Patent System," CNBC, June 27, 2018, https://www.cnbc.com/2018/06/25/high-drug-prices-caused-by-us-patent-system.html.

59   Ibid.

60   "Indian Pharmaceuticals Industry Analysis," India Brand Equity Foundation website, August 2019, https://www.ibef.org/industry/indian-pharmaceuticals-industry-analysis-presentation.

61   Ratna Devi, "India's Pharmaceutical Research Problem," *Mint*, September 15, 2017, https://www.livemint.com/Opinion/m8uzYstgqiT1rOK1GUOnVI/Indias-pharmaceutical-research-problem.html.

62   Robin Feldman, "May Your Drug Price Be Evergreen," *Oxford Journal of Law and the Biosciences* (December 7, 2018), https://papers.ssrn.com/sol3/papers.cfm?abstract_id=3061567.

63   Ratna Devi, "India's Pharmaceutical Research Problem," *Live Mint*, September 15, 2017, https://www.livemint.com/Opinion/m8uzYstgqiT1rOK1GUOnVI/Indias-pharmaceutical-research-problem.html.

64   Paul Krugman, "Trade and Trust," *New York Times*, May 22, 2015, https://www.nytimes.com/2015/05/22/opinion/paul-krugman-trade-and-trust.html; Joseph E. Stiglitz, "Don't Trade Away Our Health, *New York Times*, January 30, 2015, https://www.nytimes.com/2015/01/31/opinion/dont-trade-away-our-health.html?_r=0.

65   "The DOHA Declaration on the TRIPS Agreement and Public Health," World Health Organization website, https://www.who.int/medicines/areas/policy/doha_declaration/en/#targetText=Compulsory%20Licences&targetText=Compulsory%20licensing%20enables%20a%20competent,the%20granting%20of%20compulsory%20licences.

66   Stephen Ezell and Nigel Cory, "The Way Forward for Intellectual Property Internationally," ITIF website, April 25, 2019, https://itif.org/publications/2019/04/25/way-forward-intellectual-property-internationally.

67   James Manyika et al., "Open Data: Unlocking Innovation and Performance with Liquid Information" (report, McKinsey & Company, October 2013), https://www.mckinsey.com/~/media/McKinsey/Business%20Functions/McKinsey%20Digital/Our%20Insights/Open%20data%20Unlocking%20innovation%20and%20performance%20with%20liquid%20information/MGI_Open_data_FullReport_Oct2013.ashx.

68   Valentina Romei, "Governments Fail to Capitalise on Swaths of Open Data," *Financial Times*, October 31, 2018, https://www.ft.com/content/f8e9c2ea-b29b-11e8-87e0-d84e0d934341.

69   Ibid.

70   James Temperton, "NHS care.data Scheme Closed After Years of Controversy," *Wired*, July 6, 2016, https://www.wired.co.uk/article/care-data-nhs-england-closed.

71   "Data Trusts: Lessons from Three Pilots (Report)," The ODI, April 15, 2019, https://theodi.org/article/odi-data-trusts-report/.

72   As argued by Jenni Tennison, chief executive of the Open Data Institute, in this *Financial Times* article: "New Institutions Are Needed for the Digital Age," https://www.ft.com/content/5f46f102-6741-11e9-b809-6f0d2f5705f6.

73   Ibid.

74   Stephen Ezell and Nigel Cory, "The Way Forward for Intellectual Property Internationally," ITIF website, April 25, 2019, https://itif.org/publications/2019/04/25/way-forward-intellectual-property-internationally.

75   "Case Study: Golden Mile," Cisco website, https://www.cisco.com/c/en_in/about/case-study/golden-mile.html.

76   "Climate Strike 2015: Students Skip School Demanding Climate Actions," YouTube, March 1, 2016, https://www.youtube.com/watch?v=0GjdVgGfcb8.

77   Benjamin Jones, "EU's Rising Carbon Prices Fuels Industrial Output Exodus Fears," July 4, 2019, *Financial Times*, https://www.ft.com/content/b499932c-9d91-11e9-b8ce-8b459 ed04726.

78   Johannes Friedrich, Mengpin Ge, and Andrew Pickens, "This Interactive Chart Explains World's Top 10 Emitters, and How They've Changed," World Resources Institute, April 11, 2017, https://www.wri.org/blog/2017/04/interactive-chart-explains-worlds-top-10 -emitters-and-how-theyve-changed.

79   "Sebastian Jungermann and Emil Hristov, "European Union: Germany Extends Its Power to Review and Block Foreign Direct Investments: Catching 10% Investments and Adding Media as a Sector," Arnold&Porter, March 5, 2019, http://www.mondaq.com/germany /x/785782/Inward+Foreign+Investment/Germany+Extends+its+Power+to+Review+and +Block+Foreign+Direct+Investments+Catching+10+Investments+and+Adding+Media+ as+a+Sector.

80   For example, see Niall Ferguson's views: "The Pacific Century: Niall Ferguson on the Coming Cold War with China," Hoover Institution, March 28, 2019, https://www. hoover.org/research/pacific-century-niall-ferguson-coming-cold-war-china.

81   Bruno Maçães, *Belt and Road: A Chinese World Order* (London: Hurst, 2018).

82   Trump has complained that not just China but the US allies are doing this. For example, see: Matt Spetalnick and David Brunnstrom, "Trump, in trade feud with allies, say won't let them take advantage of U.S.," *Reuters*, June 12, 2018, https://www.reuters.com/article/ us-g7-summit-trump/trump-in-trade-feud-with-allies-say-wont-let-them-take-advan- tage-of-u-s-idUSKBN1J80WG.

Chapter 12

1   The organizers' figure; police say it was in the low hundreds of thousands. In any case, it was big: "Hong Kong Protest: 'Nearly Two Million' Join Demonstration," BBC.com, June 17, 2019, https://www.bbc.co.uk/news/world-asia-china-48656471.

2   Richard Hall and Hannah Abdel-Massih, "'All of them means all of them': How Lebanon's spontaneous protests over taxes led to calls for revolution," *The Independent*, October 21, 2019, https://www.independent.co.uk/news/world/middle-east/lebanon-protests-latest- corruption-middle-east-revolution-tax-a9165161.html.

3   "Global Disinvestment Tops $11 Trillion Mark," Business Weekly, October 22, 2019, https://www.ebusinessweekly.co.zw/global-disinvestment-tops-11-trillion-mark/.

4   "Sustainable Investing Assets Reach $12 Trillion as Reported by the USSIF Foundation's Biennial *Report on US Sustainable, Responsible and Impact Investing Trends*" (press release, Forum for Sustainable and Responsible Investment, 2019), https://www.ussif.org/files/ US%20SIF%20Trends%20Report%202018%20Release.pdf.